Predictive Analytics for Business using **R**

Predictive Analytics for Business using **R**

Russell R Barton
The Pennsylvania State University, USA

World Scientific

NEW JERSEY • LONDON • SINGAPORE • BEIJING • SHANGHAI • HONG KONG • TAIPEI • CHENNAI • TOKYO

Published by

World Scientific Publishing Co. Pte. Ltd.

5 Toh Tuck Link, Singapore 596224

USA office: 27 Warren Street, Suite 401-402, Hackensack, NJ 07601

UK office: 57 Shelton Street, Covent Garden, London WC2H 9HE

Library of Congress Cataloging-in-Publication Data
Names: Barton, Russell R., author.
Title: Predictive analytics for business using R / Russell R. Barton,
The Pennsylvania State University, USA.
Description: New Jersey : World Scientific, [2025] | Includes bibliographical references and index.
Identifiers: LCCN 2024017617 | ISBN 9789811293771 (hardcover) |
ISBN 9789811293788 (ebook) | ISBN 9789811293795 (ebook other)
Subjects: LCSH: Management--Statistical methods. | Predictive analytics. |
R (Computer program language)
Classification: LCC HD30.215 .B37 2025 | DDC 658.4/033--dc23/eng/20240516
LC record available at https://lccn.loc.gov/2024017617

British Library Cataloguing-in-Publication Data
A catalogue record for this book is available from the British Library.

For any available supplementary material, please visit
https://www.worldscientific.com/worldscibooks/10.1142/13856#t=suppl

Desk Editors: Aanand Jayaraman/Pui Yee Lum

Typeset by Stallion Press
Email: enquiries@stallionpress.com

To my wife, Robin, for her love, encouragement, and support over the years-long adventure that has led me here; and to J. Stuart Hunter, who showed me the fun of predictive analytics.

Preface

The branding of mathematical models that provide insight and decision support for practical problems as *analytics* is new, but many of the concepts and methods are old. It is now more than 100 years since William Sealy Gossett took his sabbatical from Arthur Guinness Son & Co. Ltd. to study and research confidence interval mathematics in Karl Pearson's lab at University College, London. Since then, the fields of mathematical statistics, statistical graphics, computer science, and operations research have created the rich set of methods now called analytics. Often, analytics is characterized along three poles: descriptive analytics (what do data tell us), predictive analytics (what can be forecast based on the data and with what certainty), and prescriptive analytics (how can the data inform changes to improve system performance).

This text focuses on the second pole, predictive analytics. The motivation came from three years' teaching a professional masters' course on the topic, paired with my personal interest in predictive analytics beginning in the 1970s. None of the many predictive analytics texts that I found covered the suite of topics that I thought was appropriate and not in the way that I view them. The areas of predicting a number, predicting a class, and predicting dynamic behavior are distinct, with different methods. This text is separated into three parts based on these areas. An additional theme is the threefold paradigms for research posed by Miller (2014): probability theory-based *traditional research*, empirically characterized *data-adaptive research*, and the analysis of simulation data in *model-adaptive research.* Different methods, processes, and codes are appropriate for these different paradigms, as highlighted in the text.

Further, many texts describe methods in insufficient detail to allow the student to conduct such analyses and understand the trade-offs among competing methods. Many texts fail to make a distinction between data mining and prediction. For me, characterizing a relationship is part of descriptive analytics, where I place data mining. Predictive analytics relies on probability models or cross-validation or validation studies to allow for useful characterization of prediction uncertainty — beyond a simple (or complex) description of an observed relationship.

The text also differs from existing texts in combining formal process definitions with case exercises. Many texts take a particular data set and anecdotally describe its analysis. Here, formal methods appropriate to each area are explained, and then a formal process for applying the methods is given. Often, example data are used to illustrate an approach, but the method and process description remain central.

Finally, the text is appropriate for a hybrid class structure. By hybrid, I mean that the class is a blend of lecture format and flipped classroom case analyses. In my course, one day per week was devoted to reviewing new methodology and presenting a case study charge. Another day was focused on coaching students, sometimes in teams and sometimes working individually to complete the case analysis. There were weekly quizzes to check that the reading had been done, but there were no "homework" problems assigned. Case analyses were due every week or, in some cases, after two or three weeks and were presented in slide format following a business presentation structure.

For that reason, the text does not contain homework problems. To support the hybrid class structure, at the end of each chapter, there are links to cases posted to my Google Drive: Barton (2023).

The text illustrates the application of predictive analytics methods using the R programming language. This choice was based on a number of considerations. First, I have some trust in the quality of the implementation of methods in R, particularly Base R. Unlike Excel or Python, R has been a main choice for statisticians ever since its progenitor S was developed by applied statisticians at Bell Labs in the early 1980s. Second, the language is accessible to programming novices. It is free of many arcane C-like aspects that occur in Python (such as indices for vectors starting at zero). The base version allows statements as simple as `5 + 3` or as complex as `CVgpModel <- train(sr sdpi + sddpi + spop15 + spop75, data = sLifeCycleSavings, method = "gaussprRadial", scaled = FALSE, trControl = trainMeth)`. Third, the language (and the nice development environment RStudio (Posit, 2022)) is free software and runs efficiently on a laptop. My class is conducted in an ordinary classroom. Students are able to work on cases in class using only their laptops, without special licensing arrangements.

The text is appropriate for a one-semester course in predictive analytics. It does not cover data mining methods. In our program, there is a separate data mining course. The text is divided into four parts: Part I provides an introduction to the text's perspective on predictive analytics and a chapter on the R programming environment. Part II focuses on predicting a number. Chapter 3 presents multiple linear regression under the *traditional research* paradigm. Multiple linear regression is revisited in Chapter 4 under the *data-adaptive research* paradigm, which is particularly important for observational data when model assumptions fail (i.e., independent, identically distributed normal errors). Cross-validation is used to fit these models and to characterize their prediction uncertainty. Nonlinear regression models are explored in Chapter 5. Their flexibility is demonstrated, and although probability models exist, their use belongs under the *data-adaptive research* paradigm.

Part III explores predicting a class rather than a number. Chapter 6 presents many classification methods, all fitted and characterized using cross-validation. Part IV describes predictive analytics methods when the prediction is about behavior that varies over time. Chapter 7 presents methods for forecasting time series. Chapters 8–10 move to the *model-dependent research* paradigm, where dynamic data are generated by a computer code and then analyzed using the methods described earlier. These models typically have random elements. Chapter 8 describes methods and processes for identifying appropriate probability distributions and generating artificial random data. Discrete-event dynamic simulation is the focus of the final two chapters. Chapter 9 describes the mechanics of discrete-event simulation (DES) and three different modeling perspectives for DES. Finally, Chapter 10 brings the text full circle by examining the application of predictive analytics tools, such as regression, to the computer-generated output of a DES model.

Authors often talk about the burden of writing a text. Completing the text has been a pleasure for me; I looked forward to and enjoyed my writing sessions. This effort has helped me improve the way I present methods, processes, and cases to my students. My hope is that other faculty and students may also find this coverage of predictive analytics enjoyable, understandable, and empowering.

About the Author

Russell R. Barton began his career as an analytics consultant at RCA, followed by similar roles at Econ, Inc., The Mentoris Company, and Mathtech, before returning to RCA for an eight-year stint. His projects included predicting the impact of telecommuting on urban structure, modeling exoffender post-release behavior, analyzing workers' compensation claims for hundreds of thousands of records, constructing risk models for self-insurance options, simulating semiconductor manufacturing operations, predicting satellite communications reliability, measuring videodisc quality, characterizing image errors in video monitors, and visually representing experiment results. His academic career began at Cornell University, where he was a visiting associate professor in the School of Operations Research and Industrial Engineering and the laboratory director for the Cornell Computational Optimization Project. Following Cornell, he served as an associate and then a full professor of industrial engineering at Penn State. During 1998–1999, he was a visiting professor at Ècole Centrale Paris in the Production and Logistics Research Laboratory. He moved to Penn State's Smeal College of Business in 2002 and served as the associate dean for research and M.S./Ph.D. programs, the co-director of the masters of manufacturing management degree program, and a senior associate dean for research and faculty. He was on leave from Penn State from 2010 to 2012, serving as the program director for manufacturing enterprise systems and service enterprise systems at the U.S. National Science Foundation. He is currently a distinguished professor of supply chain and information systems at the Smeal College of Business. During his academic career, he has served as a consultant to numerous firms, including Fluke, Ford, GE, GM, Kodak, Lockheed-Martin, Textron, and Xerox.

Dr. Barton holds a B.S. in electrical engineering from Princeton University and masters and Ph.D. degrees in operations research from Cornell University. He has been active at the Institute for Operations Research and the Management Sciences (INFORMS), where he has served in many volunteer and elected roles, and at the Institute for Industrial and Systems Engineers (IISE), where he is a fellow. He has been a Certified Analytics Professional® since 2013.

Dr. Barton lives in State College, PA, U.S., with his wife Robin. They have two daughters and five grandchildren. He spends his free time with family, playing golf, boating, and working on his 1937 Pontiac.

Acknowledgments

The writing of this textbook was motivated by my students in Penn State's professional master's program in business analytics. Much of the material is based on concepts covered in the course on predictive analytics; discussions and critiques from many of my students have helped me expand and clarify topics. I offer special thanks to Molly Miller, my teaching assistant, for her professional advice on wording and grammatical corrections. I would also like to thank Professor Jian Liu and an anonymous reviewer for suggestions and corrections that improved the text.

Supplementary Materials

Please note that supplementary materials of the cases and case data are provided by the author in the QR code below. The hyperlink to the google drive can also be accessed via the link https://drive.google.com/drive/folders/17dqhqUo-tkAXlSrLgkhXbqC_ErLJy0S2

While World Scientific strives to ensure that the content we link to is relevant, we do not have control over, nor do we assume responsibility for, the content, availability, or updates on the author's Google Drive. The inclusion of this link does not imply endorsement by World Scientific of the linked content.

Please also note that:

- Any information you provide or actions you take on the external site are governed by the privacy and security policies of the external site.
- World Scientific is not liable for any issues, losses, or damages arising from your use of the external link.

If you have any questions or concerns about the content found on the author's Google Drive, please contact the author directly.

Contents

Part I

Getting Started

Chapter 1

Introduction

This book presents an overview of methods categorized as *predictive analytics*. Given a set of one or more *predictor variable* values, a predictive analytics method forecasts the behavior of a system, along with a characterization of the uncertainty associated with the forecast. A simple example is the prediction of average gas mileage, given a particular speed. Mileage is the prediction, and speed is the predictor variable. So, perhaps the prediction for 60 mph is 30 mpg. Along with the prediction of mileage, a predictive analytics method typically gives a probabilistic characterization of uncertainty. For example, the method might predict that the actual average mileage will, with an approximate probability of 0.9, lie between 28.8 and 31.2 mpg.

Predictor variables and predictions can be of three types. For the mileage example, both the predictor variable and the prediction are *numbers*. But one could imagine a study of gas mileage as it depends on tire brand (e.g., Goodyear, Continental, Michelin). Then, the predictor variable would be a *class*. The prediction can also be a class variable. For example, using a complex numerical predictor variable of a digitized MRI to predict whether a tumor is cancerous or not. Finally, a predictor variable or prediction may be dynamic. In metal processing, the pattern of temperature over time can be used to predict the post-processing strength of the metal part. In this book, methods are organized by the nature of the prediction. Part I describes methods in which the prediction is a number, including regression models of various sorts; Part II has methods for predicting a class, including a variety of classifiers and characterizations of prediction error; and Part III has methods for predicting dynamic behavior, including time series forecasting and dynamic simulation.

Predictive analytics methods represent only a portion of the methods associated with *analytics*. The bundling of decision support methods under the category called analytics is relatively recent, but most of the methods have been known for a long time, some for more than 100 years. The methods have been developed in diverse fields, including agriculture, epidemiology, statistics, operations research, and computer science. As one might expect from basic human nature, identical methods have occasionally been developed and used by different disciplinary communities, consequently with different names and mathematical notations for the same method. Of course, this complicates the integration of these methods into a common analytics portfolio. When appropriate, these multiple origins and names will be highlighted, helping you to understand and work with diverse disciplines on analytics projects. Before outlining the methods and objectives of predictive analytics, let's look at the overall analytics framework in which they can be placed.

1.1 What Is Analytics?

What is *analytics*? There are many perspectives — just Google "analytics definition," and you will see! Many definitions attach the necessity of examining *data*, while others simply identify analytics as *logical analysis*. The Institute for Operations Research and the Management Sciences (or, for short, INFORMS) is a key analytics organization and offers professional certification in analytics. They define it as INFORMS (2022a): "the scientific process of transforming data into insights for the purpose of making better decisions." But this definition of analytics overemphasizes data. For example, optimization models are used in prescriptive analytics. Sometimes, the parameters of these models are varied over plausible ranges with no real "data," relying instead on expert judgment. This would be the case when exploring policy settings for as-yet-unbuilt systems. A broader definition is given by Merriam-Webster (2022): "the method of logical analysis." The Merriam-Webster definition (besides being circular) fails to capture the second part of the INFORMS definition: the purpose behind the analyses. We combine these concepts in the definition used in this book:

Definition 1 (Analytics). Analytics is the construction, validation, and logical analysis of models based on data and/or system characteristics.

Certainly, for predictive analytics, the models that we will construct, validate, and use (for prediction and characterization of prediction uncertainty) *will use data*. But the logical analysis of models permits optimization, a key aspect of analytics.

To understand the different elements of analytics, and the place of predictive analytics in the overall analytics structure, we examine the analytics domains described in the INFORMS analytics professional certification documents.

1.2 The INFORMS Analytics Framework

It is important to distinguish the analytics process from analytics tools. INFORMS established a professional certification in analytics in 2012, with the first certifications occurring in 2013. The focus was not only on specific tools but also on the process steps in a successful analytics process employing such tools. An associated body of knowledge book was assembled by Jim Cochran, with many expert academics and practitioners contributing chapters (Cochran, 2019). This summary of the analytics framework is drawn from that book. As explained in the Candidate Handbook (INFORMS, 2021), the CAP® certification requires knowledge not only of analytics methods but of the many aspects of decision support for analytics clients. The INFORMS analytics process has seven phases, or domains:

I. *Business Problem Framing*,
II. *Analytics Problem Framing*,
III. *Data*,
IV. *Methodology Selection*,

V. *Model Building*,
VI. *Deployment*, and
VII. *Model Lifecycle Management.*

We expand on these domains briefly next.

Business problem framing captures the ability to understand a business decision situation and determine whether analytics can be used to provide cost-effective decision support. Unfortunately, the emphasis on *problem* is a mischaracterization of the role of analytics in business. Analytics methods do not "solve problems" — they provide decision support. A problem is not the same thing as a question. We avoid the use of that structure here. The important issue in framing the business context is to understand what kinds of decisions need to be made, who are the decision-makers, and what kind of decision support might be possible. For example, it may be possible to forecast the length of time that a communication satellite will be operational, or, more specifically, how many communication channels may be expected to be operational each year over a ten-year horizon, affecting the forecast of revenue for the firm, and a decision on how many satellites will be needed to meet market needs and what communication channel price will be required for profitability. The decision-makers will vary from one business context to the next. Decision-makers who need analytics support include business managers, government policymakers, healthcare researchers, social service researchers and administrators, and applied researchers in many other fields.

Analytics problem framing might better be called *determining analytics approach and overall structure.* Here, the business decision is described formally in terms of decision variables, outcomes, and metrics for the quality of the outcome of the decision or decisions. For the communication satellite example, the decision variable might be how many communication channels to place on the satellite, understanding that the number will affect weight, which will affect the quantity of propellant and launch vehicle structure, and that all of these will affect satellite and launch vehicle cost. Against these costs must be weighed the benefit of the number of functional channels over the life of the satellite. An analytics model will be needed to predict the number of working satellites over time, based on existing or proposed reliability test data. Characterizing the {revenue–cost} over the life of the satellite might be the forecast metric provided for decision support.

The **data** domain is focused on the ability to identify data needs, acquire appropriate data, integrate data from disparate sources, fix or remove errors or omissions in the data ("clean" the data), and identify important relationships apparent in the data. The results, of course, can affect both the business problem framing and the analytics problem framing. For the communications satellite data, this means accessing financial data on likely costs associated with launch vehicle and satellite build directly associated with changing the number of channel amplifiers, estimating launch, and satellite and individual channel amplifier reliabilities based on historical data for similar entities. If necessary, new reliability tests may be designed and executed in order to generate the necessary reliability data.

Methodology selection will follow the analytics approach, but the specifics of the methodology might change based on the data collection. For the satellite example, perhaps the amplifier life data suggest a lognormal reliability probability model rather than a Weibull model for reliability prediction.

The **model-building** domain is at the core of the analytics value-add, where tools are combined with processes to provide decision support. Here, one or more analytic methods using probability, statistics, AI, signal analysis, simulation, or other applied mathematics techniques are combined with the data and objectives to provide *decision support*. That could be the identification of the system configuration that provides the lowest operating cost, the characterization of the most likely disease given a set of diagnostic measures, or the identification of products typically purchased together in online shopping.

Note that any particular analytics approach, say a predictive analytics framing, may well use tools from descriptive, predictive, and prescriptive analytics. For example, in building a predictive analytics regression solution, one uses descriptive analytics (a normal probability plot) to check model validity, and coefficient estimates are found using a prescriptive analytics method (least squares).

In practice, the cost of developing an analytics decision support tool can often be spread over multiple decisions. Rather than a disease diagnosis for a single patient, the tool would be used repeatedly over many patients, lowering the analytics cost per patient. This requires that the tool be automated to the extent possible, which is part of the task of **model deployment**. Further, when an analytics support tool is in regular use, it must be updated as technologies and operating situations change, and the data representations and method implementations must be monitored for correctness and errors promptly addressed. Thus, **model lifecycle management** is the last (and continuing) analytics activity in the INFORMS framework. You can find more details on these steps in the INFORMS Job Task Analysis list in Appendix A.

Full CAP® certification is intended for analytics practitioners with significant work experience (INFORMS, 2022b). The skills of a successful consultant in working with clients to identify and frame problems generally come from practice as a business consultant/analyst. The Associate CAP® is based on a subset of the elements in these domains, and certification can be achieved without extensive work experience. You can learn more about these certifications at www.certifiedanalytics.org.

1.2.1 Predictive analytics in the analytics framework

The body of knowledge for attaining either of these certifications includes many analytics methods. We can think of these as the toolkit used in an analytics project: tools that enable the analytics process. These tools are generally placed in three categories: *descriptive analytics*, *predictive analytics*, and *prescriptive analytics* (Rose, 2016). Descriptive analytics methods provide answers to the question "What happened?" or "What do the data tell us?" These methods help to turn data into insight, identifying structure and relationships that may be hard to see from the raw data. Predictive analytics methods, which are the focus of this book, provide answers to the question "What could happen?" or "What range of future outcomes are possible, given a specific set of conditions?" Prescriptive analytics tools make recommendations to decision-makers: "What should happen?" or "What operating rules for the system will give best performance, lowest operating cost, or some balance of these criteria?"

Again, it is important to distinguish the analytics process from analytics tools. While this book's focus is on understanding and correctly implementing predictive analytics tools, some attention is given to their place in the overall analytics process. We present sets of tools in the context of an analytics case, so that the business question drives the use of the tools and the insights provided by the tools are used to inform a business or policy decision. In effect, the cases provide an opportunity to explore the first five domains of the INFORMS analytics process, rather than only domains IV and V.

1.3 Predictive Analytics Objectives and Paradigms

What are the objectives of formal predictive analytics methods? Given a specific set of values for a specific set of characteristics, which we call predictor variables (sometimes called independent variables), a predictive analytics method gives a mathematical algorithm for determining two things. The first is the predicted *value.* I put value in italics because, as mentioned before, the value may be a number, the name of a class (or value of a qualitative variable), or even the prediction of dynamic behavior over time: a function. Extensions to the prediction of a function of two or more variables are also studied but are beyond the scope of this book.

Predictive analytics can be applied in three different scientific paradigms. Miller (2014) identifies these as *traditional research*, *data-adaptive research*, and *model-dependent research*. Figure 1.1, adapted from his figure, shows how data and model play different roles in different paradigms.

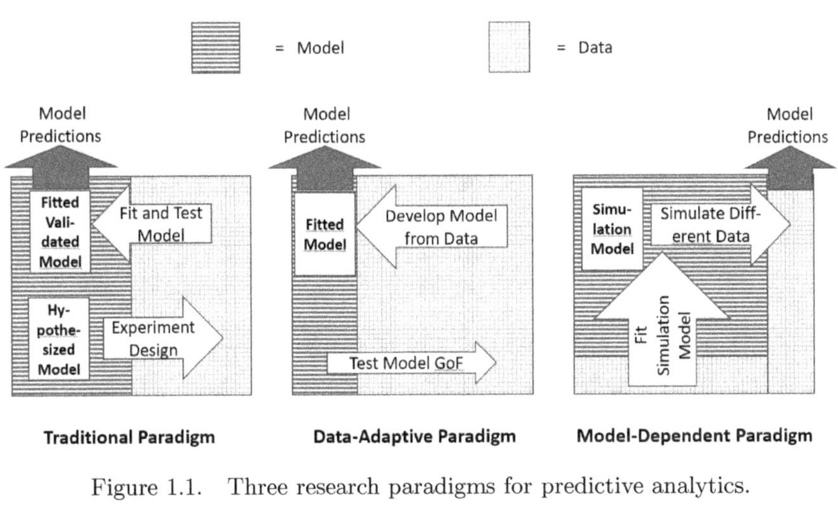

Figure 1.1. Three research paradigms for predictive analytics.

In the *traditional research* paradigm, the form of the hypothesized relationships is identified *a priori*, and then data to fit and test the model are identified, cleaned, and analyzed. This approach aligns with the following standard view of the scientific method: form a hypothesis (think of this as the general mathematical form of the predictive model); design an experiment to collect data to test the hypothesis; and test the model predictions or fit to determine whether the hypothesis was supported. Predictive analytics methods using *inferential statistics* fall into this category. Figure 1.2 gives a graphical comparison of how both descriptive and inferential statistics provide decision support to management. Inferential statistics provides predictive ability based on a hypothesized probability model whose form and sufficiency can be tested against real-world data. The fitted model (and uncertainty around the fit) can then be used to forecast future results, taking model uncertainty into account. Model uncertainty is typically characterized through confidence intervals for average behavior and prediction intervals for individual results.

As an example, consider the hypothesis that gas mileage decreases as speed increases, and it decreases at an increasing rate as speed goes up. This would imply that the decrease would not be a linear function of speed, but might be approximated by a predictive model with intercept, linear, and quadratic terms. An experiment could be designed to operate a vehicle at, say, three or four different speeds.

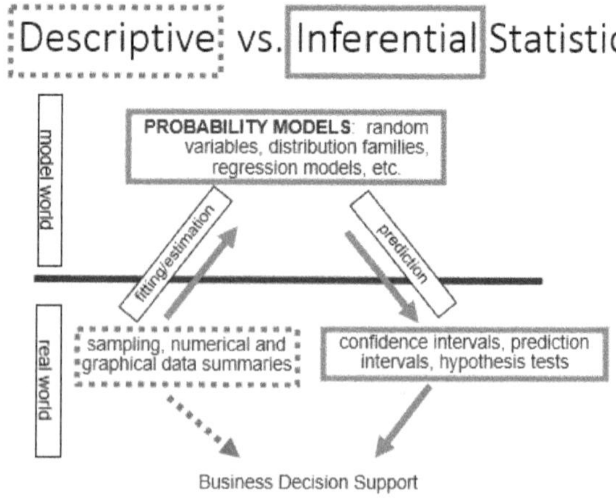

Figure 1.2. Descriptive and inferential statistics in traditional research.

The gas mileage would be recorded for each run. Multiple runs at each of the speeds might be conducted to allow for the characterization of run-to-run variation. These mileage and speed data would be used to fit a quadratic regression model, and hypotheses about the coefficients could be tested. For example, testing the null hypothesis that the linear and quadratic coefficients were nonnegative, if rejected, would give confidence that mileage decreases as speed increases and decreases with increasing rate. It is also possible to use the fitted model to predict gas mileage at other speeds and to characterize the two sources of uncertainty in the prediction: error in the fitted model and run-to-run variation inherent in the vehicle behavior.

The *data-adaptive research* paradigm often applies in observational studies when one examines a set of pre-existing data and not created through a designed experiment. Then, the data drive the model, both in form and in coefficients. Since the form was determined by the data, testing a hypothesis is not appropriate since the data used to determine the model form cannot also be used to test the hypothesized model. The typical strategy is to replace the hypothesis test with a goodness-of-fit test. To test the goodness of fit, only a portion of the data is used to determine the model form and coefficient values. This fitted model is tested on the held-out data to assess its predictive ability: How well does the predicted value for each held-out sample match the actual value? The two sets of data are often labeled *train* and *test*. When predicting a number, the average squared difference between predicted and actual (called mean squared error, or MSE) is often used to characterize the goodness of fit. More complex test/train assessment strategies are often used. For example, ten-fold cross-validation divides the data into ten equal parts, fits a model to 9/10, and computes the goodness of fit over the held-out 1/10, and this is repeated ten times, each time holding out a different tenth and computing a portion of the *cross-validation error*. In a gas mileage setting, one might imagine a rental car company recording speed and instantaneous gas mileage for a sample of cars in its fleet. The gas mileage vs. speed predictive analytics model might be a nonlinear regression or a neural network model. An overall model form might be fitted to minimize the cross-validation error summed over all ten fitting/holdout pairs.

In the *model-dependent research* paradigm, the data supporting decision-making do not come from the real world but from a model that simulates the real world, often simulating a situation that does not yet exist. Simulation models are often used to predict dynamic system behavior to allow for the comparison of alternative product or service system designs. The generated data are shown on the right side of the right-hand block. The predicted dynamic behavior allows the decision-maker to evaluate multiple performance measures, such as oscillations, rapidity of response to change, and average values of dynamically varying quantities. These models typically generate randomly varying data using fitted probability distribution models. These probability models often have parameters that must be determined from real-world data, shown at the bottom of the right-hand block. But that data are not the focus of the decision-maker's interest. For example, we need to depart from the gas mileage scenario and consider a call center design problem: alternative designs have different training and specialization for agents, different rules for assigning calls to agent types based on the nature of the call, etc. One might like to predict the average and standard deviation of call duration and the workload level for the agents, and compare these *benefit* measures against *costs* for the corresponding agent mix and training. Here, the data of interest are the time each customer spends in service and the time each agent spends in service. The data needed to fit such a simulation model would involve characterizing the random distribution of time between call arrivals and the random distribution of time for an agent of a specific training to handle a call of a specific nature. These data might be collected through an experimental pilot study.

For all three research paradigms, models can be used for prediction, as indicated by the model prediction arrows. In predictive analytics, a prediction should be accompanied by a characterization of the uncertainty in the prediction. For models under the traditional research paradigm, the hypothesized characteristics allow for formal model-based prediction and formal model-based characterization of uncertainty. For models under the data-adaptive research paradigm, prediction is model-based, but the characterization of prediction uncertainty is data-based and so has uncertain generalizability. For model-dependent prediction, the model generates data, which can be viewed as a prediction; however, the kind of data that are predicted are generally different from those used to estimate model parameters. There are often two sources of uncertainty in model-dependent predicted data: the randomness that is part of the simulation model and the error in calibrating model probability distributions and other parameters.

1.4 Distinguishing Predictive Analytics and Data Mining

The tripartite research paradigm in Figure 1.1 provides a way to understand the distinction between data mining and predictive analytics. First, data mining methods reside strictly in the data-adaptive research paradigm. Data mining seeks to identify interesting relationships through fitted models. The purpose of the model is to highlight particular structure in the data. So, in the figure, data mining methods fall in the middle portion, but without the model prediction arrow. That means the focus is more on the identification of interesting structures, with performance evaluated on the existing data, and less on characterizing predictive accuracy. The actual model types (regression and classification) are sometimes the same.

Another general characteristic of data mining scenarios is dealing with very large data sets in terms of both the number of variables and the number of records. For predictive analytics, often (but not always) the data sets are smaller. The examples in this document have 2–10 variables and range from a few tens to a few thousand records.

1.5 Text Structure and Strategy

The text is organized in three parts around the three types of prediction: predicting a number, predicting a class, and predicting dynamic behavior. In each part, chapters focus on different methods appropriate in that setting. Each method is applied in a case study that has both data and a business context. Analysis tasks include the first five domains of the INFORMS analytics process:

I. *Business Problem Framing*,
II. *Analytics Problem Framing*,
III. *Data*,
IV. *Methodology Selection*, and
V. *Model Building*.

The case study applications are developed in the R programming environment. The basics of the R programming environment using RStudio are covered in the following chapter.

Each part begins with an overview of predictive analytics tools of that type. The instructional strategy aims to (i) describe predictive analytics methods in the context of data and decisions for which they are appropriate, (ii) give mathematical descriptions of the methods along with their assumptions, strengths, and weaknesses, and (iii) illustrate their implementation in R for a case data set. Additional case study assignments are provided with associated data file links. Each assignment results in a four-part management presentation, with the parts based on my colleague Frank Archibald's structure:

1. *In Order to...* (Business Problem Framing).
2. *We Did...* (Analytics Problem Framing and Methodology Selection).
3. *Which Resulted in...* (Data, Model Building, and Results).
4. *So We Recommend...* (Decision Support Based on the Analytics).

This structure provides practice in using predictive analytics in a business context. Understanding the methods and interpretation of results is important, but an analyst needs to be able to interpret the results for management to enable informed decision-making.

Chapter 2

The R Programming Environment

All analytics for cases in the text are implemented using R. Whenever possible, commands are implemented using Base R to minimize the learning curve for beginners. Those more familiar with R might modify these commands using popular packages, such as `tidyverse` and `ggplot`. But it is important for beginners to understand the full power of Base R so that modifications introduced by these style-specific, somewhat dogmatic, programming approaches can be understood, appreciated, and selected when appropriate. Specific coding approaches for each predictive analytics method are included with the corresponding chapter. This chapter gives an overview of basic R operations, data structures, and object-oriented methods that make R a powerful programming environment.

R is a free programming environment modeled after the AT&T commercial statistical software package S (Becker, 2017). It is maintained and distributed through the Comprehensive R Archive Network, or CRAN. A Windows version is available for free download; see CRAN (2022).

The R programming language can be *interactive*. That means it can be used as a calculator, much like typing a function into a cell in Excel. But a series of commands can be assembled in a file and executed sequentially, producing multiple results. Further, R is *object-oriented*. That means it is possible to specify actions on structures that are more complex than a number or a vector. In Excel, for example, a worksheet, with all its data and perhaps functions, can be considered an *object* in R, and commands can apply to objects.

For example, the analogy to an Excel worksheet (with just data and no functions) is a *data frame* in R. You can learn more about data frames in the sections that follow.

2.1 Arithmetic in R

R can be used as a simple calculator. For example:

```
> 4+3
[1] 7
> 4*3
[1] 12
> 4^2
[1] 16
> 4^.5
[1] 2
>
```

Note that the reported result has an index number (`[1]`) to indicate the index number of the result (important if the result is, say, a matrix). In this case, there is only one value. Vectors are created in R using the concatenate (`c`) command. Also, note that commands are entered after a command prompt ">", and an R output typically has a line index printed at the start, e.g., "`[1]`". Addition, subtraction, multiplication, and division are element by element if both operands are vectors, or if one is a scalar, it is applied to all elements of the vector:

```
> c(3,4,5)
[1] 3 4 5
> c(3,4,5)*2
[1]  6  8 10
> c(3,4,5)+1
[1] 4 5 6
> c(3,4,5) + c(1,1,1)
[1] 4 5 6
> c(3,4,5)*c(1,0,2)
[1]  3  0 10
>
```

A vector is also created if a sequence is specified, for example:

```
> 1:10
[1]  1  2  3  4  5  6  7  8  9 10
```

```
> 10:1
[1] 10  9  8  7  6  5  4  3  2  1
> 1:10 + 10:1
[1] 11 11 11 11 11 11 11 11 11 11
>
```

Matrices are created using the `matrix` function. The data are provided as a vector and then wrapped into the row and column sizes specified in the command. For example, to place entries 1:12 into a 4×3 matrix:

```
> matrix(1:12,4,3)
[,1] [,2] [,3]
[1,]    1    5    9
[2,]    2    6   10
[3,]    3    7   11
[4,]    4    8   12
>
```

Note that the entries are filled column by column, which can be changed by adding `,byrow=TRUE` to the command. Also, note that the numbers in brackets now change: they represent the row and column numbers. This is not important for a small matrix, but for a matrix with hundreds of rows or columns, knowing the row or column index can be helpful.

Vector–vector, vector–matrix, and matrix–matrix products can be element by element (or outer) or as "dot" (or inner) products. Outer product multiplication is the result of the usual `*` symbol. An example was shown above for vector–vector outer product multiplication. Inner products are frequently the intent of such multiplications, however. For inner product multiplication, use `%*%`:

```
> c(3,4,5)%*%c(1,0,2)
      [,1]
[1,]    13
> c(3,4,5)%*%c(1,1,1)
      [,1]
[1,]    12
>
```

The first result is `3 * 1 + 4 * 0 + 5 * 2 = 13`. Note that the results appear as a 1×1 matrix rather than a number.

Matrix–vector and matrix–matrix operations can be either outer product (*) or inner product (%*%). For matrix–vector outer products, the vector is applied to each column, multiplying element by element:

```
> c(2,2,2,1)*matrix(1:12,4,3)
[,1] [,2] [,3]
[1,]    2   10   18
[2,]    4   12   20
[3,]    6   14   22
[4,]    4    8   12
> matrix(1:12,4,3)*c(2,2,2,1)
[,1] [,2] [,3]
[1,]    2   10   18
[2,]    4   12   20
[3,]    6   14   22
[4,]    4    8   12
> matrix(1:12,4,3)*c(5,5,1)
[,1] [,2] [,3]
[1,]    5   25    9
[2,]   10    6   50
[3,]    3   35   55
[4,]   20   40   12
>
```

In the first and second cases, the length of the vector is the same as the column length of the matrix. Each column is multiplied element by element with the same four values. The ordering of the matrix vs. the vector does not matter: the vector may come first or second. The third outer product has a vector length that does not match the column length of the matrix. For the third row in the first column, the multiplier is the final element of `(5,5,1)` $=$ `1`. Then, for the last row in the first column, the multiplying value from `(5,5,1)` wraps back around to the first element, `5`, giving the product `5 * 4 = 20`. The location of the unit-multiplied element moves up across the columns (of length 4) as the three numbers in the vector are reused.

The order of the vector and matrix matters for the inner product. When the vector is placed on the left, the result is a four-vector: the dot product of that vector with each column of the matrix. You can also think of this as a linear combination of the rows of the matrix, with each row's coefficient corresponding to that entry in the vector. So, its length must match the number of rows in each column vector of the matrix, i.e., 4. If the inner product has the vector on the right, then it produces a new column vector that is a linear combination of the column vectors. So, its length must match the number of columns, i.e., 3:

```
> c(2,2,2,1)%*%matrix(1:12,4,3)
[,1] [,2] [,3]
[1,]   16   44   72
>
> matrix(1:12,4,3)%*%c(5,5,1)
[,1]
[1,]   39
[2,]   50
[3,]   61
[4,]   72
>
```

Matrix–matrix multiplication can be an outer product (element-by-element multiplication), but caution is advised, as it can be hard to understand if the sizes of the matrices do not match. Typically, matrix–matrix multiplication refers to the inner product. Then, the number of columns in the first matrix should match the number of rows in the second:

```
> matrix(1:12,4,3)
[,1] [,2] [,3]
[1,]    1    5    9
[2,]    2    6   10
[3,]    3    7   11
[4,]    4    8   12
> matrix(1:2,3,4)
[,1] [,2] [,3] [,4]
[1,]    1    2    1    2
[2,]    2    1    2    1
[3,]    1    2    1    2
> matrix(1:12,4,3)%*%matrix(1:2,3,4)
[,1] [,2] [,3] [,4]
[1,]   20   25   20   25
[2,]   24   30   24   30
[3,]   28   35   28   35
[4,]   32   40   32   40
>
```

This multiplication result can be considered a composition of columns, each being a matrix–vector multiplication. Recall then that for each column of the second matrix, the result for each column when multiplied by the first matrix produces a new column vector that is a linear combination of the column vectors of the first matrix. For the first column of the second matrix, that gives `1 *` the column of values `(1,2,3,4)` plus `2 *` the column of values `(5,6,7,8)` plus `1 *` the column of values `(9,10,11,12)`, which results in the column `(20,24,28,32)`.

2.2 Variables in R

Like any programming language, it is helpful to reuse mathematical constructs such as matrices, vectors, and even individual values. Any construct can be given a name. These names are called *variables*. Programs often assign variable names to numerical constructs, and then operations can be defined by simply using the names of the variables. For example, the calculation of `matrix(1:12,4,3)%*%c(5,5,1)` using variables can be done as follows:

```
> my_matrix = matrix(1:12,4,3)
> my_matrix <- matrix(1:12,4,3)
> my_vector = c(5,5,1)
> my_matrix%*%my_vector
[,1]
[1,]   39
[2,]   50
[3,]   61
[4,]   72
>
```

The first two lines of the program code show that an assignment can be done in two equivalent ways: using `=` or using `<-`.

The variable names above are `my_matrix` and `my_vector`. Names can be given to numbers, vectors, matrices, and more complex structures, such as the results of a regression analysis. This is part of what makes R an object-oriented language. **It always pays to use meaningful names for variables; it makes the program code easier to understand. Be careful with your names and use a consistent style.** Otherwise, you might try to use my.matrix or myMatrix instead of my_matrix. All are legitimate names and acceptable styles to use, but it is better to stick with one style. If you are using `RStudio`, the environment helps you choose the right name. As you start to type, `RStudio` shows you a dropdown list of names (of functions or variables) that it already knows, from which you can select one.

Logical operations can be applied to matrices or vectors using their names.

Particular rows or columns of a matrix can be selected using the square bracket notation above. For example, first the full `my_matrix` then the first row, then the second column, then the submatrix of the first two rows and the second and third columns:

```
> my_matrix
[,1] [,2] [,3]
[1,]    1    5    9
[2,]    2    6   10
[3,]    3    7   11
[4,]    4    8   12
> my_matrix[1,]
[1] 1 5 9
> my_matrix[,2]
[1] 5 6 7 8
> my_matrix[1:2,2:3]
[,1] [,2]
[1,]    5    9
[2,]    6   10
>
```

2.3 Data Frames in R

So far, we have only considered numbers, vectors, and matrices as objects in R. Another important class of objects is the *data frame*. You can think of a data frame like an Excel spreadsheet. It has rows and columns, and columns have names as in Excel. Further, some columns may be text, others numbers, as in Excel. In fact, in our R sessions, we often "import" an Excel spreadsheet into R as a data frame, typically with a long name corresponding to the Excel filename. Often, the statistical and predictive analytics commands that we use in R expect the data to be in the form of a data frame, not a matrix or set of vectors.

Creating a data frame is easy; in this example, we make a data frame from three vector variables. These become the columns, whose labels are simply the names of the variables:

```
> age = c(21,17,44,32,38,65)
> height = c(66,68,71,62,68,77)
> gender = c("m","f","m","f","f","m")
```

```
> my_data = data.frame(age, height, gender)
> my_data
age height gender
1  21      66      m
2  17      68      f
3  44      71      m
4  32      62      f
5  38      68      f
6  65      77      m
>
```

2.3.1 Key operations with data frames

There are many ways to extract only a portion of a data frame. In the following, the most common is listed first: use a dollar sign after the data frame name, followed by the column that you want. Alternatively, you can identify entries in matrix notation form or by column name:

```
> my_data$height
[1] 66 68 71 62 68 77
> my_data["height"]
height
1      66
2      68
3      71
4      62
5      68
6      77
> my_data[,2]
[1] 66 68 71 62 68 77
> my_data[,"height"]
[1] 66 68 71 62 68 77
>
```

You can also subset the data from the data frame by using `c`:

```
> partial_data = my_data[c("height","gender")]
> partial_data
height gender
1      66      m
2      68      f
3      71      m
4      62      f
5      68      f
6      77      m
```

```
> partial_data = my_data[,c("height","gender")]
> partial_data
height gender
1      66      m
2      68      f
3      71      m
4      62      f
5      68      f
6      77      m
> partial_data = my_data[,2:3]
> partial_data
height gender
1      66      m
2      68      f
3      71      m
4      62      f
5      68      f
6      77      m
>
```

You can convert an existing matrix into a data frame using `as.data.frame`, but the resulting column names will be generic:

```
> my_matrix = matrix(1:12,4,3)
> df_my_matrix = as.data.frame(my_matrix)
> df_my_matrix
V1 V2 V3
1  1  5  9
2  2  6 10
3  3  7 11
4  4  8 12
>
```

You can use the **colnames** function to give meaningful names to the columns:

```
> colnames(df_my_matrix) = c("Nos. 1-4","Nos. 5-8","Nos. 9-12")
> df_my_matrix
Nos. 1-4 Nos. 5-8 Nos. 9-12
1        1        5         9
2        2        6        10
3        3        7        11
4        4        8        12
>
```

Note that when the data frame is in table form, **R always adds a column with the row numbers on the left, which is why**

the column names do not appear directly over their column data!!!. We will manually adjust that from here forward.

We see that the `summary` function performs different actions depending on the object it is summarizing. For a data frame, it presents a summary of each column. The summary type depends on whether the column is text or numeric:

```
> summary(my_data)
      age            height          gender
Min.   :17.00   Min.   :62.00   Length:6
1st Qu.:23.75   1st Qu.:66.50   Class :character
Median :35.00   Median :68.00   Mode  :character
Mean   :36.17   Mean   :68.67
3rd Qu.:42.50   3rd Qu.:70.25
Max.   :65.00   Max.   :77.00
> summary(df_my_matrix)
    Nos. 1-4       Nos. 5-8       Nos. 9-12
Min.   :1.00   Min.   :5.00   Min.   : 9.00
1st Qu.:1.75   1st Qu.:5.75   1st Qu.: 9.75
Median :2.50   Median :6.50   Median :10.50
Mean   :2.50   Mean   :6.50   Mean   :10.50
3rd Qu.:3.25   3rd Qu.:7.25   3rd Qu.:11.25
Max.   :4.00   Max.   :8.00   Max.   :12.00
>
```

2.4 Functions in R

You have already seen two functions: `c` and `matrix`. The first converts a set of elements (which need not be numbers) into a vector object, whereas the second converts a set of numbers into a matrix object. You can write your own functions.

Let's create a simple function that builds an $n \times n$ identity matrix (with ones on the diagonal). We don't really need such a function. There are two built-in functions in R that already do this: `diag()` and `Diag()`. This exercise is simply to illustrate the process. In the R session, you first define the function and then call it.

Every function you create needs a name. Pick something meaningful, but try to avoid names of likely built-in functions, such as `print`, `sqrt`, or `sum`. If you need a special sum, maybe call it `sum_of_y` or `my_sum`. You can always check to see if a function name that you have in mind is already used: just type it into the RStudio code window,

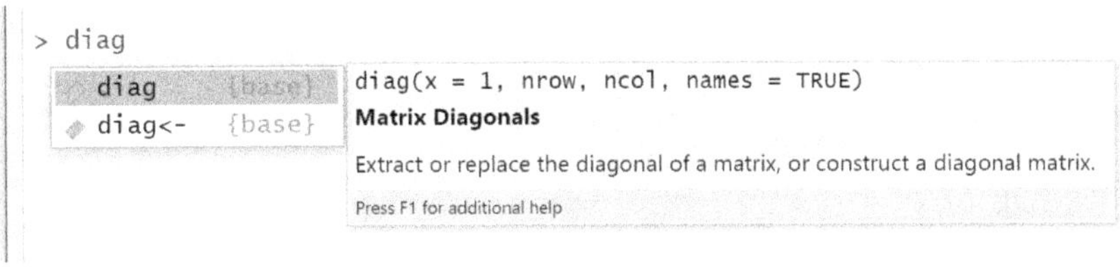

Figure 2.1. Checking for the existence of the function **diag**.

and see if it recognizes it (if so, it will autocomplete it with suggested arguments). Figure 2.1 shows a check on the name **diag**.

Here is what our function definition for creating a diagonal matrix looks like:

```
> my_diag = function(diag_val , diag_size){
    + diag_out = matrix(0,diag_size ,diag_size)
    + for(i in 1:diag_size){diag_out[i,i] = diag_val}
    + return(diag_out)
    + }
>
```

There are 10 key things to note:

1. the function name is on the left side of the equals symbol = (or you can use <-), and the function arguments or parameters belong inside the parentheses;
2. in R, function arguments or parameters are placed inside parentheses, not brackets;
3. use meaningful names for the function arguments or parameters;
4. any changes to the parameters are NOT passed outside the function, unless the parameters were declared to be GLOBAL in the calling function (this is done by using the global assign, <<- rather than the local assign, <- or =);
5. at the end of the first line, add a bracket to begin the function definition, and close the bracket after the last line of the function definition;
6. after hitting Enter for the first line, the system places a + rather than a > because it expects more input from you (the function is not yet fully defined);
7. **diag_out** is initially set to be a square matrix of all zeroes;

8. we use a `for` structure to loop over a dummy index `i` for setting the diagonal elements to `diag_val`;
9. here, the `for` loop is a single command, but it can be multiple commands (separated by line feeds or semicolons) within the brackets;
10. unless otherwise specified, functions return the value of the last object created, but it is ALWAYS a good idea to make the returned object explicit using the `return()` function.

The output of any function can be any kind of structure. Here, it is a matrix. That means we can apply the `summary` function or the `print` function to the output object. Here are the commands and results in the console window:

```
> a_diag_matrix = my_diag(3.5,5)
> summary(a_diag_matrix)
       V1             V2             V3             V4             V5
 Min.   :0.0   Min.   :0.0   Min.   :0.0   Min.   :0.0   Min.   :0.0
 1st Qu.:0.0   1st Qu.:0.0   1st Qu.:0.0   1st Qu.:0.0   1st Qu.:0.0
 Median :0.0   Median :0.0   Median :0.0   Median :0.0   Median :0.0
 Mean   :0.7   Mean   :0.7   Mean   :0.7   Mean   :0.7   Mean   :0.7
 3rd Qu.:0.0   3rd Qu.:0.0   3rd Qu.:0.0   3rd Qu.:0.0   3rd Qu.:0.0
 Max.   :3.5   Max.   :3.5   Max.   :3.5   Max.   :3.5   Max.   :3.5
> print(a_diag_matrix)
     [,1] [,2] [,3] [,4] [,5]
[1,]  3.5  0.0  0.0  0.0  0.0
[2,]  0.0  3.5  0.0  0.0  0.0
[3,]  0.0  0.0  3.5  0.0  0.0
[4,]  0.0  0.0  0.0  3.5  0.0
[5,]  0.0  0.0  0.0  0.0  3.5
>
```

After you run the function definition commands in R, you can use that function in that session. In each R session, you need to include the function definition again to use the function. But it can be tedious to reenter the function definition over and over again in each R session.

Instead, you can place the commands in a text file with the extension `.R`. These kinds of files are called *R scripts*. You can run an R script file in RStudio by opening it in the Source Editor window under the `File` tab. Then, you can select all or segments of code and click the run (right arrow) icon. You can also run a script file, such as `my_code`, by typing `my_code` in the Session window in RStudio. Let's look further at the RStudio IDE.

2.5 Script Files in R and the RStudio Integrated Development Environment

Like other programming languages, it is convenient to be able to run the same set of commands (also called *code*) repeatedly. This is particularly helpful when working to get a sequence of R statements to do what you want. If you find a mistake in a previous command, there is no need to start over; fix that command, and continue on. Before delving further, you need to understand a bit about the programming environment that we will use: `RStudio`.

Many programming languages have associated software that makes it easy to write and debug code and to run the resulting programs. These are called *Integrated Development Environments*, or *IDE*s. They typically provide a graphical Windows-based programming environment that includes text and graphical output and means to import and export code, data, and figures. A popular (and also free) IDE for R is `RStudio`. Now called `Posit`, more information and free download links can be found at Posit (2022).

Figure 2.2 shows the four panels in an RStudio session after opening a new window for creating R code, also called a *script file*. That panel at the upper left of the figure is called the *Source Editor*. It may have multiple tabs, each containing a file with some R code that you have written. As you run R code, the panel at the upper right, called *Environment*, shows you the names and values of any current variables. The lower-left window is where you execute commands in one of two ways: by typing them in directly to this *Console* window or by using your mouse to select code from one of the *Source Editor* windows and then clicking the green right-arrow icon above the *Source Editor* window. The code then appears on the console line-by-line as it is executed.

The panel at the lower right has multiple tabs with very different uses. The `Files` tab allows you to browse your folders and, in particular, click on a particular folder and make it the *working directory*.

Figure 2.2. The four panels in an RStudio session.

When you are in the folder you want, clicking the gear icon gives a dropdown list that includes `set working directory`. That means all of the R script files in that directory can be accessed without referring to the full directory path. That path can be bewilderingly long; you can see the full path using the function `getwd()`. Here is the path for one of my script files:

```
> getwd()
[1] "C:/Users/rbarton/OneDrive - The Pennsylvania State
University/Desktop/Bartons Files/Papers-Talks/PT23/SW23/R code"
>
```

In the RStudio IDE, the Source Editor window can have multiple tabs, each containing an R script that you save to your own folder. R script files are text files but have a `.R` extension to the filename rather than`.txt`. You can make this more complicated: if you have several pieces of R code in separate files, you can insert one script file (say, `my_code_2`) into another script file (say, `my_code_1`) by inserting the line `source{my_code_2}` in the `my_code_1` script file, where you want these commands to be located. RStudio will be able to find these files if that folder is your current working directory. That will happen if either you start RStudio by double-clicking one of these files.

2.5.1 R analysis strategy using functions and script files

A good overall strategy for your R analyses is to do ALL of your R session commands via script files rather than typing them interactively in the console window. This is for several reasons:

1. You can organize and reuse your codes by keeping them in one or more script files (if you want to reuse a function, put it in a separate script file).
2. If you make one code file your main program, all other script files that you use in your analyses can be accessed by including `source` commands for each R script file at the start of the main program.
3. In the same way, at the start of the main program, you can include libraries of functions available from the CRAN website, either after downloading them to your computer (once) using the `install.packages("usefulPackage")` and adding in your main file the command `library(usefulPackage)` or simply adding the `library(usefulPackage)` command and letting RStudio prompt you to download and install the package. Most packages have multiple useful functions. (Strangely, while downloading, it is called a `package`, but when using, it is called a `library`.)
4. You can open multiple script files in RStudio.
5. To run code, there is no need to type it more than once. You can simply put it in a script file, and then click the tab of the script file with the command that you want to execute if it is already open in RStudio, but if it is not open, open it using the `File` dropdown, and then run the command by placing your cursor at the start of a line and clicking the Run icon (see Figure 2.3); the cursor then moves to the next line.

Figure 2.3. The Run icon used for executing script code in an RStudio session.

6. If you click the Run icon again, it will run the next line, so you can step through your R commands without having to retype them.
7. You can run a whole group of commands by using your mouse to select them and then clicking the Run icon.
8. This allows you to keep your code organized and reuse pieces of code in different projects.

2.6 Key Descriptive Statistics Tools in R

While our focus is on *predictive analytics*, we need many tools that fall into the *descriptive analytics* categories. You may be familiar with Excel tools for descriptive analytics. These are available in R, but R has more extensive descriptive analytic tools as well.

2.6.1 Data summaries in R: Importing an Excel data file

The `summary` command has already been mentioned; it is the first way to describe a data set. We explore the `summary` command on a stock price data set that is held in an Excel file called `StockPriceData.xlsx`. This can be found in the R_codes_and_data folder in Barton (2023). A portion of the file is shown in Figure 2.4.

	A	B	C	D	E	F
1	Company	Listing	StockChgPct	RevChgPct	ProfitChgPct	IndType
2	3M	3M	35.0	-0.5	4.5	Product
3	Aetna	AETNA	49.5	4.7	-5	Service
4	AIG	AIG	-9.2	-10.2	-138.7	Service
5	Allstate	ALLSTATE	37.4	2.5	-13.5	Service
6	Alphabet	ALPHABET /	34.5	20.4	19.1	Service
7	Amazon.com	AMAZON.CC	54.4	27.1	297.8	Service
8	American Airlines Group	AMERICAN ,	13.9	-2	-64.8	Service
9	American Express	AMERICAN	33.9	-1.8	4.7	Service
10	AmerisourceBergen	AMERISOUF	12.4	8	-37.7	Service
11	Anthem	ANTHEM	62.3	7.2	-3.5	Service
12	Apple	APPLE	48.4	-7.7	-14.4	Product
13	Archer Daniels Midland	ARCHER-DA	-10.2	-7.9	-30.8	Product
14	AT&T	AT&T	-7.7	11.6	-2.8	Service
15	Bank of America Corp.	BANK OF AI	33.7	0.7	12.7	Service
16	Berkshire Hathaway	BERKSHIRE	22.9	6.1	0	Service

Figure 2.4. The Excel stock price file.

To import the Excel file into R, we first double-click on the R script file in the same folder called `R-scripts_for_book.R`. Besides opening the file, this sets RStudio's working directory to the folder that contains our R scripts and Excel data files. The Excel file `StockPriceData.xlsx` is in the same folder.

To bring the Excel data into R, we use the dropdown menu under the `File` tab, as shown in Figure 2.5. That will open a dialog box for you to select the file. In the current folder (working directory), there are only two files: an R script file and the Excel file, as seen in Figure 2.6. When `Open` is clicked, R provides a preview window showing how it intends to import the Excel data and, in the lower right, the actual R commands that will be executed. This is shown in Figure 2.7. To automate this Excel file import for additional analyses later, copy these lines from the console window (after you click `Import`) and paste them into your R script file.

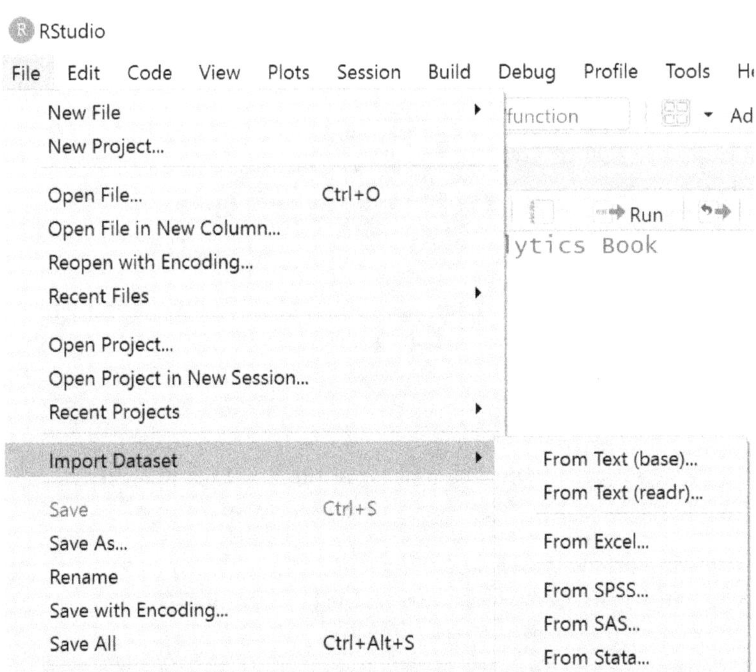

Figure 2.5. Menu to open an Excel file in an RStudio session.

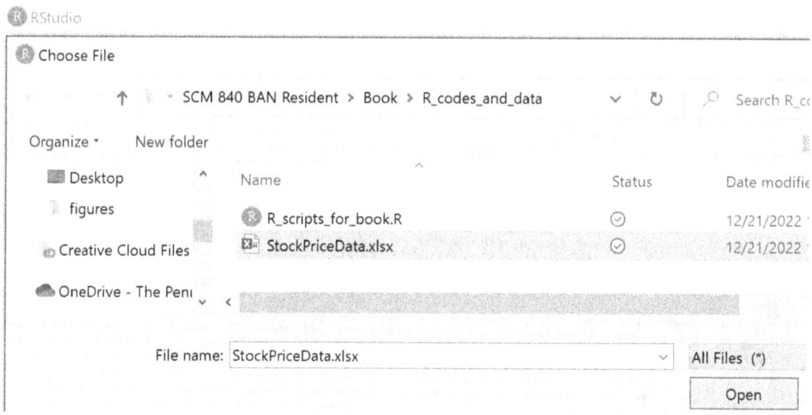

Figure 2.6. RStudio menu to select the Excel file to open.

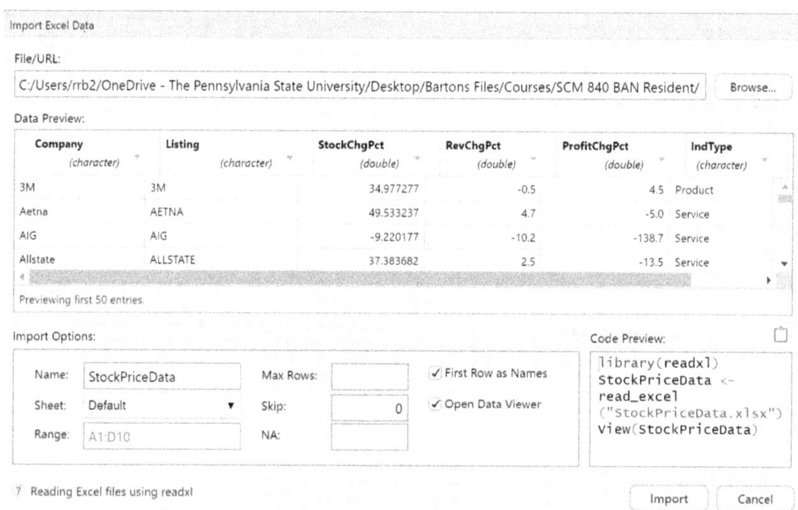

Figure 2.7. RStudio preview of the Excel file to open.

After importing the Excel file, the RStudio window will appear as shown in Figure 2.8. Here are some key things to note:

1. the commands to import the file now appear in the console window at the lower left;

Figure 2.8. RStudio after Excel file import showing the StockPriceData data frame.

2. there is a new tab at the upper left: besides the R script file, there is a tab labeled `StockPriceData` — R uses the name of the Excel file as the name of the new R data frame;
3. the data frame description appears under the `environment` tab at the upper right, showing 89 observations of 6 variables.

Now that we have a data set imported into RStudio, let's explore some key descriptive statistics capabilities of R.

2.6.2 Data summaries in R: Summary statistics

First, for any data analysis project, it is important to examine the data through plots and summaries. These can also help you identify bad data and fix or remove them — the *data cleaning* process. Also, remember that R is an object-oriented language. Among other things, this means that functions operate differently on different kinds of objects. The following is the result of applying the `summary()` function to the `StockPriceData` data frame object:

```
> summary(StockPriceData)
  Company              Listing              StockChgPct
 Length:89          Length:89          Min.   :-75.833
 Class :character   Class :character   1st Qu.:  3.448
 Mode  :character   Mode  :character   Median : 15.304
                                       Mean   : 17.867
                                       3rd Qu.: 33.730
                                       Max.   : 94.117
   RevChgPct          ProfitChgPct          IndType
 Min.   :-53.300   Min.   :-138.70   Length:89
 1st Qu.: -3.800   1st Qu.: -22.60   Class :character
 Median :  1.900   Median :  -2.70   Mode  :character
 Mean   :  4.112   Mean   :   1.14
 3rd Qu.:  6.500   3rd Qu.:  16.10
 Max.   :197.300   Max.   : 297.80
>
```

There are 89 observations of variables corresponding to the company name (**Company**), its abbreviated listing name on the stock exchange (**Listing**), the percent change in stock price over the year (**StockChgPct**), the percent revenue change (**RevChgPct**), the percent change in profit (**ProfitChgPct**), and the type of industry: product or service (**IndType**). For quantitative variables, summary statistics are provided: minimum, 25th percentile, median (50th percentile) mean, 75th percentile, and maximum values. Even this limited information allows for the identification of extremely large or small values that may be in error.

To get more statistics on the **StockPriceData** data frame, use the **describe** command. That produces standard deviation, skewness, and kurtosis values. To use **describe**, you need to attach the **psych** library. Remember, you only need to install the **psych** package once:

```
> install.packages("psych")
<<NOTE - a series of R notifications following this command>>
<<NOTE - this command only done once on your computer>>
> library(psych)
> describe(StockPriceData)
             vars  n  mean    sd median trimmed   mad     min
Company*        1 89 45.00 25.84   45.0   45.00 32.62    1.00
Listing*        2 89 45.00 25.84   45.0   45.00 32.62    1.00
StockChgPct     3 89 17.87 25.57   15.3   17.82 23.32  -75.83
RevChgPct       4 89  4.11 25.21    1.9    1.34  7.86  -53.30
ProfitChgPct    5 89  1.14 62.27   -2.7   -3.44 29.50 -138.70
IndType*        6 89  1.61  0.49    2.0    1.63  0.00    1.00
```

```
                  max   range  skew kurtosis   se
Company*        89.00   88.00  0.00    -1.24 2.74
Listing*        89.00   88.00  0.00    -1.24 2.74
StockChgPct     94.12  169.95 -0.20     1.79 2.71
RevChgPct      197.30  250.60  5.26    37.11 2.67
ProfitChgPct   297.80  436.50  2.35    10.04 6.60
IndType*         2.00    1.00 -0.43    -1.84 0.05
>
```

The summary includes the qualitative variables `Company`, `Listing`, and `IndType`. These are marked with asterisks. RStudio makes it easy to learn more. In the lower-right subwindow, click the `Help` tab and enter `describe` in the search box. Figure 2.9 shows a portion of the result. The default is set to convert text values to integers, which are then summarized. These are not useful in our setting.

2.6.3 Data summaries in R: Graphical summaries

In addition to the descriptive statistics above, there are three types of graphs that provide important initial insight into the data. Boxplots give the general distribution of the data and can be used for any quantitative variable, either over the entire data set or with separate boxplots for different levels of one or more qualitative variables. Scatter plots show relationships between two quantitative

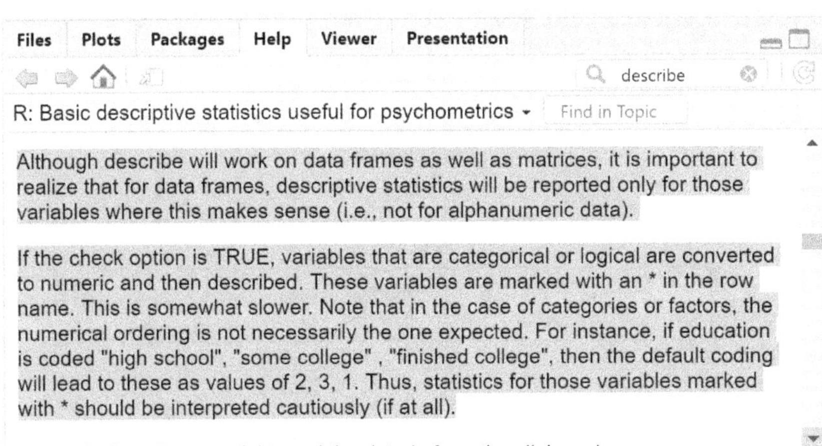

Figure 2.9. RStudio help search on describe highlighting "*" variables.

variables. They can be executed for multiple pairs of variables using the `pairs()` function in R. Finally, identifying the appropriate probability distribution for a set of data can be done using functions in R. To check whether the distribution is approximately normal, use the `qqnorm()` function in the `stats` package in R (the `stats` library is active by default in R). To check for distribution families that most closely match your data, use the Cullen and Frey graph of skewness vs. kurtosis created by the `descdist()` function in the `fitdistrplus` library (you will need to install this package once before attaching the library). Let's apply each of these methods to variables in the StockPriceData data frame.

Boxplots show quantiles and extreme values of the data visually without the clutter of individual data values, allowing an overall view of the distribution of numerical values. The box marks the middle 50% of the data, from the 0.25-quantile to the 0.75-quantile. A line divides the box at the 0.50-quantile (the median). Lines from the box extend to the most extreme data points above and below the box limits, unless extending them would make them longer than 1.5 times the length of the box. In that case, the line stops at the most extreme value that is within 1.5 times the box length, and all data points that are more extreme are marked with individual symbols: circles or asterisks. The code for a boxplot of `StockChgPct` is shown in the following and the plot in Figure 2.10. The default orientation for the boxplot is vertical, but the horizontal layout is more typical in statistical summaries, so the `horizontal=TRUE` option was added. The default provides no axis label, so the `xlab` option was added:

```
> boxplot(StockPriceData$StockChgPct , horizontal=TRUE ,
+ xlab=" Stock Price Change %")
>
```

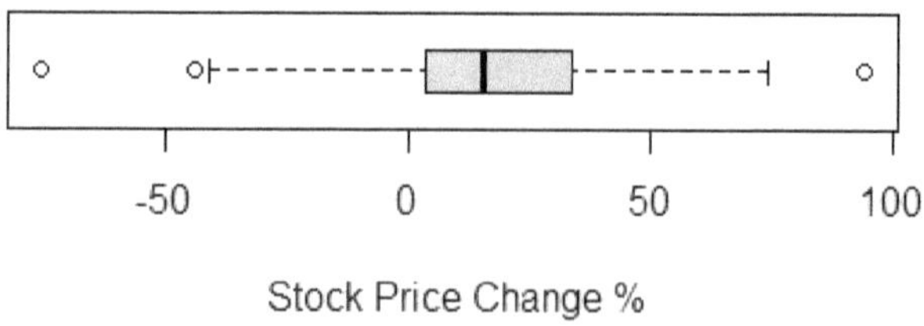

Figure 2.10. Boxplot for stock price change %.

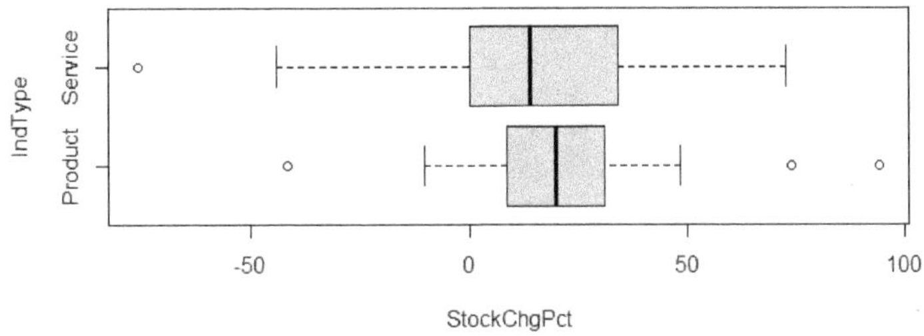

Figure 2.11. Boxplot for stock price change %.

From the box plot, we see that typical stock price changes for the year ranged from just above 0% to about 35%, with a few outliers, one gain of nearly 100%, and the greatest loss of around 75%. How does this distribution vary for product vs. service industry types? The box plot command can be used to give stock price changes *as a function of* industry type. The *as a function of* command is used in many settings in R and is denoted by a tilde (~). The command is shown as follows and the resulting box plot in Figure 2.11. Note that the labels for the axes are attached automatically and do not need to be specified by options. Also, note that the figure window must be large enough; otherwise, some of the labels will not show. From the figure, it is clear that there was more variability in stock price change for service industries than for product industries.

```
> boxplot(StockChgPct ~ IndType, data=StockPriceData,
+ horizontal = TRUE)
>
```

Scatter plots show relationships between two or more quantitative variables. Sometimes, one variable can be considered causal and the other dependent. In this case, it is usual to place the causal variable on the horizontal (x) axis. One might think that a profit increase would cause a stock price increase, so Figure 2.12 plots stock price increase vs. profit increase (again, use the *as a function of* notation). The R code for this plot is shown as follows:

```
> plot(StockChgPct ~ ProfitChgPct, data=StockPriceData)
>
```

The default large circles can be harder to visualize than small dots. One option with the plot command is to change the plot character. Plot symbol choices are numbered and can be easily found on

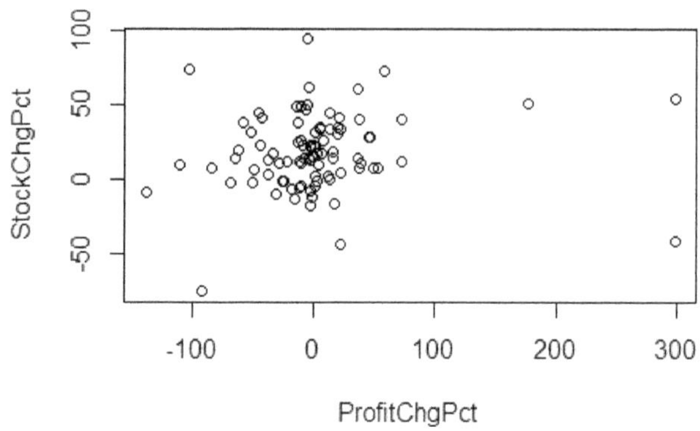

Figure 2.12. Scatter plot of stock price change % vs. profit change %.

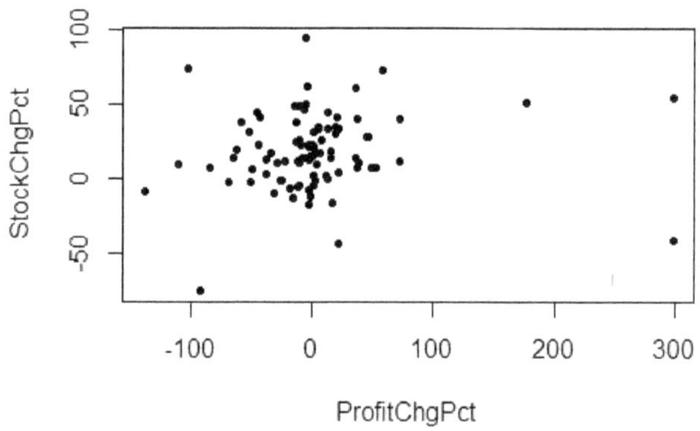

Figure 2.13. Scatter plot of stock price change % vs. profit change %.

the Web by Googling "plot characters in R" and selecting the image view. The small dot symbol has an index number of 20. The code to produce the plot in Figure 2.13 as follows:

```
> plot(StockChgPct ~ ProfitChgPct, data=StockPriceData,
+ pch=20)
>
```

Matrix plots are scatter plots of multiple quantitative variables. The R `pairs()` function produces matrix plots. It is easiest to use with the *as a function of* notation described earlier. The code (again using small dots) is as follows, and the result is shown in Figure 2.14.

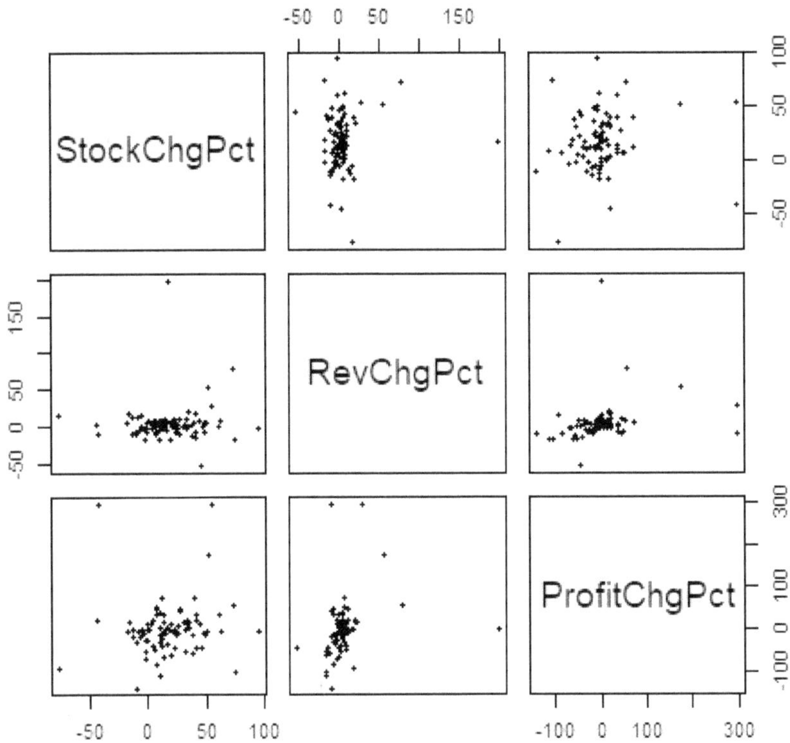

Figure 2.14. Matrix of scatter plots for stock price data.

From the matrix of plots, we see a weak positive relationship between revenue change and profit change and a weak positive relationship between stock price change and profit change.

```
> pairs(~ StockChgPct + RevChgPct + ProfitChgPct,
+ data=StockPriceData,pch=20)
>
```

Probability plots can be useful in two ways in predictive analytics. First, linear regression models for predicting a number assume that the deviations in the prediction follow a normal distribution. This can be checked by constructing a normal probability plot for the residuals of the regression model. In R, that plot is accomplished using the `qqnorm()` function. Also, many data follow a normal distribution. It is good to check if this is the case.

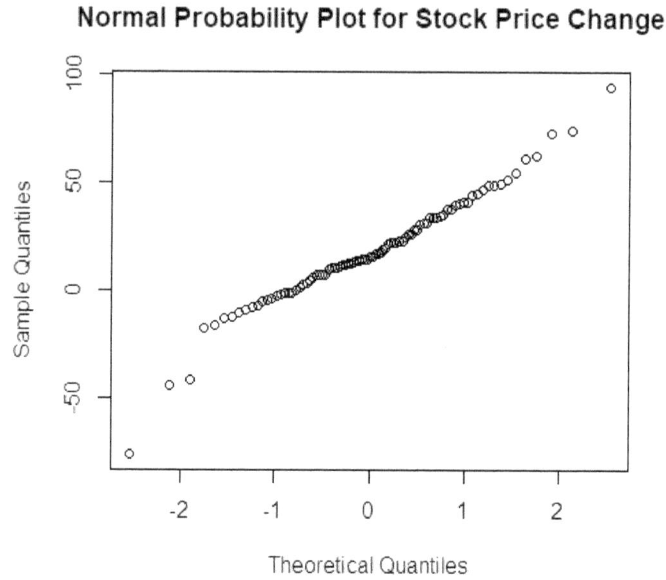

Figure 2.15. Matrix of scatter plots for stock price data.

Let's see if the stock price change data follow a normal distribution by using `qqnorm()`. The R command is as follows, and the resulting plot is shown in Figure 2.15:

```
> qqnorm(StockPriceData$StockChgPct , main=
+ "Normal Probability Plot for Stock Price Change")
>
```

The resulting plot is reasonably close to a straight line, suggesting that the data are consistent with the hypothesis of a normal distribution.

Second, in building simulation models of real systems, the inherent randomness observed in real data will usually be simulated using a known probability distribution family, such as the normal, exponential, gamma, or lognormal distribution families. Determining which family is most appropriate for a set of data is aided by examining the data skewness and kurtosis in a plot, with regions of the plot identifying potential distribution families appropriate for the data. In R, that *Cullen and Frey graph* is constructed using the `descdata()` function in the `fitdistrplus` library. Make sure that the `MASS` package is installed, and then install `fitdistrplus`.

The matrix plot shows an unusual distribution for revenue change (%). We investigate what probability distribution family might be appropriate for the revenue change data. The following code installs the required packages and attaches the `fitdistrplus` library to allow the `descdist()` function to plot the Cullen and Frey graph for `RevChgPct`. The `boot=1000` option recognizes that data can vary, and there is uncertainty about the appropriate distribution based on only one set of data. The option causes `descdist` to plot not just one skewness vs. kurtosis value but with 1,000 others based on resampling (with replacement) from the 89 data values at hand. Each resample will leave some values out and sample some values more than once, and the resulting points (plotted with small circles) represent alternative possibilities for skewness and kurtosis. Figure 2.16 shows the result. The large dot near the center is based on the original 89 observations and suggests a gamma distribution, or perhaps a beta distribution. The bootstrapped alternatives (small circles) suggest other possibilities, including exponential and lognormal distributions. All of these are potential distribution choices to represent the revenue percent change.

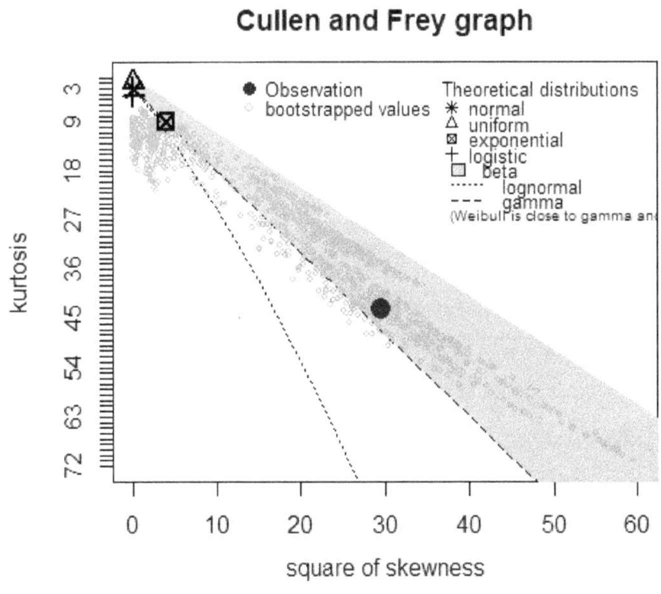

Figure 2.16. Matrix of scatter plots for stock price data.

```
> install.packages("MASS")
<<NOTE - a series of R notifications following this command>>
<<NOTE - this command only done once on your computer>>
install.packages("fitdistrplus")
<<NOTE - a series of R notifications following this command>>
<<NOTE - this command only done once on your computer>>
> library(fitdistrplus)
Loading required package: MASS
Loading required package: survival
> descdist(StockPriceData$RevChgPct, boot=1000)
summary statistics
------
min:  -53.3   max:  197.3
median:  1.9
mean:  4.11236
estimated sd:  25.21438
estimated skewness:  5.440907
estimated kurtosis:  43.31999
>
```

Additional R Functions and Code Structures

This concludes a basic introduction to R. There is much more to learn, but the rest can be picked up as you need it. Additional R functions and structures will be described in the cases that are used to illustrate the three parts that follow: predicting a number, predicting a class, and predicting dynamic behavior.

2.7 R Code Used in This Chapter

```
# R Codes for Chapter 2

# Variables in R Section
#======================
my_matrix = matrix(1:12,4,3)
my_matrix <- matrix(1:12,4,3)
my_vector = c(5,5,1)
my_matrix%*%my_vector

my_matrix[1,]
my_matrix[,2]
my_matrix[1:2,2:3]
```

```
# Data Frames in R Section
#========================
age = c(21,17,44,32,38,65)
height = c(66,68,71,62,68,77)
gender = c("m","f","m","f","f","m")
my_data = data.frame(age, height, gender)
my_data

my_data$height
my_data[,2]
my_data[,"height"]

partial_data = my_data[c("height","gender")]
partial_data
partial_data = my_data[,c("height","gender")]
partial_data
partial_data = my_data[,2:3]
partial_data

my_matrix = matrix(1:12,4,3)
df_my_matrix = as.data.frame(my_matrix)
df_my_matrix
colnames(df_my_matrix) =
c("Nos. 1-4","Nos. 5-8","Nos. 9-12")
df_my_matrix

summary(my_data)

# Functions in R Section
#======================
my_diag = function(diag_val, diag_size){
    diag_out = matrix(0,diag_size,diag_size)
    for(i in 1:diag_size){diag_out[i,i] = diag_val}
    return(diag_out)
}
a_diag_matrix = my_diag(3.5,5)
summary(a_diag_matrix)

getwd()

# Data Summaries in R: Importing an Excel Data File Subsection
#=============================================================
library(readxl)
StockPriceData <- read_excel("StockPriceData.xlsx")
```

```
# Data Summaries in R: Summary Statistics Subsection
#====================================================
summary(StockPriceData)
install.packages("psych")
library(psych)
describe(StockPriceData)

# Data Summaries in R: Graphical Summaries Subsection
#====================================================
boxplot(StockPriceData$StockChgPct, horizontal=TRUE,
xlab=" Stock Price Change %")
boxplot(StockChgPct ~ IndType, data=StockPriceData,
horizontal = TRUE)
plot(StockChgPct ~ ProfitChgPct, data=StockPriceData)
plot(StockChgPct ~ ProfitChgPct, data=StockPriceData,
pch=20)
pairs(~ StockChgPct + RevChgPct + ProfitChgPct,
data=StockPriceData,pch=20)
qqnorm(StockPriceData$StockChgPct, main=
"Normal Probability Plot for Stock Price Change")

install.packages("MASS")
install.packages("fitdistrplus")
library(fitdistrplus)
descdist(StockPriceData$RevChgPct, boot=1000)
```

Part II

Predicting a Number

Overview

In this part, our focus is on predictive analytics methods for numerical outcomes. Such predictions (along with characterization of the uncertainty in the prediction) can support many kinds of business decisions: What sales volume is likely if we institute a particular advertising strategy? What value can one expect for a home in a certain neighborhood, given its size and features? How does the average number of restaurant visits per month vary based on family income? These are just a few examples.

We will not consider the simplest cases of predicting a number, such as predicting (and characterizing the prediction uncertainty of) the mean of a population given a sample, predicting (and characterizing the prediction uncertainty of) the population standard deviation given a sample, or predicting (and characterizing the prediction uncertainty of) the 90th percentile of a population value given a sample. We focus on *conditional prediction*, where the predicted value (and uncertainty about the prediction) depends on known measured characteristics. These characteristics can be called *predictor variables*. Often, they are called *independent variables*, when they are quantitative, or *factors*, when they are qualitative. For example, predicted baseball game attendance may depend on temperature (an independent variable) and the day of the week (a qualitative factor). The numerical quantity that is predicted is called the *dependent variable* or *response*. In this case, it is the predicted attendance.

When all of the predictor variables are quantitative, the situation calls for regression models. When some predictor variables are quantitative and others qualitative, regression can still be used with careful coding of the qualitative variables. In other cases, a special class of models called *analysis of covariance* (ANOCOVA) are used. When all predictor variables are qualitative, the predictive models are often called ANOVA models. And finally, when the dependent variable is qualitative, we move from *predicting a number* to *predicting a class*, which is covered in Part II.

In the following chapters, we explore three families of methods for predicting a number: linear regression, spatial correlation (Gaussian Process) regression, and neural network regression. The first two methods fall in the traditional research paradigm, while the last one is a data-adaptive research method. These methods are some of the most popular, but there are many others, such as radial basis function regression, ANOVA models, and regression trees. References to these and other methods are given at the end of this part.

Chapter 3

Linear Regression

Linear regression is the most widely used predictive analytics tool over the past 100 years. This statistical method was motivated by Francis Galton's studies, which predicted that unusually tall parents would have children who are less unusually tall, on average, and unusually short parents would have children who are less unusually short (Galton, 1885). This phenomenon is called "regression to the mean," thus the name regression model or regression analysis. Karl Pearson, the famous statistician, gave an early exposition of the statistical method (Pearson, 1903).

Linear regression provides a theory-based flexible set of predictive analytics models that often apply to real-world data settings. The methods are computationally efficient and include well-established procedures to check model validity and characterize model error. While they have broad applicability and a solid theoretical foundation, there are still circumstances where their limitations become apparent. We cover more flexible methods (but with less theoretical support) in later chapters.

3.1 Correlation and Simple Linear Regression

We begin a review of linear regression models with the simplest case: a single independent variable and a first-order (linear) relationship.

3.1.1 Correlation and computing an estimate for ρ

Correlation is a term that characterizes the association between two numerical random quantities. Returning to the example of child height vs. parent height, we expect that tall parents will have taller children than the average (though regression suggests that they will not be quite as tall as their parents, on average). Similarly, parents with less-than-average height will tend to have children whose height is less than average (though regression suggests that they will not be quite as tall as their parents, on average). This kind of relationship is called *positive correlation*: both parent height and child height measurements tend to be on the same side of the mean, either both high or both low.

Variables that are correlated do not vary independently. The probability distribution of one variable will differ depending on the value of the second variable. In Figure 3.1, you can see that the probability distribution for Y shifts up as x increases, so the distribution of Y depends on the value of x. Further, the dashed diagonal line shows that this relationship is linear. Any nonzero slope (positive or negative) indicates correlation.

The correlation relationship is symmetric: if X is correlated with Y, then Y is correlated with X. The (linear) correlation coefficient measures the extent and linearity of this kind of relationship (based on the steepness of the slope relative to the width of the distribution).

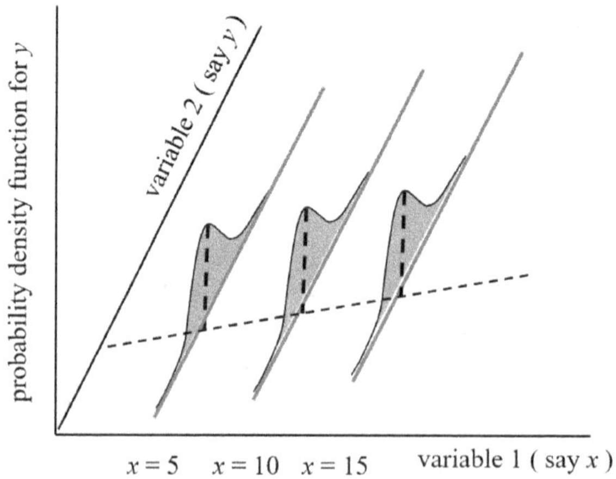

Figure 3.1. The distribution of Y depends on the value of x.

The theoretical value for the overall population is called ρ, and the value measured from sample data is called r.

A scatter plot is the easiest way to detect linear (or nonlinear) correlation. For the relationship in Figure 3.1, a sample of data might produce a scatter plot like that in Figure 3.2. Note that a scatter plot correlation can be positive or negative and strong, moderate, weak, or negligible. Because of the randomness in a sample of data, the sample scatter plot will never show zero correlation, but it can often be negligible. Figure 3.3 shows some possibilities. Note also that a scatter plot is a great way to identify unusual values in your data set. The plot at the upper right has one point that falls far outside the correlation pattern. This the data corresponding to this point should be investigated: it may well be a recording error, or may correspond to an unusual situation that should not be included in further analysis.

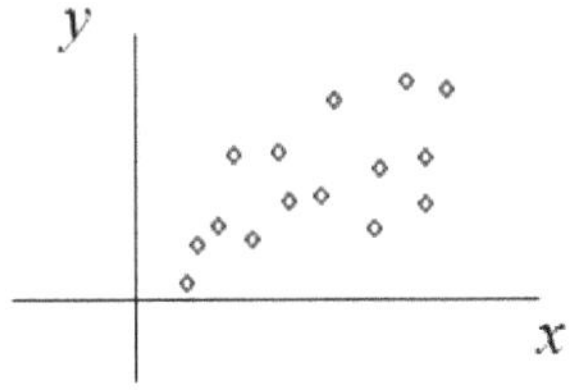

Figure 3.2. Scatter plot for an observational sample from the population shown in Figure 3.1.

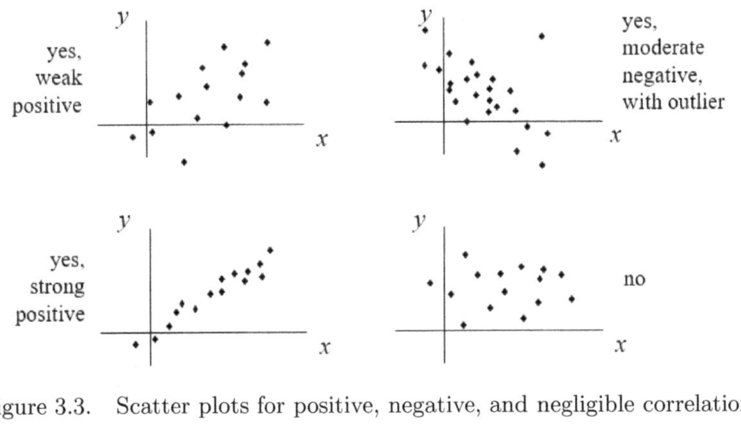

Figure 3.3. Scatter plots for positive, negative, and negligible correlation.

Computing an estimate for ρ

We compute the sample correlation, r, as the average of the product of deviations of x and y from their averages. Then, this average is further standardized by dividing by the product of the sample standard deviations of x and y. This is shown in Equation (3.1):

$$r = \frac{\sum_{j=1}^{n}(x_j - \bar{x})(y_j - \bar{y})}{(n-1)s_x s_y}. \tag{3.1}$$

This is a numerical characterization of the magnitude and sign of the correlation. An r value of $+1$ indicates perfect positive linear correlation; a value of -1 indicates perfect negative correlation. Values near zero indicate negligible correlation. Figures 3.4 and 3.5 show how the numerical calculation aligns with our intuition about positive

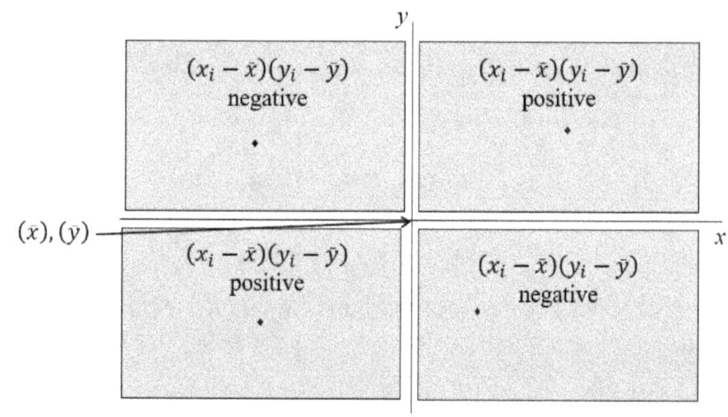

Figure 3.4. Different regions around $\bar{x}, \bar{y}$ have different signs in the correlation sum.

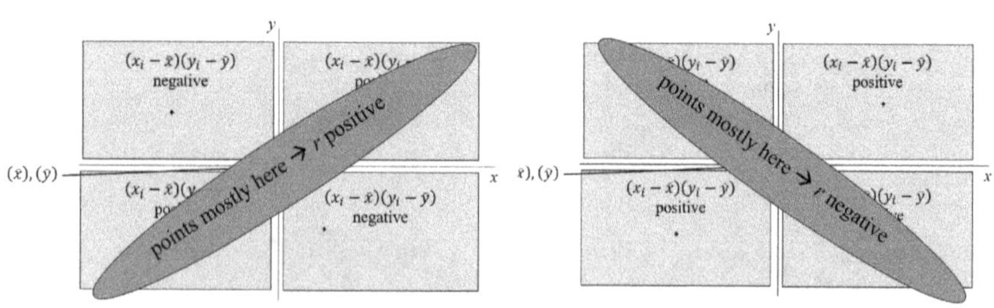

Figure 3.5. Predominance of points in these regions leads to positive or negative correlation estimate.

and negative correlation. Note that the origin in these plot is the average value for each variable, $(\bar{x}, \bar{y})$. Figure 3.4 shows four individual points, each in a different quadrant about $(\bar{x}, \bar{y})$. The product is positive when both deviations are positive or when both deviations are negative, adding a positive amount to the sum. Figure 3.5 shows that when the preponderance of points fall in these quadrants, they will dominate the sum, so the sum will be positive. Similarly, if the preponderance of points fall in the other two quadrants, the number of negative quantities in the sum will dominate. R makes it easy to compute a correlation estimate and also to test whether it is statistically significantly different from zero. The following code illustrates these commands for computing the correlation of % stock price change and % revenue change for the stock price data from Chapter 2.

```
> library(readxl)
> StockPriceData <- read_excel("StockPriceData.xlsx")
> cor(StockPriceData$StockChgPct,StockPriceData$RevChgPct)
[1] 0.06729581
> cor.test(StockPriceData$StockChgPct,
StockPriceData$RevChgPct)
Pearson's product-moment correlation
data:
StockPriceData$StockChgPct and StockPriceData$RevChgPct
t = 0.62912, df = 87, p-value = 0.5309
alternative hypothesis: true correlation is not equal to 0
95 percent confidence interval:
-0.1429645  0.2717441

sample estimates:
cor
0.06729581
>
```

The `cor()` function simply gives the sample correlation coefficient. The function `cor.test()` does much more, giving a 95% confidence interval for the true value ρ and the t statistic and p-value for the hypothesis test H_0: $\rho = 0$ vs. H_1: $\rho \neq 0$. Predictive analytics dictates that we do more than compute a predicted population correlation coefficient: we need to include this confidence interval to characterize the uncertainty that arises from the fact that the computation was based only on a sample, not the whole population.

Observational data vs. designed experiment data

This is a good opportunity to highlight the difference between *observational* data and data from a *designed experiment.* Suppose that the data in Figure 3.2 showed data from a survey where people were asked how many times they had seen a commercial advertisement for insurance in the past week (x) and how interested they were in exploring alternatives to their current insurance. This kind of data are called *observational data.* One does not know in advance whether a particular subject has seen the commercial five times, ten times, etc. One just *observes* the values that the sample provides.

In a designed experiment, a *causal* or *independent* variable (x) is deliberately set to particular values and a second, *dependent* or *response*, variable is measured for the particular settings of x. Figure 3.6 shows a possible set of experimental data. In this setting, subjects were selected randomly and then exposed to either 5, 10, 15, or 20 insurance commercials. Following the specific number of exposures for each subject, they are asked to rate their interest in exploring alternatives to their current insurance. Designed experiments are difficult to implement but can provide more reliable and precise predictions than analysis of observational data. Both settings are discussed in separate sections in the following.

Note that some researchers attempt to imitate a designed experiment by filtering their observational data. This is done on one of two ways. In the first, one identifies an event in time that should affect the correlation, samples data *before* and *after* the event, and compares them. In particular, this is the approach of a popular econometrics

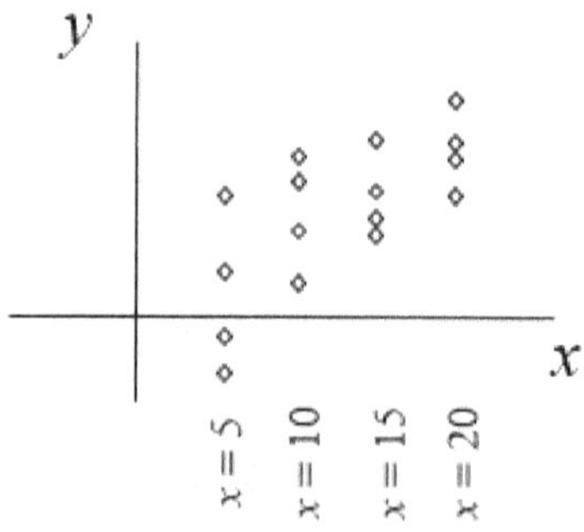

Figure 3.6. Scatter plot for a designed experiment with subjects from the population shown in Figure 3.1.

method called *difference in differences*. The second way discards some of the sample data, retaining clusters of values that are near particular settings of the hypothesized causal variable. When there is more than one causal variable, this pseudo-experimental process can be complex but can provide advantages over the raw observational data. We will see a version of this approach, called *SMOTE*, applied to predicting a class in the next part of this book.

3.1.2 Kinds of correlation

Correlation between variables arises for different reasons. Our interest is in *cause–effect* correlation: when the value of one variable *causes* changes in another. A cause–effect relationship leads to correlation, but correlation does not necessarily mean there is a cause–effect relationship. Consider the plot in Figure 3.7, which shows, for many different basketball players, their average points per game vs. the average number of fouls they commit per game. If *fouls* cause *points*, then as a coach, you should recommend that your players go out and foul the other team!!! That is not the cause of this correlation. Figure 3.8 shows the causal network that leads to the correlation between *fouls* and *points*. There is a *lurking variable*: *player skill*.

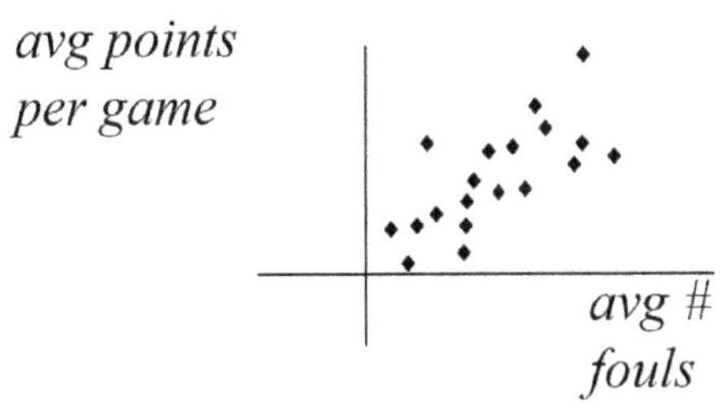

Figure 3.7. Scatter plot of basketball players average points scored vs. average fouls committed.

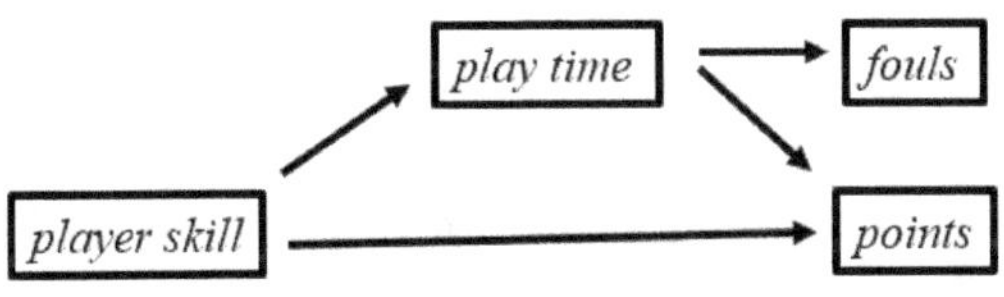

Figure 3.8. Causal structure in the basketball example.

In this case, the causal relationship is as follows: high *player skill* leads to more *play time*, and more *play time* leads to both more points and more fouls. For building a predictive analytics model, one should use *player skill* as the *independent* or *predictor* variable and *points* as the *dependent* or *response* variable. Surprisingly, researchers in industry often make this error and try to design an experiment for determining the relationship between *fouls* and *points*. Be alert to this. When it happens, search for the missing causal variable (or variables). As an alternative to the regression model, *structural equation models* build mathematical models for all relationships in the figure; these would be a set of linked regression models, one for each arrow in the figure. But structural equation modeling is beyond the scope of this text.

We see that there are in fact three kinds of correlation:

- cause–effect (our focus in regression modeling),
- lurking variable (we measure two effects, related by a missing causal variable),
- spurious (just by luck, sometimes to variables will appear to be related).

3.1.3 Simple linear regression model form

Before giving the simplest regression, let's consider a very general regression setting. When the variable we are trying to predict, Y (e.g., average points per game), varies randomly from one observation to the next, a general regression model can be written as

$$Y = f(x) + \varepsilon, \tag{3.2}$$

where, in this general form, ε represents a random perturbation to the average value, f can be any function of x, and x may be a vector of values for different predictor variables. Write Y in upper case to indicate it is a random quantity. Once we have actual samples, *they* will not vary randomly (random samples are FIXED once they have been sampled), and so sample values are represented by lowercase y. Conventional names for Y are the *dependent variable* or *response variable*, while x are *independent variables* or *predictor variables*. Also, note that we generally use italic with variable names. Now that we have a general form, we write a very simple case. *Simple linear regression* has a linear function for f (using coefficients for the intercept β_0 and slope β_1), written as

$$Y = \beta_0 + \beta_1 x + \varepsilon, \ \varepsilon \overset{\text{iid}}{\sim} N(0, \sigma^2). \tag{3.3}$$

The coefficient values β_0 and β_1 in Equation (3.3) are unknown and must be estimated from a set of (x, y) sample data. In simple linear regression under the *traditional research* paradigm, the random perturbations are assumed to be statistically independent of each other and follow a normal distribution with mean zero and unknown variance σ^2 (iid here, also written i.i.d., means independent and identically distributed). Our objective in predictive analytics for simple linear regression under the *traditional research* paradigm is to:

1. determine whether regression might be appropriate based on scatter plots of the predictor and response variable;
2. estimate the unknown values of the model parameters β_0, β_1, and σ;
3. determine the performance of the model (more on this in a moment);
4. determine the validity of the model (traditional research paradigm);
5. characterize the uncertainty in the regression model parameter estimates (estimates for the coefficients β_0 and β_1, and the parameter σ) using standard deviations for the estimates and confidence intervals for the true values;
6. use the estimates (and associated uncertainty) to predict values of Y and/or $\mathrm{E}(Y)$ and associated uncertainty by constructing prediction and/or confidence intervals if the regression model assumptions are valid and the model has predictive power.

Each of these aspects is tackled in the following sections.

3.1.4 Estimating model coefficients (βs and σ)

Estimating coefficients for simple linear regression amounts to choosing a slope and intercept that best match the data and then estimating σ as the standard deviation of the deviations of the sample values from the line (vertical distance). It makes sense that good estimates for the slope (b_1) and intercept (b_1) for the line should minimize the estimated standard deviation of the deviations from the line — that implies a best fit. The sample standard deviation of deviations from the line (residuals) is computed from the sum of squared (vertical) deviations from the line. Thus, this estimation method is called *least squares*. It is used in many other estimation tasks as well, including neural network regression, which we cover later.

Again, R makes it easy to compute these estimates and their standard deviations. In this example, we consider a real estate example based on a popular North Valley Real Estate data set. This data set is not the same (different sample size and different values), but similar principles apply. Assume that North Valley Real Estate is a small real estate office, with 124 homes sold in the past year. This firm focuses on sales of existing homes, not new construction. For this simple linear regression example, imagine that we want to determine the strength of the relationship between house selling price and house size in square feet. The actual data set has two other variables for each home sold: the number of bedrooms and the number of bathrooms (where a 1/2 bath means just a sink and toilet). Before fitting the model, we plot these variables to see if there is apparent correlation. The code for reading in the Excel data file and doing the scatter plot follows:

```
> library(readxl) # needed to read in the Excel data file
> HousePriceSimple <- read_excel("HousePriceSimple.xlsx")
> plot(HousePriceSimple$Size,HousePriceSimple$Price)
>
```

The resulting plot is shown in Figure 3.9. There appears to be a moderate positive correlation, and since we do expect people to be willing to pay more for a larger house, a cause–effect relationship seems reasonable. So, we proceed to fit the regression model. Here is the code that fits the model:

```
> regModel = lm(Price ~ Size, data = HousePriceSimple)
>
```

Note that the output of the fitting process is placed by R in the object we have called `regModel`. Because we made this assignment, no analysis is printed to the Console window. This object orientation of R makes it easy to get coefficient estimates, confidence intervals, predictions, diagnostic plots, and more. First, we would like to know

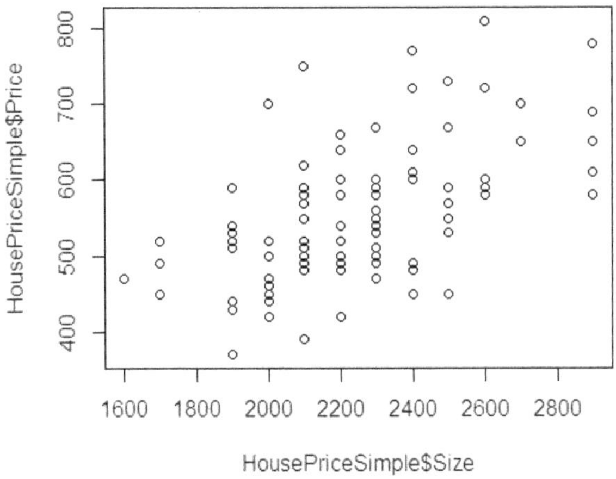

Figure 3.9. Scatter plot of sale price of house vs. size.

the fitted model form. For that, we need only part of the output from the **summary()** function. Objects have sub-objects, and these are separated from the object name by a dollar sign (**$**). At this step we only want the coefficients, and only them, not the standard deviations, nor the t-statistics testing whether they are different from zero, nor the associated p-values. That means only the first entry (column) in the coefficients piece of the summary. This suggests the following command, and the result is included.

```
> summary(regModel) $ coefficients[,1]
(Intercept)          Size
123.8169265    0.1906176
>
```

What is the practical interpretation of these coefficients? Note that EVERY ELEMENT in these statements must be included in your own summaries:

1. Average house selling price for a house that is zero square foot in size is approximately \$124,000. (This might be thought of as the value of the land with no house on it.)
2. Average house selling price increases by approximately \$190 for each additional square foot in size.

3.1.5 Simple linear regression model performance

For simple linear regression, one can plot the fitted line against the data to get a feel for the performance. This also is easy to do using R. The `plot()` command is immediately followed by an `abline()` command with a special option specifying the model:

```
> plot(HousePriceSimple$Size ,HousePriceSimple$Price)
> abline(lm(Price ~ Size, data = HousePriceSimple))
```

The result in shown in Figure 3.10.

Regression model performance is usually summarized in an analysis of variance (ANOVA) table. This contains the performance information for the regression model: how much of the variability in the data is explained by the fitted model. The performance of the model is characterized by the sum of squared deviations from the mean captured by the regression model, called *sum of squares regression*, or *SSR*, vs. the sum of squared deviations of the regression model prediction to the actual value, called *sum of squared error*, or *SSE*. Often, an ANOVA table also includes the total of these two sums of squares, called *SS Total*, or *SST*. Note that SST is also equal to the sum of squared differences between the individual dependent variable values and the overall average. A good regression model will have SSR as a large fraction of SST, and SSE will be small relative to SST. The ratio SSR/SST is called R^2, or the *coefficient of determination*, and interpreted as *the fraction of variation in the*

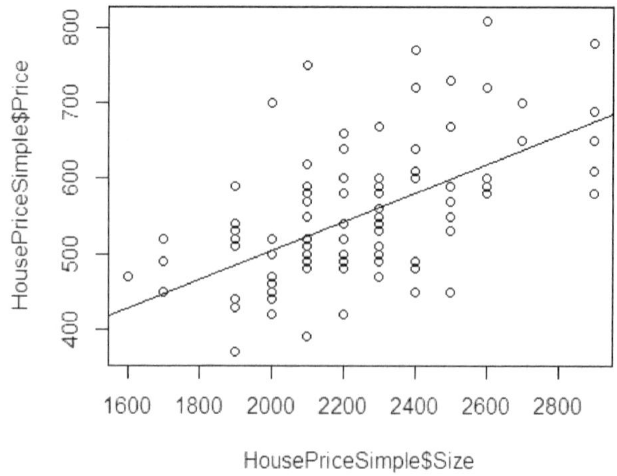

Figure 3.10. Scatter plot of sale price of house vs. size.

data that is captured by the regression model. The second column af the ANOVA table divides each total by its *degrees of freedom.* These are called mean squares and are used to construct hypothesis tests for the model. In particular, the quantity $SSE/(n-2)$ is called the mean squared error, or MSE, and it estimates σ^2.

Again, this is easy to compute in R using the `anova()` function applied to the `lm()` regression model output object. We also want the R^2 value. Here is the result for our example:

```
> anova(regModel)
Analysis of Variance Table

Response: Price
           Df Sum Sq Mean Sq F value    Pr(>F)
Size        1 276709  276709  50.395 9.054e-11 ***
Residuals 122 669884    5491

> summary(regModel)$r.squared
[1] 0.2923209
>
```

In the ANOVA table above, SSR and SSE are labeled "Sum Sq" for "Size" and "Residuals," respectively. Computing SST as $276709 + 669884 = 946593$, let's compute R^2 directly as $276709/946593 \approx 0.29$. A precise calculation is provided in the variable `summary(regModel)$r.squared` shown in the listing above. In simple linear regression, the R^2 value is related to the correlation by $R^2 = r^2$; that is, R^2 is the square of the correlation coefficient. This is easy to see by computing the square of the correlation coefficient directly in R:

```
> cor(HousePriceSimple$Size,HousePriceSimple$Price)^2
[1] 0.2923209
>
```

An R^2 of 29% is not particularly strong. We expect that the selling price of a house depends on more than just the size. We explore *multiple regression* models that add the number of bedrooms and number of bathrooms in the following section, and then the R^2 will increase to more than 80%.

While the ANOVA includes an F statistic and a p-value (`Pr(>F)`), these are only used in the *traditional research* setting, and only after *model validity checks.* These are discussed in the following.

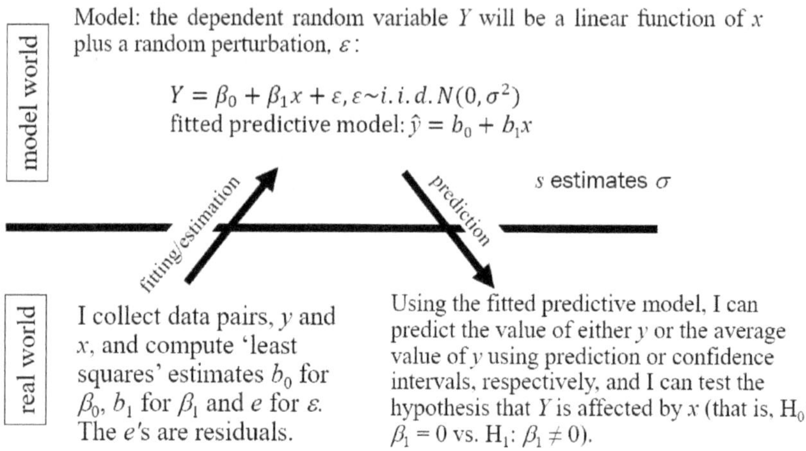

Figure 3.11. Simple linear regression in the traditional research paradigm.

3.1.6 Regression in the traditional research paradigm

Figure 3.11 shows how simple linear regression is used in the *traditional research* paradigm. This is the realm of inferential statistics. One begins in the real world at the lower left with data and scatter plots of the data. That leads to the model world, where the proposed model is simple linear regression. In the model world, there are key assumptions about the random error terms: they must be independent, identically distributed (mean of zero and equal variance), and have a normal distribution. The fitted predictive model can be characterized statistically because of these assumptions. Model uncertainty can be estimated and used to allow the errors in model predictions to be formally characterized, as we will see later in this section. But you cannot assume that these conditions hold for your data; you need to check the validity of the assumptions.

3.1.7 Simple linear regression model validity checks

Determining the validity of the model in the *traditional research* paradigm requires checking the following conditions, using the associated plots:

1. independence: autocorrelation (`acf()`) plot for residuals;

2. identically distributed (equal mean, sometimes referred to as the "linearity" assumption): plots of residuals vs. predicted, and residuals vs. each independent variable;
3. identically distributed (equal variance): plot of square root of standardized residuals vs. predicted;
4. normal distribution of residuals: residuals probability plot;
5. overly influential points (outliers): Cook's distance leverage plot.

Each of these checks can be done graphically. Table 3.1 shows the six kinds of plots, what they validate, and how they are coded in R.

The resulting plots for the House Price vs. Size simple linear regression are shown in Figure 3.12. None of the plots indicate a violation of the linear regression assumptions.

The **autocorrelation plot of residuals** at the upper left shows how large is the correlation between adjacent residual values in the data set the adjacencies are 0, 1, 2,... up to 20. Of course, zero adjacency means correlation of a residual with itself, which is always 1. The dashed lines indicate the 95% limits of ordinary variation. For the independence assumption to hold, only about 5% of the autocorrelations should fall beyond the line (at most one of the twenty). We see that only one falls beyond the limit (besides lag zero which does not count), so the independence assumption is not violated.

Table 3.1. Graphical methods for linear regression model validation.

Validity Check	**Graph**	**R Command**
Independence	Autocorrelation Plot	`acf(regModel$residuals)`
Identical Mean	Residual vs. Predicted Plot	`plot(regModel)`
Identical Mean	Residual vs. Predictor Plot	`plot(data$predictor, regModel$residual)`
Identical Variance	Sqrt(Residuals) vs. Predicted Plot	`plot(regModel)`
Normal Distribution for Error	Normal Probability Plot	`plot(regModel)`
Outliers with Undue Influence	Cook's Distance Plot	`plot(regModel)`

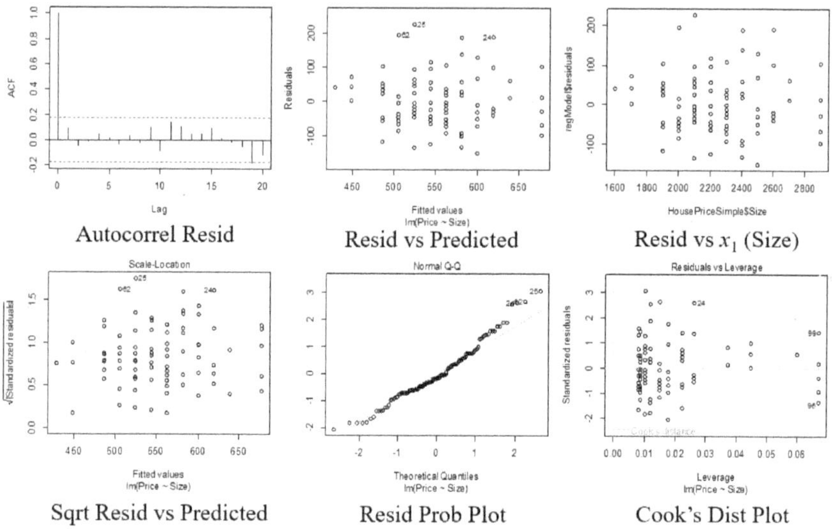

Figure 3.12. Six linear regression diagnostic plots for the house price example.

The **scatter plot of residuals vs. predicted** shows no pattern. It can be curved or V-shaped, which would indicate that there are one or more terms missing from the model.

The **scatter plot of residuals vs. predictor variable (Size)** plot shows no apparent pattern. It could be curved or V shaped, which would indicate a missing predictor variable or perhaps the need to a squared term in addition to the linear term for size. These two scatter plots show that the identical mean part of the i.i.d. requirement is not violated.

The **square root of residuals plot** shows uniform vertical spread across the predicted (fitted) values. Important: There are fewer data points at the extreme lower and upper predicted values, so the vertical spread looks less, but this is an artifact from smaller number of samples in those areas. This scatter plot shows that the identical variance part of the i.i.d. requirement is not violated.

The **residual probability plot** shows the ordered residuals vs. normal distribution quantiles falling on a fairly straight line, and so the normal distribution assumption is not violated.

Finally, **Cook's distance plot** shows no points falling outside the limit lines. In fact, the limit lines are FAR from the data and do not appear at all in the plot! This scatter plot shows that there are no outliers unduly influencing the fitted regression coefficients.

For the house price example, the fitted regression model passes all validity checks.

3.1.8 Hypothesis testing for overall model and individual coefficients

If the fitted regression model passes the validity checks in Section 3.1.7, then the p-values from hypothesis tests and confidence and prediction intervals can be considered valid. In this section, we interpret the hypothesis tests for coefficients and the overall regression model. These can be collected from either the `anova()` or `summary()` functions in R. In the following, we show the code for each and the resulting output for the house price example.

```
> anova(regModel)
Analysis of Variance Table

Response: Price
           Df Sum Sq Mean Sq F value    Pr(>F)
Size        1 276709  276709  50.395 9.054e-11 ***
Residuals 122 669884    5491
---
Signif. codes:  0 *** 0.001 ** 0.01 * 0.05 . 0.1   1
>
```

The `anova()` function output provides an F statistic and p-value for the hypothesis test: H_0: $\beta_1 = 0$ vs. H_1: $\beta_1 \neq 0$.

For simple linear regression, this is equivalent to a test on the significance of the overall model (the significance of the intercept does not contribute to the overall test). We see that the F statistic is very large and the p-value is very small, so we can reject the hypothesis that house size has no effect on house selling price.

For hypothesis testing of individual coefficients and the overall model, all can be found in the output of the `summary()` function; the `anova()` function is not really needed for hypothesis testing.

In the `Coefficients:` section of the `summary()` output, we see t statistics and p-values for individual model coefficients for each of the following hypothesis tests: H_0: $\beta_0 = 0$ vs. H_1: $\beta_0 \neq 0$, and H_0: $\beta_1 = 0$ vs. H_1: $\beta_1 \neq 0$.

Asterisks are printed next to coefficients with statistically significant p-values for their hypothesis test, according to the `Signif.codes` output line. The p-value for the intercept, 0.0419, is marginally less than 0.05, so the intercept can be considered (marginally) different from zero. One might interpret the intercept — the selling price of a house with zero square feet — as the average lot value (property with no house). The `summary()` output also provides the F statistic and p-value for the overall regression model as the last line of the output. Again, because there is only one predictor variable, the p-value is the same as that for testing the hypothesis for β_1. It says that the overall model has statistically significant (though perhaps not practically significant) predictive ability.

```
> summary(regModel)

Call:
lm(formula = Price ~ Size, data = HousePriceSimple)

Residuals:
    Min      1Q  Median     3Q    Max
-150.36  -45.29  -13.18  41.43 225.89

Coefficients:
             Estimate  Std. Error t value Pr(>|t|)
(Intercept) 123.81693   60.22201   2.056   0.0419 *
Size          0.19062    0.02685   7.099 9.05e-11 ***
---
Signif. codes:  0 *** 0.001 ** 0.01 * 0.05 . 0.1   1

Residual standard error: 74.1 on 122 degrees of freedom
Multiple R-squared:  0.2923, Adjusted R-squared:  0.2865
F-statistic: 50.39 on 1 and 122 DF,  p-value: 9.054e-11
>
```

Again, when validity checks are successful, confidence intervals for the true but unknown model coefficients (βs) are valid. These are computed in R by applying the `confint()` function to the fitted regression model. The code and result for the house price example are shown as follows.

```
> confint(regModel)
                2.5 %       97.5 %
(Intercept) 4.601435 243.0324177
Size        0.137462   0.2437731
>
```

What is the practical interpretation of these coefficients? Note that EVERY ELEMENT in these statements must be included in your own summaries:

1. Average house selling price for a house that is zero square foot in size falls between approximately \$4,600 and \$243,000, with 95% confidence. (This might be considered the value of the land with no house on it.)
2. Average house selling price increases between approximately \$137 and \$244 for each additional square foot in size, with 95% confidence.

3.1.9 Prediction and prediction uncertainty for simple linear regression

The predictive power of a fitted regression model is the ability to predict values of the dependent variable given specific settings of the independent variable, for example, predicting the mean house selling price for homes of size 2,500 square feet. Beyond simply an estimate, in the *traditional research* setting with a valid model, one can characterize the uncertainty in the mean value by a *confidence interval* and characterize uncertainty for an individual house selling price by a *prediction interval.* The formulas for computing the confidence and prediction intervals at a particular value of the predictor variable, say x, have the following general form:

$$\text{response estimate } \hat{y}(x) \pm t\text{-multiplier} \times \text{standard error.} \tag{3.4}$$

How does this work? The standard error will be the square root of a custom regression-based multiplier times the MSE. The formulas differ for confidence and prediction intervals which we show in the following. The t-multiplier is just the critical t value for the significance (α, e.g., 0.05) chosen, with the degrees of freedom (df) of the MSE. The degrees of freedom for a linear regression for MSE

will always be $n-$(the number of regression coefficients), where n is the total sample size (number of x, y pairs) for the fitted regression. For simple linear regression, we estimate an intercept and a slope, so $df = n - 2$. For a 95% confidence ($\alpha = .05$) interval for a forecast mean value $\text{E}(Y)$ at a particular value of x, say x^*, the formula would be

$$CI = (\text{b}_0 + \text{b}_1 x^*) \pm t_{(.975,n-2)} \times \sqrt{\text{MSE} \times \left(\frac{1}{n} + \frac{(x^* - \bar{x})^2}{SSx}\right)}, \tag{3.5}$$

where SSx is the sum of squared deviations of the sample x values from their average, i.e., $\sum_{i=1}^{n} (x_i - \bar{x})^2$, and $\text{b}_0 + \text{b}_1 x^* = \hat{y}(x^*)$, where b_0 and b_1 are the least-squares estimates for intercept and slope, respectively.

The prediction interval multiplier is larger since prediction for an individual selling price (not the average) must take into account the variability in selling price among houses with the same price. That adds a "1" multiplier to the MSE, giving

$$CI = (\text{b}_0 + \text{b}_1 x^*) \pm t_{(.975,n-2)} \times \sqrt{\text{MSE} \times \left(1 + \frac{1}{n} + \frac{(x^* - \bar{x})^2}{SSx}\right)}. \tag{3.6}$$

These computations are easily accomplished in R, particularly if the default 95% intervals are used. Consider the house price example, where a forecast is desired for the size $x = 2500$. Suppose that in addition to the predicted house selling price, both confidence and prediction intervals are desired. This is done in R using the `predict()` function. Note that the regression model `regModel` must first be fitted using the `lm()` function. Also, prediction can be done at one or more x values, but they must be placed in a data frame first to use the `predict()` function. In this case, there is only one prediction. The data frame with the value of x (Size) for prediction is named `new.dat`. The entry in the `data.frame()` function must be named "Size" so that `predict()` can match it to the data frame used in fitting the regression model. `predict()` is invoked twice, once for the confidence interval and once for the prediction interval. Both also provide the nominal regression model prediction $\hat{y}$, called `fit`.

```
> new.dat <- data.frame(Size = 2500)
> predict(regModel, newdata = new.dat)
1
600.3609
> predict(regModel, newdata = new.dat,
          interval = 'confidence')
       fit     lwr      upr
1 600.3609 580.842 619.8798
> predict(regModel, newdata = new.dat,
          interval = 'prediction')
       fit     lwr      upr
1 600.3609 452.379 748.3428
>
```

What is the practical interpretation of these coefficients? Note that EVERY ELEMENT in these statements must be included in your own summaries:

1. The regression model forecast average house selling price for a house that is 2,500 square feet in size is approximately \$600,000.
2. Taking sampling error into account, the forecast average house selling price for a house that is 2,500 square feet in size falls between approximately \$580,000 and \$620,000, with 95% confidence.
3. Taking sampling error and selling price variation into account, for any individual 2,500 square foot house, the forecast selling price will fall between approximately \$452,000 and \$748,000.

3.1.10 Managerial interpretation for simple linear regression

Simple linear regression models are actually fairly complex in terms of how validity checks are done and how prediction and confidence intervals are calculated. One must be careful and precise in describing the results in managerial terms. There is a list of items to be discussed, and the following text suggests appropriate wording:

- Examine scatter plot: "A plot of house selling price vs. house size suggests moderate positive correlation. House size seems reasonable as having a causal effect on house price, so we pursue constructing a regression model with house size as the predictor variable."

- Model passes validity tests: "The regression model passes all validity tests, so the p-values are meaningful."
- Overall p-value less than 0.05: "The regression model has statistically significant predictive power." (This may happen even with a small R-squared.)
- Coefficient p-value less than 0.05: "This term has a statistically significant effect on the response. A unit increase in its value produces an estimated change of bb in the response" (where bb is the estimated coefficient) (At this point it is good to add the confidence interval as follows.) "The 95% confidence interval for the coefficient value captures uncertainty in the estimate bb. The confidence interval is (ll, uu)." (Here, ll is the lower limit, while uu is the upper limit.)
- Coefficient p-value greater than 0.05: "This term's affect on the response is not statistically significant — the coefficient is not statistically different from zero." (No need to give the estimate, no need to give a confidence interval.)
- R-squared: "The R-squared of approximately 0.xx means that xx% of the variability in the response is captured by the regression model predictions." and "The correlation of predicted versus actual values is approximately sqrt(0.xx), or 0.yy." Say "the practical prediction ability of the model is weak" if 0.xx < 0.5 or "moderate" if 0.5 < 0.xx< 0.8 or "strong" if 0.8 < 0.xx. If the model is weak or moderate say "additional predictor variables should be found and added to the model." (Note: for simple linear regression, the p-value for the model and the coefficient will be THE SAME.)
- R-squared > 0.8 (actual value a judgment call): for strong prediction ability, you can offer forecast values with associated confidence and prediction intervals. Say "Based on the fitted regression model, a predictor value of x* is forecast to give a mean response of $yhat$. Taking sampling error into account, a 95% confidence interval for the mean response is $(ylowc, yhic)$." ($yhat$ is the regression model prediction, and $ylowc$ and $yhic$ are the confidence interval limits for a prediction at x*.) Then, say: "For predictor value(s) $x*$, taking sampling error and response variation into account, individual responses will vary between $(ylowp, yhip)$ with 95% confidence." ($ylowp$ and $yhip$ are the confidence interval limits for a prediction at $x*$.)

Using these guidelines, the following managerial summary is appropriate for the house price vs. size simple linear regression model:

- The regression model of house selling price vs. size passes all validity tests, so the p-values are meaningful.
- Since the overall p-value for the model is 0.9054e−11, much less than 0.05, the fitted regression model has statistically significant predictive power.
- Since the p-value for the coefficient for house size is 0.9054e−11, much less than 0.05, house size has a statistically significant effect on the selling price. A 1 sq ft. increase in house size produces an estimated increase of \$190 in the average selling price. The 95% confidence interval for the coefficient value captures uncertainty in the estimate 0.19. The confidence interval is (0.14, 0.4), or, in dollars, (\$140, \$400).
- The R-squared of approximately 0.29 means that 29% of the variability in the house selling price is captured by the regression model predictions. The correlation of predicted vs. actual values is approximately sqrt(0.29), or 0.54. The practical prediction ability of the model is weak, with an R-squared of only 29% . Additional predictor variables should be found and added to the model. Prediction is not useful with such a low R-squared value.

3.2 Multiple Linear Regression

Very often, effective prediction depends on modeling the effects of multiple predictor (or independent) variables on a response. The independent variables are represented by a vector x (one component for each predictor variable) rather than a single number. The individual components of x would be indexed as $x_1, x_2, x_3, \ldots, x_p$. While the regression model now will be quite different from the simple linear regression model shown in Equation (3.3), there are only small changes to the model fitting and validity checks and managerial interpretation. First, we present the multiple regression model form.

3.2.1 Multiple regression model form

Building from the general regression form in Equation (3.2), we write $f(x)$ as a linear combination of d known functions of x, each function indexed by j; we call each such function $g_j(x)$ (remember, x is now a vector with p components). The form for $f(x)$ is then $f(x) = \beta_0 + \sum_{j=1}^{d} \beta_j g_j(x)$, where the unknown multiplier coefficients β_j will be estimated from sample data. The multiple linear regression model is then

$$Y = \beta_0 + \sum_{j=1}^{d} \beta_j g_j(x) + \varepsilon,\ \varepsilon \overset{\text{iid}}{\sim} N(0, \sigma^2). \tag{3.7}$$

Now, the g functions can be simple or complex. For example, we can capture the simple linear regression model of Equation (3.3) by having $d = 1$ with $g_1(x) = x$, where x is a one-dimensional vector. For the house price multiple regression we consider next, there are three predictor variables with only linear terms the structure; therefore, for this case, $d = 3$, $g_1(x) = x_1$, $g_2(x) = x_2$, $g_3(x) = x_3$, with x a three-dimensional vector, x_1 = size in square feet, x_2 = number of bedrooms, and x_3 = number of baths.

But there is great flexibility for the g functions in multiple linear regression. Possible g functions for multiple linear regression models include products of x components such as x_1x_2, powers such as x_2^2, logarithms, $\log(x_3)$, and any other function of the x components that you can think of.

The *linearity* comes from the way the unknown coefficients appear in the model. The response is a *linear combination* of the g functions, where the linear combination coefficients (βs) must be estimated from sample data. The structure of the sample data will not be (x, y) pairs but rows of a data frame containing in each row the values $\{y, x_1, x_2, \dots\}$.

3.2.2 Estimating model coefficients (βs) and σ

Estimating coefficients for the simple linear regression amounts to choosing estimates for all of the βs in Equation (3.7) in a way that best matches the responses in the sample data and then estimating σ as the standard deviation of the deviations of the sample responses from the response predicted by Equation (3.7), with estimates substituted for the β values. As for simple linear regression, it makes sense that good estimates for the coefficients for the model should minimize the estimated standard deviation of the deviations of actual values from predicted values — that implies a best fit. The sample standard deviation of deviations of the sample responses (y_i) from the predictions ($\hat{y}_i$) is computed from the sum of squared deviations. Thus, for multiple linear regression, we estimate the unknown coefficients using *least squares*.

Again, R makes it easy to compute these estimates and their standard deviations. In this example, we expand the real estate example to include two additional predictor variables in the model: the number of bedrooms and the number of bathrooms (where a 1/2 bath means just a sink and toilet).

As for the simple linear regression case, before fitting the model, IT IS IMPORTANT to summarize the data and produce scatter plots for all variables to see if there is apparent correlation. But now, there are more to plot: we are not only interested in the scatter plot of each predictor variable against the response, but also (for reasons that will be explained later) we want to plot predictor variables against each other to check for correlation among predictor variables, which can be problematic. R provides a convenient function to do all possible pairs of variables. It is called the `pairs()` function. The code for reading in the Excel data file, providing a data summary, and doing the scatter plots follows:

```
> library(readxl)
> HousePriceSimple <- read_excel("HousePriceSimple.xlsx")
> summary(HousePriceSimple) # summarize the data
pairs(HousePriceSimple)
>
```

The resulting plot is shown in Figure 3.13. For each small plot, look across its row to find the name of the vertical axis, and look up and down its column to find the name of the horizontal axis. The top row shows plots with Price on the vertical axis. All of the predictor variables (Bedrooms, Size, and Baths) show moderate positive correlation and since we do expect people to be willing to pay more for a larger house, a house with more bedrooms, and a house with more bathrooms. We see weak to moderate positive correlation among the predictor variables as well. This correlation increases the variance of the coefficient estimates, making us less certain about the true model. But since there are no high correlations, this effect will be small. It is measured by the *variance inflation factor*, or *VIF*, which is discussed later in Section 3.3.6.

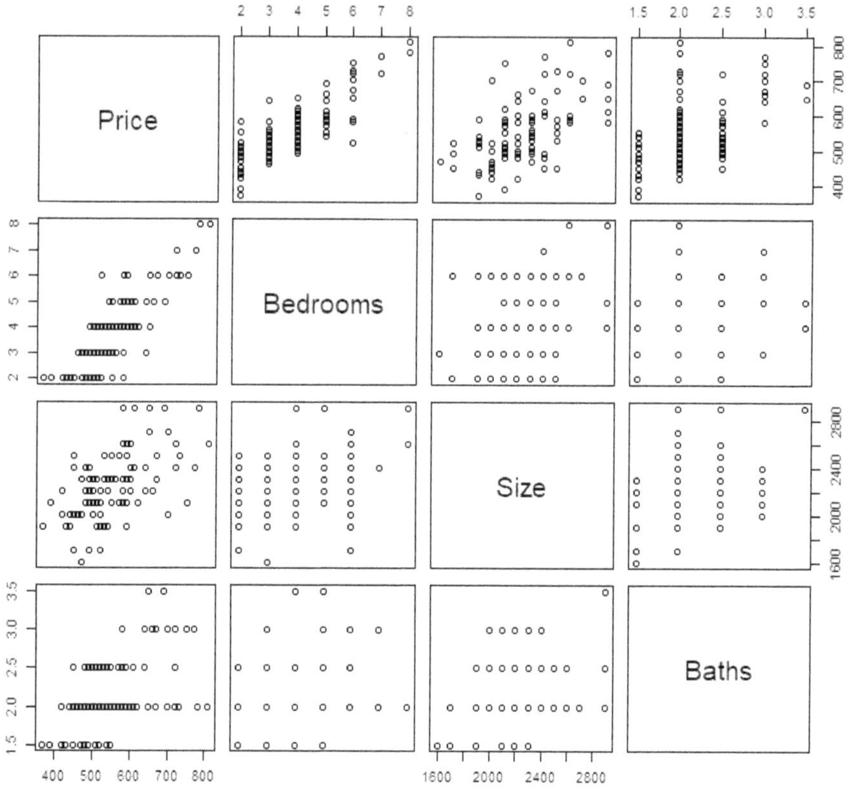

Figure 3.13. Matrix plot for the house price variables.

As for the simple linear regression case, a cause–effect relationship seems reasonable for all of the predictor variables. So, we proceed to fit the regression model. The form compared with that for simple linear regression just adds two predictor variables using the "+" sign.

```
> regModel = lm(Price ~ Size + Bedrooms + Baths,
               data = HousePriceSimple)
>
```

As before, the output of the fitting process will be placed in the object called `regModel`. And because we made this assignment of the output to `regModel`, no analysis is printed to the Console window. Even though this regression model is quite different from the previous simple linear regression model, the object orientation of R makes the process identical to get coefficient estimates, confidence intervals, predictions, diagnostic plots, and more.

The command to generate the model coefficient estimates is identical to that used for simple linear regression, but of course the results are different.

```
> summary(regModel)$coefficients[,1]
 (Intercept)          Size      Bedrooms         Baths
130.87080665    0.06636542   40.89318153   55.11095193
>
```

What is the practical interpretation of these coefficients? Note that EVERY ELEMENT in these statements must be included in your own summaries:

1. Average house selling price for a house that is zero square foot in size is approximately \$131,000. (This might be thought of as the value of the land with no house on it.)
2. All other predictors held the same, average house selling price increases by approximately \$66 for each additional square foot in size.
3. All other predictors held the same, average house selling price increases by approximately \$41,000 for each additional bedroom.
4. All other predictors held the same, average house selling price increases by approximately \$55,000 for each additional bathroom.

3.2.3 Multiple linear regression model performance

For simple linear regression, one can plot the fitted line against the actual data to get a feel for the performance, whereas in multiple regression, that is not possible because there is not just one predictor variable. However, one can plot the actual data vs. the predicted response. If the fit is good, these should (approximately) match, and so the points will fall on a diagonal line with slope 1. This also is easy to do using R using the `plot()` function. We need the `predict()` function that we saw previously in Section 3.1.9. Here, instead of passing it a single value, we give it the entire data frame used to fit the model. Then, it will generate a regression model prediction for each set of x values in the sample data that we can compare with the actual value. The `plot()` command is immediately followed by

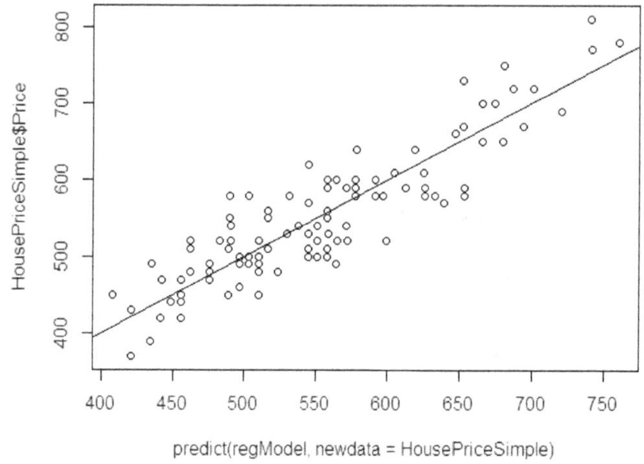

Figure 3.14. Scatter plot of sale price of house vs. size.

an **abline(0,1)** command since the predicted and actual should fall on a 45 degree line, with intercept 0 and slope 1:

```
> plot(predict(regModel , newdata = HousePriceSimple),
HousePriceSimple$Price)
> abline(0,1) # points near line if predicted ~ actual
>
```

The result in shown in Figure 3.14. This plot can be compared with the Price vs. Size scatter plot in Figure 3.10. The points in Figure 3.14 do seem to fall closer to the line. This means we should expect a higher R^2 value.

Regression model performance is summarized in the ANOVA table. Again, this is easy to compute in R, using the **anova()** function applied to the lm() regression model output object. For the house price regression, the R command and result is shown as follows.

```
> anova(regModel)
Analysis of Variance Table

Response: Price
           Df Sum Sq Mean Sq F value    Pr(>F)
Size        1 276709  276709 181.812 < 2.2e-16 ***
Bedrooms    1 428839  428839 281.770 < 2.2e-16 ***
Baths       1  58411   58411  38.379 8.466e-09 ***
Residuals 120 182634    1522
>
```

The table has more rows than that for simple linear regression. Now, the SSR is broken into contributions from Size, then the added contribution to regression sum of squares from Bedrooms, and finally the added contribution from Baths relative to a regression model with only Size and Bedrooms. SSR can be computed as the sum of these three.

Similarly to simple linear regression, the second column af the ANOVA table divides each total by its degrees of freedom. Recall that the quantity SSE/df is called the mean squared error, or MSE, and it estimates σ^2. But now, there are four parameters to be fitted: the intercept β_0 and the three coefficients $\beta_1, \beta_2, \beta_3$. So, the *df* is $n - 4 = 120$ rather than $n - 2 = 122$.

Our main focus in assessing performance is for the overall model. That performance depends on the ratio $SSR/SST = R^2$, also called the coefficient of determination. Similarly to simple linear regression again, it is the fraction of variation in the data that is captured by the regression model. Computing SSR requires adding the three components (Size, Bedrooms, and Baths) in the ANOVA table, and computing SST requires adding all four, but that is not necessary. We use the same command as in the simple linear regression case. Here is the code and result for our example:

```
> summary(regModel)$r.squared
[1] 0.8070621
>
```

As expected, the percent of variation explained by the regression model has increased: from 29% for the model with only the Size predictor variable to approximately 81% by adding Bedrooms and Baths to help predict selling price. Before further characterization of the model using the *traditional research* paradigm, we need to do checks for model validity.

3.2.4 Multiple regression model validity checks

We follow the procedure described in Section 3.1.7 using plots to determine the five aspects of validity of the model in the *traditional research* paradigm:

1. independence;
2. identically distributed (equal mean);
3. identically distributed (equal variance);

4. normal distribution of residuals;
5. overly influential points (outliers).

Again, each of these checks should be done graphically. Table 3.1 shows the kinds of plots, what they validate, and how they are coded in R. Note that in the multiple regression house price case, there will be three "Residual vs. Predictor" plots rather than just one, and so there will be eight validity plots in total. These plots are shown in Figure 3.15. As in the case of the simple linear regression case, the plots show that none of the model assumptions are violated.

3.2.5 Hypothesis testing for overall model and individual coefficients

If the fitted regression model passes the validity checks in Section 3.2.4, then the p-values from hypothesis tests and confidence and prediction intervals can be considered valid. In this section, we interpret the hypothesis tests for coefficients and the overall regression model. These can be collected from either the `anova()` or `summary()` functions in R. We showed in Section 3.1.8 that all of the key results are produced by the `summary()` function, and so the results of the `anova()` function will not be shown. The following is the code and resulting `summary()` output for the house price example.

```
> summary(regModel)

Call:
lm(formula = Price ~ Size + Bedrooms + Baths,
                data = HousePriceSimple)
Residuals:
Min      1Q     Median    3Q     Max
-79.27 -30.67   -3.14   27.77   90.20

Coefficients:
                 Estimate Std. Error t value Pr(>|t|)
(Intercept) 130.87081    33.23694    3.938 0.000139 ***
Size          0.06637     0.01579    4.204 5.08e-05 ***
Bedrooms     40.89318     2.69625   15.167  < 2e-16 ***
Baths        55.11095     8.89588    6.195 8.47e-09 ***
---
Signif. codes:  0 *** 0.001 ** 0.01 * 0.05 . 0.1   1

Residual standard error: 39.01 on 120 degrees of freedom
Multiple R-squared:  0.8071,    Adjusted R-squared:  0.8022
F-statistic: 167.3 on 3 and 120 DF,  p-value: < 2.2e-16
>
```

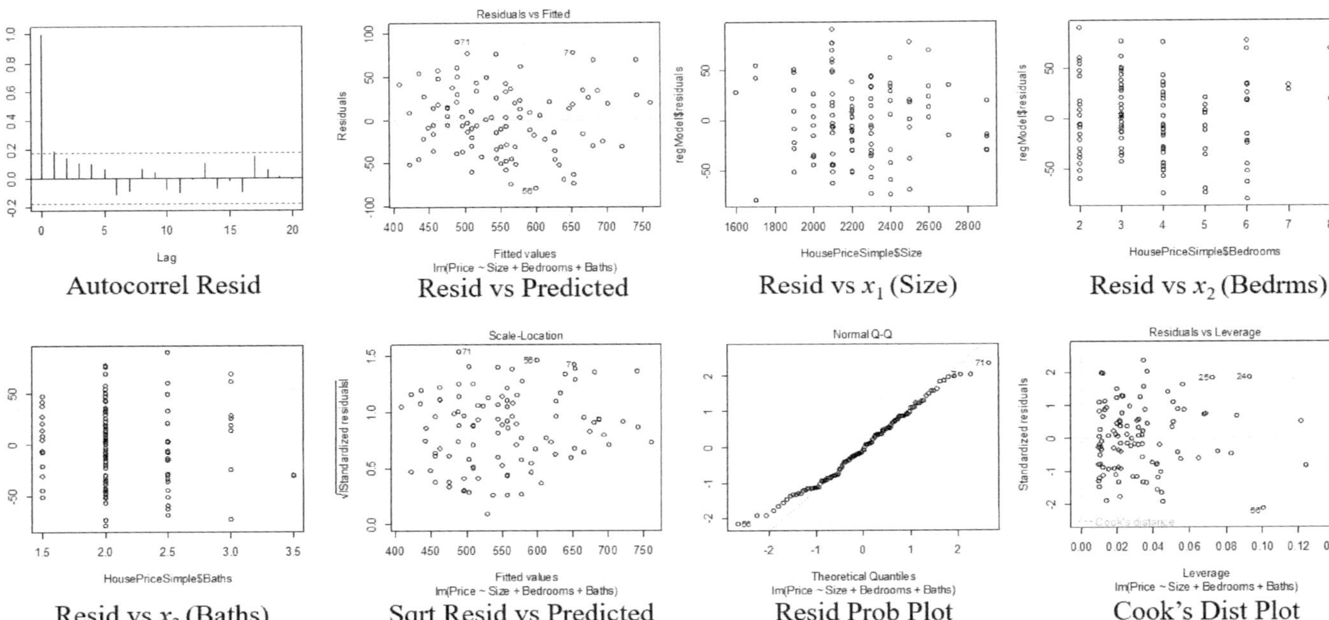

Figure 3.15. Eight multiple linear regression diagnostic plots for the house price example.

The `summary()` function output provides a t statistic and p-value for each of the following hypothesis tests:

H_0: $\beta_0 = 0$ vs. H_1: $\beta_0 \neq 0$.
H_0: $\beta_1 = 0$ vs. H_1: $\beta_1 \neq 0$.
H_0: $\beta_2 = 0$ vs. H_1: $\beta_2 \neq 0$.
H_0: $\beta_3 = 0$ vs. H_1: $\beta_3 \neq 0$.

Asterisks are printed next to coefficients with statistically significant p-values for their hypothesis test, according to the `Signif.codes` output line. We see that all p-values are much smaller than 0.05, and so all terms in the multiple regression model would be declared significantly different from zero.

The last line of the output shows the F statistic and p-value for the overall model. This corresponds to the hypothesis test

H_0: $\beta_1 = \beta_2 = \beta_3 = 0$ vs. H_1: At least one of $\{\beta_1, \beta_2, \beta_3\} \neq 0$.

The result in F statistic is very large, and the p-value is much smaller than 0.05. This means that the overall model has statistically significant (and, in this case, practically significant since $R^2 \approx .81$) predictive ability.

Again, when validity checks are successful, confidence intervals for the true but unknown model coefficients (βs) are valid. These are computed in R by applying the `confint()` function to the fitted regression model. The code is identical to that for the simple linear regression house price example, but the result is different for the multiple regression case.

```
> confint(regModel)
                 2.5 %       97.5 %
(Intercept) 65.06398037 196.67763292
Size         0.03510914   0.09762171
Bedrooms    35.55479762  46.23156543
Baths       37.49773281  72.72417105
>
```

What is the practical interpretation of these coefficients? Note that EVERY ELEMENT in these statements must be included in your own summaries:

- Average house selling price for a house that is zero square foot in size falls between approximately \$65,000 and \$197,000, with 95%

confidence. (This might be considered the value of the land with no house on it.)

- All other predictors held the same, average house selling price increases between approximately \$35 and \$97 for each additional square foot in size, with 95% confidence.
- All other predictors held the same, average house selling price increases between approximately \$36,000 and \$46,000 for each additional bedroom, with 95% confidence.
- All other predictors held the same, average house selling price increases between approximately \$37,000 and \$73,000 for each additional bathroom, with 95% confidence.

3.2.6 Prediction and prediction uncertainty for multiple linear regression

Formulas for computing the confidence and prediction intervals for the response at a particular value of the predictor variable, say the vector x, still follow the general form in Equation (3.4), but now the formula for standard error involves matrix computations. Details are postponed to Section 3.3.7. These computations in R use the same commands as for simple linear regression, with a 95% significance default value. Note that the regression model `regModel` must be fitted first using the `lm()` function. Also, prediction can be done at one or more x values, but they must be placed in a data frame first to use the `predict()` function.

We used the multiple prediction capability of `predict()` with the multiple linear regression house price example in Section 3.2.3 to generate the actual vs. predicted scatter plot (no `interval =` option was used with `predict()` there). For this multiple linear regression model, the R^2 is high enough to permit use for prediction. In the following, we show two predictions: the first for a house of 2,500 square feet with four bedrooms and three bathrooms, the second for a house of 2,800 square feet with three bedrooms and three bathrooms. `predict()` includes the nominal prediction in addition to the upper and lower prediction and confidence interval limits, useful for the following managerial interpretation. As before, the data frame columns must be named "Size," "Bedrooms," and "Baths' so that `predict()` can match it to the data frame used in fitting the regression model.

```
> new.dat = data.frame(Size = 2500, Bedrooms = 4, Baths = 3)
> new.dat = rbind(new.dat, c(2800,3,3))
> predict(regModel, newdata = new.dat,
          interval = 'confidence')
       fit      lwr      upr
1 625.6900 608.7113 642.6686
2 604.7064 580.7187 628.6941
> predict(regModel, newdata = new.dat,
          interval = 'prediction')
       fit      lwr      upr
1 625.6900 546.6046 704.7753
2 604.7064 523.8260 685.5868
>
```

What is the practical interpretation of these coefficients? Note that EVERY ELEMENT in these statements must be included in your own summaries:

- The regression model forecast average house selling price for a house that is 2,500 square feet in size with four bedrooms and three bathrooms is approximately \$626,000.
- Taking sampling error into account, the forecast average house selling price for a house that is 2,500 square feet in size with four bedrooms and three bathrooms falls between approximately \$609,000 and \$643,000, with 95% confidence.
- Taking sampling error and selling price variation into account, for any individual 2,500 square foot house with four bedrooms and three bathrooms, the forecast selling price will fall between approximately \$546,000 and \$705,000.
- The regression model forecast average house selling price for a house that is 2,800 square feet in size with three bedrooms and three bathrooms is approximately \$605,000.
- Taking sampling error into account, the forecast average house selling price for a house that is 2,800 square feet in size with three bedrooms and three bathrooms falls between approximately \$581,000 and \$629,000, with 95% confidence.
- Taking sampling error and selling price variation into account, for any individual 2,800 square foot house with three bedrooms and three bathrooms, the forecast selling price will fall between approximately \$524,000 and \$686,000.

3.2.7 Managerial interpretation for multiple linear regression: The house price study

Multiple linear regression models are more complex than simple linear regression, and so it is even more important to be careful and precise in describing the results in managerial terms. The same guidelines presented in Section 3.1.10 apply. Using these guidelines, the following managerial summary is appropriate for the House Price vs. Size, Bedrooms, and Baths multiple linear regression model:

- Examine scatter plot: "Plots of house selling price vs. house size, number of bedrooms, and number of bathrooms suggest moderate positive correlation for all three. House size, number of bedrooms, and number of bathrooms seem reasonable as having causal effect on house price, so we pursue constructing a regression model with house size, number of bedrooms, and number of bathrooms as predictor variables."
- The regression model of house selling price as a linear function of size, number of bedrooms, and number of bathrooms passes all validity tests, so the p-values are meaningful.
- Since the overall p-value for the model is less than 2.2e−16, much less than 0.05, the fitted regression model has statistically significant predictive power.
- Since the p-value for the coefficient for house size is 5.08e−05, much less than 0.05, house size has a statistically significant effect on the selling price. All other predictor variables held constant, a 1 sq. ft. increase in house size produces an estimated increase of \$66 in the average selling price. The 95% confidence interval for the coefficient value captures uncertainty in the estimate 0.066. The confidence interval is (0.035, 0.098), or, in dollars, (\$35, \$98).
- Since the p-value for the coefficient for bedrooms is less than 2e−16, much less than 0.05, the number of bedrooms has a statistically significant effect on the selling price. All other predictor variables held constant, an additional bedroom produces an estimated increase of \$41,000 in the average selling price. The 95% confidence interval for the coefficient value captures uncertainty in the estimate 41. The confidence interval is (36, 46), or, in dollars, (\$36,000, \$46,000).

- Since the p-value for the coefficient for bathrooms is 8.47e−09, much less than 0.05, house size has a statistically significant effect on the selling price. All other predictor variables held constant, an additional bathroom produces an estimated increase of $55,000 in the average selling price. The 95% confidence interval for the coefficient value captures uncertainty in the estimate 55. The confidence interval is (37, 73), or, in dollars, ($37,000, $73,000).
- The R^2 of approximately 0.81 means that 81% of the variability in the house selling price is captured by the regression model predictions. The correlation of predicted vs. actual values is approximately sqrt(0.81), or 0.9. The practical prediction ability of the model is strong, but additional predictors could be found that would further increase R^2. We can use this model to predict house selling price.
- The regression model forecast average house selling price for a house that is 2,500 square feet in size with four bedrooms and three bathrooms is approximately $626,000.
- Taking sampling error into account, the forecast average house selling price for a house that is 2,500 square feet in size with four bedrooms and three bathrooms falls between approximately $609,000 and $643,000, with 95% confidence.
- Taking sampling error and selling price variation into account, for any individual 2,500 square foot house with four bedrooms and three bathrooms, the forecast selling price will fall between approximately $547,000 and $705,000.
- The regression model forecast average house selling price for a house that is 2,800 square feet in size with three bedrooms and three bathrooms is approximately $605,000.
- Taking sampling error into account, the forecast average house selling price for a house that is 2,800 square feet in size with three bedrooms and three bathrooms falls between approximately $581,000 and $629,000, with 95% confidence.
- Taking sampling error and selling price variation into account, for any individual 2,800 square foot house with three bedrooms and three bathrooms, the forecast selling price will fall between approximately $524,000 and $686,000.

3.3 Special Issues in Linear Regression

Linear regression (both simple linear and multiple) provides an important tool for predictive analytics. But successful application of linear regression is not always straightforward. Sometimes, the graphical validity checks indicate violation of the assumptions required for a *traditional research* approach: residuals that violate normality, equal mean, equal variance, or independence. The following sections discuss transformations of variables and additional model terms that can address some of these issues.

When dealing with nonlinear relationships using linear regression, the approach is sometimes called *curvilinear regression*. Often, curvilinear regression models are better behaved and easier to interpret when the predictor variables are scaled to ± 1. Additional sections discuss this issue. Although we identified earlier that ANOCOVA is an appropriate model for a mix of qualitative and quantitative predictor variables, it is possible to incorporate qualitative predictor variables in a linear regression setting. Finally, we compare regression strategies in two different settings: when data are observed without managerial control, and when data come from a controlled designed experiment.

3.3.1 Nonlinear transformations of Y

Sometimes, a multiple (or simple) regression model fails to pass the validity checks because of curvature and heteroskedasticity. In this case, transforming y is a good strategy. The revised regression model in Equation (3.7) would use a transformed value of Y, such as $\log(Y)$, for the dependent variable. *Heteroskedasticity* is a fancy statistical term for *unequal variance*. This arises naturally in a number of settings. For example, when communication or service systems get congested, delay times increase but also become more variable. This can be calculated exactly for very simple waiting line systems using probability. For example, consider a single-server system where customers arrive randomly according to an exponential distribution at a rate of λ (mean time between arrivals is $1/\lambda$), and the time it takes the server to complete one customer is also random, with an exponential distribution with rate μ (mean service time is $1/\mu$). Then, the time in the system (waiting + service) is random with an exponential distribution with rate $\mu - \lambda$, and the mean can be computed to be $\text{E}(W) = 1/(\mu - \lambda)$. If we think of this relationship as a function of service rate μ, the relationship is not linear. But worse, the variance of time in system, $\text{Var}(W)$, is $\text{Var}(W) = 1/(\mu - \lambda)^2$, which is not constant; it is a nonlinear function of service rate as well. Further, the randomness about the mean is not normal; it is exponential.

In this and other business process settings, theoretical models can help identify transformations to the response or the predictor variable that will both make the relationship more linear and make the variance more constant across different response levels. Let's start with the single-server example above. Two transformations suggest themselves. First, the exponential distribution violates the assumption of normally distributed error. There are complex ways to transform the y values to have a normal distribution, but a simple logarithmic transform does a pretty good job. We will also see that this transformation can reduce the differences in variance for different means.

The log transform for y

To fix the deviation from a normal distribution, we apply the log transformation to a sample of 1,000 Y values and their logarithms created using the following R commands.

```
> y = rexp(1000, rate = 1)
> log_y = log(y)
>
```

Figure 3.16 gives a comparison of the histograms of y and $log(y)$. It shows a closer approximation to the bell shape for the log-transformed values. Normal probability plots provide a better graphical assessment of normality than histograms. Normal probability plots for y and $log(y)$ data are shown in Figure 3.17. Again, the logarithm transform reduces the curvature greatly, perhaps making the normality assumption acceptable.

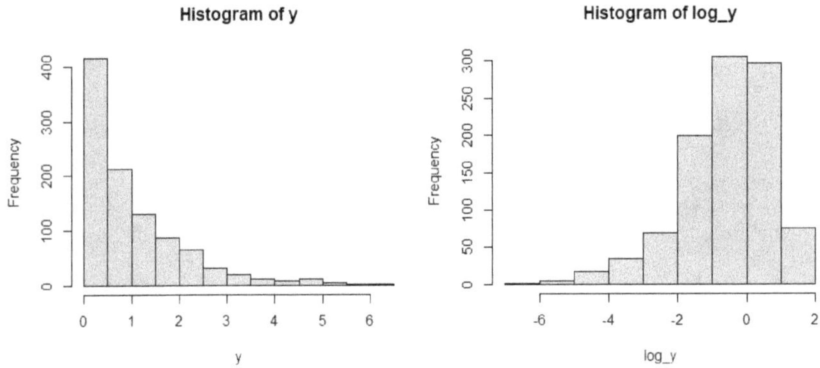

Figure 3.16. Histogram for $log(y)$ more normal than for y.

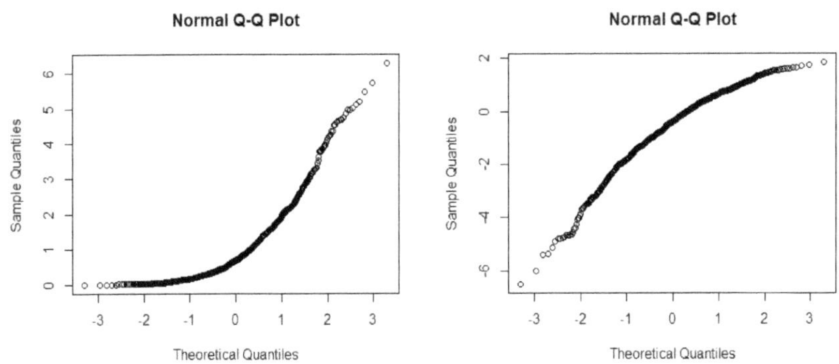

Figure 3.17. Normal probability plot for $log(y)$ straighter than for y.

The R commands for generating these plots are straightforward.

```
> hist(y)
> hist(log_y)
> qqnorm(y)
> qqnorm(log_y)
>
```

The log transform can also improve equal variance across different response levels. Figure 3.18 shows samples from a queueing system with different service rates ($x = \mu$, where $1/\mu$ is mean service time). Note the nonlinearity in the plot with untransformed y on the left and better behavior for the plot on the right using the log transform of y. Not only are the variances more equal across values of the predictor variable but the relationship is more linear. Further,

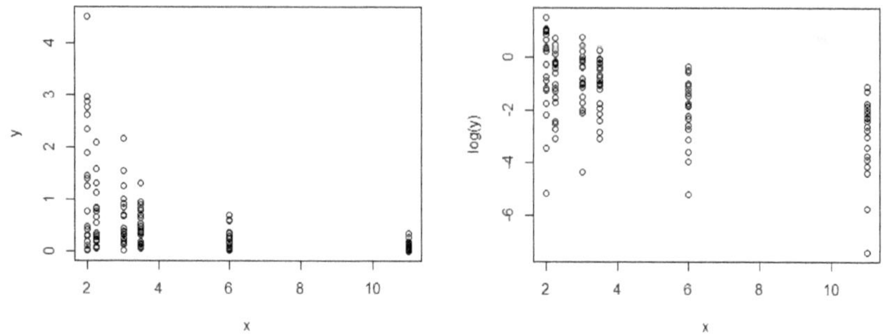

Figure 3.18. Scatter plot for $log(y)$ vs. μ straighter than for y vs. μ.

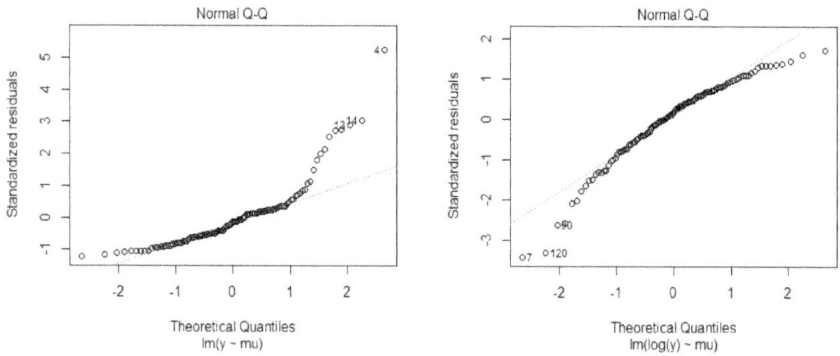

Figure 3.19. Normal plot for $log(y)$ straighter than for y.

Figure 3.19 shows that the deviations from normality are smaller, as shown in the probability plots.

The Box–Cox transformation family

A second transformation strategy was proposed by Box and Cox (1964). The main purpose is to transform the variations to follow a normal distribution, but this transformation usually reduces the nonlinearity of the response as well. It actually consists of a family of transformations, parameterized by λ_{BC} (not to be confused with the arrival rate λ in the service example). The usual definition *assumes that the y values are positive.* Given a value for λ_{BC}, The Box–Cox transformation is $BC(y, \lambda_{BC}) = (y^{\lambda_{BC}} - 1)/\lambda_{BC}$ if $\lambda_{BC} \neq 0$ and $BC(y, \lambda_{BC}) = \log(y)$ if $\lambda_{BC} \approx 0$. Given a set of data, there is a process for choosing the appropriate λ_{BC}; see the Box and Cox article if you are interested. For our purposes, we only need R to do the computation. For the regression example above, the code follows (it is not shown as part of an interactive session, so the > prompts are not present).

```
# find Box-Cox Transform
# the boxcox function resides in the MASS library
library(MASS)
regModel = lm(y ~ mu, data = xy_data)
bcFit = boxcox(y ~ mu, data = xy_data)
bc_lambda = bcFit$x[which.max(bcFit$y)]

# Do regression with bc transformed y
bc_lambda
plot(xy_data$mu,((xy_data$y^bc_lambda-1)/bc_lambda),
     xlab = "x", ylab = "BoxCox Xform y")
bcRegModel = lm(((y^bc_lambda-1)/bc_lambda) ~ x,
                data = xy_data)
plot(regModel, add.smooth=F, ask = F)
```

Note that to use the `boxcox` function, you need the `MASS` library. Figure 3.20 shows the *likelihood* curve from the `boxcox` function used to choose λ_{BC}. The maximum likelihood value occurs at about 0.14. Using this value for λ_{BC} gives the scatter plot and normal plot shown in Figure 3.21. The results are similar to the log transform plots above, perhaps with a bit more nonlinearity in the scatter plot. Note, however, that the Box–Cox λ_{BC} of 0.14 is quite close to zero, which would correspond to the log transformation. So, one would expect similar results in this case.

When NOT to transform y

When a scatter plot shows linear structure but heterogeneous variance (heteroskedasticity in the regression), then a nonlinear transformation to get homogeneous variance will destroy the linearity — probably not a good strategy. In this case, *weighted least squares* is a good option. Rather than counting the squared deviations from the fitted line equally in the least-squares sum of squares, points at which high variance is observed are given less weight since less is known about the true value.

The weight for sample i must be determined by an estimated σ_i. In designed experiments, that can be computed by the sample standard

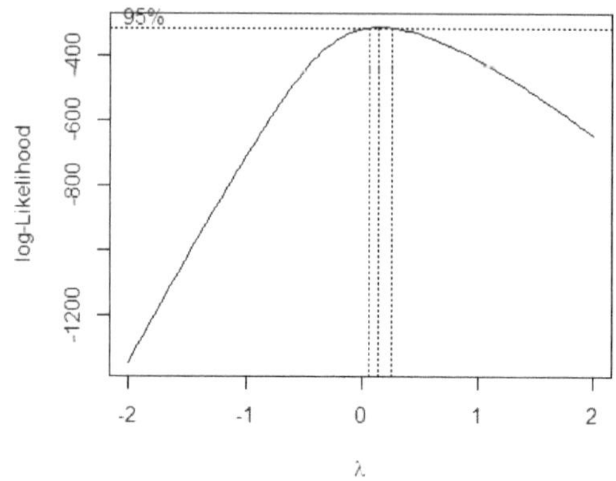

Figure 3.20. Box–Cox likelihood plot for the service system example.

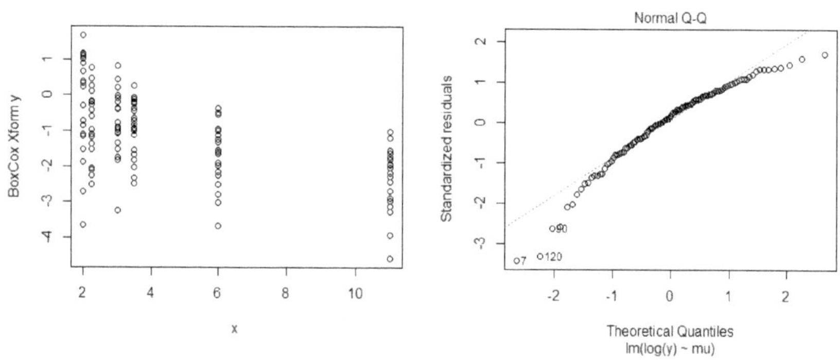

Figure 3.21. Scatter plot and normal plot for Box–Cox (y) similar to log transform in Figures 3.18 and 3.19.

deviation of y over repeated observations with the same x value. For observational data, one can estimate σ_i by fitting a second regression line to the absolute value of all residuals vs. either predicted value $\hat{y}$ from an unweighted fit or vs. the corresponding y. Using residuals vs. $\hat{y}$, the R code would be as follows (it is not shown as part of an interactive session, so the > prompts are not present). Note the final weighted least-squares regression model is called `wtRegModel`.

```
# need unweighted model to get residual estimates
regModel = lm(y ~ mu, data = xy_data)
# second regression model to predict sigma for each x,y pair
wtModel = lm(abs(regModel$residuals) ~
regModel$fitted.values)
# use the regression predicted value as estimate for sigma,
```

```
#     then square it and invert it to get the weight
wtVals = 1/wtModel$fitted.values^2
# third regression model is weighted least squares
wtRegModel <- lm(y ~ mu, data = xy_data ,
weights = wtVals)
```

Weighted least squares can be unsatisfactory when the randomness in the data is very different from a normal distribution, say a binomial distribution for a "yes/no" response or an exponential distribution for a waiting time response. When a nonlinear tranformation of y is unsatisfactory, an alternative to weighted least squares is to use the more complex *generalized linear model* presented in Section 3.5. Other options and more details can be found online, for example at the Penn State Statistics Website at https://online.stat.psu.edu/stat501/lesson/13/13.1.

3.3.2 Transforming x and adding nonlinear g terms to the model

When a scatter plot shows that the response is a nonlinear function of one or more predictor variables but the variance remains stable across different values (homogeneous), then a transformation of Y values will not work: any transformation that makes the response more linear will result in unequal variances across values of the predictor variable. This will also be the case if there is a curved pattern in the residuals vs. the predicted plot with stable variance across the prediction range.

The solution is to transform the predictor variable or variables rather than transforming y. This can be done in two ways: a direct transform of x, such as $x' = log(x)$, or adding a term nonlinear in x to the model, such as x^2. In the latter case, the model would be a multiple regression model including both x and x^2 terms. Either case will result in the prediction being a curve when plotted in the y vs. x space.

Figure 3.22 shows the most common curvature patterns and possible transformations of x to linearize the response. The first shows the typical pattern when a $\log(x)$ transform is appropriate. The second shows a typical pattern when an x^2 term should be added to the model. Finally, the third pattern suggests that using $1/x$ rather than

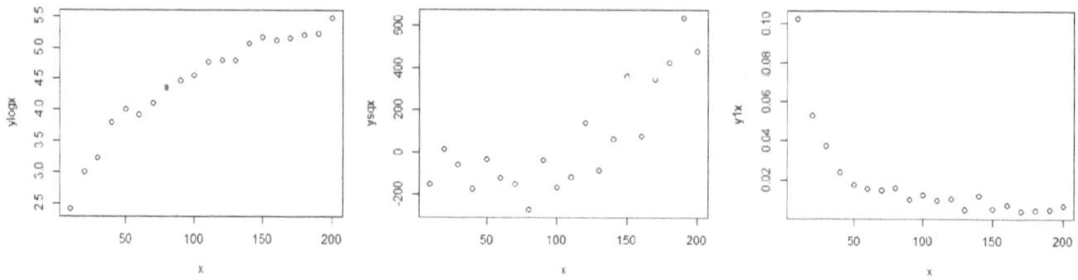

Figure 3.22. Patterns in scatter plots suggesting log, square, and inverse transformations of x.

x might linearize the response function and remove structure from the residuals plot.

We examine only one of these cases in more detail. The following code shows the regression model for the data where an inverse transformation for x is appropriate (scatter plot at right in Figure 3.22). It is not shown as part of an interactive session, so the > prompts are not present.

```
# analysis when an inverse transform for x is appropriate
x=seq(from = 10, to = 200,by=10)
y1x = 1/x + .003*rnorm(20)
plot(x,y1x)

# do analysis using x where y related to 1/x
# fit the regression model
regModel = lm(y1x ~ x)
# just used for showing fitted model
summary(regModel)$coefficients[,1]
# do plots to check model validity
acf(regModel$residuals)
plot(regModel, ask=F, add.smooth=F)
plot(x,regModel$residuals)
```

The resulting validity plots for a regression using untransformed x are shown in Figure 3.23. The autocorrelation plot looks fine — all values are inside the dashed lines. The residuals vs. predicted and residuals vs. x show structure: a curvature, so the validity check fails. The square root of residuals does not indicate a problem with unstable variance, but there is an outlier, also appearing as a leverage point in Cook's plot. The normal probability plot looks adequate except for the outlier. For comparison with the transformed model that we fit next, we show the performance in terms of R^2 and the

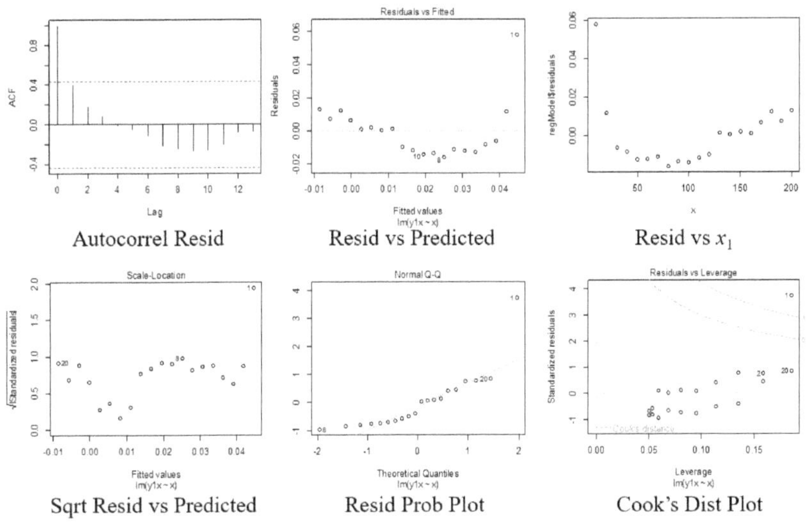

Figure 3.23. Six linear regression diagnostic plots for the untransformed x.

ANOVA table for this invalid model. Note that the value of R^2 is only 0.495.

```
> summary(regModel)$coefficients[,1]
 (Intercept)             x
0.0474516470 -0.0002798624

> anova(regModel)
Analysis of Variance Table

Response: y1x
          Df    Sum Sq   Mean Sq F value    Pr(>F)
x          1 0.0052085 0.0052085  17.667 0.0005344 ***
Residuals 18 0.0053067 0.0002948

> summary(regModel)$r.squared
[1] 0.4953309
>
```

The pattern in the scatter plot in Figure 3.22 suggests an inverse transform; therefore, we create a new variable `xinv = 1/x` and redo the regression analysis. The code is as follows. It is not shown as part of an interactive session, so the > prompts are not present.

```
# do analysis using 1/x
# fit the regression model
xinv = 1/x
plot(xinv, y1x)
regModel = lm(y1x ~ xinv)
# just used for showing fitted model
summary(regModel)$coefficients[,1]

# do plots to check model validity
acf(regModel$residuals)
plot(regModel, ask=F, add.smooth=F)
plot(xinv,regModel$residuals)

# show ANOVA table for regression model
anova(regModel)
# pull out the R-squared value from the summary
summary(regModel)$r.squared
# show standard deviation estimates and p-values
summary(regModel)
# compute confidence intervals for model coefficients
confint(regModel)
```

The scatter plot in Figure 3.24 of the response vs. $1/x$ shows a more linear pattern. The validity plots are shown in Figure 3.25. Now, all results look reasonable, and validity is supported. Even the outlier in Cook's plot is less extreme. Further, the model performance is greatly improved, with an R^2 of 0.985. The following interactive

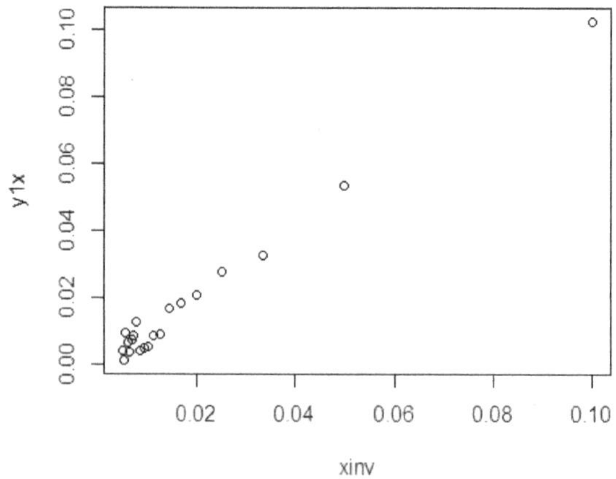

Figure 3.24. Plot of response vs. $1/x$.

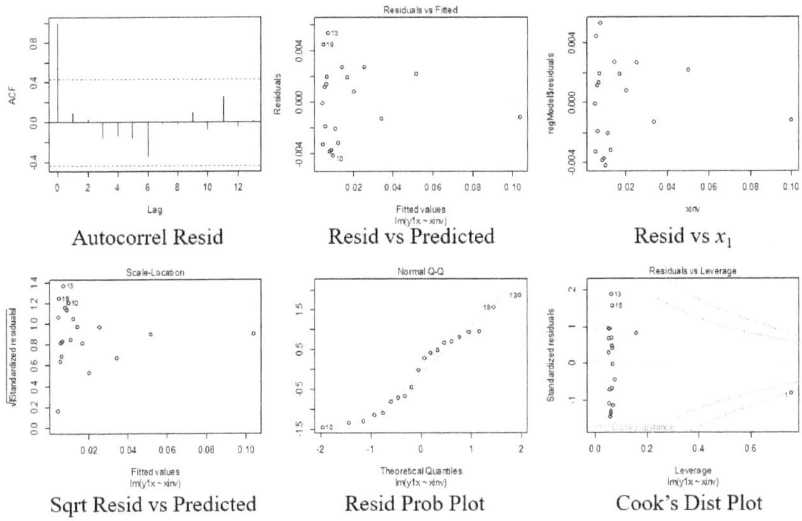

Figure 3.25. Six linear regression diagnostic plots for the model with $1/x$.

session shows the overall model summary with p-values and confidence intervals for the coefficients. These are now reliable since the model with transformed x passed all validity checks.

```
> summary(regModel)
Call:
lm(formula = y1x ~ xinv)

Residuals:
   Min          1Q        Median       3Q         Max
-0.0041601 -0.0023270  0.0003644  0.0020197  0.0053394

Coefficients:
              Estimate Std. Error t value Pr(>|t|)
(Intercept) -0.0007284  0.0008541  -0.853    0.405
xinv         1.0447958  0.0302332  34.558   <2e-16 ***
---

Residual standard error: 0.002945 on 18 degrees of freedom
Multiple R-squared:  0.9852,  Adjusted R-squared:  0.9843
F-statistic:  1194 on 1 and 18 DF,  p-value: < 2.2e-16
```

```
> # compute confidence intervals for model coefficients
> confint(regModel)
                   2.5 %      97.5 %
(Intercept) -0.002522818 0.001065972
xinv         0.981278178 1.108313480
>
```

3.3.3 Scaling predictor variables to ± 1

When nonlinear regression terms, such as x^2 or x_1x_2, are placed in a regression function *in addition to the x term*, then rescaling the x values to ± 1 becomes important. To understand why, consider the data in Figure 3.26, which plots x^2 vs. x for values between $x = 10$ and $x = 200$, the range of values in the previous section. These values are highly correlated — it seems the name *independent variables* does not apply here! The result is that in building the regression model, it will be difficult to determine how much of the prediction should come from x and how much should come from x^2. This phenomenon in regression is called *multicollinearity*. Fortunately, multicollinearity arising from having x and x^2 in the same model (or x_1, x_2, and x_1x_2 in the same model) can easily be fixed by scaling the predictor variables to the range $[-1, 1]$. When we look at that relationship, shown in Figure 3.27, we see what we mentally imagined: two very different effects. This is why scaling is important.

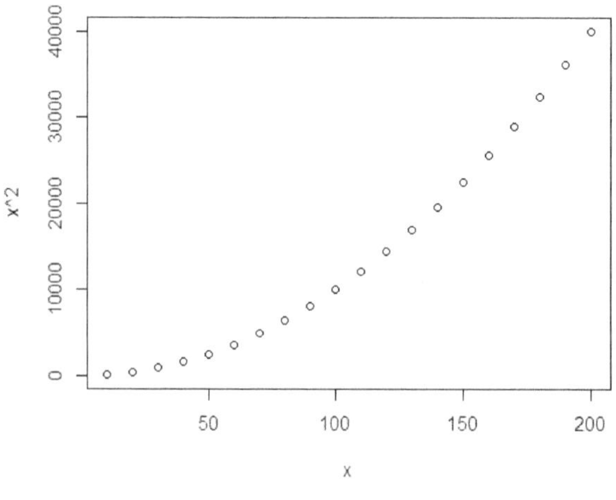

Figure 3.26. High correlation of x^2 and x over the range [10, 200].

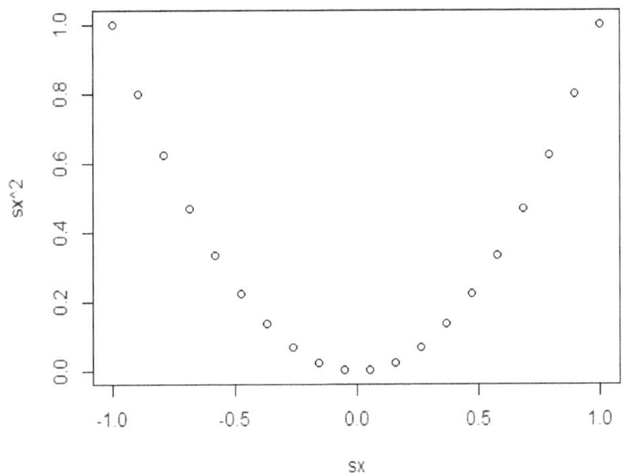

Figure 3.27. Zero correlation of x^2 and x over the range $[-1, +1]$, scaled x.

The resulting model fit and diagnostics are the same whether scaled or original predictor variables are used. The only thing that changes are the values of the regression coefficients and the confidence in those values. When the correlation is high, there is greater uncertainty.

A statistical measure of this correlation is called the *variance inflation factor*, or *VIF*. When the *VIF* is greater than 10 (some people use 5), there is real concern about keeping that term in the regression model. *VIF* for the jth term measures how much the other regression terms capture what this term can predict. To describe it mathematically, define R_j^2 to be the R^2 value for a regression model, with the other predictors predicting $g_j(x)$ rather than y as the dependent variable. Then, *VIF* is defined as

$$VIF = \frac{1}{1 - R_j^2}. \tag{3.8}$$

If the correlation of the jth term with the other regression model terms is high, the R_j^2 will be near one, and the denominator will shrink toward zero, giving a very large *VIF*. Again, the impact will not be on the R^2 of the fitted model, nor will it impact the validity plots. It will only affect the p-values and confidence intervals for individual regression model coefficients.

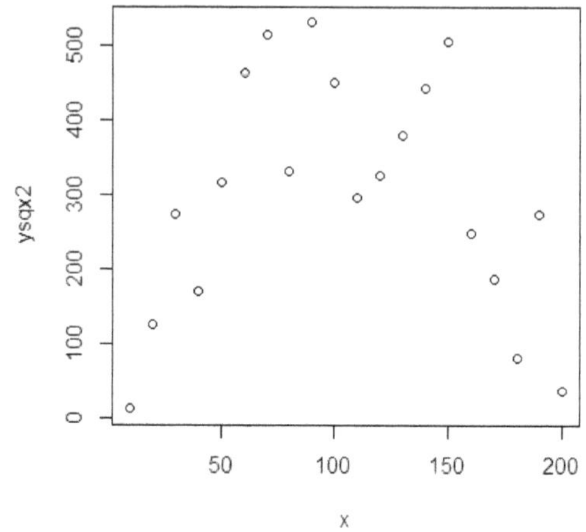

Figure 3.28. Another pattern indicating the need for x^2 term.

To illustrate this issue, we analyze the data in Figure 3.28, first without ± 1 scaling and then with scaling. This is another pattern where a quadratic term in x should be added to the model. Unlike the center plot in Figure 3.22, the quadratic coefficient will be negative in this case. In fact, the response looks almost purely (negative) quadratic. The R code and output (not including the validity check plots) are shown as follows.

```
> regModel = lm(ysqx2 ~ x + I(x^2))
> # just used for showing fitted model
> summary(regModel)$coefficients[,1]
(Intercept)            x       I(x^2)
-22.82576910   8.89817927  -0.04277448
> # show ANOVA table for regression model
> anova(regModel)
Analysis of Variance Table

Response: ysqx2
          Df Sum Sq Mean Sq F value    Pr(>F)
x          1    474     474  0.0497    0.8263
I(x^2)     1 321214  321214 33.6422 2.131e-05 ***
Residuals 17 162315    9548
---
>
> # pull out the R-squared value from the summary
> summary(regModel)$r.squared
[1] 0.6646407
```

```
> # need package "rms" to compute VIF
> library(rms)
> vif(regModel)
x   I(x^2)
17.70455 17.70455
> # do plots to check model validity
> acf(regModel$residuals)
> plot(regModel, ask=F, add.smooth=F)
> plot(x,regModel$residuals)
> confint(regModel)
                   2.5 %       97.5 %
(Intercept) -176.20341784 130.55187963
x              5.53436979  12.26198875
I(x^2)        -0.05833368  -0.02721529
>
```

Here are the R^2, the problematic *VIF*, the regression coefficients, and the 95% confidence intervals for the regression coefficients.

```
> summary(regModel)$r.squared
[1] 0.6646407
> library(rms)
> vif(regModel)
x   I(x^2)
17.70455 17.70455
>
> summary(regModel)$coefficients[,1]
(Intercept)            x       I(x^2)
-22.82576910   8.89817927  -0.04277448
>
> confint(regModel)
                   2.5 %       97.5 %
(Intercept) -176.20341784 130.55187963
x              5.53436979  12.26198875
I(x^2)        -0.05833368  -0.02721529
>
```

Note particularly the value for the linear coefficient. It is much larger than zero; yet, looking at Figure 3.28, the function seems to be almost entirely a negative quadratic over the range of the data. Uncertainty in the contribution of x at its highest value is between 5.534(200) and 12.262(200), or [1107, 2452]. And the contribution of the quadratic is much smaller than the scatter plot indicates. The coefficient is only $.0428/8.898 \approx 0.005$, or only about 1/2% that of the linear effect.

Next, we fit the same model with one small change, replacing x with sx using the following code:

```
scalpm1 = function(x){(x-(min(x)+max(x))/2)/
                        (.5*(max(x)-min(x)))}
sx = scalpm1(x).
```

It is not shown as part of an interactive session, so the > prompts are not present. The sx values are scaled to ± 1. The new regression model is:

```
> regModel = lm(ysqx ~ sx + I(sx^2))
>
```

The following are just the three summarized parts of the regression output to compare with the output from the unscaled regression model.

```
> summary(regModel)$r.squared
[1] 0.6646407
> library(rms)
> vif(regModel)
sx I(sx^2)
1       1
>
> summary(regModel)$coefficients [,1]
(Intercept)          sx      I(sx^2)
439.894370    -8.023922 -386.039717
>
> confint(regModel)
                 2.5 %      97.5 %
(Intercept)  370.60157   509.18717
sx           -83.97127    67.92342
I(sx^2)     -526.46142 -245.61801
>
```

The R^2 value is unchanged at 0.66. But the *VIF* has decreased from a value of 17.7 to a value of 1, the minimum possible value. Multicollinearity has been removed. The coefficients are much different. We see how to interpret them in the following paragraphs. Now, the coefficient for the linear term is near zero, and the uncertainty in the contribution of x at its highest value is between $-84(1)$ and $68(1)$, or $[-84, 68]$, much smaller than uncertainty about the linear contribution in the unscaled case: [1107, 2452]. Now, the relative impact of the quadratic term is much larger: the linear coefficient is only about 2% of the magnitude of the quadratic coefficient. The correct magnitude and higher precision for the linear- and quadratic-term coefficients give better information to management on the magnitude of the linear vs. quadratic effects.

One complication is added: explaining the model coefficients to management. But in fact, this can be easier to explain, at least for the intercept. Remember the house selling price example, where the intercept was explained as "the house selling price for a house of zero square feet." We were able to interpret this as the price of land, but often this interpretation for the intercept makes no sense when $x = 0$ is outside the practical range of x. Interpreting the intercept for a scaled x regression model is easy:

Scaled x regression intercept: *The value of the intercept is the average response one can expect when the predictor variable is at the middle of its range.*

If there are only linear terms in the model — no x^2 or $x_1 x_2$ terms, then the linear-term coefficients are also easy to interpret:

Scaled x regression coefficients (only linear terms): *Linear coefficients for a scaled x regression when only linear terms appear measure the average change in response when the predictor variable changes from its middle value to its highest value.* This characterizes the CHANGE in response; to predict the actual response, add the change plus the intercept.

When there are both linear and quadratic terms in the model, they must be explained by their joint effect. This is more complicated but still explainable:

Scaled x regression coefficients (x and x^2 terms): *The average change in response when the predictor variable changes from its middle value to its highest value is the sum of the linear and quadratic coefficients.* This characterizes the CHANGE in response; to predict the actual response, add the change plus the intercept.

This managerial interpretation is given as follows for the regression model with scaled x that we just fitted:

- When x is at the center of its range, about 105, the response is predicted to average, about 440. (This is where $sx = 0$.)
- When x moves from the center of its range to the high end, about 200, the average response is predicted to decrease by

$-8(1) - 386(1^2) = -394$. (This is where $sx = 1$.) The predicted average response would be $440 - 394 = 46$.

- When x moves from the center of its range to the low end, about 10, the average response is predicted to decrease by $-8(-1) - 386((-1)^2) = -378$. (This is where $sx = -1$.) The predicted average response would be $440 - 378 = 62$.

3.3.4 Going beyond scaling: Making model terms orthogonal

Scaling x values to ± 1 makes the quadratic and linear terms independent, but problems remain in multicollinearity with the intercept. And higher-order g functions (e.g., cubic) for model terms will introduce new correlations. Figure 3.29 shows the plots for constant, linear, quadratic, and cubic functions for x between zero and one. One can think of one measure of the multicollinearity as the dot product of the vector of values for one function against the other. The dot product of the quadratic function against the linear function is symmetric about zero, except that below $x = 0$, the values for the linear function are negative. This means that the two halves of the dot product will cancel, giving zero.

This fails when we compute the dot product of the constant function values with the quadratic function values since the constant function is always 1 and the quadratic values are always greater than or equal to zero. Similarly, the cubic and linear functions are positive and negative together, always producing a positive dot product. So, even with ± 1 scaling, multicollinearity exists between the intercept and quadratic and between the linear and cubic.

The solution is something called *orthogonal polynomials.* You might think of these as the decorrelated quadratic, cubic, etc., portions. The plots in Figure 3.30 make the concept clear: the new quadratic and cubic plots make intuitive sense as characterizing something distinctly different from the linear and intercept functions. While their g functions are complex, they are easy to compute in R. The plots in Figure 3.30 were constructed with the following code. It is not shown as part of an interactive session, so the > prompts are not present.

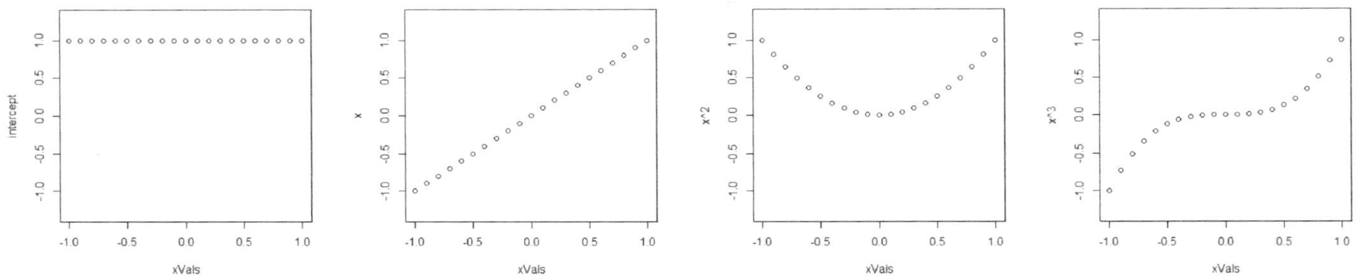

Figure 3.29. Scaling to ±1 leaves some multicollinearity in model terms.

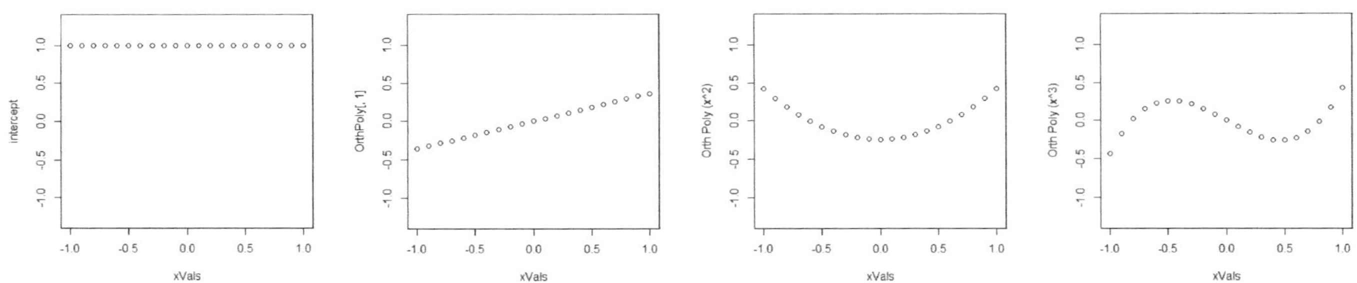

Figure 3.30. Orthogonal polynomials eliminate multicollinearity in x.

```
xVals = seq(from = -1, to = 1, by = .1)
intercept = rep(1,length(xVals))  # the intercept (constant)
OrthPoly = poly(xVals, degree = 3)
# rescale them so that linear goes between -1 and +1
# column 1 is linear, 2 quadratic, 3 cubic,
#    so [1,1] is first (most negative) value of x
OrthPoly = OrthPoly/abs(OrthPoly[1,1])
plot(xVals, intercept, ylim = c(-1.3,1.3))
plot(xVals, OrthPoly[,1], ylim = c(-1.3,1.3))
plot(xVals, OrthPoly[,2], ylab = "Orth Poly (x^2)",
     ylim = c(-1.3,1.3))
plot(xVals, OrthPoly[,3], ylab = "Orth Poly (x^3)",
     ylim = c(-1.3,1.3))
```

While multicollinearity is removed, interpretation now becomes difficult because the range of the orthogonal polynomial representations for x, x^2 and x^3 vary: [−3.60375, 3.60375] for OP(x), and [−0.24481103, 0.42285541] for OP(x^2) and [−0.43329786, 0.43329786] for OP(x^2). For this reason, orthogonal polynomials are rarely used for prediction in business settings. While coefficient uncertainty is reduced, interpretation of the coefficients for management is nearly impossible. In business settings, orthogonal polynomials are used primarily for hypothesis testing on the significance of the coefficients.

How would the quadratic regression model from the previous section be coded to employ orthogonal polynomials? The `lm()` function accepts `poly()` in the model specification, making this easy! The code and results are as follows. Since *VIF* does not show the confounding of the intercept and the quadratic term, there is no difference between the *VIF* reported in the following and that for the scaled x regression above.

The validity checking plots remain identical to the two regressions above, supporting model validity again. But now the intercept (constant) effect has been correctly separated from the intercept. Note that the confidence interval for the intercept is narrower than for the scaled regression, which is narrower than for the unscaled regression.

We will not use orthogonal polynomials further because of the difficulty in explaining the coefficients to management.

```
> regModel = lm(ysqx2 ~ poly(sx, degree = 2))
> # just used for showing fitted model
> summary(regModel)$coefficients[,1]
(Intercept) poly(sx, degree = 2)1 poly(sx, degree = 2)2
```

```
297.6692                  -21.7808                  -566.7579
>
> # show ANOVA table for regression model
> anova(regModel)
Analysis of Variance Table

Response: ysqx2
                     Df Sum Sq Mean Sq F value    Pr(>F)
poly(sx, degree = 2)  2 321689  160844  16.846 9.265e-05 ***
Residuals            17 162315    9548
---
>
> # pull out the R-squared value from the summary
> summary(regModel)$r.squared
[1] 0.6646407
> # need package "rms" to compute VIF
> library(rms)
> vif(regModel)
poly(sx, degree = 2)1 poly(sx, degree = 2)2
1                     1
> # do plots to check model validity
> acf(regModel$residuals)
> plot(regModel, ask=F, add.smooth=F)
> plot(sx,regModel$residuals)
> confint(regModel)
                          2.5 %    97.5 %
(Intercept)            251.5709  343.7675
poly(sx, degree = 2)1 -227.9386  184.3770
poly(sx, degree = 2)2 -772.9157 -360.6001
>
```

3.3.5 Handling qualitative independent variables

All of the regression models that we have considered so far involved predictor or independent variables that were *quantitative*. But often, we wish to predict a response variable as a function of one or more qualitative variables. We revisit the house price case from Section 3.2, with slightly different data. There are three townships in the North Valley area, which we call "North," "Central," and "South." Homes in the central township demand higher prices than those in the north, and those in the north more than those in the south, which have relatively lower values. The following shows the first six records of the data frame in R. All columns are labeled `<dbl>`, meaning *double precision real numbers*, except for Twp, which is labeled `<chr>`, which means *character* — a qualitative variable. While there are still 124 records with matching house characteristics as in Section 3.2, this data set has different prices that account for township-to-township differences.

```
  Price Bedrooms  Size  Baths  Twp
  <dbl>    <dbl> <dbl> <dbl> <chr>
1  590        4  2300   2    Central
2  445        4  2100   2    North
3  460        3  2300   2    South
4  425        2  2200   2.5  North
5  300        2  2100   1.5  South
6  510        2  2100   2    Central
```

We complete the analysis of this more complex model using R. But first, we need to discuss the model form.

There are two approaches for response modeling when some predictor variables are quantitative and others are qualitative. One method, mentioned earlier, is to construct a mixed model called an analysis of covariance, or ANOCOVA, model. Recall the simple linear regression model in Equation (3.3):

$$Y = \beta_0 + \beta_1 x + \varepsilon,\ \varepsilon \overset{\text{iid}}{\sim} N(0, \sigma^2).$$

Consider a model with an additional qualitative variable v whose unknown effect for the kth level is denoted γ_k. Suppose that there were three levels, so $k \in \{1, 2, 3\}$. The ANOCOVA model would be written as

$$Y(x, v_k) = \beta_0 + \beta_1(x - \bar{x}) + \gamma_k + \varepsilon, \quad \sum_{k=1}^{3} \gamma_k = 0,\ \varepsilon \overset{\text{iid}}{\sim} N(0, \sigma^2). \tag{3.9}$$

Note that the γ_k values are deviations from the average over all three townships, and so they sum to zero. If all variables are qualitative, only effect terms such as γ_k would be present in the model (no βs), and the model would be called an ANOVA model.

ANOVA and ANOCOVA models and their analysis are beyond the scope of this text. We pursue a second approach, where we construct a regression model (all quantitative predictors) by replacing the qualitative variable with a set of 0–1 indicator variables. There will be one less indicator variable than the number of levels of the qualitative variable. For the house price case, we select the value of

v (Township, or Twp for short) from the set {"North." "Central," "South"}. So, we create $3-1 = 2$ indicator variables. These are sometimes called *dummy variables*. Since we expect houses in the central township to have highest value, we pick that qualitative value as the reference. Understand, though, that we could pick any of the three as the reference.

We create two new quantitative predictor variables, North and South, (you can consider these to be x_4 and x_5, respectively). we leave out the reference level. When the qualitative variable Twp equals "North," set the indicator variable x_4 (North) $= 1$, and $= 0$ otherwise. When the qualitative variable Twp equals "South," set the indicator variable x_5 (South) $= 1$, and $= 0$ otherwise. Here is the corresponding code in R:

```
> HousePriceTwp=
> read_excel("HousePriceSimpleWithTownship.xlsx")

> # create two indicator dummy variables
> HousePriceTwp$North=
    ifelse(HousePriceTwp$Twp=="North",1,0)
> HousePriceTwp$South=
    ifelse(HousePriceTwp$Twp=="South",1,0)

> # remove qualitative variable "Twp"
> HousePriceTwp=
    HousePriceTwp[,!names(HousePriceTwp)
                  %in% c("Twp")]
>
```

Note two things: first, there is no indicator variable for `Twp=="Central"`. With both indicators set to zero, the model predicts the selling price in the central township. Second, after creating the indicator variables, the variable "Twp" is deleted from the data frame so that the `pairs()` function and `lm()` can operate against the entire data frame. Also, note that at most one of the indicator variables will be 1 for any particular observation. The house is in only one township. Both indicators will be zero if the house is in the central township.

Now, let's examine the results and give a managerial interpretation. First, we present the code for the regression, assessment of practical predictive power, validity checks, and finally uncertainty

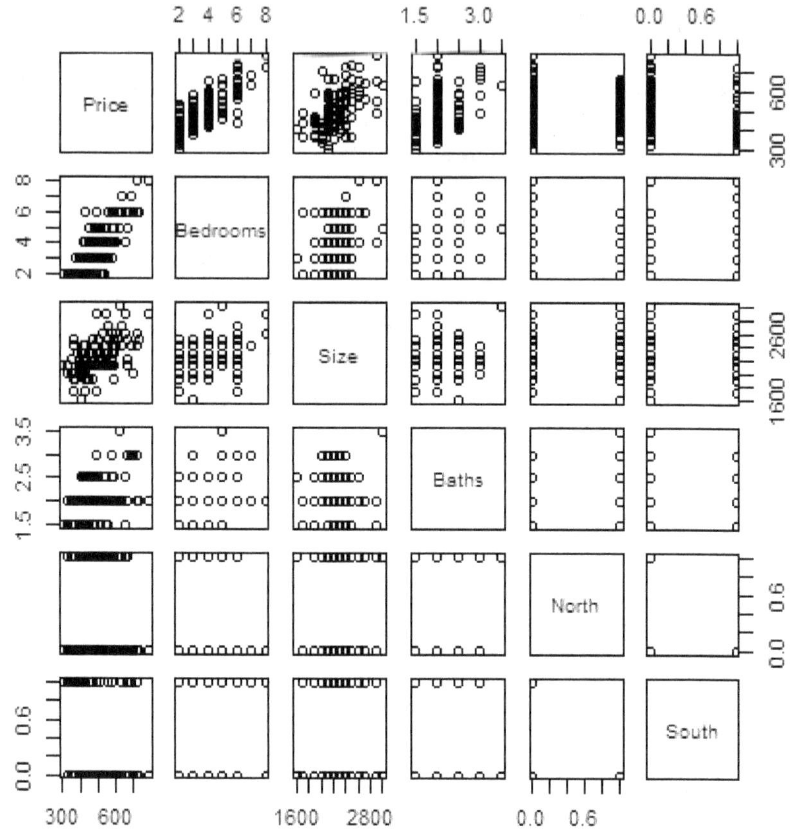

Figure 3.31. Matrix plot for the house case with township indicator variables.

characterization, including forecast selling price, confidence, and prediction intervals for the same 2,500 square feet, four-bedroom, three-bath house that we considered earlier, but now for each of the three townships separately.

The following is the code and resulting output. For brevity, the plots are omitted, except for the `pairs()` plot in Figure 3.31, which gives some hint that house prices in both the North and South townships are lower than the reference (Central) township.

```
> pairs(HousePriceTwp)
> # regression model fitting command is below
> regModel = lm(Price ~ Size + Bedrooms + Baths + North
                        + South, data = HousePriceTwp)
> summary(regModel)$coefficients[,1] # just used for
#                                      showing fitted model
```

```
(Intercept)          Size      Bedrooms         Baths
84.26698857    0.09349491   38.28247222   56.06323236
       North          South
-69.58891985 -96.04525194
>
> # assess regression model performance
> # first plot actual vs predicted
> plot(predict(regModel, newdata = HousePriceTwp),
       HousePriceTwp$Price)
> abline(0,1) # points should fall near diagonal if
#                 predicted ~ actual

> summary(regModel)$r.squared # pull out the R-squared value
#                                from the summary
[1] 0.8485353

> # do diagnostic plots for model validity
> acf(regModel$residuals)
> plot(regModel, ask=F, add.smooth=F)
> plot(HousePriceTwp$Size,regModel$residuals)
> plot(HousePriceTwp$Bedrooms, regModel$residuals)
> plot(HousePriceTwp$Baths,regModel$residuals)
> plot(HousePriceTwp$North, regModel$residuals)
> plot(HousePriceTwp$South,regModel$residuals)
>
>
> anova(regModel) # print ANOVA table for regression model
Analysis of Variance Table


Response: Price
           Df Sum Sq Mean Sq  F value    Pr(>F)
Size        1 297558  297558 192.9352 < 2.2e-16 ***
Bedrooms    1 442924  442924 287.1897 < 2.2e-16 ***
Baths       1  77498   77498  50.2492  1.07e-10 ***
North       1  10686   10686   6.9287  0.009617 **
South       1 190866  190866 123.7569 < 2.2e-16 ***
Residuals 118 181988    1542
---
> summary(regModel) # used to show standard deviation
#                      estimates and p-values
Call:
lm(formula = Price ~ Size + Bedrooms + Baths + North
                 + South, data = HousePriceTwp)
Residuals:
 Min     1Q   Median     3Q    Max
-79.32 -30.98  -1.53  26.41  88.72

Coefficients:
             Estimate Std. Error t value Pr(>|t|)
(Intercept)  84.26699   37.24853   2.262   0.0255 *
```

```
Size            0.09349     0.01553    6.020 2.02e-08 ***
Bedrooms       38.28247     2.80172   13.664  < 2e-16 ***
Baths          56.06323     9.07342    6.179 9.50e-09 ***
North         -69.58892     8.82717   -7.883 1.77e-12 ***
South         -96.04525     8.63358  -11.125  < 2e-16 ***
---
Residual standard error: 39.27 on 118 degrees of freedom
Multiple R-squared:  0.8485,    Adjusted R-squared:  0.8421
F-statistic: 132.2 on 5 and 118 DF,  p-value: < 2.2e-16

> confint(regModel)
                    2.5 %      97.5 %
(Intercept)    10.50475653 158.0292206
Size            0.06273997   0.1242498
Bedrooms       32.73430919  43.8306353
Baths          38.09538945  74.0310753
North         -87.06912067 -52.1087190
South        -113.14210060 -78.9484033
>
> # confidence,prediction intervals for North,South,Central
> new.dat=data.frame(Size = 2500, Bedrooms = 4, Baths = 3,
                     North = 1, South = 0)
                     ># add two more rows
> new.dat=rbind(new.dat,data.frame(Size = 2500, Bedrooms = 4,
                      Baths = 3, North = 0, South = 1))
> new.dat=rbind(new.dat,data.frame(Size = 2500, Bedrooms = 4,
                      Baths = 3, North = 0, South = 0))

># give forecast CI
> predict(regModel,newdata=new.dat,interval='confidence')
       fit      lwr      upr
1 569.7349 548.3247 591.1451
2 543.2786 520.3977 566.1595
3 639.3239 617.6728 660.9749
># give forecast CI
> predict(regModel,newdata=new.dat,interval='prediction')
       fit      lwr      upr
1 569.7349 489.0729 650.3970
2 543.2786 462.2137 624.3434
3 639.3239 558.5975 720.0502
>
```

Next, we interpret key parts of this output in the special way required when indicator variables are included. It is important to note that, since only linear terms are included in the regression, *the predictor (x) variables are NOT scaled to* ± 1. First is the interpretation of the coefficient estimates and confidence intervals, based on this selected output:

```
> summary(regModel)$coefficients[,1]

(Intercept)          Size       Bedrooms         Baths
84.26698857    0.09349491   38.28247222   56.06323236
          North          South
   -69.58891985 -96.04525194

# compute confidence intervals for model coefficients
> confint(regModel)
                     2.5 %       97.5 %
(Intercept)    10.50475653  158.0292206
Size            0.06273997    0.1242498
Bedrooms       32.73430919   43.8306353
Baths          38.09538945   74.0310753
North         -87.06912067  -52.1087190
South        -113.14210060  -78.9484033
>
```

- Average house selling price for a house that is zero square foot in size is estimated at \$84,000, and the true mean value falls between approximately \$10,500 and \$158,000, with 95% confidence.
- All other predictors held the same, for each additional square foot in size, average house selling price increase is estimated to be \$93, and the true mean increase falls between approximately \$62 and \$124 with 95% confidence.
- All other predictors held the same, for each additional bedroom, average house selling price increase is estimated to be \$38,000, and the true mean increase falls between approximately \$33,000 and \$44,000 with 95% confidence.
- All other predictors held the same, for each additional bathroom, average house selling price increase is estimated to be \$56,000, and the true mean increase falls between approximately \$38,000 and \$74,000 for each additional bathroom, with 95% confidence.
- All other predictors held the same, houses sold in the North township are estimated to sell for \$70,000 less than in the Central township, and the true mean decrease falls between approximately \$52,000 and \$87,000 less, with 95% confidence.
- All other predictors held the same, houses sold in the South township are estimated to sell for \$96,000 less than in the Central township, and the true mean decrease falls between approximately \$79,000 and \$113,000 less, with 95% confidence.

Next is the interpretation of the three forecasts for selling price of a 2,500 square feet four-bedroom three-bath house, based on this selected output:

```
> new.dat = data.frame(Size=2500, Bedrooms=4, Baths=3,
                            North=1, South=0)
> new.dat = rbind(new.dat,data.frame(Size=2500, Bedrooms=4,
                                        Baths=3, North=0, South=1))
> new.dat = rbind(new.dat,data.frame(Size=2500, Bedrooms=4,
                                        Baths=3, North=0, South=0))

> predict(regModel,newdata=new.dat,interval='confidence')
       fit      lwr      upr
1 569.7349 548.3247 591.1451
2 543.2786 520.3977 566.1595
3 639.3239 617.6728 660.9749

> predict(regModel,newdata=new.dat,interval='prediction')
       fit      lwr      upr
1 569.7349 489.0729 650.3970
2 543.2786 462.2137 624.3434
3 639.3239 558.5975 720.0502
>
```

- The regression model forecast average house selling price for a North township house that is 2,500 square feet in size with four bedrooms and three bathrooms is approximately \$570,000.
- Taking sampling error into account, the forecast average house selling price for a North township house that is 2,500 square feet in size with four bedrooms and three bathrooms falls between approximately \$548,000 and \$591,000, with 95% confidence.
- Taking sampling error and selling price variation into account, for any individual 2,500 square foot house with four bedrooms and three bathrooms in North township, the forecast selling price will fall between approximately \$489,000 and \$650,000.
- The regression model forecast average house selling price for a South township house that is 2,500 square feet in size with four bedrooms and three bathrooms is approximately \$543,000.
- Taking sampling error into account, the forecast average house selling price for a South township house that is 2,500 square feet in size with four bedrooms and three bathrooms falls between approximately \$520,000 and \$566,000, with 95% confidence.
- Taking sampling error and selling price variation into account, for any individual 2,500 square foot house with four bedrooms and

three bathrooms in the South township, the forecast selling price will fall between approximately \$462,000 and \$624,000.
- The regression model forecast average house selling price for a Central township house that is 2,500 square feet in size with four bedrooms and three bathrooms is approximately \$639,000.
- Taking sampling error into account, the forecast average house selling price for a Central township house that is 2,500 square feet in size with four bedrooms and three bathrooms falls between approximately \$618,000 and \$661,000, with 95% confidence.
- Taking sampling error and selling price variation into account, for any individual 2,500 square foot house with four bedrooms and three bathrooms in Central township, the forecast selling price will fall between approximately \$559,000 and \$720,000.

3.3.6 Multiple regression with observational or cross-sectional data

Many business studies deal with observational data. For the house price study, the data consisted of the complete information on sales for one year for North Valley Real Estate. For the stock price data study in Chapter 2, the regression model used data from a specific period for the 89 companies listed on the New York Stock Exchange. In both of these studies, time was not taken into account in the modeling. The data were snapshots in time. This kind of observational data (when time is not a factor) is called *cross-sectional data* and are probably the most common type of observational data.

Observational data are problematic for predictive analytics under the *traditional research* paradigm. In this section, we explain the problems and how best to address them if one wants to use regression models with observational data in this setting. If these problems cannot be resolved, regression can be applied under the *data-adaptive research* paradigm. We show how to do this in the following chapter.

There are three concerns in building regression models for observational data under the *traditional research* paradigm. The first is easily addressed. Dealing with the second issue is more subtle. The third issue can make regression under the *traditional research* paradigm impossible:

1. If the form of the model (predictor variables and model terms involving them) is determined from the data, the regression will be overfit to the data at hand, and its predictive ability based on the same data will be overly optimistic. p-values will be overly small, and confidence and prediction intervals will be overly tight and not trustworthy, even if all validity plots are satisfactory.
2. Predictor variables in observational studies often exhibit high correlation, driven by unobserved (*lurking*) variables (see Section 3.1.2), or the structure of the population or the sampling process for the observational data.
3. Observational studies are typically *unbalanced*. That means that the levels of one predictor variable do not occur with the same frequency across all levels of a second predictor variable.

For the first issue, coefficients are custom-fitted to the observational data at hand, but more problematic is the selection of predictor variables and model terms *based on the same data used to fit the model and determine p-values*. The model was *designed* to fit a particular set of data, violating the *traditional research* paradigm that assumes a theory-driven model.

The solution is to base the model form on hypothesized relationships from common knowledge or prior studies. For the house price study, common knowledge suggests that house selling price will increase for greater size, more bedrooms, and more bathrooms. The simplest model is linear, and in our study, that worked well, so the model form was not modified by the observational data (other than fitting the coefficient values). In some cases, common knowledge can suggest a nonlinear form: propensity to various activities (including responsiveness to a salary increase) is often based on % of income, which suggests the linear relationship is with the logarithm of income.

To address the first issue then, one needs to think carefully about a plausible conceptual model before examining the data set in any detail. The conceptual model should include predictor variables and terms (linear, log, quadratic, etc.) based on theory or common sense and predictor variables identified in previous studies. Chances are that for any study that you undertake, you can find a similar one in the literature via Google or a library search. To quote Reichenheim & Coutinho (2010):

> "Multivariate regression models should be avoided when assumptions for causal inference from cross-sectional data do not hold."

Multicollinearity is a concern for regression using observational data. But an even greater concern is when multicollinearity is driven by unobserved *lurking* variables since the cause–effect structure is lost and prediction becomes risky. Unmeasured but important predictor variables correlated with the observed predictor variables are sometimes called *unmeasured confounders*. As we saw in Section 3.1.2, changes in lurking variables can cause joint changes in the predictor variables. For example, in an observational study of the effects of drinking alcohol and smoking on cancer, high stress may affect both drinking alcohol and smoking. For the house price study, human occupancy count is a lurking variable that implies that a house with more bedrooms should have more bathrooms. In observational studies, predictor variables may be correlated for other reasons. For example, houses with large size tend to have more bedrooms, but there is no obvious lurking variable.

When multicollinearity is significant, the importance of predictor variables cannot be judged independently because there is nonzero, often substantial correlation among the predictor variables. The *VIF* value is one indicator of this effect confounding in an observational sample (discussed in Section 3.3.3). When the *VIF* is large, necessarily at least one high-*VIF* variable should be excluded from the model. Ideally, common knowledge can drive the choice, keeping variables higher up the causal chain and deleting their dependents. One must assume that the observed dependency is likely to continue in the predictive setting, either due to the continuing presence of a *lurking variable* or due to continuing inherent correlation structure in the population. Large *VIF* often results in unrealistically large positive and negative regression coefficients, whose effects cancel in the prediction.

There are methods to fit regression models with constraints on the magnitude of the regression coefficients. Ridge regression constrains the sum of squared coefficient values (Euclidean or L^2 norm). For technical aspects of ridge regression, see Hoerl & Kennard (2000). Ridge regression does not result in zero coefficients for any of the model terms. A better choice may be the least absolute shrinkage and selection operator (LASSO), which constrains the sum of absolute values in a way that can result in zero values for some regression coefficients, effectively accomplishing both the removal of coefficient anomalies and the selection of important predictor variables. For technical aspects of LASSO regression, see Tibshirani (1996). Unfortunately, both ridge and LASSO regression do not provide straightforward calculations for confidence intervals and p-values. As a consequence, they are more appropriate for regression under the *data-adaptive research* paradigm, which is the subject of Chapter 4.

The third issue is imbalance in the values of the predictor variables. Consider a set of observational data where cancer incidence is the dependent variable and smoking, age, and sex are predictor variables. Suppose that there is a real effect for sex (males more likely than females to get cancer) but that in our observational sample, the fraction of females who were smokers was larger than the fraction of males who were smokers. Then, a scatter plot of cancer incidence vs. sex might show little effect, and the corresponding correlation and single-variable regression might show no statistical significance. But if a regression model were fitted with all three predictor variables, sex would be recognized to have an effect *after taking into account age and smoking*. This phenomenon is sometimes called *residual confounding*. It can be addressed by including all likely predictors in the model and only using backward elimination to determine unimportant predictors. Alternatively, best-subsets regression finds among all subsets of variables the model with the best performance, in terms of R^2, adjusted R^2, or another measure of fit (Hocking & Leslie, 1967; Rencher & Pun, 1980). Some authors argue that for observational data, model selection based on the data used to fit the final model is risky: all *a priori* determined model terms should be retained (Thorpe, 2017).

If imbalance occurs for an unmeasured variable, the *traditional research* paradigm cannot be supported. For the cancer example, that could include unmeasured values of ethnicity, geographic location, and occupation. When unmeasured predictor variables are not balanced across the levels of the measured predictors, their effect appears associated with the other predictor variables. If the imbalance comes from correlation patterns that are stable, then this is less of a worry. But prediction to arbitrary combinations of predictor variables in this case is risky, and the characterization of prediction error will be too small. However, we will be able to fit a predictive regression model and give empirical confidence and prediction intervals in this case under the *data-adaptive research* paradigm. That approach is the topic of Chapter 4.

Special validity concerns for observational data

Observational studies require the researcher to address two common concerns in this setting: *common methods bias* and *endogeneity.*

Common methods bias occurs when building regression models for survey data. This arises because individual respondents may have a *response style* that they use in surveys. For example, rather than paying careful attention to each question, they might focus on *middle response* categories, never using high or low. Others might consistently choose the *extreme response* categories. The former will deflate observed correlations relative to actual relations, while the latter will inflate them. A third style is called *agreement tendency,* where positive ratings are generally given.

Addressing common methods bias can be done through the design of the survey, called *procedural controls* or *ex ante* methods, or through modified statistical methods, called *statistical controls* or *ex post* methods.

To minimize the impact of middle response and extreme response styles through procedural controls, a key strategy is to change the response scales: some with fewer levels (as few as two), and some with more. To minimize the impact of the agreement tendency style, some question scales should be set in such a way that higher ratings correspond to higher agreement, while others are scaled in such a way that lower scores indicate higher agreement. Another important strategy is to collect predictor variable data from respondents but collect dependent variable data from a secondary source that can be linked to a respondent. For example, one might ask about working environment characteristics from employees at different firms and collect turnover rate data not from them, but from separate company sources.

Statistical controls cannot completely compensate for a survey design that admits common methods bias. Harman's single-factor test is a widely used technique, but this is beyond the scope of this text. For more information on handling common methods bias, see Baumgartner & Steenkamp (2001) and Kock *et al.* (2021).

Endogeneity occurs with observational data when a variable in the model is affected by other variables that are either included or not included in the model. The variable in the model is called *endogenous*. This situation can make the predictor variable or variables dependent on the missing or *lurking* variable or variables, violating two principles required in the *traditional research* paradigm: i.i.d. errors, and the assumption that all the model predictor variables *independently cause* the changes in the response variable. In the case of endogeneity from a factor external to the model, the *lurking* variable causes changes in the response AND the predictor variables. Ignoring this destroys the ability to characterize model error in terms of coefficient estimates and forecasts. If the *lurking* or included variable that drives the endogenous variable is known, it is called an *instrumental* variable.

When the instrumental variable is known and measured, endogeneity can be detected by including the instrumental variable in the regression and checking the VIF with the predictor variables. Then, endogeneity can be handled by constructing two regression models: one uses the instrumental variable to predict the endogenous predictor variable or variables, and the predicted values are then used in the primary regression model. Two-stage least squares and the more complex structural equation modeling can be used in the face of endogeneity, but they are beyond the scope of this text. For more on the risks of endogeneity, see Semadeni *et al.* (2014).

Life-cycle savings example

We illustrate regression with observational data using the `LifeCycleSavings` data set in the R `datasets` library. It consists of 50 observations of five variables:

- aggregate personal savings rate,
- percent of population under 15 years old,
- percent of population over 75 years old,
- per-capita disposable income, and
- growth rate of disposable income.

It is a good example of an observational data set that can be analyzed via regression under the *traditional research* paradigm. The theory providing a hypothesized model was developed by the famous economist Franco Modigliani. The regression model proposed in the

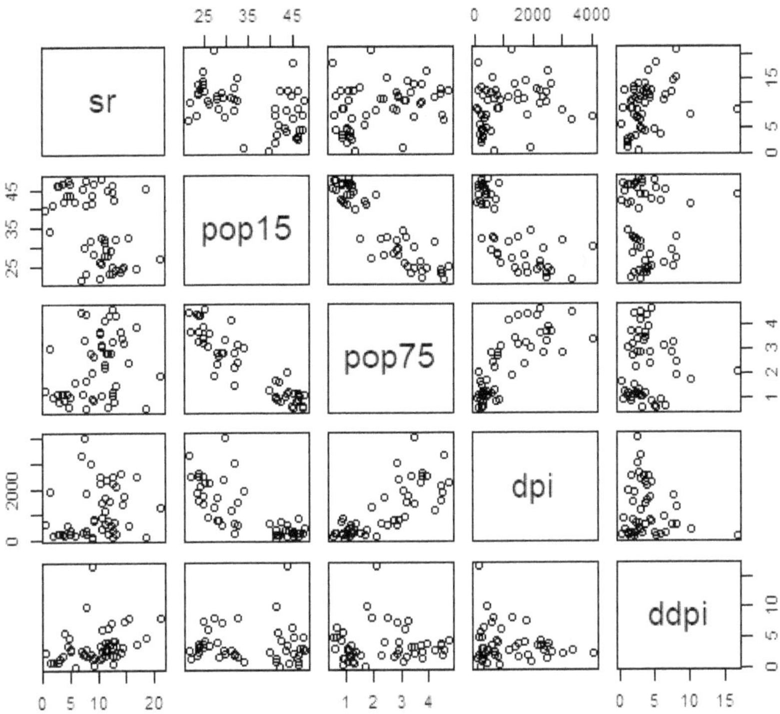

Figure 3.32. Matrix plot for life-cycle data.

`LifeCycleData` description is

$$Y = \beta_0 + \beta_1 x_1 + \beta_2 x_2 + \beta_3 x_3 + \beta_4 x_4 + \varepsilon, \varepsilon \overset{\text{iid}}{\sim} N(0, \sigma^2), \qquad (3.10)$$

where Y is aggregate personal savings, x_1 is per-capita disposable income, x_2 is growth rate of personal income, x_3 is the percent of population less that 15 years old, and x_4 is the percent of population older than 75. The data set contains values for 50 different countries. Each of these measures is averaged over the decade 1960–1970. For more information, see Belsley *et al.* (2013).

Because we have a theoretical model (Equation (3.10)), the analysis of this observational data can be conducted under the *traditional research* paradigm. We expect to see relationships between savings rate and the four variables mentioned above. First, we check the matrix plot (via `pairs(LifeCycleSavings)`). This is shown in Figure 3.32.

Three interesting characteristics are apparent: first, looking across the top row, there appears a slight negative relationship between pop15 (the percent of population younger than 15) and the dependent variable sr (savings rate). But with observational data, it is often difficult to see all important relationships from the matrix plot. The second important characteristic is the clear negative correlation between pop15 and pop75. That is not a surprise since countries with a higher fraction of youthful population are likely to have a lower fraction of older population. A second correlation is apparent: pop75 is positively correlated with dpi (disposable personal income). This is also not a surprise. These correlations help us predict what will happen in the regression modeling activity: because of these correlations, it is likely that two of these three predictor variables will be dropped from the final model. Further, since among these three, only pop15 shows any correlation with savings rate in the pairs() plot, that is the likely variable to remain.

Suppose that our ultimate predictive analytics objective is to predict savings rate for countries with 3% population over 75, 35% population under 15, $2,000 disposable personal income, and 10% rate of change of income. We begin by fitting the full regression model and then examine coefficients, R^2, and *VIF* before going any further with analysis and prediction. The code for these steps and resulting output is as follows. (Note: attach() allows you to use variable names without the data frame name. BUT within one R session, only do the attach() command ONCE or you will see warnings with Masked in them.)

```
> library(datasets)
> attach(LifeCycleSavings)
> pairs(LifeCycleSavings)
> regModel = lm(sr ~ dpi + ddpi + pop15 + pop75)
> summary(regModel)$coefficients
                 Estimate    Std. Error    t value     Pr(>|t|)
(Intercept) 28.5660865407 7.3545161062  3.8841558 0.0003338249
dpi         -0.0003369019 0.0009311072 -0.3618293 0.7191731554
ddpi         0.4096949279 0.1961971276  2.0881801 0.0424711387
pop15       -0.4611931471 0.1446422248 -3.1885098 0.0026030189
pop75       -1.6914976767 1.0835989307 -1.5609998 0.1255297940
> summary(regModel)$r.squared
[1] 0.3384564
> library(rms)
> vif(regModel)
   dpi     ddpi    pop15    pop75
2.884369 1.074309 5.937661 6.629105
>
```

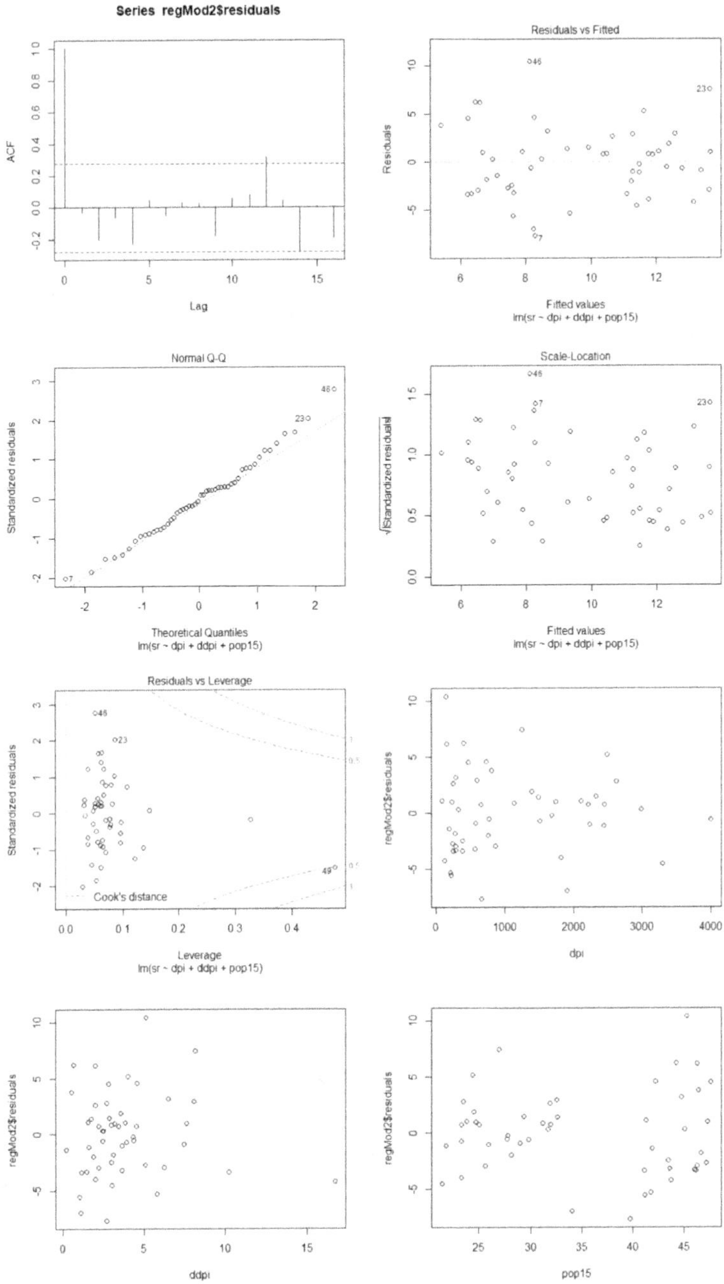

Figure 3.33. LifeCycleSavings without **pop75** validity plots.

The *VIF* is high for pop15 and pop75. Dropping the highest gives the revised model and the following results. The value of R^2 decreases slightly from 0.34 to 0.30. Such low values for R^2 are not uncommon in observational studies.

```
> # two VIF values > 5, delete largest (pop75)
> regModel2 = lm(sr ~ dpi + ddpi + pop15)
> summary(regModel2)$coefficients
                 Estimate   Std. Error   t value     Pr(>|t|)
(Intercept) 19.2771686683 4.3888974032  4.392258 6.533416e-05
dpi         -0.0008703878 0.0008795403 -0.989594 3.275496e-01
ddpi         0.3929354505 0.1989389516  1.975156 5.426908e-02
pop15       -0.2883861300 0.0945353962 -3.050562 3.783754e-03
> summary(regModel2)$r.squared
[1] 0.3026342
> library(rms)
> vif(regModel2)
     dpi     ddpi    pop15
2.495779 1.071092 2.459559
>
```

Now, the *VIF* values are less than five, and the validity plots are checked. The results are shown in Figure 3.33. The autocorrelation plot shows one value beyond the statistical limits, but the value is only slightly beyond, and with a 95% interval, one might expect one or two to slightly exceed the limits. Since none of the other plots indicate violation of the i.i.d. normal assumptions, the coefficient p-values can be examined to determine whether any predictor variables should be dropped. That code and the results are as follows.

```
> summary(regModel2)

Call:
lm(formula = sr ~ dpi + ddpi + pop15)

Residuals:
    Min      1Q  Median      3Q     Max
-7.6889 -2.8813  0.0296  1.7989 10.4330

Coefficients:
              Estimate Std. Error t value Pr(>|t|)
(Intercept) 19.2771687  4.3888974   4.392 6.53e-05 ***
dpi         -0.0008704  0.0008795  -0.990  0.32755
ddpi         0.3929355  0.1989390   1.975  0.05427 .
pop15       -0.2883861  0.0945354  -3.051  0.00378 **
---
Residual standard error: 3.862 on 46 degrees of freedom
```

```
Multiple R-squared:  0.3026,  Adjusted R-squared:  0.2572
F-statistic: 6.654 on 3 and 46 DF,  p-value: 0.0007941
>
```

The p-value for dpi is high at 0.33, and so the variable is dropped. The revised plots (not shown) are satisfactory, and the *VIF* for the remaining two variables is quite low. The code and results for the summary and coefficient confidence intervals are shown as follows.

```
> regModel3 = lm(sr ~ ddpi + pop15)
> summary(regModel)$r.squared
[1] 0.287788
> library(rms)
> vif(regModel3)
    ddpi     pop15
1.002293 1.002293
> summary(regModel3)
Call:
lm(formula = sr ~ ddpi + pop15)

Residuals:
    Min      1Q  Median      3Q     Max
-7.5831 -2.8632  0.0453  2.2273 10.4753

Coefficients:
            Estimate Std. Error t value Pr(>|t|)
(Intercept) 15.59958    2.33439   6.682 2.48e-08 ***
ddpi         0.44283    0.19240   2.302 0.025837 *
pop15       -0.21638    0.06033  -3.586 0.000796 ***
---
Residual standard error: 3.861 on 47 degrees of freedom
Multiple R-squared:  0.2878,  Adjusted R-squared:  0.2575
F-statistic: 9.496 on 2 and 47 DF,  p-value: 0.0003438
>
> # give confidence intervals for regression coefficients
> confint(regModel3)
                  2.5 %      97.5 %
(Intercept) 10.90337994 20.29577158
ddpi         0.05576858  0.82989175
pop15       -0.33775402 -0.09499838
>
```

R^2 again decreased slightly from 0.30 to 0.29. The remaining two predictor variables have small p-values, so their coefficients are statistically different from zero. An increase of 1% in the rate of personal income increase results in approximately 0.44% increase in personal savings rate, on average, with a 95% confidence interval for the effect as between 0.06% and 0.82%. On the other hand, an increase of 1% in the fraction of country population younger than 15 years is associated with a decrease in the average personal savings rate of approximately 0.21%, with a 95% confidence interval for the effect as between (negative) 0.09% and 0.34%.

Next, we use the model for prediction. We do not expect a highly predictive model, given the very low R^2 value. To predict savings rate for countries with 3% population over 75, 35% population under 15, $2,000 disposable personal income, and 10% rate of change of income, we ignore the settings of % population over 75 and disposable personal income since these variables were eliminated from the regression model. The R code and results are shown as follows.

```
> new.dat = data.frame(ddpi = 10, pop15 = 35)
> predict(regModel3, new.dat, interval = "confidence")
       fit      lwr     upr
1 12.45471 9.801022 15.1084

> predict(regModel3, new.dat, interval = "prediction")
       fit      lwr      upr
1 12.45471 4.247059 20.66236
>
```

In managerial terms, the model has low predictive power. The average predicted personal savings rate for all countries with 3% population over 75, 35% population under 15, $2,000 disposable personal income, and 10% rate of change of income is approximately 12%, with a 95% confidence interval of 9.8% to 15.1%. Taking into account country-to-country variation, savings rate for an individual country with these demographic characteristics will fall between 4.2% and 20.7% with 95% confidence. The intervals are wide, perhaps not useful, due to the low R^2 of the model.

Checklist for regression with observational data

The 11-step general process for regression outlined in Section 3.4 requires some modification when dealing with observational data. Here is a checklist of special considerations:

- Between steps 1 and 2, add the following activity: Using common knowledge or results from previously published studies, identify the preliminary form of the model. That means identifying all potential predictor variables, any expected interactions (these require cross-product terms in the model), and any nonlinear relationships that might require transformed y, transformed x, or polynomial terms in x variables.

- As part of Step 6: A high VIF can be viewed as a concern for endogeneity. Since two-stage least squares is beyond the scope of this text, here the appropriate action is limited to deleting the highest-VIF model term (or one of the highest if there is a tie) and refitting the model. Repeat this as needed.
- In steps 10 and 11, add the following: Emphasize any concern about validity raised by (i) model form not matching an *a priori* guess, (ii) high *VIF*, or (iii) high imbalance.
- As part of step 3, check for large imbalance for qualitative variables. This can be checked by using a special form of the `summary` command. For example, to summarize balance for three qualitative predictor variables "A," "B," and "C," in data frame "myData," the R command is as follows.

```
> summary(cbind(A,B,C) ~ A + B + C, data = myData)
```

3.3.7 Designing experiments to fit multiple regression models

Often in business we are presented with data and are asked to find predictive models. Alternatively, we conduct a survey and use survey results to construct a model, or we take an entire set of data for a time period, such as a quarter or a year, and develop a predictive model. These regression models are based on *observational data.* But sometimes, we are able to design experiments where we deliberately vary the predictor variables and observe the response. This is called a *designed experiment.* Designed experiments are often used in marketing studies, product design, and with simulation models of processes, as we will see in Chapter 10. In this section, we explain the advantages of designed experiments, common structures, and interpreting results visually for designed experiments.

Basics of a designed experiment

We explore the basics of designed experiments for regression models through a machining example. Suppose that you use a machine to drill a precise hole for a laptop hinge mechanism. Because the hole must be precise, drill bits must be replaced when they wear out. Figure 3.34 shows an image of a drill bit in action (Photo by Greg Rosenke on Unsplash). When the drilling force is increased, drill time is shorter: the hole is completed more quickly, but the added heat means the drill bit wear-out rate will be greater. When the drilling speed (in revolutions per minute, or RPM) is increased, one expects that drilling time will be shorter, under a fixed force. For a particular force, suppose that past experience says that the drill bit wear rate decreases as RPM speed increases from a very low value to a certain mid-level RPM, but then beyond that RPM, excess heat again causes higher wear rate and shorter time until wear-out.

Management wants to decide on pressure and RPM settings that will maximize their profits. Rather than run all possible settings to determine wear and speed, it is possible to run just enough settings to fit predictive models — regression models in this case. Providing guidance to management requires two regression models: one regression model that predicts how long it takes to drill each hinge (shorter time means greater productivity and profit) and a second regression

Figure 3.34. A drill bit in action.

model that predicts the wear-out rate, which will determine the number of hinges that can be drilled before the drill wears out and the process must be stopped while the drill bit is replaced (adding cost for drill bits and hurting productivity and profit).

This is one kind of experiment, called a *response surface* experiment, where the objective is to fit a predictive regression model. It is also necessary if we want to use the model for *system optimization* (choosing the pressure and speed that give maximum profit) and if we further want to study *system robustness* (how much profitability is hurt if pressure and speed settings drift a little).

There are two other categories of experiments that are not explored here. *Comparison experiments* characterize the response of two or more system configurations to see which is the best (often a single qualitative variable called a *factor*). *Screening experiments* are used to identify which of many independent variables have significant effect on the response.

In a designed experiment, the predictor variables are set by the experimenter, and then experimental "runs" are performed at the prescribed settings. For the drilling study, speed and pressure are set for each run, and then wear-out rate and time to drill each hinge are measured. Designing the experiment means deciding what settings of pressure and speed (RPM) will be used in the experiment. How many different settings and in what combinations? and How many repeated runs using the same conditions should be done? Repeated runs under the same conditions are called *replications* and only exist in designed experiments. When the experiment is conducted, the predictor variables (pressure and speed) can be set by the experimenter. Here is where the term *independent variables* comes from. How one sets the RPM can be decided independently of how one sets the pressure.

The topic of design of experiments is typically covered in a one- or two-semester graduate course. Here, we can only give brief coverage of some key aspects. To learn more, see for example Barton (1999) and Wu & Hamada (2009).

To keep the discussion brief, we focus on only one of the two required regression models: predicting tool wear-out rate as a function of pressure and RPM. Before developing the experiment design, we present a high-level process for experiment design in a regression setting. We follow this for the drilling study. For more details on the experiment design process and tools, see the references above.

Experiment design process

1. Determine the objectives for the fitted regression model. Goal hierarchy plots can be helpful for this.
2. Identify variables. There are multiple kinds of variables. First, identify *dependent or response* and *independent or predictor* variables relevant to the study objective. For complex systems, cause–effect diagrams can be helpful. BE ALERT to falsely identifying intermediate variables as independent variables. We called these variables "lurking" variables in the discussion of correlation earlier in this chapter. So, "number of fouls" is an intermediate variable: it is correlated with "number of points" but cannot be set independently by the experimenter. Think of independent predictor variables as having values that can be set *independently*; there should be a virtual or real "knob" that can set the value. If the value of the variable you are considering will change if you change other independent variables, it is intermediate, NOT independent, and should not be in the study.
3. Based on prior data or educated guess, determine qualitatively the relationship between each independent variable and each dependent variable over the practical range. *A priori* plots can be helpful for this.
4. Determine levels to use for each variable. Independent variables expected to have a linear effect on the dependent variable only need to be run at high and low levels; independent variable with curved effect will need at least a quadratic term in the model and so should be run at a minimum of three different levels: low, mid, and high.
5. Given the practical range to be studied for each independent variable, scale the upper and lower limits for each variable to $+/-$ 1.
6. Determine the run conditions to be used in the experiment. Take all possible combinations of selected levels of all independent variables. This is called a *factorial design.* If this is too many run conditions, select a fraction of them. The fraction must be selected in an intelligent way: do a Web search for "fractional factorial designs" or refer to Barton (1999) for details. *Note*: If there is more than one dependent variable, but they are affected by the

same set of independent variables, then a single experiment design to fit multiple regression models is warranted. If the independent variables affecting each of the dependent variables are different, separate experiment designs should be constructed for each dependent variable.

7. Construct a table of independent variable settings for these runs. Add extra rows that are copies of the rows above if you want to conduct any *replications*. Have a key that identifies mapping of -1, 0, and $+1$ back to the original independent variable values.
8. Assign a random run order to the experimental conditions in the table.
9. Conduct the experiment, and for each run, record the independent variable (x) and response (y) values.

On completion of the designed experiment, one has a set of data for conducting a regression analysis. For this, follow the process described elsewhere in this chapter.

Now, we apply this process to the drilling study.

Determine objectives

The objective of this study is to understand how speed and pressure settings for the drill affect drill wear-out, as part of an initiative to maximize profit. It is good to place goals in perspective for management to gain support for the effort that will be required and to make sure that the short-term objectives are consistent with the overall goals of the organization.

Goal hierarchy plots provide a graphical means to do this and to simultaneously identify resources that will be needed to conduct the simulation study. These plots were developed as part of a special decision-making procedure called the "analytic hierarchy process" (Saaty, 1980). Figure 3.35 shows a simple goal hierarchy plot for the drilling study. The business objective appears at the top: it is to increase profit. Optimizing the pressure and speed settings will lead to increased profit, but these settings depend on knowledge about how pressure and speed affect wear-out and drilling time. Gaining this knowledge requires experiments with various pressure and speed

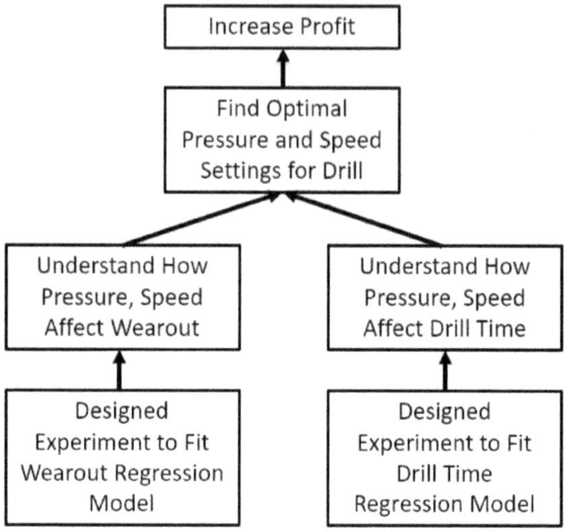

Figure 3.35. Goal hierarchy plot for the drilling study.

settings so that regression models can be fit that will describe how pressure and speed affect wear-out and drilling time.

Identify variables

In the brief discussion above, we identified the key independent variables as speed (RPM) and pressure (PSI). Note that on the machine, there are "knobs" to adjust these, so we are confident that they are truly independent variables. In fact, it is better to think of the independent variables as "pressure knob PSI setting" and "speed knob RPM setting" since the actual pressure and speed will not generally be known, but will be determined by the knob settings (so they are actually intermediate variables!). Although not needed here, a cause–effect diagram can be a useful tool for determining independent variables of interest. These diagrams place a dependent variable in a box on the right of the diagram, with a horizontal line extending to the left. Then, one identifies variables that affect the dependent variable, connecting them to the horizontal line with diagonal lines. If these variables are themselves affected by other variables, then additional lines are added to the diagram. There is one diagram for each dependent variable. Independent variables have no branches impinging on them. The others are intermediate variables and cannot be set independently.

Figure 3.36 shows a cause–effect diagram for wear-out time for the drilling study. Note two important features. First, the independent variables that will be varied in the study are highlighted: the pressure knob and the speed knob. Note that drill composition has an effect but is not included in the study. Yet, we know it has an effect, so it must be *held constant* over the duration of the experiment, and the particular alloy that was used must be *recorded.* In any experimental study, the values of ALL held-constant factors need to be recorded for the fitted regression model to have predictive power; it is only predictive under the specified settings of the held-constant variables.

Note also that the shop conditions of temperature and humidity are *nuisance variables*; they can be measured but not controlled exactly. They often vary randomly about some average that may or may not be controllable. These and other random nuisance variables are why it is important to randomize the order of running the experiment conditions. Otherwise, a trending change in a nuisance variable could be falsely identified as an independent variable effect.

Determine qualitative relationships

We determine the relationship between the independent predictor variables and wear-out time qualitatively by making rough plots of

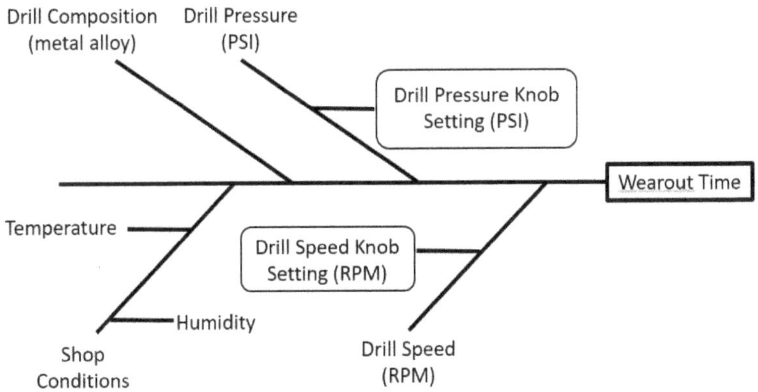

Figure 3.36. Cause–effect diagram for wear-out time for the drilling study.

the relationships that we expect to find. These are just qualitative guesses at the effects.

Recall the earlier description:

> "When the drilling force is increased, drill time is shorter: the hole is completed more quickly, but the added heat means the drill bit wear-out rate will be greater. When the drilling speed (in revolutions per minute, or RPM) is increased, one expects that drilling time will be shorter, under a fixed force. For a particular force, suppose that past experience says that the drill bit wear rate decreases as RPM speed increases from a very low value to a certain mid-level RPM, but then beyond that RPM, excess heat again causes higher wear rate and shorter time until wear-out."

This suggests the plots shown in Figure 3.37. Here, we have assumed that the practical range for pressure is 5–50 psi, and the practical range for speed is 200–1000 RPM. Note that the plots have no y-axis marks. If we knew the effects well enough to plot with axis values, we wouldn't need to design an experiment to fit a predictive model!

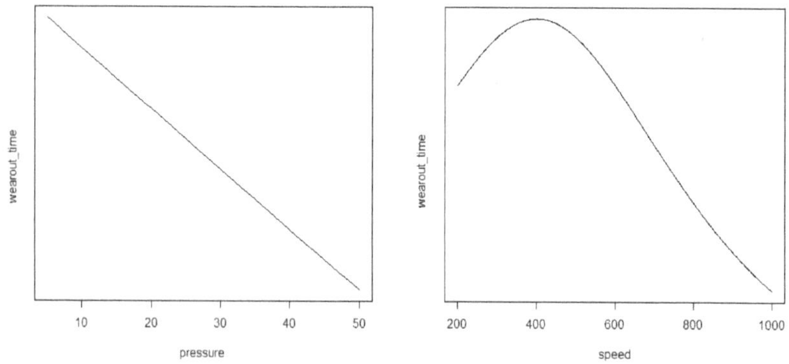

Figure 3.37. *A priori* effect plots for the independent variables pressure and speed.

Determine number of levels for each independent variable

Since the speed effect is nonlinear, we need to conduct experiments at three different values. Three different values will allow us to fit an x^2 term. If the nonlinear relationship is more complicated, we might want to use four or five levels for speed. For pressure, given that we expect roughly linear behavior, only two levels are required.

Scale-independent variables to $+/-$ 1

This step requires little further explanation. We set sPressure $= -1$ when Pressure $= 5$, and sPressure $= +1$ when Pressure $= 50$. Similarly, set sSpeed to -1 when Speed $= 200$, sSpeed $= 0$ when Speed $= 600$, and sSpeed $= +1$ when Speed $= 1000$.

Determine run conditions for the experiment

If we run all possible combinations of sPressure and sSpeed levels, there are $2 \times 3 = 6$ run conditions. This is called a *full factorial* design. This does not require many runs and is therefore our design choice.

Construct table of settings for runs

These are shown in Table 3.2. The table shows that we plan to make two replications of each run condition. Further, the random run order has been established. It is shown in the first column.

Conduct experiment; record y values

If we were able to conduct this experiment, we would have a resulting data frame with columns sPressure, sSpeed, and WearoutTime. It would have twelve rows, one for each run. We could then proceed to build a regression model and follow the usual process for determining predictive ability, validity, and confidence and prediction intervals to characterize prediction uncertainty. While we do not have actual data, we examine an artificial data set below, in particular to show the advantage of factorial designed experiments on VIF.

Table 3.2. A factorial design for two predictor variables at two and three levels.

Order	x_1 (sPressure)	x_2 (sSpeed)
4	−1	−1
10	+1	−1
11	−1	0
7	+1	0
2	−1	+1
12	+1	+1
6	−1	−1
3	+1	−1
8	−1	0
1	+1	0
5	−1	+1
9	+1	+1

Analyzing data from a factorial experiment

The data in the table below are artificial, but their analysis will let us show how designed experiments provide ideal settings for regression modeling. The following code shows the creation of the design and result, with the design including simulated WearoutTime measurements, the regression model, and the resulting output. Most figures have been omitted; all pass the required validity tests. One additional diagnostic plot is included and shown in Figure 3.38. It is important to be sure that no trend in nuisance variables is present in the data. Such a trend would appear in the Residuals vs. Order plot. There is no apparent trend, and so all validity tests are passed. Two aspects of this output should be highlighted:

- The *VIF* for all factors is 1. This is a characteristic of factorial designed experiments and a key advantage.
- For a perfectly balanced experimental design (such as a factorial design or balanced fractional–factorial design), there will be NO OUTLIERS. The grid layout leads to the leverage for each extreme point of d/n, for d model terms and n runs. For our experiment, that is $4/12 = 0.3333$, and Cook's distance plot is not useful. The error "`hat values (leverages) are all = 0.3333333 and there are no factor predictors; no plot no. 5`" appears in the

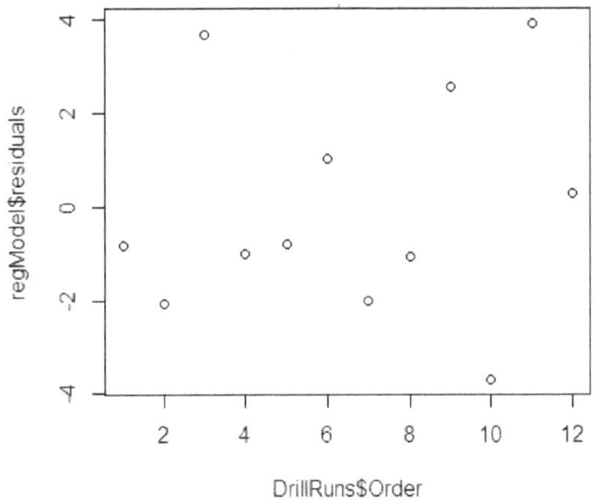

Figure 3.38. Residuals vs. run order diagnostic plot for drilling study.

following output. It can be ignored: we do not need Cook's distance plot for regression with a factorial designed experiment.

```
> # set data frame for DOE
> # create grid
> set.seed(54321)
> DrillRuns = expand.grid(sPressure = c(-1,1),sSpeed = c(-1,0,1))
> # add replicate runs
> DrillRuns = rbind(DrillRuns,DrillRuns)
> # add column of random run order
> RandOrder = sample(x = 1:length(DrillRuns[,1]),replace=FALSE)
> DrillRuns = cbind(RandOrder,DrillRuns)
> # add column names Order Pressure Speed
> colnames(DrillRuns) = c("Order","sPressure","sSpeed")
>
> DrillRuns
   Order sPressure sSpeed
1      4        -1     -1
2     10         1     -1
3     11        -1      0
4      7         1      0
5      2        -1      1
6     12         1      1
7      6        -1     -1
8      3         1     -1
9      8        -1      0
10     1         1      0
11     5        -1      1
12     9         1      1
>
```

```
> DrillRuns  # updated to include WearoutTime
   Order sPressure sSpeed WearoutTime
1      4        -1     -1   16.394409
2     10         1     -1    8.172896
3     11        -1      0   14.066942
4      7         1      0    2.594537
5      2        -1      1   22.145003
6     12         1      1   18.960414
7      6        -1     -1   18.432151
8      3         1     -1   15.566358
9      8        -1      0    9.054725
10     1         1      0    3.769924
11     5        -1      1   23.408463
12     9         1      1   21.243634
>
> regModel = lm(WearoutTime ~ sPressure+sSpeed+I(sSpeed^2),
              data=DrillRuns)
>
> summary(regModel)$coefficients[,1]
(Intercept)  sPressure    sSpeed  I(sSpeed^2)
7.371532    -2.766161    3.398963   10.668884
> summary(regModel)$r.squared
[1] 0.8866917
>
> anova(regModel)
Analysis of Variance Table

Response: WearoutTime
            Df  Sum Sq Mean Sq F value   Pr(>F)
sPressure    1  91.820  91.820  11.785 0.008917 **
sSpeed       1  92.424  92.424  11.862 0.008770 **
I(sSpeed^2)  1 303.534 303.534  38.957 0.000248 ***
Residuals    8  62.332   7.791
---

> library(rms)
> vif(regModel)
sPressure    sSpeed   I(sSpeed^2)
   1           1           1
> # do plots to check model validity
> acf(regModel$residuals)
> plot(regModel, ask=F, add.smooth=F)
   hat values (leverages) are all = 0.3333333
   and there are no factor predictors; no plot no. 5
> plot(DrillRuns$sPressure,regModel$residuals)
> plot(DrillRuns$sSpeed,regModel$residuals)
> plot(DrillRuns$Order,regModel$residuals)
```

```
> # model valid, hypothesis test p-values and confidence
  intervals
> summary(regModel)

Call:
lm(formula = WearoutTime ~ sPressure + sSpeed + I(sSpeed^2),
data = DrillRuns)

Residuals:
Min       1Q  Median      3Q     Max
-3.7024 -1.3149 -0.8163  1.4110  3.9292

Coefficients:
            Estimate Std. Error t value Pr(>|t|)
(Intercept)   7.3715     1.3957   5.282 0.000745 ***
sPressure    -2.7662     0.8058  -3.433 0.008917 **
sSpeed        3.3990     0.9869   3.444 0.008770 **
I(sSpeed^2)  10.6689     1.7093   6.242 0.000248 ***

Residual standard error: 2.791 on 8 degrees of freedom
Multiple R-squared:  0.8867,    Adjusted R-squared:  0.8442
F-statistic: 20.87 on 3 and 8 DF,  p-value: 0.0003868

> confint(regModel)
                2.5 %     97.5 %
(Intercept)  4.153131 10.5899333
sPressure   -4.624306 -0.9080162
sSpeed       1.123209  5.6747160
I(sSpeed^2)  6.727164 14.6106042
>
```

The analysis of this artificial data allows us to see the three key advantages of a designed experiment:

1. The *traditional research* paradigm is strongly supported: predictor variables and their effects on the response are explicitly hypothesized, and experiments are run to test those hypotheses. There is no "data snooping."
2. Factorial and fractional–factorial designs provide independence of the predictor variables. *VIF* values are 1, and the *p*-values and coefficient estimates do not change based on their order in the model.
3. There will be no outliers with a factorial or fractional–factorial design. We do not need Cook's distance plot.

3.4 The Overall Process for Linear Regression in the *Traditional Research* Paradigm

In the previous sections, we followed a formal procedure for constructing and interpreting linear regression models in the *traditional research* paradigm. It is worth summarizing the steps, integrating what we have covered in different sections:

1. Determine the objectives of the predictive model based on managerial needs.
2. Summarize the data with a descriptive summary, scatter plots (matrix plot), (perhaps boxplots with qualitative predictors), and discussion.
3. Based on plots and expectations, propose a regression model form. Justify any transformations and/or nonlinear terms (including interactions) that you propose. Identify indicator variables if you are including qualitative variables as predictors. Include a mathematical presentation with βs, ε, and the i.i.d. statement.
4. Show and interpret for management the fitted regression model.
5. Assess the practical predictive ability with a fitted line plot and discussion of R^2.
6. If the fitted model has practical predictive power, perform model validity checks; plots with comments. Also, check *VIF*: a value greater than 10 suggests removal of the predictor variable with the highest *VIF*.
7. If the validity checks are passed, then uncertainty characterization using the i.i.d. normal error assumption will be valid. If the validity checks are not passed, return to step 3 and revise the model to include additional transformations, interaction, and/or nonlinear terms. If this fails, seek additional predictor variables or move to a data-centric regression analysis (Chapter 4).
8. If the validity checks are passed, then continue. Show appropriate tables and discuss the sigma estimate and p-values for coefficients and the overall model.
9. Show and discuss confidence intervals for coefficients in managerial terms.
10. Show and discuss forecast confidence and prediction intervals for desired configurations. Do this in managerial terms.

11. Give useful overall managerial summary and recommendation on use of the fitted regression model.

3.5 The General Linear Model and the Generalized Linear Model

Sometimes, variance stabilizing transformations make the response more complex rather than less complex. Or, in some common situations, there is no variance stabilizing transformation that will make the randomness in the transformed Y follow a normal distribution with equal variance at all predicted values. The *generalized linear model* provides a more flexible regression model form that allows different probability distributions for ε and more complex response functions. Before introducing the generalized linear model, we frame the regression models above as *general linear models.* As we will see, there is an important distinction between general linear models (GLMs) and generalized linear models (GLIMs).

3.5.1 The general linear model

Simple and multiple linear regression, ANOVA, and ANOCOVA models are all special cases of the GLM. The GLM is usually written in matrix form, as shown in the following.

Consider the multiple regression case. To represent that equation in matrix form, construct a matrix containing a row for each observation in the data set, where all values in the first column are 1 (for the intercept). call that column "column 0." Then, add columns to the matrix corresponding to all terms in the model: that is, let "column j" contain the values of $g_j(x)$. The ith row uses the value of the predictor variables (x) from the ith observation in the data set. This matrix is typically called X.

When only linear terms are included in the model, then X will have $d+1$ columns: the ith row of the matrix begins with a 1 and is followed by the values of the d predictor variables for the ith observation in the data set. Columns might be added to X for interaction, quadratic, and/or transformed variables (which sometimes replace one or more original predictor variables x_j).

To use the matrix form, construct a response vector $\vec{y}$. The ith entry in the vector $\vec{y}$ contains the response for the ith observation in the data set. When constructing the probability model, the (random) observation vector is written as $\vec{Y}$ rather than $\vec{y}$. The lowercase $\vec{y}$ denotes observed values in the data set, which are known sample values from the random variable vector $\vec{Y}$.

The random ε component is written as a random vector $\vec{\varepsilon}$, where each ε_i is normally distributed and has the same unknown variance σ^2. A random vector having a normal distribution is characterized by a mean vector and a variance/covariance matrix. For multiple regression, the mean is zero for each entry and the variance (diagonal entries of the variance-covariance matrix) are all equal to σ^2 for each element of the random observation vector. Because we assume that the ε values are independent, all covariances between them are zero. The resulting variance-covariance matrix has σ^2 values on the diagonal and zero on all off-diagonal elements. In the matrix form of (3.7), this is usually written as the unknown scalar σ^2 times the identity matrix, denoted I.

The matrix form of Equation (3.7) typically omits the vector symbols over Y and ε, but they remain vectors. Similarly, we did not use the vector symbol for x in Equation (3.7). The matrix form is

$$Y = X\beta + \varepsilon \; \varepsilon \sim N(0, \sigma^2 I). \tag{3.11}$$

The form can be used for multiple linear regression, ANOVA, and ANOCOVA models, although for the latter two structures, additional constraints and structure apply. Equation (3.11) presents the (matrix) form of the GLM. It will be important to recognize the difference between GLMs and GLIMs in terms of how $\mathrm{E}(Y)$ is represented. Since the mean value of ε in Equation (3.11) is zero, we have

$$\mu_Y = \mathrm{E}(Y|X) = X\beta, \tag{3.12}$$

where μ is the vector of mean values for Y. Each element of $\mathrm{E}(Y)$ is computed from the ith row of X as $X_i\beta$. X_i is more than just the (row) vector of predictor variables for the ith observation, say x_i, because the vector includes an initial 1 and possibly added $g_j(x_i)$ terms.

The least-squares estimates s for σ and $\vec{b}$ for $\vec{\beta}$ can be computed in matrix form. For $\vec{\beta}$, the least-squares estimate vector is computed as

$$b = (X'X)^{-1}X'y, \tag{3.13}$$

where X' is the transpose (of rows with columns) of X. The estimate for σ is $SSE/(n-(d+1))$. After simplifying the matrix form of SSE, it is

$$s = \frac{y'y - b'X'y}{n-d-1}. \tag{3.14}$$

3.5.2 The generalized linear model

As mentioned at the end of Section 3.3.1, transforming y values does not always produce simple regression models with residuals that appear normally distributed. In some cases, a variance stabilizing transformation changes a simple linear response to a highly nonlinear response, requiring quadratic or other complex g functions to be added to the regression model. In other cases, the assumption of randomness that follows a normal distribution cannot be accomplished by a transformation. For many commonly occurring cases, a GLIM is the correct model choice.

The GLIM extends the structure in Equation (3.11) in two ways. First, the expected value of Y can be a more complex function of $X'\beta$ than is shown in Equation (3.12). The GLIM allows

$$\mathscr{g}(\mu_Y) = \mathscr{g}(\mathrm{E}(Y|X)) = X\beta. \tag{3.15}$$

The function $\mathscr{g}$ is called the *link function.* It applies element by element each element of the μ_Y vector. It allows the linear form $X\beta$ to predict some nonlinear function of the mean of Y. It is different conceptually from the g functions applied to the predictor variables. The link function is also different from the same transform function applied to Y values directly since a nonlinear transform on individual Y values does not transform the mean of Y in the same way.

Second, for a GLIM, the requirement that the random variation have a normal distribution is relaxed, allowing for alternatives from a special family of distributions: the *regular exponential family.* The regular exponential family is different from the exponential distribution family, although it includes these and many others with which we are familiar: normal, gamma, and binomial families to name a few. Unfortunately, the name regular exponential family is often shortened to just exponential family, leading to confusion.

Table 3.3. Distribution families and link functions for GLIMs.

Distribution for Y	**Link Function Name**	**Link Function g**
Normal (Gaussian)	Identity	$g(\mu) = \mu$
Binomial (Percent)	Logit	$g(\mu) = \ln\left(\frac{\mu}{1-\mu}\right)$
Poisson (Count)	Log	$g(\mu) = \ln(\mu)$
Exponential, Gamma	Negative Inverse	$g(\mu) = -1/\mu$

Choice of a particular distribution family in the regular exponential family identifies a particular link function g for the corresponding GLIM. The relationship between the probability distribution family for the random behavior in the response and the appropriate link function is shown in Table 3.3. Once one identifies the likely probability distribution for the random Y values, the appropriate link function is known.

Note that GLMs are a special case of GLIMs; see row 1 of Table 3.3. But also, note the following:

A Caution: Often GLIMs are referred to as GLMs; this is bad form but common and leads to confusion. In fact, the R function that implements GLIM is called `glm`.

3.5.3 Fitting and prediction for GLIMs in R: Time-in-system example

Fitting a GLIM in R is very similar to fitting an ordinary regression model (GLM) using `lm`. The only difference is that the fitting function is called `glm` and the distribution family (first column in Table 3.3) must be specified using the `family =` option.

We fit a GLIM for the exponential time-in-system data discussed in Section 3.3.1. The data are shown in Figure 3.18. We compare the results for ordinary linear regression using `lm`, linear regression against the log transform of Y discussed in Section 3.3.1, and the GLIM using `glm` with the exponential, gamma family option (fourth row of Table 3.3). Note that gamma must be specified in the call to `glm()`: `glm` does not allow the `family = Exponential` option; it is equivalent to the `family = Gamma` option and so it is considered redundant. Strangely, the `family = Gamma` option is the only one capitalized. Other choices for family are **gaussian**, **binomial**, and **poisson**.

For comparison, the R code for fitting and summarizing the three regression models is discussed next. The full R code for this example may be found at the end of this chapter. First, the simple linear regression model using `lm` produces the following:

```
> # do GLM regression using lm
> regModel = lm(TimeInSystem ~ MeanServRate,
  data = xy_data)
> summary(regModel)

Call:
lm(formula = TimeInSystem ~ MeanServRate, data = xy_data)

Residuals:
Min       1Q   Median      3Q      Max
-0.6970 -0.3876 -0.1329  0.1155  2.5796

Coefficients:
Estimate Std. Error t value Pr(>|t|)
(Intercept)   0.86760    0.09967   8.705 2.26e-14 ***
MeanServRate -0.08082    0.01784  -4.531 1.42e-05 ***
---

Residual standard error: 0.6126 on 118 degrees of freedom
Multiple R-squared:  0.1482,  Adjusted R-squared:  0.141
F-statistic: 20.53 on 1 and 118 DF,  p-value: 1.416e-05
>
```

The summary shows that the p-value for the predictor variable `MeanServRate` is about 1.4×10^{-5}. Since there is only one predictor variable, the p-value for a null model is the same. While this is good, the predictive ability is not strong, as indicated by the low R^2 of about 0.14.

Next is the regression using the log transform for Y:

```
> # do GLM regression using lm and ln Y
> regModel = lm(log(TimeInSystem) ~ MeanServRate,
  data = xy_data)
> summary(regModel)

Call:
lm(formula = log(TimeInSystem) ~ MeanServRate,
 data = xy_data)
```

```
Residuals:
Min       1Q   Median      3Q      Max
-7.4352  -0.7757  0.2063  0.9955  2.2476

Coefficients:
Estimate Std. Error t value Pr(>|t|)
(Intercept)   -0.42539    0.23932  -1.777   0.0781 .
MeanServRate  -0.26391    0.04283  -6.161 1.03e-08 ***
---

Residual standard error: 1.471 on 118 degrees of freedom
Multiple R-squared:  0.2434,   Adjusted R-squared:  0.237
F-statistic: 37.96 on 1 and 118 DF,  p-value: 1.033e-08
>
```

Both p-value (1.0×10^{-8}) and R^2 (0.24) show superior predictive ability, as expected.

Unfortunately, GLIM summaries from `glm` do not have the same form as GLM summaries from `lm`. The following is the code for fitting the GLIM and the resulting summary:

```
> # do GLIM regression using glm
> glimModel = glm(TimeInSystem ~ MeanServRate,
+                 family = Gamma(), data = xy_data)
> summary(glimModel)

Call:
glm(formula = TimeInSystem ~
MeanServRate, family = Gamma(),
data = xy_data)

Coefficients:
Estimate Std. Error t value Pr(>|t|)
(Intercept)    -0.9433     0.4609  -2.047   0.0429 *
MeanServRate    0.9841     0.1765   5.574  1.6e-07 ***
---

(Dispersion parameter for Gamma family taken to be
 1.077892)

Null deviance: 225.68  on 119  degrees of freedom
Residual deviance: 164.18  on 118  degrees of freedom
AIC: 15.249

Number of Fisher Scoring iterations: 6
>
```

First, note that the fitting command matches that for the `lm()` function, but with the added option `family = Gamma()`. The output of the `summary()` function is somewhat different. One can see that the *p*-value for the model is small (1.6×10^{-7}), better than for the ordinary regression but not as small as for regression using $\log(Y)$ as the dependent variable. But the value R^2 does not appear, and an additional characteristic, AIC, appears. AIC, the Akaike information criterion, is useful for comparing different models with different numbers of predictor variable terms, a bit like adjusted R^2. However, unlike adjusted R^2, the AIC value does not link directory to quality of fit; it should only be used to compare alternative models. The lowest AIC value would indicate the best model.

An analogous quantity for R^2 is the *fraction of deviance explained*, called R^2_D. It is 1 − (residual deviance/null deviance). For more information, see Martin & Hall (2016). The computation is implemented in R in `r2d()` (Shumake, 2023). This produces the usual R^2 for ordinary regression (that is, when `family = gaussian()` is specified in `glm()`). The R^2_D value is easily computed as $1 - (164.18/225.68) \approx .27$, higher than for the ordinary and log transform regression models.

Last, the summary shows `Number of Fisher Scoring iterations: 6`. For GLMs and GLIMs, the β coefficient estimates are chosen to maximize the *likelihood* function. For GLMs, this is equivalent to least squares. For GLIMs, maximum likelihood is not generally the same as least squares and cannot be solved by linear algebra. An iterative optimization procedure based on Newton's method is employed to search for the optimal β estimates. Finding satisfactory values required six iterations, a relatively small number, so the fit can be trusted.

The difference in quality of fit between the GLMs and the GLIM can be seen in the plot of predicted mean time in system vs. service rate. Recall from Section 3.3.1 the relationship is *mean time in system* $= 1/(\mu - \lambda)$, where μ is the mean service rate and λ is the mean arrival rate. For the data shown in Figure 3.18, $\lambda = 1$ and μ takes on values 2, 2.25, 3, 3.5, 6, and 11. Figure 3.39 shows the plot of the true mean time in system values along with predictions from the three models fitted to the sample data. Only the GLIM provides

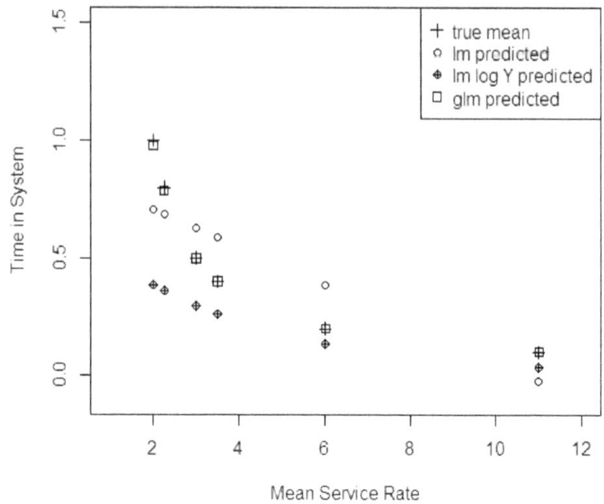

Figure 3.39. GLM predictions for mean time in system are inferior to the GLIM predictions.

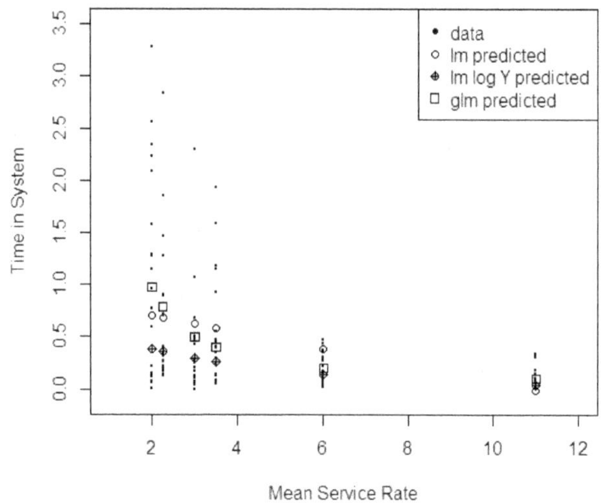

Figure 3.40. GLM vs. GLIM predictive ability is difficult to judge against data.

a good prediction. This would not be obvious if we did not know the formula for the true value. When plotted against the original data as in Figure 3.40, both the regression using $\log(Y)$ and the GLIM seem to provide reasonable fits.

3.6 The Overall Process for Generalized Linear Models in the *Traditional Research* Paradigm

In Section 3.4, we gave a formal procedure for constructing and interpreting linear regression models under the *traditional research* paradigm. The process for GLIMs generally depends on the specific link function. The overall process here is necessarily abbreviated because of this:

1. Determine the objectives of the predictive model based on managerial needs.
2. Summarize the data with a descriptive summary, scatter plots (matrix plot), (perhaps boxplots with qualitative predictors), and discussion.
3. Based on plots and expectations, identify the probability distribution family associated with the randomness in the response. Include a mathematical presentation with βs, link function, and probability distribution family.
4. Show and interpret for management the fitted GLIM. Assess the practical predictive ability with a predicted means vs. actual data plot and discussion of R_D^2.
5. Validity checks are difficult for GLIMs. If fit is good, discuss the p-values for the model coefficients.
6. Confidence and prediction intervals for desired configurations are not directly available for GLIMs fitted using `glm`. Approximations based on standard deviation or use of `ciTools` is beyond the scope of this text.
7. Give useful overall managerial summary and recommendation based on predictions from the fitted GLIM.

3.7 Cases Supporting Chapter 3

The HousePriceRegression is an introductory case relying on material in Sections 3.1 and 3.2. The case description slides and data can be found online in the HousePriceSimple folder of Barton (2023).

The RanchAndGarden case explores transformations and nonlinear terms, discussed in Section 3.3. The case description slides and data can be found online in the RanchAndGardenTransformations folder of Barton (2023).

The DodgersRegressionQualitativeVariables case examines coding qualitative predictor variables as 0–1 dummy variables and the interpretation issues associated with such regressions. It also supports material covered in Section 3.3. The DodgersRegressionQualitativeVariables folder of Barton (2023) contains case description slides and data.

The GasMileageDOE case does not involve data analysis; it asks students to construct an experiment design based on their own understanding of factors affecting automobile fuel efficiency (MPG). Design of experiments topics are covered in Section 3.3.7. The case description slides and data can be found online in the GasMileageDOE folder of Barton (2023).

The BostonHousingRegressionPart1 case explores the problems of predictive analytics in the *traditional research* paradigm when the data are observational, not from a designed experiment. This is a transition case as the text moves from the *traditional research* paradigm for regression in Chapter 3 to regression under the *data-adaptive research* paradigm covered in Chapters 4 and 5. Key topics are covered in Section 3.3.6. The case description slides and data can be found online in the BostonHousingRegressionTraditional folder of Barton (2023).

3.8 R Code Used in Chapter 3

```
# Code for House Price Case Simple Linear Regression

library(readxl) # needed to read in the Excel data file
# read the Excel file
HousePriceSimple <- read_excel("HousePriceSimple.xlsx")
# summarize the data
summary(HousePriceSimple)
# scatter plot of data
plot(HousePriceSimple$Size ,HousePriceSimple$Price)

# fit the regression model
regModel = lm(Price ~ Size, data = HousePriceSimple)
 # just used for showing fitted model
 summary(regModel)$coefficients[,1]

 # do plots to check model validity
 acf(regModel$residuals)
plot(regModel, ask=F, add.smooth=F)
plot(HousePriceSimple$Size ,regModel$residuals)
```

```
# show ANOVA table for regression model
anova(regModel)
# pull out the R-squared value from the summary
summary(regModel)$r.squared
# used to show standard deviation estimates and p-values
summary(regModel)
# compute confidence intervals for model coefficients
confint(regModel)

# predict selling price for a 2500 sq ft home

# put desired forecast in a data frame
new.dat <- data.frame(Size = 2500)
# give forecast CI
predict(regModel, newdata = new.dat,
        interval = 'confidence')
# give forecast PI
predict(regModel, newdata = new.dat,
        interval = 'prediction')


# Code for House Price Case Multiple Linear Regression

library(readxl) # needed to read in the Excel data file
# read the Excel file
HousePriceSimple <- read_excel("HousePriceSimple.xlsx")
summary(HousePriceSimple) # summarize the data
# do a matrix plot to check for obvious correlations
pairs(HousePriceSimple)

# regression model fitting command is below
regModel = lm(Price ~ Size + Bedrooms + Baths,
              data = HousePriceSimple)
# just used for showing fitted model
summary(regModel)$coefficients[,1]

# assess regression model performance
# first plot actual vs predicted
plot(predict(regModel, newdata = HousePriceSimple),
     HousePriceSimple$Price)
# points should fall near diagonal if predicted ~ actual
abline(0,1)
# pull out the R-squared value from the summary
summary(regModel)$r.squared

# assess regression model validity
# do diagnostic plots for model validity
acf(regModel$residuals)
plot(regModel, ask=F, add.smooth=F)
plot(HousePriceSimple$Size,regModel$residuals)
```

```
plot(HousePriceSimple$Bedrooms, regModel$residuals)
plot(HousePriceSimple$Baths ,regModel$residuals)

# print ANOVA table for regression model
anova(regModel)
# show standard deviation estimates and p-values
summary(regModel)
# compute confidence intervals for model coefficients
confint(regModel)

# model forecasts with confidence and prediction intervals
# put desired forecast in data frame
new.dat = data.frame(Size = 2500, Bedrooms = 4, Baths = 3)
new.dat = rbind(new.dat, c(2800,3,3))
 # give forecast CI
 predict(regModel, newdata = new.dat,
         interval = 'confidence')
# give forecast PI
predict(regModel, newdata = new.dat,
        interval = 'prediction')

# R code for nonlinear transformations of y=============
# approximately fix normality
y = rexp(1000, rate = 1)
log_y = log(y)
hist(y)
hist(log_y)
qqnorm(y)
qqnorm(log_y)

# approximately fix heteroskedasticity
y1 = rexp(20, rate = 1)
y1.25 = rexp(20, rate = 1.25)
y2 = rexp(20, rate = 2)
y2.5 = rexp(20, rate = 2.5)
y5 = rexp(20, rate = 5)
y10 =rexp(20, rate = 10)

xy1 = cbind(rep(1,20),y1)
xy1.25 = cbind(rep(1.25,20),y1.25)
xy2 = cbind(rep(2,20),y2)
xy2.5 = cbind(rep(2.5,20),y2.5)
xy5 = cbind(rep(5,20),y5)
xy10 = cbind(rep(10,20),y10)

xy_data = rbind(xy1,xy1.25,xy2,xy2.5,xy5,xy10)
xy_data[,1] = 1/xy_data[,1]
xy_data = as.data.frame(xy_data)
colnames(xy_data) = c("x","y")
```

```
# read same data every time - pull from stored version
#xy_data = read.csv("xy_data.csv")
plot(xy_data)

# optional - save xy_data
write.csv("xy_data")

# do regression using x, y
regModel = lm(y ~ x, data = xy_data)
plot(regModel, add.smooth=F, ask = F)

# do regression using x, log(y)
regModel = lm(log(y) ~ x, data = xy_data)
plot(regModel, add.smooth=F, ask = F)

# do regression using mu, y
# compute mu = rate + lambda, assume lambda = 1
xy_data$mu = 1+ (1/xy_data$x)

# do regression using mu, y
plot(xy_data$mu,xy_data$y, xlab = "x", ylab = "y")
regModel = lm(y ~ mu, data = xy_data)
plot(regModel, add.smooth=F, ask = F)

# do regression using mu, log(y)
plot(xy_data$mu,log(xy_data$y), xlab = "x", ylab = "log(y)")
regModel = lm(log(y) ~ mu, data = xy_data)
plot(regModel, add.smooth=F, ask = F)

# find Box Cox Transform
library(MASS) # the boxcox function in the MASS library
regModel = lm(y ~ mu, data = xy_data)
bcFit = boxcox(y ~ mu, data = xy_data)
bc_lambda = bcFit$x[which.max(bcFit$y)]

# Do regression with bc transformed y
bc_lambda
plot(xy_data$mu,((xy_data$y^bc_lambda-1)/bc_lambda),
     xlab = "x", ylab = "BoxCox Xform y")
BCRegModel = lm(((y^bc_lambda-1)/bc_lambda) ~ x,
                data = xy_data)
plot(BCRegModel, add.smooth=F, ask = F)


# R code for x variable transformations and rescaling=====
set.seed = 1234566
x=seq(from = 10, to = 200,by=10)
ylogx = log(x) + .1*rnorm(20)
plot(x,ylogx)
ysqx = -5*x + .04*x^2 + 100*rnorm(20)
```

```
plot(x,ysqx)
ysqx2 = 8*x - .04*x^2 + 100*rnorm(20)
plot(x,ysqx2)
y1x = 1/x + .003*rnorm(20)
plot(x,y1x)

# do analysis using x where y related to 1/x
# fit the regression model
regModel = lm(y1x ~ x)
# just used for showing fitted model
summary(regModel)$coefficients[,1]

# do plots to check model validity
acf(regModel$residuals)
plot(regModel, ask=F, add.smooth=F)
plot(x,regModel$residuals)

# show ANOVA table for regression model
anova(regModel)
# pull out the R-squared value from the summary
summary(regModel)$r.squared



# do analysis using 1/x
# fit the regression model
xinv = 1/x
plot(xinv, y1x)
regModel = lm(y1x ~ xinv)
# just used for showing fitted model
summary(regModel)$coefficients[,1]

# do plots to check model validity
acf(regModel$residuals)
plot(regModel, ask=F, add.smooth=F)
plot(xinv,regModel$residuals)

# show ANOVA table for regression model
anova(regModel)
# pull out the R-squared value from the summary
summary(regModel)$r.squared
# used to show standard deviation estimates and p-values
summary(regModel)
# compute confidence intervals for model coefficients
confint(regModel)



# use ysqx2 in quadratic model with unscaled x
plot(x, x^2)
```

```
regModel = lm(ysqx2 ~ x + I(x^2))
# just used for showing fitted model
summary(regModel)$coefficients[,1]
# show ANOVA table for regression model
anova(regModel)
# pull out the R-squared value from the summary
summary(regModel)$r.squared
# need package "rms" to compute VIF
library(rms)
vif(regModel)
# do plots to check model validity
acf(regModel$residuals)
plot(regModel, ask=F, add.smooth=F)
plot(x,regModel$residuals)
confint(regModel)


# use ysqx2 in quadratic model with scaled x
scalpm1 = function(x){(x-(min(x)+max(x))/2)/
                       (.5*(max(x)-min(x)))}
sx=scalpm1(x)
plot(sx, sx^2)
regModel = lm(ysqx2 ~ sx + I(sx^2))
# just used for showing fitted model
summary(regModel)$coefficients[,1]
# show ANOVA table for regression model
anova(regModel)
# pull out the R-squared value from the summary
summary(regModel)$r.squared
# need package "rms" to compute VIF
library(rms)
vif(regModel)
# do plots to check model validity
acf(regModel$residuals)
plot(regModel, ask=F, add.smooth=F)
plot(sx,regModel$residuals)
confint(regModel)

# Orth Poly regression at end of section 3.3.4==========
regModel = lm(ysqx2 ~ poly(sx, degree = 2))
# just used for showing fitted model
summary(regModel)$coefficients[,1]
# show ANOVA table for regression model
anova(regModel)
# pull out the R-squared value from the summary
summary(regModel)$r.squared
# need package "rms" to compute VIF
library(rms)
vif(regModel)
# do plots to check model validity
```

```
acf(regModel$residuals)
plot(regModel, ask=F, add.smooth=F)
plot(ox,regModel$residuals)
confint(regModel)

# R code for orthogonal polynomials section 3.3.4=========
# create x values between -1 and +1 spaced by .1
xVals = seq(from = -1, to = 1, by = .1)
# create the intercept (constant) function
intercept = rep(1,length(xVals))
x = xVals      # linear g function
x2 = xVals^2   # quadratic g function
x3 = xVals^3   # cubic g function
plot(xVals, intercept, ylim = c(-1.3,1.3))
plot(xVals, x, ylim = c(-1.3,1.3))
plot(xVals, x2, ylab = "x^2",ylim = c(-1.3,1.3))
plot(xVals, x3, ylab = "x^3", ylim = c(-1.3,1.3))
OrthPoly = poly(xVals, degree = 3)
plot(xVals, intercept, ylim = c(-1.3,1.3))
plot(xVals, OrthPoly[,1], ylim = c(-1.3,1.3))
plot(xVals, OrthPoly[,2], ylab = "Orth Poly (x^2)",
ylim = c(-1.3,1.3))
plot(xVals, OrthPoly[,3], ylab = "Orth Poly (x^3)",
ylim = c(-1.3,1.3))

# R code for LifeCycleSavings regression section 3.3.6 ======

library(datasets)
pairs(LifeCycleSavings)
# the attach() command eliminates need for data =
  LifeCycleSavings
attach(LifeCycleSavings)
regModel = lm(sr ~ dpi + ddpi + pop15 + pop75)
summary(regModel)$coefficients
summary(regModel)$r.squared
library(rms)
vif(regModel)

# two VIF values > 5, delete largest (pop75)
regModel2 = lm(sr ~ dpi + ddpi + pop15)
summary(regModel2)$coefficients
summary(regModel2)$r.squared
library(rms)
vif(regModel2)

# model VIF OK, check validity plots
acf(regModel2$residuals)
plot(regModel2, ask = F, add.smooth = F)
plot(dpi,regModel2$residuals)
```

```
plot(ddpi,regModel2$residuals)
plot(pop15,regModel2$residuals)

# diagnostic plots OK, get model summary
summary(regModel2)

# drop term with highest p-value (dpi at .328)
regModel3 = lm(sr ~ ddpi + pop15)
summary(regModel3)$coefficients
summary(regModel3)$r.squared
library(rms)
vif(regModel3)

# model VIF OK, check validity plots
acf(regModel3$residuals)
plot(regModel3, ask = F, add.smooth = F)
plot(ddpi,regModel3$residuals)
plot(pop15,regModel3$residuals)

# diagnostic plots OK, get model summary
summary(regModel3)
summary(regModel3)$coefficients[,2]
summary(regModel3)$r.squared

# give confidence intervals for regression coefficients
confint(regModel3)

# predict savings rate for 3% population over 75,
#   35% population under 15, 2000 disposable personal
#   income and 10% rate of change of income
# NOTE: since pop75 and dpi removed from the model, leave
#       them out of prediction dataframe
new.dat = data.frame(ddpi = 10, pop15 = 35)
predict(regModel3, new.dat, interval = "confidence")
predict(regModel3, new.dat, interval = "prediction")

# R code for DOE section 3.3.7 in book ====================
# first, generate artificial data for a priori plots
# for pressure, decreasing linear wearout time,
# for speed, increasing then decreasing
pressure = 5:50
speed = 200:1000
scalpm1 = function(x){(x-(min(x)+max(x))/2)/(.5*(max(x)-min(x)))}
s_pressure = scalpm1(pressure)
s_speed = scalpm1(speed)
# a priori plots
wear_rate = 1/(1.1-s_pressure)
plot(pressure, wear_rate, type = 'l', yaxt = 'n')
```

```
wearout_time = 1/wear_rate
plot(pressure, wearout_time, type = 'l', yaxt = 'n')
wear_rate = 7 + 5*(s_speed + .5)^2
plot(speed, wear_rate, type = 'l', yaxt = 'n')
wearout_time = 1/wear_rate
plot(speed, wearout_time, type = 'l', yaxt = 'n')


# set data frame for DOE
# create grid
set.seed(54321)
DrillRuns = expand.grid(sPressure = c(-1, 1),sSpeed = c(-1,0,1))
# add replicate runs
DrillRuns = rbind(DrillRuns,DrillRuns)
# add column of random run order
RandOrder = sample(x = 1:length(DrillRuns[,1]),replace = FALSE)
DrillRuns = cbind(RandOrder,DrillRuns)
# add column names Order Pressure Speed
colnames(DrillRuns) = c("Order", "sPressure", "sSpeed")
DrillRuns

# make artificial runs using above
# create mean values
wear_rate = 1/(1.1-DrillRuns$sPressure)
DrillRuns$WearoutTime = 3/wear_rate + 7 +
5*(DrillRuns$sSpeed + .5)^2
# boxplot(DrillRuns$WearoutTime)
# add normal(0,2) error
DrillRuns$WearoutTime = DrillRuns$WearoutTime +
rnorm(length(DrillRuns$WearoutTime),0,4)
DrillRuns
regModel = lm(WearoutTime ~ sPressure+sSpeed+I(sSpeed^2),
data = DrillRuns)
summary(regModel)$coefficients[,1]
summary(regModel)$r.squared
anova(regModel)
library(rms)
vif(regModel)
# do plots to check model validity
acf(regModel$residuals)
plot(regModel, ask=F, add.smooth=F)
plot(DrillRuns$sPressure,regModel$residuals)
plot(DrillRuns$sSpeed,regModel$residuals)
plot(DrillRuns$Order,regModel$residuals)
# model valid, hypothesis test p-values and confidence intervals
summary(regModel)
confint(regModel)
```

```
# R code for GLIM for Exponential Y=============

# generate time in system values
#  for lambda = 1 and mu = 2,2.25,3,3.5,6,11
# only do once then store for repeatability
y1 = rexp(20, rate = 1)
y1.25 = rexp(20, rate = 1.25)
y2 = rexp(20, rate = 2)
y2.5 = rexp(20, rate = 2.5)
y5 = rexp(20, rate = 5)
y10 =rexp(20, rate = 10)

xy1 = cbind(rep(2,20),y1)
xy1.25 = cbind(rep(2.25,20),y1.25)
xy2 = cbind(rep(3,20),y2)
xy2.5 = cbind(rep(3.5,20),y2.5)
xy5 = cbind(rep(6,20),y5)
xy10 = cbind(rep(11,20),y10)

xy_data = rbind(xy1,xy1.25,xy2,xy2.5,xy5,xy10)
xy_data = as.data.frame(xy_data)
colnames(xy_data) = c("MeanServRate","TimeInSystem")
# after running above - save xy_data as glim_xy_data
# DO THIS ONCE - THEN RESULTS BELOW USE THAT DATA FILE
#write.csv(xy_data,"glim_xy_data.csv")
# later, read fixed simulated data set glim_xy_data.csv
xy_data = read.csv("glim_xy_data.csv")
plot(xy_data$MeanServRate, xy_data$TimeInSystem,
xlab = "Mean Service Rate", ylab = "Time in System")

# do GLM regression using lm
regModel = lm(TimeInSystem ~ MeanServRate, data = xy_data)
summary(regModel)
MSRvals = c(2,2.25,3,3.5,6,11)
predVals = data.frame(MeanServRate = MSRvals)
lmYhat = predict(regModel,newdata = predVals)
plot(xy_data$MeanServRate, xy_data$TimeInSystem,
xlim = c(1,12),ylim = c(-.1,3.5), pch=20, cex = .5,
xlab = "Mean Service Rate", ylab = "Time in System")
points(MSRvals,lmYhat,pch=1)

# do GLM regression using lm and ln Y
regModel = lm(log(TimeInSystem) ~ MeanServRate, data = xy_data)
summary(regModel)
MSRvals = c(2,2.25,3,3.5,6,11)
predVals = data.frame(MeanServRate = MSRvals)
lnlmYhat = exp(predict(regModel,newdata = predVals))
points(MSRvals,lnlmYhat,pch=10)
legend( x = "topright",
legend = c("data", "lm predicted",
```

```
"lm log Y predicted","glm predicted"),
pch = c(20,1,10,0))

# do GLIM regression using glm
glimModel = glm(TimeInSystem ~ MeanServRate ,
family = Gamma(), data = xy_data)
summary(glimModel)
predVals = data.frame(MeanServRate = MSRvals)
# note that predict() for glm predicts g(mu) not mu
# glm uses Inverse instead of Negative Inverse for g(mu_Y)
# so need 1/prediction
glimYhat = 1/predict(glimModel,newdata = predVals)
points(MSRvals, glimYhat, pch = 0)

# plot of means without data vs true mean time in system
plot(MSRvals,lmYhat,
xlim = c(1,12),ylim = c(-.1,1.5), pch = 1,
xlab = "Mean Service Rate", ylab = "Time in System")
points(MSRvals,1/(MSRvals-1),pch = 3)
points(MSRvals, glimYhat, pch = 0)
points(MSRvals,lnlmYhat,pch = 10)
legend( x = "topright",
legend = c("true mean", "lm predicted",
"lm log Y predicted","glm predicted"),
pch = c(3,1,10,0))
```

Chapter 4

Regression Under the Data-Adaptive Research Paradigm

While there are situations where theory predicts the model structure for regression using observational data, this modeling process is often exploratory. In such cases, predictive analytics lacks the theoretical framework of a *traditional research* paradigm to validate predictions and characterize prediction uncertainty. For the observational data sets discussed earlier, there are theoretical expectations for the model structure and at least the sign, if not the magnitude, of model coefficients. However, we will explore how predictive analytics can be applied in the absence of theory, letting the data both specify the predictive regression model and characterize the model prediction error. This general approach also means that we can employ regression modeling methods where there is little or no theory and yet still provide a characterization of forecast uncertainty.

4.1 Cross-Validation for Fitting and Characterizing Regression Prediction Error

When one cannot *a priori* describe the key variables and qualitative relationships expected for a regression modeling scenario, key relationships can be identified through an *exploratory study*. In such a study, plots and correlations of potential predictor variables give a hint to relationships, and a regression model (with perhaps interaction and other nonlinear terms) is fitted to the observational data.

In this setting, cross-validation (CV) provides a way to empirically assess prediction uncertainty for regression under the *data-adaptive research* paradigm.

CV is an empirical approach for fitting and assessing predictive analytics models, including regression and other model types. It is based on an old idea, used historically in applied statistics. To empirically test the predictive ability of a regression model, fit the model using only a portion of the data (the *train* portion) and then assess the quality of prediction on the portion of the data not used to fit the model (the *held-out* or *test* portion). Since the *test* portion was not used to fit the model, error is independently assessed.

> *Note*: it is important that the observations in the *test* portion of the data be selected randomly.

4.1.1 Train-and-test root mean squared error for error characterization

This train-and-test approach is at the center of fitting and assessing prediction error using CV. Figure 4.1 shows how the data set might be divided for a single train-and-test analysis. The regression model is fit to the train portion of the data, in this case consisting of the full data set less a *randomly selected* fraction (in this case, 10%) for the *test* data set. After fitting the parameters, the prediction error is computed by comparing the prediction $\hat{y}$ with the observed value y for each observation in the *test* data set. The left-out percent is often described as $1/k$; in this instance, $k = 10$.

But how is prediction error measured, and how is this used to establish forecast confidence and prediction intervals? With CV in the *data-adaptive research* framework, prediction error is usually

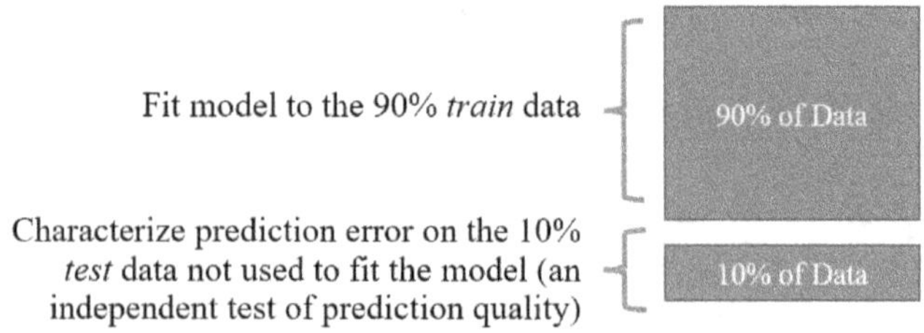

Figure 4.1. Assessment of prediction error by simple CV with 10% test data.

characterized by a function of the *test SSE* that is computed similarly to that in regression under the *traditional research* paradigm. The function is the square root of the average squared prediction error, called the root mean squared error, or *RMSE*:

$$RMSE_1 = \sqrt{SSE_1/n_k} = \sqrt{MSE_1}, \tag{4.1}$$

where n_k is the number of observations in the *test* data set and

$$SSE_1 = \sum_{i=1}^{n_k}(y_i - \hat{y}_i)^2. \tag{4.2}$$

If the full data set has n observations, then $n_k = n/k$. The subscript on *RMSE*, *SSE*, and *MSE* in Equation (4.1) indicates that there is one instance of train-and-test assessment. We will see in the following section that this can be repeated and averaged.

If one finds the error over the test set to be approximately normally distributed, then an approximate 95% prediction interval for the vector of predictor variable values $x = x^*$ can be computed as

$$\text{PI for } Y(x^*) = \hat{y}(x^*) \pm 2RMSE_1, \tag{4.3}$$

where $\hat{y}$ is from the regression model fitted to the full set of data. Equation (4.3) is an approximation to the 95% prediction interval for regression under the *traditional research* paradigm:

$$PI = \hat{y}(x^*) \pm t_{(.975,n'-d)}\sqrt{MSE\left(1+\frac{1}{n'}+g(x^*)'(g(X)'g(X))^{-1}g(x^*)\right)}, \tag{4.4}$$

where the prediction is for an x^* that gives the d-dimensional vector of model terms $g(x^*)$ (including the intercept as $g_0(x^*) = 1$) and $g(X)$ is the matrix with one row for each observation and one column for each of the g function values for that observation. For a CV regression, the value of n is $n' = ((k-1)/k) \times n$. Then, as the overall sample size n increases, $1/n'$ decreases. It turns out that $g(x^*)'(g(X)'g(X))^{-1}g(x^*)$ can be written as C/n' for some constant, C; hence, this term also becomes smaller as n increases. So, for large n, the quantity inside the square root is simply $MSE \times 1$, or *MSE*. Also, for large n, say larger than 100, the value of $t_{(.975,n'-d)}$ is close to the normal distribution value of $1.96 \approx 2$. So, for reasonably large n, Equation (4.3) is a good approximation to Equation (4.4).

4.1.2 *k*-fold CV

By randomly selecting a $1/k$ fraction to leave out of the fit, one may, by bad luck, either leave out a set of values that are quite typical, resulting in a small $RMSE_1$, or leave out an unusual set of observations, resulting in a very large $RMSE_1$. So, it would be better to divide the data set into k portions and repeat the CV assessment k times, leaving out a different fraction each time. This extension of the train-and-test method is called *k-fold cross-validation*, or *k-fold CV*. This is illustrated in Figure 4.2 for $k = 10$. *Note*: it is important that the data rows are randomly shuffled before dividing into k parts.

Now, we have k repeated train-and-test instances, each time leaving out a different $1/k$ of the data, fitting using the remainder, and computing MSE_j over the jth left-out $1/k$ fraction. Some sources define the overall $RMSE_k$ as the average of k computed $RMSE_j$ values from each train-and-test instance. But it is more appropriate to first average the MSE_j values over the k folds and then compute the square root of the average MSE. That k-fold CV we call $RMSE_k$, and its formula is shown in Equation (4.5). The prediction interval formula based on k-fold CV then matches Equation (4.3), with $RMSE_k$ replacing $RMSE_1$:

$$RMSE_{k\text{-fold}} = \sqrt{\frac{1}{k}\sum_{j=1}^{k} SSE_j/n_k} = \sqrt{\frac{1}{k}\sum_{j=1}^{k} MSE_j} = \sqrt{\sum_{i=1}^{n} SSE_i/n}. \tag{4.5}$$

Choosing *k*

In the examples here, why was k chosen as 10? In CV, choosing the value of k involves a trade-off between low bias in the forecast coverage percentage induced by modeling with fewer observations when k is small and high variance in the predictions when k is large. The most extreme case is to choose $k = n$. This is called *leave-one-out* cross-validation, or *LOOCV*, and has two problems. First, if n is large, say 10,000, it means that 10,000 regression models must be fit and evaluated — a lot of work. Second, strange behavior in portions of the response surface where there is data will always be captured since all but one observation is used to fit each model. But strange behavior that is not in the span of observations will

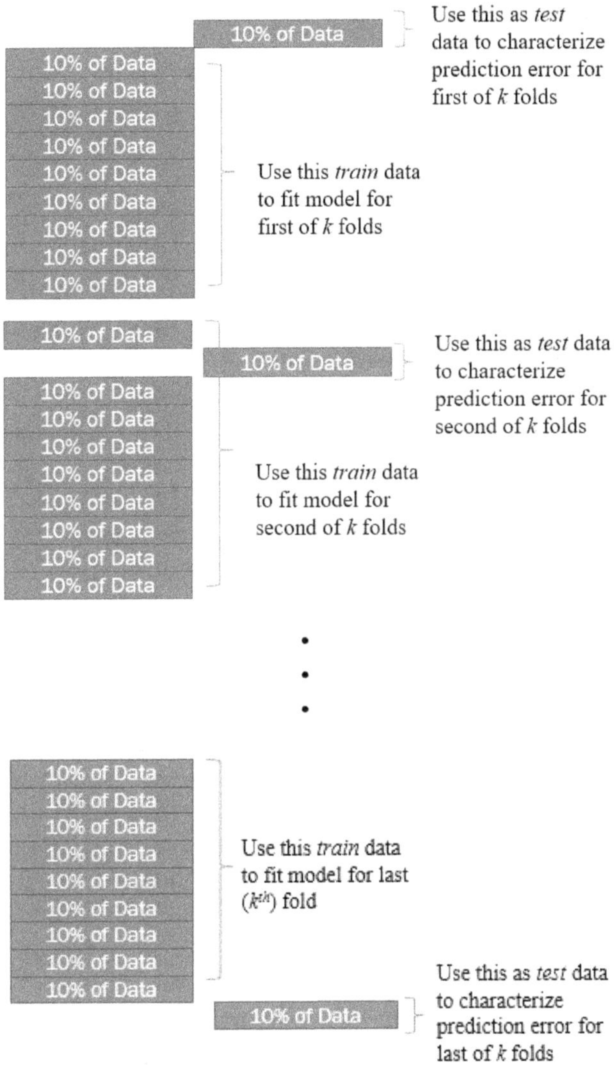

Figure 4.2. Process for k-fold CV with $k = 10$.

be missed. It is fairer to characterize this by leaving out larger portions of the observed data during the fitting process. Kohavi (1995) shows that k values between 10 and 20 tend to balance these two errors and perform well, although other alternatives can further improve performance.

It is important to recognize that these coverages are approximate. Bates *et al.* (2023) show that 10-fold CV prediction intervals in a regression setting can result in significantly lower coverage, with examples of actual 82% coverage for a nominal 90% prediction interval.

4.1.3 Alternatives to k-fold CV

There are several alternatives to k-fold CV that have been studied by researchers. *Complete CV* chooses all possible splits into k subsets and averages *RMSE* from all of these. The computational burden can be huge. Note that complete CV occurs automatically when $k = n$. A simpler approach is *repeated CV*. In this case, several instances of k-fold CV are conducted, but not all possible combinations. In each instance, the process follows that in Figure 4.2; however, each time, the order of the full data set is randomly reassigned.

In *stratified CV*, the k subsamples are selected to each have a balance of predictor variable values found in the overall data set — to the extent possible. The expectation is lower variance and bias for the standard deviation of the *RMSE* and R^2 estimates.

In these cases, the extra effort does not guarantee improved performance; performance can actually deteriorate. So, the added complexity comes with risk. In addition, software for ordinary k-fold CV is readily available, whereas availability for other options is less certain and, when present, requires longer computational time. The recommended strategy is to employ $k = 10$ in the CV estimation of model uncertainty.

4.2 Using k-Fold CV in R via `caret`

The `caret` package in R implements k-fold and other *data-adaptive research* methods for fitting and uncertainty characterization regression and classification. There are three key characteristics to keep in mind when using this approach:

1. the particular fitting and uncertainty characterization method (k-fold, repeated k-fold, LOOCV, or bootstrap) is specified by the `trainControl()` function;

2. the command to fit the model is `train()` rather than `lm()`, while specifying `method = "lm"` as an argument to the `train()` command; and
3. the regression object from `train()` has a different structure from that of `lm()`, so the commands to access coefficients, R^2, etc., are different.

Many model types can be fitted using `caret`. Several regression and classification methods can be found in Chapter 7 of the `caret` online manual (Kuhn, 2019).

Revisiting the Modigliani life-cycle savings example

These differences are illustrated by an example. We reanalyze the Modigliani life-cycle savings model from Section 3.3.6. In that section, we concluded with a model having one dependent variable and two independent variables. It consists of 50 observations:

- aggregate personal savings rate (dependent variable),
- percent of population under 15 years old (pop15), and
- growth rate of disposable income (ddpi).

We include the output coefficient estimates, R^2, and prediction intervals from the ordinary linear regression analysis in Section 3.3.6. The results are as follows.

```
> summary(regModel3)$coefficients
              Estimate Std. Error   t value     Pr(>|t|)
(Intercept) 15.5995758 2.33439442  6.682494 2.479591e-08
ddpi         0.4428302 0.19240135  2.301596 2.583739e-02
pop15       -0.2163762 0.06033473 -3.586263 7.959672e-04
> summary(regMod3)$r.squared
[1] 0.287788
> summary(regMod3)$sigma
[1] 3.860746
>
> # predict savings rate for 3% population over 75,
> #   35% population under 15, 2000 disposable personal
> #   income and 10% rate of change of income
> # NOTE: since pop75 and dpi removed from the model,
> #       leave them out of prediction dataframe
> new.dat = data.frame(ddpi = 10, pop15 = 35)
> predict(regModel3, new.dat, interval = "confidence")
```

```
       fit       lwr      upr
1 12.45471 9.801022 15.1084
> predict(regModel3 , new.dat, interval = "prediction")
       fit       lwr       upr
1 12.45471 4.247059 20.66236
>
```

Using CV with linear regression will not change the coefficient estimates, but it gives two important results:

1. a robust estimate of R^2 and an estimated standard deviation for that estimate, and
2. a robust estimate of the standard deviation of prediction error: *RMSE*.

The following are the code and corresponding results for the model fitted using `train()`. Note that 10-fold CV is indicated by `trainControl(method = "cv", number = 10)`.

```
> # Cross-validation regression code
> # Important for repeatable results to set the random
    number seed;
> #   this effects the random split into 10 subsets
      of data
> set.seed(80111973)
> library(caret) # needed for cross validation
> trainMeth = trainControl(method = "cv", number = 10)
> # NOTE: need data = for caret train() function
> CVregModel <- train(sr ~ ddpi + pop15, data =
  LifeCycleSavings,
+                     method = "lm", trControl
                      = trainMeth)
>
> CVregModel$finalModel$coefficients
(Intercept)        ddpi       pop15
15.5995758   0.4428302  -0.2163762
# the CV-based estimate used for prediction intervals
> CVregModel$results$RMSE
[1] 3.690107
> CVregModel$results$RMSESD
[1] 1.542347
> CVregModel$results$Rsquared
[1] 0.4203932
> CVregModel$results$RsquaredSD
[1] 0.336205
>
```

```
> # Create predicted values at existing data points
> predictValCVreg = predict(CVregModel,LifeCycleSavings
                     [2:5])
> # plot actual vs predicted
> plot(predictValCVreg,LifeCycleSavings[,1],
> xlab = "Predicted Savings Rate",
> ylab = "Actual Savings Rate")

> # Must create residuals manually (actual-predicted)
> residValCVreg = LifeCycleSavings[,1] - predictValCVreg
> acf(residValCVreg)
> qqnorm(residValCVreg)
> plot(LifeCycleSavings$ddpi,residValCVreg)
> plot(LifeCycleSavings$pop15,residValCVreg)

> # Constructing approximate confidence intervals from a
    CV-trained
> # model is beyond the scope of this course. But
    constructing
> # approximate prediction intervals is fairly easy to do:
    just
> # use the predicted value +/- 2*sigma_hat and remember
    that
> # RMSE can be used as sigma_hat, the estimate of sigma
> # (for a normal interval we would use 1.96*sigma)
#
# from ordinary regression case in Ch 3
> predictVals = predict(CVregModel,new.dat)
> pUpper = predictVals+2*CVregModel$results$RMSE
> pLower = predictVals-2*CVregModel$results$RMSE
>
> print("Approximate Prediction Intervals")
[1] "Approximate Prediction Intervals"
> print(cbind(predictVals,pLower,pUpper))
  predictVals   pLower   pUpper
1    12.45471 5.074495 19.83493
>
```

Note that the commands used to print the coefficients, R^2, *RMSE*, and the (empirical) 95% prediction interval for a CV-fitted model using `train()` are different from those used for a model fitted using `lm`. The coefficient estimates are identical to those from `lm()`. This is because the CV for regression is ONLY used to characterize the fit and prediction error.

Table 4.1. A comparison of `lm()` and `train()` results.

Quantity	`lm()` **Result**	`train()` **Result**
Intercept Coeff. Est.	15.60	15.60
s.d. (Int. Est.)	2.334	N.A.
ddpi Coeff. Est.	0.4428	0.4428
s.d. (ddpi Est.)	0.1924	N.A.
pop15 Coeff. Est.	−0.2164	−0.2164
s.d. (pop15 Est.)	0.0603	N.A.
R^2	0.2878	0.4204
s.d. (R^2)	N.A.	0.3362
$RMSE$	3.861	3.690
s.d. ($RMSE$)	N.A.	1.542
Prediction	12.45	12.45
Lower PI	4.247	5.074
Upper PI	20.66	19.83

Table 4.1 compares the *traditional research* (`lm()`) estimates with the *data-adaptive research* (`train()`) estimates for regression coefficients, R^2, and *RMSE*. The table shows that `lm()` and `train()` produce the same regression coefficient estimates and the same predicted value at ddpi = 10, pop15 = 35. The table indicates a higher estimated R^2 from the CV assessment and a lower *RMSE*. As a consequence, the prediction interval for `lm()` is slightly larger than that of `train()`. This may be due to a few outlier data points, which all contribute to a smaller R^2 for ordinary regression but may only appear in the left-out 10% a few times (*SSE* is only computed over the 10%), weakening their average effect. Nonetheless, there are only small differences between the *RMSE*, R^2, and prediction intervals found using ordinary regression and regression via CV. Since the `lm()` model passed the *traditional research* validity tests, this similarity in prediction intervals gives some confidence in the empirical CV approach to characterizing prediction uncertainty.

Missing from the `train()` results are coefficient estimate standard deviations and confidence intervals. The `lm()` results are based on a probability model that is supported in the *traditional research* paradigm. That model does not hold in the *data-adaptive research* paradigm. Empirical standard deviations for coefficient estimates from `train()` could be based on the coefficient variation over the

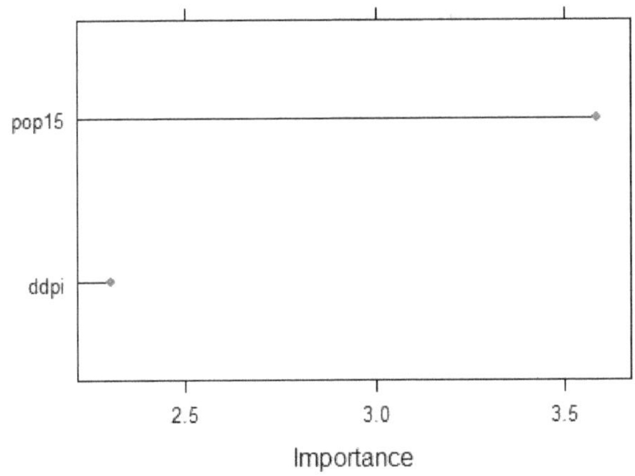

Figure 4.3. Variable importance plot from `train()` fit for the life-cycle model.

10 folds. Unfortunately, the coefficient estimates from each fold are not available in the output from the `train()` function; therefore, the standard deviations (s.d.) of the coefficient estimates for `train()` is denoted by "N.A." in the table. Instead, `train()` provides a graphical representation of the empirical relative importance of the regression coefficients: a decomposition of the sum of squares, much like that provided by `anova()` but graphically. The code to generate the plot is as follows:

```
> plot(varImp(CVregModel, scale = FALSE))
>
```

The result is shown in Figure 4.3. Clearly, the percentage of the population under age 15 drives the largest part of the prediction of the aggregate personal savings rate.

As a benefit of CV, the repeated fitting of models by `train()` gives empirical estimates of variation for model R^2 and *RMSE*, which are not provided in the `lm()` output. In particular, note the very high standard deviation for R^2. This means that the R^2 value varied a great deal from one fold to the next. This high variability means that we can place little confidence in the value of 0.4204. It is also likely that this high variation would occur for the R^2 estimated from a different full data set, and so this casts doubt on the 0.2878 value as well. While the s.d. for *RMSE* is not as large, it still indicates high uncertainty in the value; therefore, prediction intervals will not likely be reliable, despite the already large size of the prediction intervals — a point to consider. Remember that this work received the Nobel Prize in Economics (but there was more to it).

4.3 The Overall Process for Linear Regression Under a *Data-Adaptive Research* Paradigm

In the previous sections, we identified a different procedure for constructing and interpreting linear regression models under a *data-adaptive research* paradigm. The following is a step-by-step summary of that procedure:

1. Determine the objectives of the predictive model based on managerial needs.
2. Summarize the observational data with a descriptive summary, scatter plots (matrix plot; or perhaps boxplots with qualitative predictors), and discussion.
3. Choose a general regression model based on the observed structure, and include nonlinear terms that may be useful in fitting the data. Create dummy indicator variables if you are including qualitative variables as predictors. Show a mathematical presentation with βs and ε, BUT DO NOT INCLUDE the i.i.d. normal statement.
4. Fit the proposed model via k-fold CV using `train()` with $k = 10$.
5. Show and interpret for management the fitted regression model coefficients. Use the variable importance plot to identify the important predictor variables. Assess the practical predictive ability with a fitted line plot, $RMSE_{k\text{-fold}}$, and R^2 discussion.
6. Even though we do not expect a theoretical model, create a subset of the diagnostic plots: the acf of residuals, residuals vs. predictors, and the normal probability plot of residuals.
7. Show and discuss *empirical* forecast prediction intervals for desired configurations x^* by using $RMSE_{k\text{-fold}}$. Describe the resulting prediction intervals in managerial terms, highlighting their empirical nature, without the theoretical foundation.
8. Give a useful overall managerial summary and recommendation on the application of the fitted regression model, with predictions for any key levels of interest to management.

4.4 Case Supporting Chapters 4 and 5

The multi-segment case BostonHousingRegressionPart2 supports the material in Chapters 4 and 5. Multiple linear regression, Gaussian process regression, and neural network regression methods are all applied to the Boston housing data. All analyses are conducted under the *data-adaptive research* paradigm. This case extends over multiple weeks. The case description slides and data can be found online in the BostonHousingRegressionCV folder of Barton (2023).

4.5 R Code Used in Chapter 4

```
# R code for LifeCycleSavings regression section 4.2
  ======

library(datasets)
pairs(LifeCycleSavings)
# the attach() command removes the need for
data=LifeCycleSavings attach(LifeCycleSavings)
regModel = lm(sr ~ dpi + ddpi + pop15 + pop75)
summary(regModel)$coefficients
summary(regModel)$r.squared
library(rms)
vif(regModel)

# two VIF values > 5, delete largest (pop75)
regModel2 = lm(sr ~ dpi + ddpi + pop15)
summary(regModel2)$coefficients
summary(regModel2)$r.squared
library(rms)
vif(regModel2)

# model VIF OK, check validity plots
acf(regModel2$residuals)
plot(regModel2, ask = F, add.smooth = F)
plot(dpi,regModel2$residuals)
plot(ddpi,regModel2$residuals)
plot(pop15,regModel2$residuals)

# diagnostic plots OK, get model summary
summary(regModel2)
```

```
# drop term with highest p-value (dpi at .328)
regModel3 = lm(sr ~ ddpi + pop15)
summary(regModel3)$coefficients
summary(regModel3)$r.squared
library(rms)
vif(regModel3)

# model VIF OK, check validity plots
acf(regModel3$residuals)
plot(regModel3, ask = F, add.smooth = F)
plot(ddpi,regModel3$residuals)
plot(pop15,regModel3$residuals)

# diagnostic plots OK, get model summary
summary(regModel3)
summary(regModel3)$coefficients
summary(regModel3)$r.squared
summary(regModel3)$sigma

# give confidence intervals for regression coefficients
confint(regModel3)

# predict savings rate for 3% population over 75,
#   35% population under 15, 2000 disposable personal
#   income and 10% rate of change of income


# NOTE: since pop75 and dpi removed from the model, leave
#       them out of prediction dataframe
new.dat = data.frame(ddpi = 10, pop15 = 35)
predict(regModel3, new.dat, interval = "confidence")
predict(regModel3, new.dat, interval = "prediction")


# Now add on cv to 3rd model
# Cross-validation regression code
# Important for repeatable results to set the random
#   number seed - this effects the random split into
    10 subsets of data set.seed(80111973)
library(caret) # needed for cross validation
trainMeth = trainControl(method = "cv", number = 10)

# NOTE: need data = for caret train() function
CVregModel <- train(sr ~ ddpi + pop15,
data = LifeCycleSavings,
```

```
method = "lm", trControl = trainMeth)

CVregModel$finalModel$coefficients
# the CV-based estimate RMSE is used for prediction
  intervals
CVregModel$results$RMSE
CVregModel$results$RMSESD
CVregModel$results$Rsquared
CVregModel$results$RsquaredSD

# Create predicted values at existing data points
predictValCVreg = predict(CVregModel,LifeCycleSavings
[2:5])
# plot actual vs predicted
plot(predictValCVreg,LifeCycleSavings[,1],
xlab = "Predicted Savings Rate",
ylab = "Actual Savings Rate")

# Must create residuals manually (actual-predicted)
residValCVreg = LifeCycleSavings[,1] - predictValCVreg
acf(residValCVreg)
qqnorm(residValCVreg)
plot(LifeCycleSavings$ddpi,residValCVreg)
plot(LifeCycleSavings$pop15,residValCVreg)

CVregModel
CVregModel$resample
plot(varImp(CVregModel, scale = FALSE))

# Constructing approximate confidence intervals from a
  CV-trained
# model is beyond the scope of this course. But
  constructing
# approximate prediction intervals is fairly easy to do:
  just use
# the predicted value +/- 2*sigma_hat and remember that
  RMSE can
# be used as sigma_hat, the estimate of sigma (for a
# normal interval we would use 1.96*sigma)




# from ordinary regression case in Ch 3
predictVals = predict(CVregModel,new.dat)
```

```
pUpper = predictVals+2*CVregModel$results$RMSE
pLower = predictVals-2*CVregModel$results$RMSE

print("Approximate Prediction Intervals")
print(cbind(predictVals,pLower,pUpper))
```

Chapter 5

Nontraditional Regression (Machine Learning)

In addition to multiple linear regression, many other regression strategies are available in the *data-adaptive research* paradigm. Typically, they (along with related classification methods discussed in Part II) are called *machine learning* (ML) methods. In this chapter, we discuss the general approach to fitting ML regression models and using them for prediction. We give details on two such approaches: spatial correlation (also known as Gaussian process or Kriging) regression, and neural network regression.

5.1 Machine Learning Concepts and Methods

Machine learning encompasses a broad collection of computer-based predictive models. It includes regression models of many sorts, classification methods (which are discussed in Part II of the text), clustering methods important for unsupervised learning, and time series models. The term "machine learning" originated with Robert Neeley, who in 1962 developed a computer program to predict the outcome of a checkers game based on the current position of pieces (the state) and the next move. This is a clustering, classification, and optimization problem. You can imagine that there are too many possible states to consider (about 5×10^{20} — more than 100 times the 7×10^{18} grains of sand on our planet). So, the cleverness in ML for checkers is deciding which states to explore and whether for each the game needs to be played to a conclusion. ML is really a bad but catchy name. It explains NOTHING about what is going on. There is no "machine" in the usual sense. The primary use of these methods is for data mining (detecting structure and relationships) or predictive analytics (using such relationships for prediction).

A modern objective that has been achieved through ML is recommender systems. For example, based on previous movies that you have watched, NETFLIX will recommend ones that you might like. The recommender system identifies movies that it *predicts* you will enjoy. The ML (predictive analytics) method will use data on your previous choices and similar data from people who made previous choices like yours. This is a clustering and classification ML problem.

Figure 5.1 shows a collection of ML methods. On the left are the methods for predicting a number (Part I of this text). On the right are methods for predicting a class (e.g., winning or losing a checkers game, having or not having a disease; Part II of this text). The shaded methods are covered in this text. For predicting a number, we see that there are many methods in addition to multiple linear regression. Multiple linear regression can be included as a ML method. We explain two other methods in this chapter: *Gaussian process* (GP) regression and *neural network* regression. But there are many others.

What is missing from our coverage? Multilayer neural networks are used only for very sophisticated modeling and are beyond the scope of this text. Spline models, radial basis function (RBF) regression, and multivariate adaptive regression splines (MARS) are useful alternatives, but they are conceptually more difficult and their

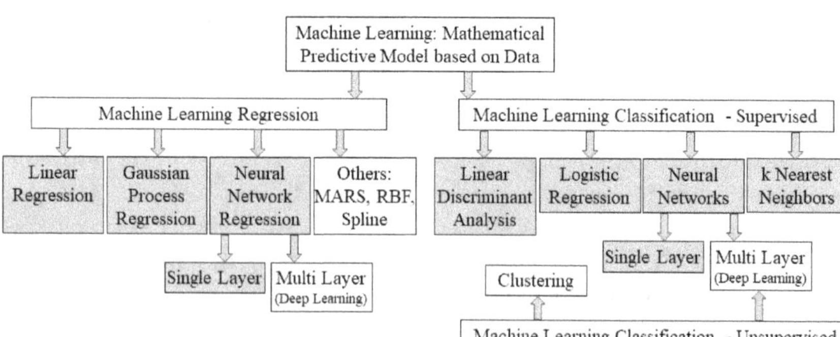

Figure 5.1. Machine learning encompasses many methods.

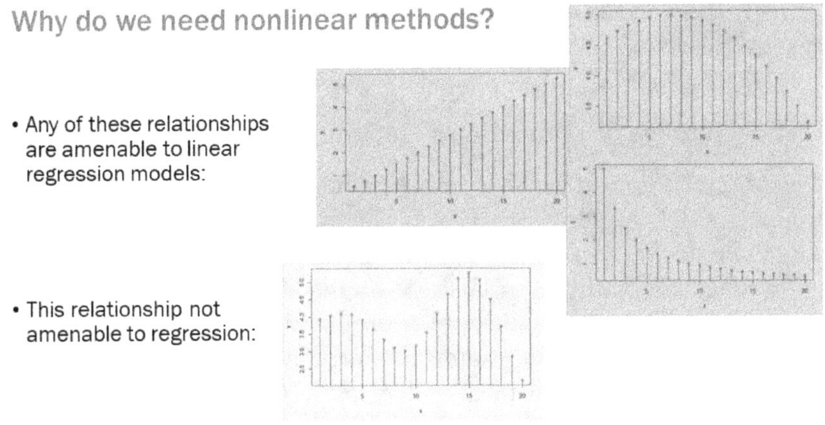

Figure 5.2. Some response functions are not amenable to linear regression.

performance can be unreliable. The focus in this text is on prediction, not data mining. Unsupervised learning falls more into the latter category and is beyond our scope. Classification and regression trees are missing from the figure. They are extremely useful and popular, but they overlap with data mining and are not included in this text.

Why do we need nonlinear methods?

In Section 3.3, we examined the flexibility of multiple linear regression terms to capture nonlinearity in the response. But the process was difficult. Should we transform x? or y? Which transform should we use? Should we use a Box–Cox transformation? What if structure remains in the residuals? Figure 5.2 highlights the situation. Three of the four responses are amenable to linear regression. Only the image at the lower left is not. It would be ideal to specify some very general expected behavior and have the fitting process figure out the rest.

5.2 Spatial Correlation (Gaussian Process) Regression

GP regression takes several forms and has different names: GP models, spatial correlation models, and Kriging models are commonly used names. GP models refer to a particular form of spatial correlation model, and they are our focus here. Google "Gaussian process regression," and you will find that it is quite popular. Further,

GP regression software is readily available in R, and specific R packages are discussed in the following.

5.2.1 History of spatial correlation modeling

The original application of spatial correlation models was to gold mining. In that application, Y_i was the gold concentration found in a borehole drilled at position x_i, where x_i is a vector $(x_{i,1}, x_{i,2})$ with $x_{i,1}$ = longitude and $x_{i,2}$ = latitude at the ith drilled location. The objective was to forecast the gold concentration, $Y(x)$, at intermediate locations — for mining potential and mine valuation.

The key idea, natural in a geological setting, is that concentrations at nearby locations should be similar (either high or low); this is a *spatial correlation* of Y values in x-space. Spatial correlation models were motivated by the ideas of Danie Gerhardus Krige (1919–2013), a South African statistician and mining engineer. His paper, "A statistical approach to some basic mine valuation problems on the Witwatersrand," (Krige, 1951) was expanded by Matheron (1960), who applied the name Kriging (but, in French, "*Krigeage*").

The original method was designed for modeling stochastic responses, meaning that in addition to the overall trend of the response, there was a local small-scale variation. This stochastic variability was modeled with a *nugget*, analogous to the ε in linear regression. Recent popularity has been led by the pioneering paper on predicting the output of an engineering, medical, or social computer simulation model by Sacks *et al.* (1989). Even for forecasting deterministic computer model output, a small nugget (say, 0.0001) often improves the fit. In 2010, an alternative modeling form for stochastic computer simulation model responses allowing differing magnitudes for local nugget values was developed by researchers at Northwestern University (Ankenman *et al.*, 2010). That local nugget variation is implemented in one of the methods presented in the following (`mlegp`).

5.2.2 The intuition behind spatial correlation prediction

GP regression and other spatial correlation models build on a very intuitive concept: the value of an unobserved response function $Y(x)$

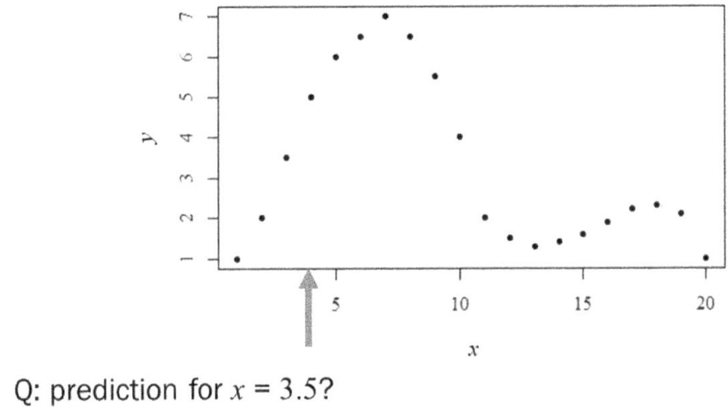

Figure 5.3. How to predict $y(3.5)$ for a nonlinear response function?

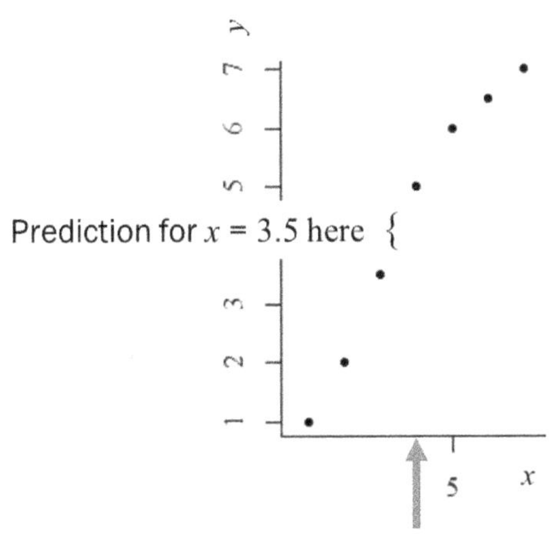

Figure 5.4. Intuitive strategy for prediction uses values of neighbors.

should be similar to that of an observed $Y(x_0)$ for x values that are near x_0. Consider the data set in Figure 5.3. The nature of the response suggests that multiple linear regression is not a good candidate for a predictive model. How might one predict the response, say at $x = 3.5$?

It makes sense that the value would fall between the nearby observed values at $x = 3$ and $x = 4$. An intuitive prediction interval is shown in Figure 5.4. That is how GP models work: they assume that the unobserved Y values are *correlated* with the observed Y values that are nearby in x-space. That is, they exhibit *spatial correlation.*

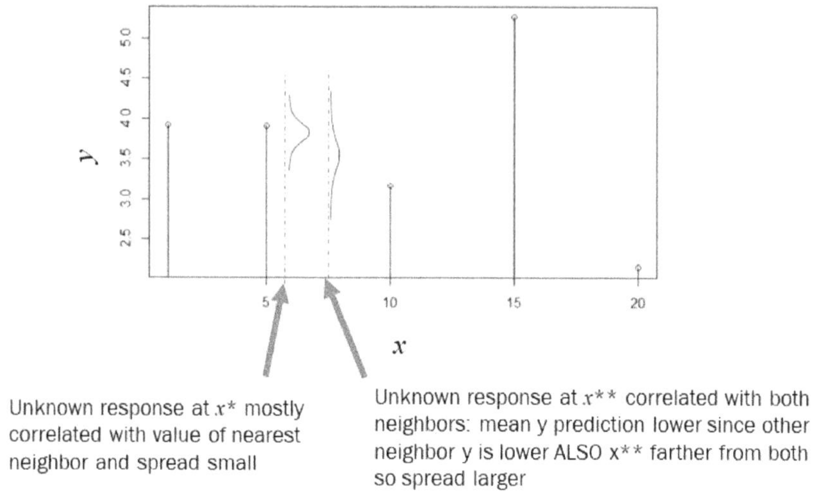

Figure 5.5. Spatial correlation prediction uncertainty for x^* and x^{**}.

The GP model assumes a normally distributed uncertainty around each predicted value. In Figure 5.5, the unknown response at x^* is mostly correlated with the value of its nearest neighbor, and since the corresponding x values are close, the spread is small. But the unknown response at x^{**} is correlated with both neighbors about equally; therefore, the mean y prediction is lower since the other neighboring y is lower. Also, since x^{**} is farther from both neighbors, the uncertainty spread is larger. The correlation decreases exponentially with the squared distance. In both cases, the GP model assumes that the uncertainty about a predicted y has a normal or Gaussian distribution, with greater variance the farther you are from known points (and less dependence to be similar to the neighboring y values). We use the normal distribution to formulate GP regression, but the formulation is more complex than for linear regression due to the special correlation structure.

5.2.3 Form of the GP model

A GP model assumes that the response values have a multivariate normal distribution, correlated with each other, where the correlation is high for nearby responses (nearby in terms of predictor space: their x values). This correlation exponentially decreases as the distance of the predictor variable vectors increase, typically as the square of the distance. This form makes the correlation magnitude for $Y(x)$ follow the shape of a normal distribution centered at x. Before showing the form of the model, it will be helpful to review the notation for a multivariate normal distribution. First, consider the univariate (ordinary) normal distribution for a single random quantity Y with a mean of μ and a standard deviation of σ:

$$Y \sim N(\mu, \sigma^2),\ f_Y(y) = \frac{1}{\sigma\sqrt{2\pi}} e^{-\frac{(y-\mu)^2}{2\sigma^2}} = \frac{1}{\sqrt{2\pi\sigma^2}} e^{-\frac{(y-\mu)(\sigma^2)^{-1}(y-\mu)}{2}}. \tag{5.1}$$

The usual form is in the middle, and we simply moved some terms on the right-hand form of the density to make it easier to see the analogy for the multivariate normal density. To generalize the right-most density in Equation (5.1) to the case where Y is a vector of values, we need to replace σ, the variance of a univariate Y, with Σ, the variance-covariance matrix for a random vector Y. Then, the σ^2 in the denominator is replaced by the determinant of the variance-covariance matrix, and $(\sigma^2)^{-1}$ is replaced by the inverse of the variance-covariance matrix. That form is shown in Equation (5.2). Remember, Σ is a matrix, and Y and y and μ are all vectors. For intuition, you can think of Y and y as having an element for each one of the rows in the data set, say n observations, so n elements in Y and y:

$$Y \sim MVN(\mu, \Sigma),\ f_Y(y) = \frac{1}{\sqrt{2\pi \det \Sigma}} e^{-\frac{(y-\mu)\Sigma^{-1}(y-\mu)}{2}}. \tag{5.2}$$

Now, we can talk about the form of the GP model. The general form is

$$Y = \beta_0 + \sum_{j=1}^{d} \beta_j g_j(x) + M(x) + \varepsilon,\ \varepsilon \overset{\text{iid}}{\sim} N(0, \sigma^2), \tag{5.3}$$

where $M(x)$ represents the spatial correlation part of the model. It is a random function with a mean of zero and a special correlation structure. Consider a set of $M()$ values $(M(x_1), M(x_2), \ldots, M(x_n))$ at different predictor values, $(x_1, x_2, \ldots, x_n)$, where x_i is a vector corresponding to the values of the predictor variables for the ith observation. Then,

$$(M(x_1), M(x_2), \ldots, M(x_n)) \sim MVN(0, \Sigma_M), \quad (5.4)$$

and Σ_M is a product of the overall variance of observed Y values (σ^2_{GP}, a number not a vector) times the spatial correlation matrix R_M. The correlation function depends on the scaled (coordinate-by-coordinate) squared distance between points. Usually, we simply use Euclidean distance: so, the scaled squared distance between two predictor vectors x_i and x_j is $\sum_{k=1}^{p} \theta_k (x_{ik} - x_{jk})^2$, where there is a scaling factor θ_k that can be different for each coordinate k. This is important if one variable is measured in millions of dollars and the other in tens of minutes. It *should* mean that we don't have to worry about scaling the predictors to ± 1, but the R software still works better if we do the scaling.

Now, we can write the formula for Σ_M:

$$\Sigma_M = \sigma^2_{\text{GP}} R_M, \; R_M[i,j] = e^{-\sum_{k=1}^{p} \theta_k (x_{ik} - x_{jk})^2}. \quad (5.5)$$

In fact, typically all of the variation in Y across x values can be captured by $M(x)$, and so the usual structure for a GP model only has an intercept, $M(x)$, and ε. The model is (expanding the definition of $M(x)$):

$$Y = \beta_0 + M(x) + \varepsilon, \; M(x) \sim MVN(0, \Sigma_M), \; \varepsilon \overset{\text{iid}}{\sim} N(0, \sigma^2). \quad (5.6)$$

Let's compare the form of GP regression in Equation (5.6) with multiple linear regression. The multiple linear regression is given by

$$Y = \beta_0 + \sum_{j=1}^{d} \beta_j g_j(x) + \varepsilon, \; \varepsilon \text{ i.i.d. } \sim N(0, \sigma^2). \quad (5.7)$$

For multiple regression, we estimate βs with bs and σ with s. Then, prediction is possible using the bs and s. For GP regression, we have to estimate β_0 with b_0, σ_{GP} with s_{GP}, Σ_ε with $\widehat{\Sigma_\varepsilon}$ (which is the *nugget*), and θs with $\hat{\theta}$s. The estimation is more complex than for linear regression. But once the estimates are found, prediction is possible. We need two more terms to show the formula. First, we need the correlation vector for the predicted point x^*, say r. The jth element of that vector is defined using the formula in (5.5):

$$r_j = e^{-\sum_{k=1}^{p} \theta_k (x^* - x_{jk})^2}.$$

And we need to get a combined variance-covariance matrix $\widehat{V} = \widehat{\Sigma_M} + \widehat{\Sigma_\varepsilon}$. The prediction formula is

$$\hat{y}(x^*) = b_0 + s_{\text{GP}} r' \widehat{V}^{-1} (y_{\text{obs}} - b_0 \mathbf{1}_n), \tag{5.8}$$

where y_{obs} is the vector of n observed responses in the fitting data set and $\mathbf{1}$ is a vector of ones, the same length as the vector of responses, n.

All this is rather complicated, but GP models work very well, and because of the model structure, they permit prediction intervals based on the normal distribution. Fortunately, understanding the approach at a high level is all that is needed. All of the details are handled by the R functions that are discussed in the following section.

5.2.4 GP regression using R

There are a number of different packages that provide GP regression in R. These include `DiceKriging` (with regression command `km`), `gausspr` (with regression command `gausspr` or `gaussprRadial` in caret), `GPfit` (with regression command `GP_fit`), `laGP` (with regression command `newGP`), `mlegp` (with regression command `mlegp`), and `RobustGASP` (with regression command `ppgasp`). We focus on `mlegp` and `gausspr`.

The R function `mlegp` is attractive because it allows the nugget to be set differently at each observed x. Recall in linear regression our concern about having equal variance (vertical spread) across all values of each predictor variable. With this package, if there are replications or if the variance vs. x value can be estimated, then unequal variance is not a problem. Most GP fitting functions, including `gausspr` require the nugget to be the same at every x. But in using `mlegp`, it is important to set the nugget carefully to balance fitting with mean reversion. In statistical settings, this will rarely be a problem: we can estimate the nugget from a preliminary multiple regression fit and use the resulting *MSE*.

Unfortunately, `mlegp` is not an option in the caret `train()` function. We have to do that fitting manually. In the following example, we do not use cross-validation, and we do not set separate nugget values for each coordinate because there is only one predictor variable.

To better understand the commands to fit and predict for **mlegp**, we compare them with commands for multiple linear regression. It is not shown as part of an interactive session, so the > prompts are not present.

```
# Here is the code for fitting and predicting for a set of
#   prediction values with linear regression.

# Linear regression with x^2
LinRegMod = lm(y ~ x + I(x^2), data = myData)
xpreds = data.frame(x=matrix((1:100)/5,100,1))
ypreds = predict(LinRegMod,xpreds)

# Now the code for fitting and predicting with mlegp
#   (using the sigma estimate from a preliminary
    linear regression)
# Note that constantmean=1 means to use only beta_0 for the
#   regression model part
sig2Est = (summary(LinRegMod)$sigma)^2
GPmodel = mlegp(x,y,constantMean=1,nugget=sig2Est,
                nugget.known=1)
xpreds = matrix((1:100)/5,100,1)
ypreds = predict(GPmodel,xpreds)

# If there are repeated observations at the same x values, then
#   use this form, computing means at for each set of
#   replications and sample variance of y's. This ASSUMES that
#   ALL x values have 'reps' replications and that the
#   data are sorted to keep replications together in groups.
groupID = rep(1:nDOEpts, each = reps)
grp_x = tapply(x, groupID, FUN=mean)
grp_meany = tapply(y, groupID, FUN=mean)
grp_vary = tapply(y, groupID, FUN=var)
# Nugget in this case set as the sample variance,
#   different for each x
sig2Est = grp_vary/reps
GPmodel = mlegp(grp_x,grp_meany,constantMean=1,nugget=sig2Est,
                nugget.known=1)
xpreds = matrix((1:100)/5,100,1)
ypreds = predict(GPmodel,xpreds)
```

The risk in modeling with **mlegp** is choosing a bad nugget value. If the preliminary regression model is a poor fit, then its MSE (and square root, sigma: in the code, this is squared and assigned to **sig2est**) will be too large and the GP model will be overly smooth. An alternative is to plot y vs. x for a single predictor and make a judgment about the prediction uncertainty (vertical spread) at a single

x value. You could think of such an interval as $\pm 2\sigma$ or 4σ total length. Taking one-fourth of that value and squaring it might make a good nugget choice.

Fortunately, there is an alternative. The caret package offers GP as one model choice. It is gausspr using the "radial" option, so the method name is `gaussprRadial`. The cross-validation activity automatically handles fitting the GP model. You can specify a nugget value with the `sigma =` argument in the `CVgpModel` statement, but it is not needed. That command sequence takes the following form. It is not shown as part of an interactive session, so the > prompts are not present.

```
# Using the sigma estimate from a preliminary linear regression
# Note that sigma, not sigma^2 used here and is optional
sigEst = summary(LinRegMod)$sigma
trainMeth = trainControl(method = "cv", number = 10)
# To specify a nugget, add 'sigma =sigEst' to train()
#   (or any other value that you choose)
CVgpModel <- train(y ~ ., data = MyData,
sigma = sigEst,
method = "gaussprRadial",
trControl = trainMeth)
xpreds =data.frame(x = (1:100)/5)
ypreds = predict(CVgpModel,xpreds)
```

For the `CVgpModel`, prediction requires the predictor variable values to be in a data frame, indicated both by `data = MyData,` in the `train` command and in the form of `xpreds` for the `predict` command above. This was also necessary for the `lm` because the `data =` option was used there. It was not required for the `mlegp` fitting command. Another consequence is that plotting the response against a set of possible predictor variable values requires the predictor in the data frame to be converted back to a numeric vector. For example, for `xpreds$x`, rather than just `xpreds` as seen in the following, where line plotting commands for `lm`, `mlegp`, and `train` models are compared. The code is not shown as part of an interactive session, so the > prompts are not present.

```
# actual vs predicted lines for fitted lm model
lines(xpreds$x,ypreds,xlab = "x", ylab = "y")

# actual vs predicted lines for fitted mlegp model
lines(xpreds,ypreds,xlab = "x", ylab = "y")

# actual vs predicted lines for CV fitted gaussprRadial model
lines(xpreds$x,ypreds,xlab = "x", ylab = "y")
```

An example GP model and prediction using R

Consider the data set shown in Figure 5.3. The actual data entered in R is shown as follows.

```
> x = 1:20
> y = as.vector(c(1,2,3.5,5,6,6.5,7,6.5,5.5,4,2,1.5,1.3,
                          1.4,1.6,1.9,2.2,2.3,2.1,1.0))
> myData = data.frame(y,x)
>
```

Remember that when using GP under `train` in caret, the model is described in terms of a data frame, and the usual structure places the dependent variable first. Next, we explore fitting the model and predicting over a large number of values between 1/5 and 20.

Since we want to explore setting the nugget using the MSE from regression, (actually the square root, called sigma), we first fit a quadratic regression model. The code is as follows, and the resulting fit is shown in Figure 5.6. It is not shown as part of an interactive session, so the > prompts are not present.

```
# Linear regression with x^2
LinRegMod = lm(y ~ x + I(x^2), data = myData)
xpreds = data.frame(x=matrix((1:100)/5,100,1))
ypreds = predict(LinRegMod,xpreds)
# actual vs predicted for fitted model
par(family = "serif")
plot(x,y,pch = 20, xlab = "x", ylab = "y")
lines(xpreds$x,ypreds,xlab = "x", ylab = "y")
```

Next, we consider **mlegp** using the MSE for a nugget estimate. The code is not shown as part of an interactive session, so the > prompts are not present. The resulting fit is shown in Figure 5.7.

```
library("mlegp")
sig2Est = (summary(LinRegMod)$sigma)^2
GPmodel = mlegp(x,y,constantMean=1,nugget=sig2Est,
nugget.known=1)
xpreds = matrix((1:100)/5,100,1)
ypreds = predict(GPmodel,xpreds)
# actual vs predicted for fitted model
par(family = "serif")
plot(x,y,pch = 20, xlab = "x", ylab = "y")
lines(xpreds,ypreds,xlab = "x", ylab = "y")
```

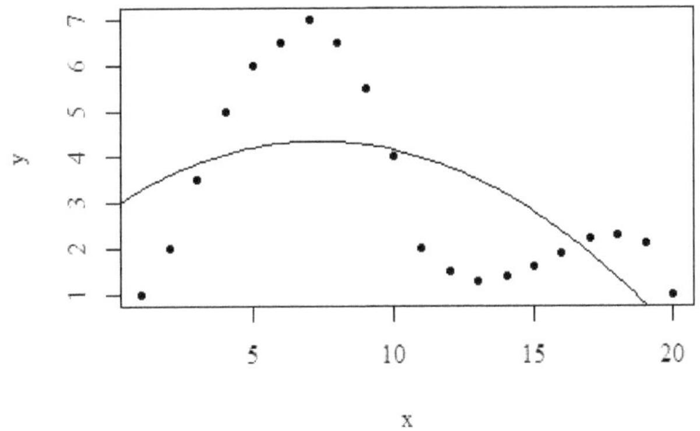

Figure 5.6. Linear regression quadratic model fit is poor.

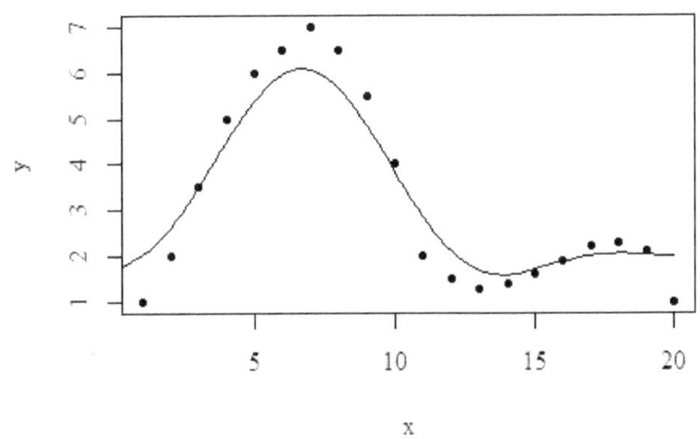

Figure 5.7. GP using `mlegp` with MSE nugget fit is fair.

Because the regression fit is poor, the value of the *MSE* is large, and so the resulting value of `(summary(LinRegMod)$sigma)`^2 is large: about 3. The result is an overly smooth fit. This function has much less variation around a smooth curve. Looking at the vertical distance between adjacent points, it looks like the variability from a smooth curve might be +/− 0.2. Letting this be +/− 2 σ gives $\sigma = 0.1$ or $\sigma^2 = 0.01$. The next fit used a fixed value of `nugget = .01`. The code is not shown as part of an interactive session, so the > prompts are not present. The result is in Figure 5.8. Now, the fit with a small nugget is very good.

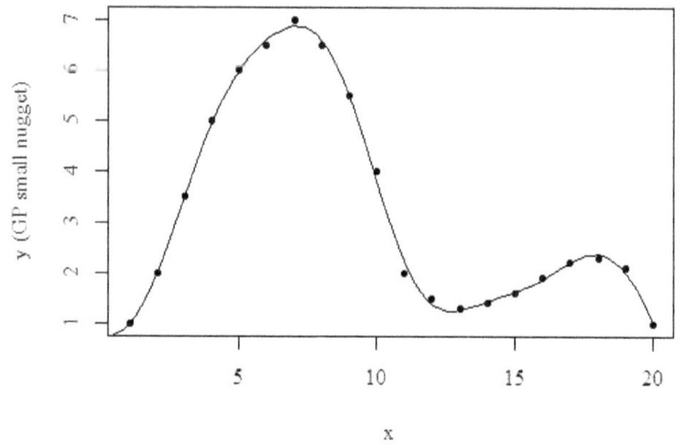

Figure 5.8. GP using **mlegp** with small nugget fit is good.

```
# Gaussian Process fit using mlegp with nugget based MSE
library("mlegp")
sig2Est = (summary(LinRegMod)$sigma)^2
GPmodel = mlegp(x,y,constantMean=1,nugget=sig2Est,
nugget.known=1)
xpreds = matrix((1:100)/5,100,1)
ypreds = predict(GPmodel,xpreds)
# actual vs predicted for fitted model
par(family = "serif")
plot(x,y,pch = 20, xlab = "x", ylab = "y")
lines(xpreds,ypreds,xlab = "x", ylab = "y")
```

Next, we explore the CV GP model fit using `train()` with the `model = gaussprRadial` option. Because this function is nearly deterministic (as evidenced by the very small nugget that gives a good fit), cross-validation will likely produce an inferior fit. The code for fitting `gausspr` via the caret `train` function and plotting predictions is as follows, and the resulting fit is shown in Figure 5.9. The code is not shown as part of an interactive session, so the > prompts are not present.

```
# GP using cv modeling via caret
library(caret)
trainMeth = trainControl(method = "cv", number = 10)
# To specify a nugget, add 'sigma = sigEst,' to train()
sigEst = summary(LinRegMod)$sigma
```

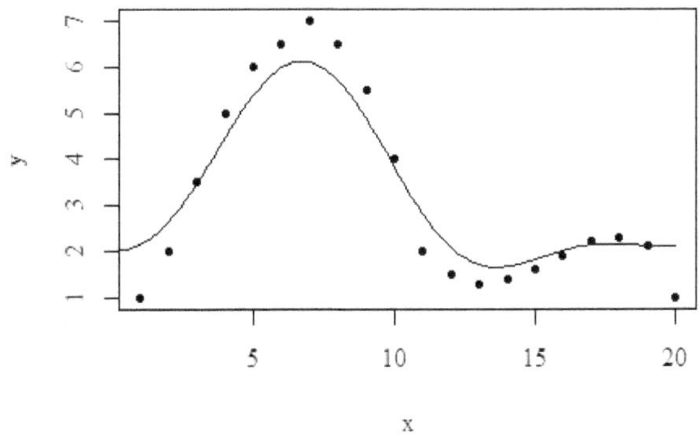

Figure 5.9. GP using **gausspr** in caret **train**.

```
CVgpModel <- train(y ~ x,
data = myData,
method = "gaussprRadial",
trControl = trainMeth)
# Fitting done, do prediction with CVgpModel
xpreds =data.frame(x = (1:100)/5)
ypreds = predict(CVgpModel,xpreds)
par(family = "serif")
plot(x,y,pch = 20, xlab = "x", ylab = "y")
lines(xpreds$x,ypreds,xlab = "x", ylab = "y")
```

The fit in Figure 5.9 is overly smooth. This problem is less severe when fitting data with larger inherent variability.

5.2.5 Life-cycle savings GP model and prediction

In this section, we revisit the Modigliani life-cycle savings model explored in Section 3.3.6 and Chapter 4. Recall that the data set is in the R **datasets** library and consists of observations of five variables for 50 different countries:

- aggregate personal savings rate,
- percent of population under 15 years old,
- percent of population over 75 years old,
- per-capita disposable income, and
- growth rate of disposable income.

The multiple linear regression model developed in Chapter 4 and fitted using the caret `train()` function is shown in the following session:

```
> trainMeth = trainControl(method = "cv", number = 10)
>
> # NOTE: need data = for caret train() function
> CVregModel <- train(sr ~ ddpi + pop15,
                      data = LifeCycleSavings,
+                     method = "lm", trControl = trainMeth)
> CVregModel$finalModel$coefficients
(Intercept)        ddpi       pop15
15.5995758   0.4428302  -0.2163762
# the CV-based RMSE estimate used for prediction intervals
> CVregModel$results$RMSE
[1] 3.873001
> CVregModel$results$RMSESD
[1] 0.9332545
> CVregModel$results$Rsquared
[1] 0.3553619
> CVregModel$results$RsquaredSD
[1] 0.2971349

> new.dat = data.frame(ddpi = 10, pop15 = 35)
> predictVals = predict(CVregModel,new.dat)
> pUpper = predictVals+2*CVregModel$results$RMSE
> pLower = predictVals-2*CVregModel$results$RMSE
>
> print("Approximate Prediction Intervals")
[1] "Approximate Prediction Intervals"
> print(cbind(predictVals,pLower,pUpper))
  predictVals   pLower   pUpper
1    12.45471 5.043567 19.86585
>
```

We compare these results with those of the GP model for prediction, *RMSE*, R^2, and the 95% prediction interval for the CV model fit. Again, a reminder that for CV model fits, the only forecast available is a prediction interval: the 95% likely range for *a future observation* given a particular setting of the predictor variables. A confidence interval would be the 95% likely range for *the average of all possible future observations* given a particular setting of the predictor variables. The latter are not available with cross-validation modeling using `train()`.

Because we had a single predictor variable in the previous example, we did not scale it to ±1. But for regression with multiple variables and a nonlinear response, it is necessary to scale the predictor variables to ± 1. That step is done first for the GP regression, and after scaling, the new data must be declared a data frame or the method fails. Second, when predicting for a new value of the predictor variables, the vector in its original scaling must also be converted to ± 1. That is done using the original predictor values to set the scale. It requires a new function: `scalpm1_only1`. The following is the code and results of the GP model fit and forecast.

```
> # Redo model using GP (gausspr)
> # Scaling important for ML models - create scaled data frame
> sLifeCycleSavings = NULL
> scalpm1 = function(x){(x-(min(x)+max(x))/2)/
                        (.5*(max(x)-min(x)))}
> sLifeCycleSavings$sr = LifeCycleSavings$sr
> sLifeCycleSavings$sdpi = scalpm1(LifeCycleSavings$dpi)
> sLifeCycleSavings$sddpi = scalpm1(LifeCycleSavings$ddpi)
> sLifeCycleSavings$spop15 = scalpm1(LifeCycleSavings$pop15)
> sLifeCycleSavings$spop75 = scalpm1(LifeCycleSavings$pop75)
> sLifeCycleSavings = as.data.frame(sLifeCycleSavings)
>
> trainMeth = trainControl(method = "cv", number = 10)
>
> # NOTE: need data = for caret train() function
> # NOTE: sigma = is optional
> CVgpModel <- train(sr ~ sdpi + sddpi + spop15 + spop75,
+                    data = sLifeCycleSavings,
+                    method = "gausspr Radial",
+                    scaled = FALSE,
+                    trControl = trainMeth)

>
> #CVgpModel$results$thetas # this DOES NOT WORK
> #   fitted theta model parameters not informative
> CVgpModel$results$sigma # the estimated nugget for best fit
[1] 0.5803128
> # the CV-based RMSE estimate used for prediction intervals
> CVgpModel$results$RMSE
[1] 4.058122
> CVgpModel$results$RMSESD
[1] 1.132456
> CVgpModel$results$Rsquared
[1] 0.2818378
> CVgpModel$results$RsquaredSD
[1] 0.2928297

> # Now new.dat must be in scaled units, and uses all predictors,
> #   so others set to midrange.
> sdpi0 = 0 # not specified in new.dat, just set to mid range
> spop750 = 0 # not specified in new.dat, just set to mid range
```

```
> scalpm1_only1 = function(x0,x)
                  {(x0-(min(x)+max(x))/2)/(.5*(max(x)-min(x)))}
> sddpi0 = scalpm1_only1(10,LifeCycleSavings$ddpi)
> spop150 = scalpm1_only1(35,LifeCycleSavings$pop15)
> snew.dat = data.frame(sdpi = sdpi0,sddpi=sddpi0,spop15=spop150,
                        spop75=spop750)
> predictVals = predict(CVgpModel,snew.dat)
> pUpper = predictVals+2*CVgpModel$results$RMSE
> pLower = predictVals-2*CVgpModel$results$RMSE
>
> print("Approximate Prediction Intervals")
[1] "Approximate Prediction Intervals"
> print(cbind(predictVals,pLower,pUpper))
predictVals      pLower    pUpper
[1,]     7.887547  -0.6333839  16.40848
>
```

A comparison of the caret results for model predictive power and predictive uncertainty using regression (from Chapter 4) and the GP regression is shown in Table 5.1.

It appears that the added nonlinearity capability of GP resulted in consistent overfitting — perhaps trying to fit the few outliers mentioned in Chapter 4. The result is a lower R^2, a higher *RMSE*, and a larger prediction interval. The simpler linear regression with cross-validation to properly capture the outlier impact has smaller prediction uncertainty; this suggests that the relationship (as proposed by Modigliani) is indeed linear (more justification for the Nobel Prize!). In this case, where the response is really a linear function, the nonlinear flexibility provided by GP models leads to harmful overfitting.

Table 5.1. A comparison of `lm()` and `train()` results.

Quantity	`lm()` **result**	`gausspr()` **result**
R^2	0.4204	0.2818
s.d.(R^2)	0.3362	0.2928
$RMSE$	3.690	4.058
s.d.($RMSE$)	1.542	1.132
Prediction	12.45	10.12
Lower PI	5.074	2.007
Upper PI	19.83	18.24

Key lesson: For regression with observational data in the *data-adaptive research* paradigm, it is wise to first try a multiple linear regression fit with only linear terms, evaluated via cross-validation. Then, more complex nonlinear regression models should only be adopted if there is significant improvement in R^2, *RMSE*, and prediction intervals.

Note that, as part of cross-validation modeling, diagnostic plots are also important. Even for the GP model, it is important to show the predicted vs. actual and residuals plots. Residuals with caret are computed separately using the prediction results. Here is the session generating the key plots for the GP model using caret's `train()` function.

```
> # Create predicted values at existing data points
> predictValCVgp = predict(CVgpModel,sLifeCycleSavings[2:5])
> # plot actual vs predicted
> plot(predictValCVgp,sLifeCycleSavings[,1],
+      xlab = "Predicted Savings Rate",
+      ylab = "Actual Savings Rate")
>
> # Must create residuals manually (actual-predicted)
> residValCVgp = sLifeCycleSavings[,1] - predictValCVgp
> acf(residValCVgp)
> qqnorm(residValCVgp)
> plot(LifeCycleSavings$dpi,residValCVgp)
> plot(LifeCycleSavings$ddpi,residValCVgp)
> plot(LifeCycleSavings$pop15,residValCVgp)
> plot(LifeCycleSavings$pop75,residValCVgp)
>
```

5.2.6 Strengths and weaknesses of GP regression

GP regression provides many advantages. As we have seen, it is very flexible and can fit any smoothly varying response function. Multiple packages are available in R. Using these packages, it is easy and computationally fast to fit (train) a model and make predictions with prediction uncertainty based on the model form.

On the other hand, there are three weaknesses. First, the method suffers from a phenomenon named "mean reversion." Figure 5.10 illustrates the phenomenon for an extreme prediction relative to observed x values. When the predictor value is far from any of the values in the training set, the resulting prediction will just be the

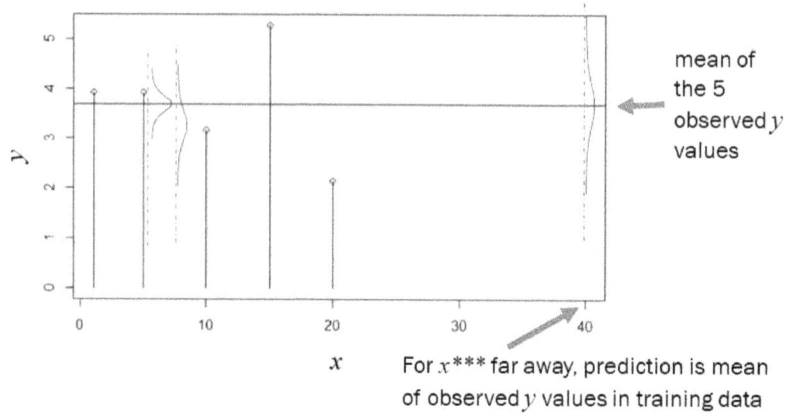

Figure 5.10. GP models predict the mean for x far from training data.

mean of the entire set of training y values. To summarize, *GP models can suffer from mean reversion.*

This is related to the second problem. The rate of mean reversion depends on the value of the *nugget.* A zero nugget provides a smooth interpolation of the observed y values but has rapid mean reversion. A large nugget gives a more slowly varying approximation that does not pass through each y value and is slower to revert to the mean. Figure 5.11 from Erickson *et al.* (2018) shows fitted GP predictions from three different GP software packages: DiceKriging, laGP, and mlegp. What differs is not their method, but the default value for the nugget. The method labeled "mlegpE" is similar to the method in mlegp, but allows the software to automatically estimate (E) the nugget. Perhaps it was chosen as zero — the authors do not mention it. The result is a rapid mean reversion between observed values and a useless approximation. The method labeled "laGPE" is similar to the method in laGP, but allows the software to automatically estimate (E) the nugget. The automatic nugget choice in this case resulted in a very good fit with no evidence of mean reversion between points. The version of DiceKriging used had Gaussian spatial correlation representation (there are others), and so it was called "Dice2." The authors state that this software chose the smallest nugget that would make the parameter estimation numerically stable. This apparently was a large nugget since the response is over-smoothed and again does not approximate the data very well. To summarize the second

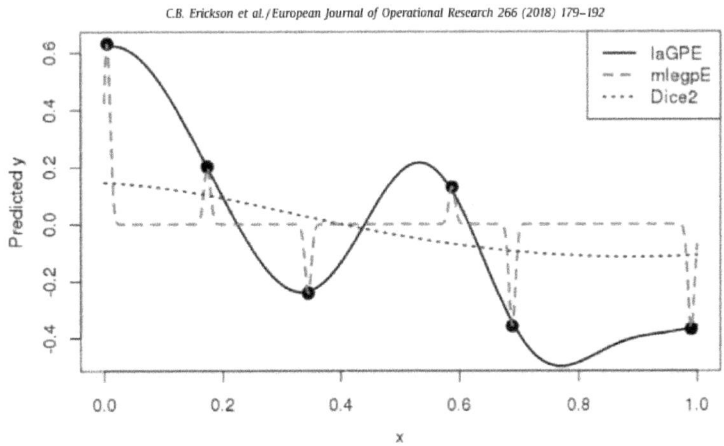

Figure 5.11. GP models predict the mean for x far from training data (Erickson *et al.*, 2018).

problem: *regardless of the GP software chosen, the nugget must be chosen carefully to balance close fit against rapid mean reversion.* Fortunately, most GP regression methods in R offer an automatic nugget estimation that is reasonably good.

Third, as we saw in the life-cycle savings example, if the underlying relationship is truly linear, the overfitting of the GP model will be correctly characterized by the cross-validation results. To summarize, *GP models will overfit simple linear relationships, resulting in R^2, RMSE, and prediction intervals that are inferior to linear regression.*

5.3 Neural Network Regression

When nonlinear regression models are called for, neural network regression is an option. Neural networks have become very popular in analytics and are typically what people are thinking of when they refer to "machine learning" or "deep learning." In this section, we learn a bit about their history, show the mathematical and graphical form, and describe the practical strengths and weaknesses. The implementation using the caret `train()` function is illustrated for the two examples covered in the earlier sections.

5.3.1 History of neural network modeling

The history of artificial neural networks is almost as long as that of GP models. Bernard Widrow and Marcian Hoff developed computer models called "ADALINE" and "MADALINE" while at Stanford University in 1959. The names are acronyms: MADALINE is Multiple ADAptive LINear Elements. ADALINE was designed to predict the next bit in a string of bits from a digital signal. MADALINE was used to identify and filter echoes from digitized audio transmissions. These networks consisted of sequences of connected processing nodes that were often called *perceptrons.*

Neural networks are attractive for nonlinear regression for the same reason as GP models. They can approximate any smoothly varying response function. Kurt Hornik, Maxwell Stinchcombe, and Halbert White showed in 1989 that multilayer feed-forward networks with as few as one hidden layer are universal approximators (Hornik *et al.*, 1989).

5.3.2 The intuition behind neural network prediction

The intuition behind neural network models is quite different from that for GP models. The initial concept was to mimic the "firing" of neurons in animal brains. The computational model for a single neuron (perceptron) is shown in Figure 5.12. Numeric inputs to the neuron (typically from the output of other neurons) are combined in a weighted sum. That sum is used as the argument for a nonlinear threshold function called an *activation function.* A commonly used activation function is $g(x) = 1/(1+e^{-x})$, which is called the *sigmoid* function. It is shown at the lower right of the figure.

Each node takes as input x (a weighted sum of previous node outputs) and produces $g(x)$, often called a_i for the ith node. Nodes are usually arranged in vertical groups, with input nodes on the far left and output nodes on the far right. For regression, there is a single output node. When neural networks are used for classification, there are often multiple nodes in the output layer, one for each value of the class variable. Each vertical group is called a *layer.* For ordinary *feedforward* neural networks, links go from left to right, from nodes in one layer to nodes in the next layer. More complex link structures exist for *recurrent* and *recursive* networks.

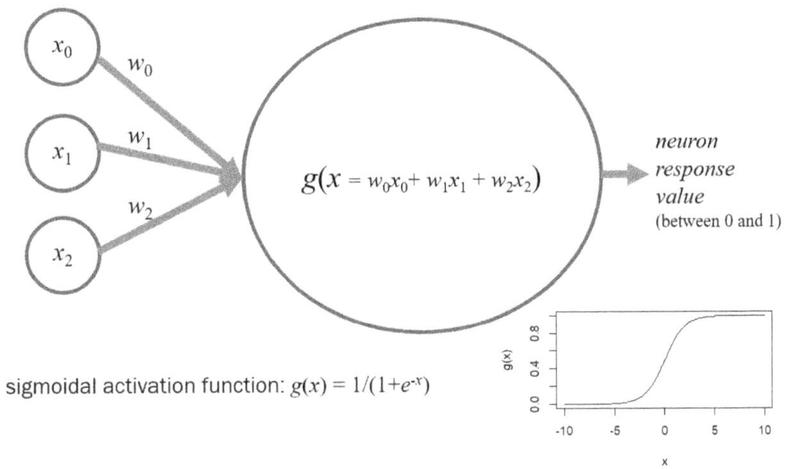

Figure 5.12. Computational model of a neuron.

Although the form of the activation function could be different for each node (neuron), it is typically kept the same. The one exception is for the output node when using a neural network for regression modeling. Usual activation functions such as that in Figure 5.12 produce values between 0 and 1, and so if the response variable is not scaled to $[0, 1]$, then the output node activation function would need to be different. In this case, a linear activation function is used: $g(x) = x$.

5.3.3 Form of the neural network model

How does neural network fitting and prediction work? It is easier to understand visually for a method that we already understand: linear regression. Figure 5.13 shows a neural network representation for multiple linear regression with two predictor variables, x_1 and x_2. This simple regression example shows the neural network computational structure. Inputs are combined as a weighted sum at a node, and the output is the activation function applied to this weighted sum. In this case, the activation function is simple: $g(x) = x$.

While Figure 5.13 shows a neural network representation for the regression model, Figure 5.14 shows the same figure but using typical neural network model notation: bs replaced by ws, with the activation function represented as $g(x)$. Neural networks always have nodes

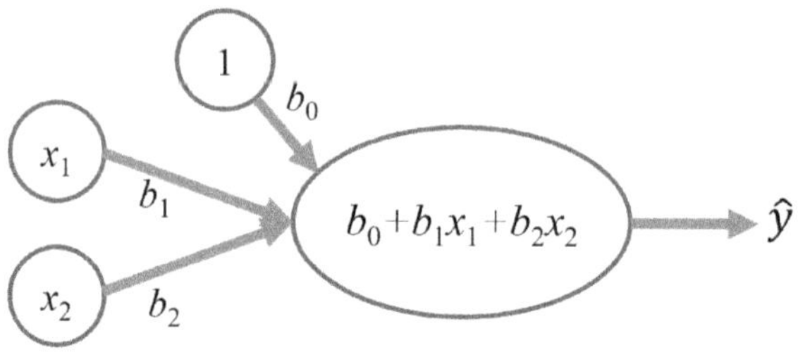

Figure 5.13. Multiple regression in a neural network representation.

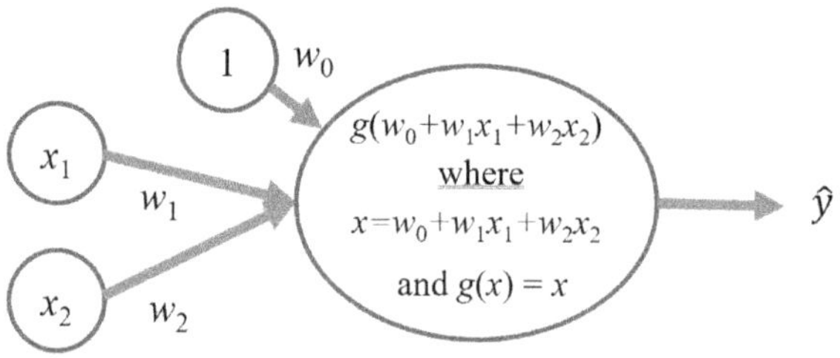

Figure 5.14. Multiple regression in a neural network representation.

equivalent to the b_0 (intercept) node. They occur for every node at every layer of the network and are called *bias nodes* — here, w_0. If you think of the output of a node (neuron) as *activated* or *on* when the value is near 1, then bias nodes are always *on*: their value is always 1.

Figure 5.15 shows a computational representation for a more complex neural network model from Ramasamy *et al.* (2021). In the figure, the general argument of the activation functions is called θ rather than x, and the bias nodes are not shown but represented by the b_j values in the formulas above each layer. For this example, the hidden and final nodes use different activation functions: f and g. For regression, it is often the case that the activation function for the final node is just the identity: $g(x) = x$.

The mathematical form for the neural network regression model in Figure 5.15 is written by simply nesting the models from each layer. Since there is no underlying theory for the form and it is just trying to *learn* the response function, the w values are best estimates. There are no Greek letter equivalents used in neural network modeling. So, the left-hand side of the equation will be $\hat{y}$, not y. For this example,

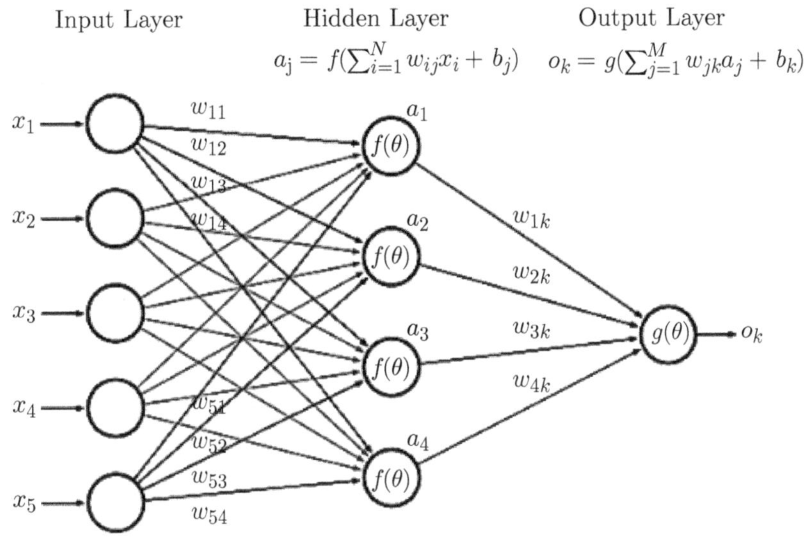

Figure 5.15. A general single hidden layer neural network representation (from Ramasamy *et al.*, 2021) under Creative Commons Attribution 4.0 International Public License.

if $g(\theta) = \theta$ (as expected for a regression application), writing the bias terms b_j as w_{0j} and the output node bias as w_{0k}, the complete mathematical representation analogous to the GP prediction equation in (5.8) is shown in Equation (5.9):

$$\hat{y}(x^*) = \sum_{j=0}^{M} w_{jk} g\left(\sum_{i=0}^{N} w_{ij} x_i\right). \tag{5.9}$$

It is important to understand that the g function result in the equation is *different* for each value of the index j.

5.3.4 Choosing weights for the neural network model

How do we find the weights $\{w_{ij}\}$ and $\{w_{jk}\}$ for the model in Equation (5.9)? There is good news and bad news for the answer. First, the good news: similarly to multiple linear regression, the w values are found using *least squares*, that is, minimizing *SSE*, where $SSE = \sum_{i=1}^{n}(y - \hat{y})^2$. The bad news: unlike multiple linear regression, this cannot be solved by a bit of linear algebra; it is a nasty nonlinear optimization problem. Given a starting set of w values, the partial derivative of *SSE* with respect to each w coefficient is computed. This is a gradient vector; to minimize *SSE*, a sequence of steps in the negative gradient direction leads to new values of w (a vector), and new gradient values are computed at the new w. An efficient iterative method computes gradient elements hierarchically using the *chain rule* from calculus. This method is called *backpropagation*. When used in a gradient-step optimization approach, it is not an efficient method and has similar problems to the gradient descent method, which we discuss in the following section.

5.3.5 Neural network regression using R

There are a number of different packages that provide neural network regression in R. Many model types can be fitted using the `caret train()` function; see Chapter 7 of the caret online manual (Kuhn, 2019). These include:

- `nnet` (single hidden layer good; robust),
- `avNNet` (based on nnet; good),
- `deepnet` (command `dnn`; quite good but `nnet` preferred by Mahdi *et al.* (2022)),
- `neuralnet` (good for classification, less so for regression),
- `mlp` (has multiple hidden layers, and you specify total nodes), and
- `mlpML` (has multiple layers, and you specify nodes in layers 1, 2, 3).

This discussion focuses on two of these methods: `neuralnet` and `nnet`. For regression, Mahdi *et al.* (2022) found `nnet` to give superior performance. While `neuralnet` works well for classification problems (we revisit it in Part II), it is difficult to fit for regression applications. Before we illustrate this, we need to explain a bit more about the fitting mechanism.

It is important to see how the gradient descent search process can fail because, in practice, the software may fit w values using a gradient-based method and can fail to fit a model — or in some cases, just predict a constant response! This is especially a problem for neural networks in a regression setting. Figure 5.16 shows a well-behaved *SSE* function, with a starting point in $\{w_1, w_2\}$ space at the base of the thin arrow with box attached. The minimum value is the

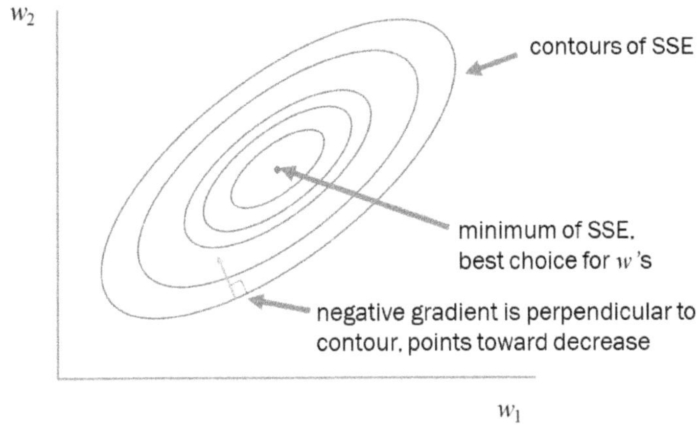

Figure 5.16. Negative gradient and contours of SSE surface as function of w_1, w_2.

dot at the center, the values for $\{w_1, w_2\}$ that would provide the best fit. The direction of steepest descent is the negative gradient, which is always perpendicular to the *SSE* function contour lines.

The search for better$\{w_1, w_2\}$ values would proceed in this direction. The size of the step must be chosen at each iteration. If the step size chosen is too large, the search will oscillate around the optimal value and fail to find a good $\{w_1, w_2\}$ value. This is illustrated in Figure 5.17. This issue can be addressed by reducing the step size each time by some factor less than one. The initial size is specified by `learningrate` for the `neuralnet` method, and the rate of decrease is specified by `learningrate.factor`. These only apply when the fitting method chosen is backpropagation: `algorithm = 'backprop'`.

But problems can still occur if the step size is too small or is reduced too quickly. There are two possible difficulties. First, the search process will not continue indefinitely, and one typically specifies a maximum number of steps (`stepmax` for neuralnet; `maxit` for nnet). With a small step size, the search may reach the maximum number of steps before coming close to the minimum. This is shown in Figure 5.18. Alternatively, the function may be less well behaved and have several local minima. A shorter initial step size is more likely to lead to a minimum that is nearby, not necessarily a very low *SSE* value. That situation is shown in Figure 5.19.

More sophisticated search methods approximate both the first and second derivatives, making searches on the examples above very

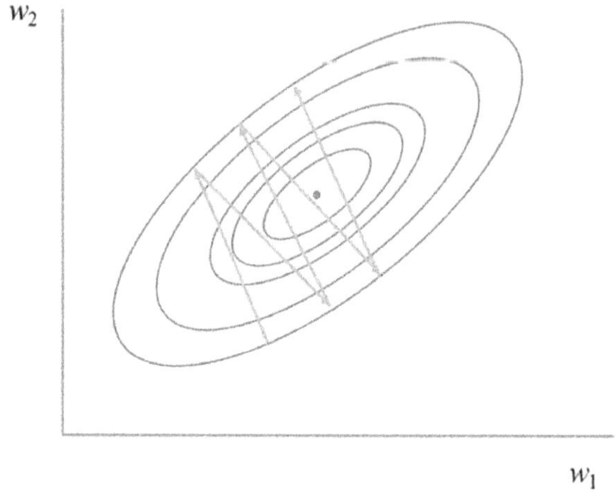

Figure 5.17. Negative gradient search with large step fails to find good $\{w_1, w_2\}$ value.

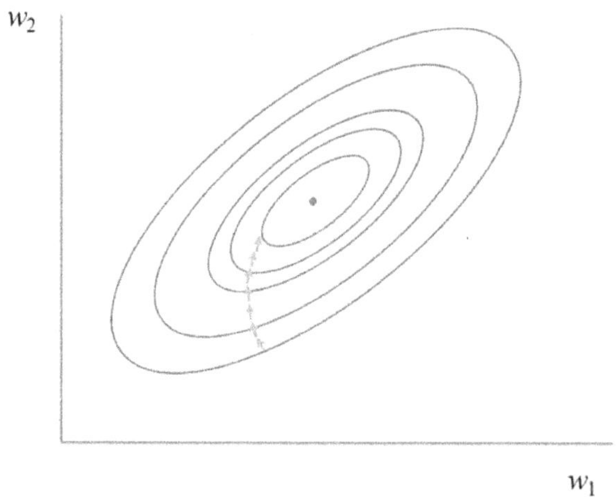

Figure 5.18. Negative gradient search with small step but not enough steps to find good $\{w_1, w_2\}$ value.

efficient. The nnet routine uses such an approach and is relatively robust. Unfortunately, the real contours of most neural network regression *SSE* functions are more complex, with many local minima, and even nnet can fail to find good weight values and return "NA" rather than a solution.

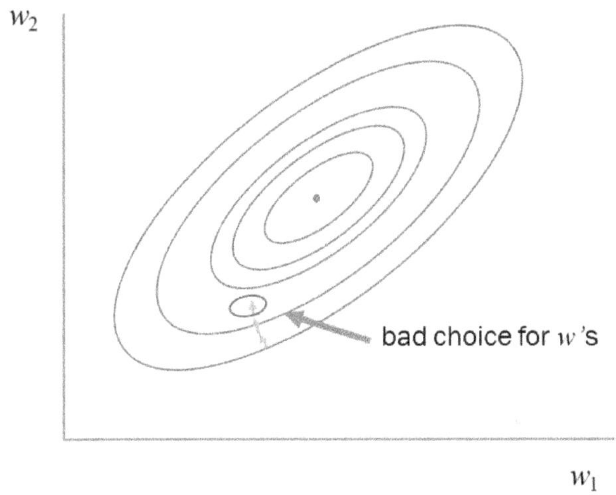

Figure 5.19. Negative gradient search with small step finds local minimum with inferior $\{w_1, w_2\}$ value.

An example neural network model and prediction using R

Consider again the data set shown in Figure 5.3. The actual data coded in R is shown as follows.

```
x = 1:20
y = as.vector(c(1,2,3.5,5,6,6.5,7,6.5,5.5,4,2,1.5,1.3,
                 1.4,1.6,1.9,2.2,2.3,2.1,1.0))
myData = data.frame(y,x)
```

Remember that when using regression models under **train** in caret, the model is described in terms of a data frame, and the usual structure places the dependent variable first. Next, we explore neural network regression fitting, and predicting for a large number of values between 1/5 and 20. This is done using both `method = 'nnet'` and `method = 'neuralnet'`.

The codes for fitting take different arguments and are thus shown separately in the following. The code is not shown as part of an interactive session, so the > prompts are not present. Note also that it is important in this case to scale the predictor variable x to $+/-$ 1, so the `scalpm1()` function is used, and `sx` is used as the predictor variable.

```
# Scaling predictor using scalpm1
scalpm1 = function(x){(x-(min(x)+max(x))/2)/
                      (.5*(max(x)-min(x)))}
myData$sx = scalpm1(myData$x)

# Fitting neural network with caret using nnet
CVnnModel <- train(y ~ sx,
                   data = myData,
                   method = "nnet",
                   trace = F,
                   trControl = trainMeth,
                   linout = TRUE)

# Fitting neural network with caret using nnet
CVnnModel <- train(y ~ sx,
                   data = myData,
                   method = "neuralnet",
                   threshold = .1,
                   trControl = trainMeth,
                   linear.output = TRUE)
```

The key differences between `nnet` and `neuralnet` are as follows: (i) step-by-step updates need to be suppressed with the `nnet` method via `trace = F`; and (ii) the `neuralnet` method runs very long if the stopping threshold for *SSE* improvement is not set to a fairly large fraction, e.g., `threshold =.1` or `.01`. The full code is in the last section of this chapter.

Figure 5.20 compares the performance of the fitted models with two versions of GP regression from Section 5.2: with a small nugget, and with the `mlegp` automatically chosen nugget. Both neural network approximations capture much of the response shape, but there are significant errors in prediction on the right side. Only the small nugget GP model performs well there. Remember, in higher dimensions, the quality of fit can only be judged by the *RMSE*, the R^2, and the actual vs. predicted plot.

5.3.6 Life-cycle savings neural network model and prediction

In this section, we revisit the Modigliani life-cycle savings model explored in Section 3.3.6, Chapter 4, and in the previous section on GP regression. The fitting and prediction commands are very similar

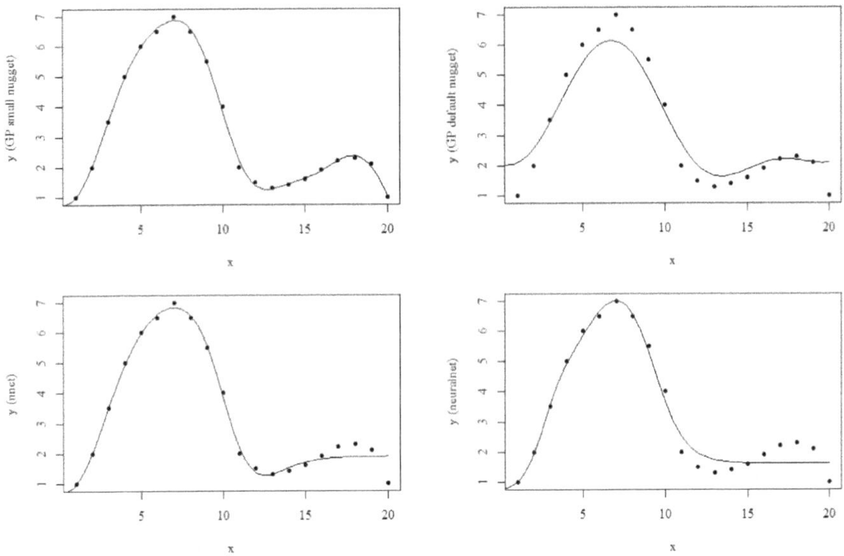

Figure 5.20. A comparison of GP and neural network models on a nonlinear function.

to those for the GP **gaussprRadial** model shown in the previous section. The code is not shown as part of an interactive session, so the > prompts are not present. Full details of the code are in Section 5.6.

```
# caret model using nnet
CVnnModel <- train(sr ~ sdpi + sddpi + spop15 + spop75,
data = sLifeCycleSavings,
method = "nnet",
trace = F,
trControl = trainMeth,
linout = TRUE)

#c caret model using neuralnet
CVnnModel <- train(sr ~ sdpi + sddpi + spop15 + spop75,
data = sLifeCycleSavings,
method = "neuralnet",
threshold = .1,
trControl = trainMeth,
linear.output = TRUE)
```

There are also important changes in recovering *RMSE* and R^2. The cross-validation `train()` procedure considered different network topologies, so the results contain several different models. It is necessary to select the index of the best model (in terms of *RMSE*) when reporting results. The following code shows how this is done: finding the index of the model with the lowest *RMSE* and using that index (**minIndex**) to reference **RMSESD**, **R-squared**, and **R-squaredSD**. The code is not shown as part of an interactive session, so the > prompts are not present.

```
CVnnRMSE = min(CVnnModel$results["RMSE"],na.rm=TRUE)
CVnnRMSE

minIndex = which(CVnnModel$results["RMSE"] ==
min(CVnnModel$results["RMSE"],na.rm=TRUE))

CVnnRsquared = CVnnModel$results[,"Rsquared"][minIndex]
CVnnRsquared

CvnnRMSESD = CVnnModel$results[,"RMSESD"][minIndex]
CVnnRMSESD

CVnnRsquaredSD = CVnnModel$results[,"RsquaredSD"][minIndex]
CVnnRsquaredSD
```

While the variable importance plot gives some insight on how the model uses the predictor variables, there is a special package that will plot a neural network model created by **nnet**. The edges are black for positive weights, gray for negative weights, and thick for the weights of greater magnitude. Figure 5.21 shows the plot for the Modigliani data fitted with **nnet**. Clearly, the pop15 variable drives the prediction, with a negative weight.

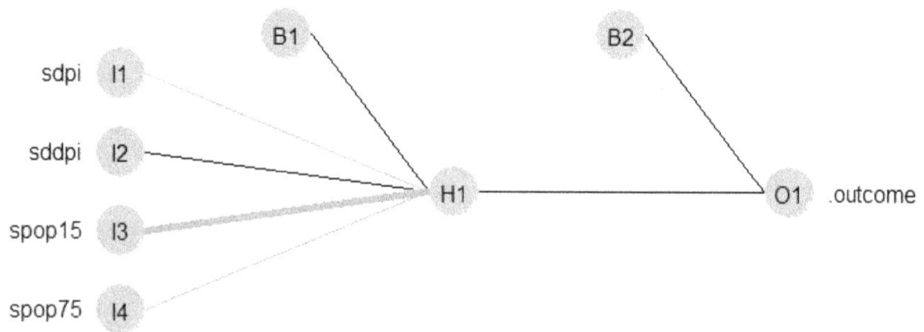

Figure 5.21. Fitted neural network (**nnet**) for the Modigliani data.

Fitting using **nnet** gives easy access to a detailed list of link weights and the network architecture. The session commands and results are shown as follows.

```
> # Get network weights and network structure
> print(CVnnModel$finalModel$wts)
[1] 5.971843 -10.605392 15.407398 -51.576351 -13.173896 7.051157
[7] 5.339793
> print(CVnnModel$finalModel$n)
[1] 4 1 1
>
```

The list (4 1 1) indicates four input nodes, one hidden node, and one output node. The weights are listed in order from top to bottom on the left of the network in Figure 5.21 and then moving right. For example, the first weight of 5.971843 is for the link from B1 to H1 in Figure 5.21; the weight −51.576351 is for the link from I3 to H1.

Table 5.2 augments Table 5.1 to provide a comparison of caret `train()` fits to the Modigliani data for three methods: multiple linear regression, GP regression, and neural network regression. Both **nnet** and **neuralnet** neural network methods are included.

In this augmented table, the neural network model **nnet** provides comparable performance to linear regression, with slightly higher R^2 (good) and slightly higher $RMSE$ (bad). Multiple linear regression remains the best performer because the relationship is approximately linear. Further, the multiple linear regression coefficients are interpretable. The remarks at the end of Section 5.2.5 bear repeating.

Key lesson: For regression with observational data in the *data-adaptive research* paradigm, it is wise to first try a multiple linear regression fit with only linear terms, evaluated via cross-validation.

Table 5.2. A comparison of `lm()` and `train()` results.

Quantity	`lm` **result**	`gausspr` **result**	`nnet` **result**	`neuralnet` **result**
R^2	0.4204	0.2818	0.4480	0.4178
s.d.(R^2)	0.3362	0.2928	0.2187	0.3437
$RMSE$	3.690	4.058	3.737	3.894
s.d.($RMSE$)	1.542	1.132	1.297	.6821
Prediction	12.45	10.12	12.39	9.772
Lower PI	5.074	2.007	4.913	1.983
Upper PI	19.83	18.24	19.86	17.56

Then, more complex GP or neural network regression models should only be adopted if there is significant improvement in R^2, $RMSE$, and prediction intervals.

5.3.7 Strengths and weaknesses of neural network regression

Like GP regression, neural network regression models offer the advantage of built-in nonlinear fit from the nested weighted combination of nonlinear activation functions. Neural network models can fit complex shapes. Further, with multiple output nodes, they can fit multiple response variables simultaneously. The models have great flexibility in the number of layers, number of nodes per layer, and layer interconnections.

But neural network regression has weaknesses as well. There is no underlying statistical or physical model justification, which make prediction quality assessment totally dependent on cross-validation. Strangely, it is difficult, sometimes impossible, to fit simple responses, such as linear responses. It is also difficult to fit responses with large random variation, and prediction intervals are complex for stochastic response functions, which are beyond the scope of this text. Finally, neural network models can take extensive computing time to fit, and sometimes the fitting process fails. This issue is compounded by the need for multiple fits in order to conduct a cross-validation assessment of model predictive error.

5.4 The Overall Process for Machine Learning Predictive Analytics

The process for ML regression is set in the *data-adaptive research* paradigm. It matches that for multiple linear regression in Section 4.3. The following is a summary of these steps:

1. Determine the objectives of the predictive model based on managerial needs.
2. Summarize the observational data with a descriptive summary, scatter plots (matrix plot), (perhaps boxplots with qualitative predictors), and discussion.

3. Unless there are nonlinearities apparent in the scatter plots that are beyond the capability of multiple linear regression, first try a multiple linear regression model following the process in Section 4.3. Create dummy indicator variables if you are including qualitative variables as predictors. Show a mathematical presentation with βs and ε, BUT DO NOT INCLUDE the i.i.d. normal statement. Fit the multiple linear regression via k-fold CV using `train()` with $k = 10$. If the resulting regression produces a low R^2 or the validity check residual plots show problematic curvature (see Figure 5.2), then choose a nonlinear ML method for a better fit (for this text, either GP or neural network, but there are others).
4. If warranted, fit the proposed nonlinear ML model via k-fold CV using `train()` with $k = 10$. If the resulting performance in terms of R^2, $RMSE_{k\text{-fold}}$, and prediction interval width is superior to that of the multiple regression model, then adopt the nonlinear ML model.
5. Show and interpret for management the chosen regression model (either ML or linear regression). Use the variable importance plot to identify the important predictor variables. Assess the practical predictive ability with a fitted line plot, $RMSE_{k\text{-fold}}$, and R^2 discussion.
6. Even though we do not expect a theoretical model, do a subset of the diagnostic plots: acf of residuals, residuals vs. predictors, and normal probability plot of residuals.
7. Show and discuss *empirical* forecast prediction intervals for desired configurations x^* by using $RMSE_{k\text{-fold}}$. Describe the resulting prediction intervals in managerial terms, highlighting its empirical nature, without theoretical foundation.
8. Give useful overall managerial summary and recommendation on use of the fitted regression model, with predictions for any key levels of interest to management.

5.5 Case Supporting Chapters 4 and 5

The multi-segment case BostonHousingRegressionPart2 supports the material in Chapters 4 and 5. Multiple linear regression, GP regression, and neural network regression methods are all applied to the

Boston housing data. All analyses are conducted under the *data-adaptive research* paradigm. This case extends over multiple weeks. The case description slides and data can be found online in the BostonHousingRegressionCV folder of Barton (2023).

5.6 R Code Used in Chapter 5

```
# Example response not good for regression ===========

x = 1:20
y = as.vector(c(1,2,3.5,5,6,6.5,7,6.5,5.5,4,2,1.5,1.3,
1.4,1.6,1.9,2.2,2.3,2.1,1.0))
myData = data.frame(y,x)
plot(x,y, pch = 20)

# Linear regression with x^2
LinRegMod = lm(y ~ x + I(x^2), data = myData)
xpreds = data.frame(x=matrix((1:100)/5,100,1))
ypreds = predict(LinRegMod,xpreds)
# actual vs predicted for fitted model
par(family = "serif")
plot(x,y,pch = 20, xlab = "x", ylab = "y (lm)")
lines(xpreds$x,ypreds)

# No scaling of x or y needed with GP models
# GP fit using mlegp with nugget based MSE
library("mlegp")
sig2Est = (summary(LinRegMod)$sigma)^2
GPmodel = mlegp(x,y,constantMean=1,nugget=sig2Est,
nugget.known=1)
xpreds = matrix((1:100)/5,100,1)
ypreds = predict(GPmodel,xpreds)
# actual vs predicted for fitted model
par(family = "serif")
plot(x,y,pch = 20, xlab = "x", ylab = "y (GP lm MSE nugget)")
lines(xpreds,ypreds)


# No scaling of x or y needed with GP models
# GP fit using mlegp with small nugget, 1/2 vertical gap^2
GPmodel = mlegp(x,y,constantMean=1,nugget=.01,
nugget.known=1)
xpreds = matrix((1:100)/5,100,1)
ypreds = predict(GPmodel,xpreds)
# actual vs predicted for fitted model
par(family = "serif")
plot(x,y,pch = 20, xlab = "x", ylab = "y (GP small nugget)")
lines(xpreds,ypreds)
```

```
# for repeatable randomness in caret, use set.seed
set.seed(80111901)
# GP using cv modeling via caret
library(caret)
trainMeth = trainControl(method = "cv", number = 10)
# To specify a nugget, add 'sigma =,' to train()
sigEst = summary(LinRegMod)$sigma
CVgpModel <- train(y ~ x,
data = myData,
method = "gaussprRadial",
trControl = trainMeth)
xpreds =data.frame(x = (1:100)/5)
ypreds = predict(CVgpModel,xpreds)
par(family = "serif")
plot(x,y,pch = 20, xlab = "x", ylab = "y (GP default nugget)")
lines(xpreds$x,ypreds)

# Give prediction at x = 3.5
xpreds =data.frame(x = 3.5)
ypreds = predict(CVgpModel,xpreds)

print("predicted value at x = 3.5")
print(ypreds)

# NN using cv modeling via caret nnet
# Scaling of x variables advised
scalpm1 = function(x){(x-(min(x)+max(x))/2)/(.5*(max(x)-min(x)))}
myData$sx = scalpm1(myData$x)
# For prediction at x = 3.5
scalpm1_only1 = function(x0,x)
                    {(x0-(min(x)+max(x))/2)/(.5*(max(x)-min(x)))}

trainMeth = trainControl(method = "cv", number = 10)
CVnnModel <- train(y ~ sx,
data = myData,
method = "nnet",
trace = F,
trControl = trainMeth,
linout = TRUE)

sxpreds =data.frame(sx = scalpm1((1:100)/5))
ypreds = predict(CVnnModel,sxpreds)
par(family = "serif")
# Note even though model uses sx, can plot against x
#  since they are in the same order as sx
xpreds = data.frame(x = (1:100)/5)
plot(x,y,pch = 20, xlab = "x", ylab = "y (nnet)")
lines(xpreds$x,ypreds)
```

```
# Give prediction at x = 3.5
sxpreds = data.frame(sx = scalpm1_only1(3.5,x))
ypreds = predict(CVnnModel,sxpreds)

print("predicted value at x = 3.5")
print(ypreds)


# NN using cv modeling via caret neuralnet
trainMeth = trainControl(method = "cv", number = 10)
CVnnModel <- train(y ~ sx,
data = myData,
method = "neuralnet",
threshold = .1,
trControl = trainMeth,
linear.output = TRUE)


sxpreds =data.frame(sx = scalpm1((1:100)/5))
ypreds = predict(CVnnModel,sxpreds)
par(family = "serif")
# Note even though model uses sx, can plot against x
#  since they are in the same order as sx
xpreds = data.frame(x = (1:100)/5)
plot(x,y,pch = 20, xlab = "x", ylab = "y (nnet)")
lines(xpreds$x,ypreds)

# Give prediction at x = 3.5
sxpreds = data.frame(sx = scalpm1_only1(3.5,x))
ypreds = predict(CVnnModel,sxpreds)

print("predicted value at x = 3.5")
print(ypreds)




# Modigliani LifeCycleData with lm gausspr nnet
and neuralnet =====

library(datasets)
pairs(LifeCycleSavings)
regModel = lm(sr ~ dpi + ddpi + pop15 + pop75,
data = LifeCycleSavings)
summary(regModel)$coefficients
summary(regModel)$r.squared
library(rms)
vif(regModel)
```

```
# two VIF values > 5, delete largest (pop75)
regModel2 = lm(sr ~ dpi + ddpi + pop15,
               data = LifeCycleSavings)
summary(regModel2)$coefficients
summary(regModel2)$r.squared
library(rms)
vif(regModel2)

# model VIF OK, check validity plots
acf(regModel2$residuals)
plot(regModel2, ask = F, add.smooth = F)
plot(LifeCycleSavings$dpi ,regModel2$residuals)
plot(LifeCycleSavings$ddpi ,regModel2$residuals)
plot(LifeCycleSavings$pop15 ,regModel2$residuals)

# diagnostic plots OK, get model summary
summary(regModel2)

# drop term with highest p-value (dpi at .328)
regModel3 = lm(sr ~ ddpi + pop15, data = LifeCycleSavings)
summary(regModel3)$coefficients
summary(regModel3)$r.squared
vif(regModel3)

# model VIF OK, check validity plots
acf(regModel3$residuals)
plot(regModel3, ask = F, add.smooth = F)
plot(LifeCycleSavings$ddpi ,regModel3$residuals)
plot(LifeCycleSavings$pop15 ,regModel3$residuals)

# diagnostic plots OK, get model summary
summary(regModel3)
summary(regModel3)$coefficients
summary(regModel3)$r.squared
summary(regModel3)$sigma

# give confidence intervals for regression coefficients
confint(regModel3)
# plot actual vs predicted
predModel3 = predict(regModel3,new.data = LifeCycleSavings)
plot(predModel3,LifeCycleSavings[,1],
xlab = "Predicted Savings Rate",
ylab = "Actual Savings Rate")

# predict savings rate for 3% population over 75,
#   35% population under 15, 2000 disposable personal
#   income and 10% rate of change of income
# NOTE: since pop75 and dpi removed from the model, leave
#       them out of prediction dataframe
new.dat = data.frame(ddpi = 10, pop15 = 35)
```

```
predict(regModel3, new.dat, interval = "confidence")
predict(regModel3, new.dat, interval = "prediction")

# Now add on cv to 3rd model
# Cross-validation regression code
# Important for repeatable results to set the
    random number seed -
#   this effects the random split into 10 subsets of data
set.seed(80111973)
library(caret) # needed for cross validation
trainMeth = trainControl(method = "cv", number = 10)


# NOTE: need data = for caret train() function
CVregModel <- train(sr ~ ddpi + pop15, data = LifeCycleSavings,
method = "lm", trControl = trainMeth)


CVregModel$finalModel$coefficients
# The CV-based RMSE estimate used for prediction intervals
CVregModel$results$RMSE
CVregModel$results$RMSESD
CVregModel$results$Rsquared
CVregModel$results$RsquaredSD

# Create predicted values at existing data points
predictValCVreg = predict(CVregModel,LifeCycleSavings[2:5])
# plot actual vs predicted
plot(predictValCVreg,LifeCycleSavings[,1],
xlab = "Predicted Savings Rate",
ylab = "Actual Savings Rate")

# Must create residuals manually (actual-predicted)
residValCVreg = LifeCycleSavings[,1] - predictValCVreg
acf(residValCVreg)
qqnorm(residValCVreg)
plot(LifeCycleSavings$ddpi,residValCVreg)
plot(LifeCycleSavings$pop15,residValCVreg)


CVregModel
CVregModel$resample
plot(varImp(CVregModel, scale = FALSE))



# Constructing approximate confidence intervals from
# a CV-trained model is beyond the scope of this course.
# But constructing approximate prediction intervals is fairly
# easy to do: just use the predicted value +/- 2*sigma_hat and
```

```
# remember that RMSE can be used as sigma_hat, the estimate
# of sigma (for a normal interval we would use 1.96*sigma)
# new.dat from ordinary regression case in Ch 4
predictVals = predict(CVregModel,new.dat)
pUpper = predictVals+2*CVregModel$results$RMSE
pLower = predictVals-2*CVregModel$results$RMSE

print("Approximate Prediction Intervals")
print(cbind(predictVals,pLower,pUpper))

#====================================================
# Redo model using GP (gausspr)
# Scaling important for ML models - create scaled data frame

sLifeCycleSavings = NULL
scalpm1 = function(x){(x-(min(x)+max(x))/2)/(.5*(max(x)-min(x)))}
sLifeCycleSavings$sr = LifeCycleSavings$sr
sLifeCycleSavings$sdpi = scalpm1(LifeCycleSavings$dpi)
sLifeCycleSavings$sddpi = scalpm1(LifeCycleSavings$ddpi)
sLifeCycleSavings$spop15 = scalpm1(LifeCycleSavings$pop15)
sLifeCycleSavings$spop75 = scalpm1(LifeCycleSavings$pop75)
sLifeCycleSavings = as.data.frame(sLifeCycleSavings)

trainMeth = trainControl(method = "cv", number = 10)

library(tictoc)
tic()
# NOTE: need data = for caret train() function
# NOTE: sigma = 3.69 is optional
CVgpModel <- train(sr ~ sdpi + sddpi + spop15 + spop75,
data = sLifeCycleSavings,
method = "gaussprRadial",
scaled = FALSE,
trControl = trainMeth)
toc()

#CVgpModel$results$thetas # this DOES NOT WORK
#   fitted theta model parameters not informative
CVgpModel$results$sigma # the estimated nugget for best fit
# The CV-based RMSE estimate used for prediction intervals
CVgpModel$results$RMSE
CVgpModel$results$RMSESD
CVgpModel$results$Rsquared
CVgpModel$results$RsquaredSD

# Create predicted values at existing data points
predictValCVgp = predict(CVgpModel,sLifeCycleSavings[2:5])
# plot actual vs predicted
plot(predictValCVgp,sLifeCycleSavings[,1],
```

```
xlab = "Predicted Savings Rate",
ylab = "Actual Savings Rate")

# Must create residuals manually (actual-predicted)
residValCVgp = sLifeCycleSavings[,1] - predictValCVgp
acf(residValCVgp)
qqnorm(residValCVgp)
plot(LifeCycleSavings$dpi,residValCVgp)
plot(LifeCycleSavings$ddpi,residValCVgp)
plot(LifeCycleSavings$pop15,residValCVgp)
plot(LifeCycleSavings$pop75,residValCVgp)

CVgpModel$resample
plot(varImp(CVgpModel, scale = FALSE))



# Constructing approximate confidence intervals from
# a CV-trained model is beyond the scope of this course.
# But constructing approximate prediction intervals is fairly
# easy to do: just use the predicted value +/- 2*sigma_hat and
# remember that RMSE can be used as sigma_hat, the estimate
# of sigma (for a normal interval we would use 1.96*sigma)
# Now the new.dat must be in scaled units, and uses
#   all predictors, so others set to midrange.
sdpi0 = 0 # not specified in new.dat, just set to mid range
spop750 = 0 # not specified in new.dat, just set to mid range
# New function to scale one candidate prediction x to +/-1
scalpm1_only1 = function(x0,x)
{(x0-(min(x)+max(x))/2)/(.5*(max(x)-min(x)))}
sddpi0 = scalpm1_only1(10,LifeCycleSavings$ddpi)
spop150 = scalpm1_only1(35,LifeCycleSavings$pop15)
snew.dat = data.frame(sdpi=sdpi0,sddpi=sddpi0,spop15=spop150,
spop75=spop750)
predictVals = predict(CVgpModel,snew.dat)
pUpper = predictVals+2*CVgpModel$results$RMSE
pLower = predictVals-2*CVgpModel$results$RMSE

print("Approximate Prediction Intervals")
print(cbind(predictVals,pLower,pUpper))

#=====================================================
# Redo model using NN (nnet)
# Scaling important for ML models - create scaled data frame
# NOTE: SCLAING HAPPENED ABOVE in the GP SECTION

trainMeth = trainControl(method = "cv", number = 10)

tic()
```

```
# NOTE: need data = for caret train() function
# NOTE: need scaled predictors created above
CVnnModel <- train(sr ~ sdpi + sddpi + spop15 + spop75,
data = sLifeCycleSavings,
method = "nnet",
trace = F,
trControl = trainMeth,
linout = TRUE)
toc()

# Method for finding RMSE and R-squared different from GP or lm
CVnnRMSE = min(CVnnModel$results["RMSE"],na.rm=TRUE)
CVnnRMSE
minIndex = which(CVnnModel$results["RMSE"] ==
min(CVnnModel$results["RMSE"],na.rm=TRUE))
CVnnRsquared = CVnnModel$results[,"Rsquared"][minIndex]
CVnnRsquared

CvnnRMSESD = CVnnModel$results[,"RMSESD"][minIndex]
CvnnRMSESD

CVnnRsquaredSD = CVnnModel$results[,"RsquaredSD"][minIndex]
CVnnRsquaredSD

# Create predicted values at existing data points
predictValCVnn = predict(CVnnModel,sLifeCycleSavings[2:5])
# plot actual vs predicted
plot(predictValCVnn,sLifeCycleSavings[,1],
xlab = "Predicted Savings Rate",
ylab = "Actual Savings Rate")

# Must create residuals manually (actual-predicted)
residValCVnn = sLifeCycleSavings[,1] - predictValCVnn
acf(residValCVnn)
qqnorm(residValCVnn)
plot(LifeCycleSavings$dpi,residValCVnn)
plot(LifeCycleSavings$ddpi,residValCVnn)
plot(LifeCycleSavings$pop15,residValCVnn)
plot(LifeCycleSavings$pop75,residValCVnn)

CVnnModel$resample

# Characterize model with varImp plot and network plot
plot(varImp(CVnnModel, scale = FALSE))
library(devtools) # do install.packages("devtools")
 the first time
source_url('https://gist.githubusercontent.com/fawda123/7471137/
      raw/466c1474d0a505ff044412703516c34f1a4684a5/nnet_plot_
      update.r')
plot.nnet(CVnnModel, nid=T)
```

```
# Get network weights and network structure
print(CVnnModel$finalModel$wts)
print(CVnnModel$finalModel$n)


# As for the GP regression new.dat must be in scaled units,
# and uses all predictors,  so others set to midrange.
# All snew.dat values set above in GP regression analysis.

predictVals = predict(CVnnModel,snew.dat)
pUpper = predictVals+2*CVnnRMSE
pLower = predictVals-2*CVnnRMSE

print("Approximate Prediction Intervals")
print(cbind(predictVals,pLower,pUpper))

#========================================================
# Redo model using NN (neuralnet)
# Scaling important for ML models - create scaled data frame
# NOTE: SCALING HAPPENED ABOVE in the GP SECTION

trainMeth = trainControl(method = "cv", number = 10)

tic()
# NOTE: need data = for caret train() function
# NOTE: need scaled predictors created above
CVnnModel <- train(sr ~ sdpi + sddpi + spop15 + spop75,
data = sLifeCycleSavings,
method = "neuralnet",
threshold = .1,
trControl = trainMeth,
linear.output = TRUE)
toc()

# Method for finding RMSE and R-squared different from GP or lm
CVnnRMSE = min(CVnnModel$results["RMSE"],na.rm=TRUE)
CVnnRMSE
minIndex = which(CVnnModel$results["RMSE"] ==
min(CVnnModel$results["RMSE"],na.rm=TRUE))
CVnnRsquared = CVnnModel$results[,"Rsquared"][minIndex]
CVnnRsquared

CvnnRMSESD = CVnnModel$results[,"RMSESD"][minIndex]
CvnnRMSESD

CVnnRsquaredSD = CVnnModel$results[,"RsquaredSD"][minIndex]
CVnnRsquaredSD
```

```
# Create predicted values at existing data points
predictValCVnn = predict(CVnnModel,sLifeCycleSavings[2:5])
# plot actual vs predicted
plot(predictValCVnn,sLifeCycleSavings[,1],
xlab = "Predicted Savings Rate",
ylab = "Actual Savings Rate")

# Must create residuals manually (actual-predicted)
residValCVnn = sLifeCycleSavings[,1] - predictValCVnn
acf(residValCVnn)
qqnorm(residValCVnn)
plot(LifeCycleSavings$dpi,residValCVnn)
plot(LifeCycleSavings$ddpi,residValCVnn)
plot(LifeCycleSavings$pop15,residValCVnn)
plot(LifeCycleSavings$pop75,residValCVnn)

CVnnModel$resample
# Characterize model with varImp plot and network plot
plot(varImp(CVnnModel, scale = FALSE))



# As for the GP regression new.dat must be in scaled units,
# and uses all predictors, so others set to midrange.
# All snew.dat values set above in GP regression analysis.

predictVals = predict(CVnnModel,snew.dat)
pUpper = predictVals+2*CVnnRMSE
pLower = predictVals-2*CVnnRMSE

print("Approximate Prediction Intervals")
print(cbind(predictVals,pLower,pUpper))
```

Part III

Predicting a Class

Overview

In this part, our focus is on predictive analytics methods for qualitative outcomes. Such predictions (along with characterization of the uncertainty in the prediction) can support many kinds of business decisions: How can I decide whether a customer will likely repay a loan, or should be turned down as a default risk? Which characteristics of my credit card holders help identify whether a particular incentive would result in increased spending on their part? Which blood measurements help identify the presence or absence of COVID-19, and is the predictive accuracy superior to existing antigen rapid tests?

Four methods for predicting a class are presented in the following chapter: two are relatively straightforward, and two are complex. The methods are implemented using R, and their performance is compared for predicting the satisfaction of airline passengers.

Chapter 6

Classification for Predictive Analytics

When an outcome to be predicted is qualitative, such as *pass* vs. *fail*, *disease present* vs. *disease not present*, or *borrower will default* vs. *borrower will not default*, then the appropriate type of analysis is called *classification*, or, sometimes, *machine learning*. The number of classes can be more than two. For example, given a set of symptoms, indicate one of a dozen possible disease types. Or, given counts of certain words in a text, determine what the subject is (to allow an appropriate AI bot response). In this chapter, we explain the purpose of such classifiers, show measures of their imperfect nature, and explain their use for prediction.

6.1 Classification Purpose and Performance

Classification predictive analytics uses the value of predictor variables to identify the likely value of a qualitative dependent or response variable. For a loan default classification, the predictor variables could include individual characteristics, such as age, income over the past three years, occupation, region of residence, marital status, current debt, and environmental characteristics, such as area unemployment rate and recent unemployment rate change, current interest rate, and recent interest rate change. The dependent variable data are qualitative and often represented by two classes: "will not default on loan" and "will default on loan." When the response variable has only two classes, it can be coded as 0 or 1. For the loan default, say "0" means "will not default" and "1" means "will default." But it is often left in character form, usually with "yes" and "no" values.

In R, this means that the response variable in the data frame must have type *factor*. Nonetheless, most classifiers compute an intermediate numerical quantity between zero and one, which we call the *score*. These methods also choose a *threshold*, p_0. For a given set of predictor variable values, if the predicted score is above the threshold, then the predicted class is class 1. If the predicted score is below the threshold, the predicted class is class 0. Often, the score is considered the probability of being in class 1, and so the threshold is often by default set to $p_0 = 0.5$.

When the response variable has more than two class values, it is sometimes left in character form, for example in predicting phone preference based on personal characteristics, the classes might be "iPhone," "Samsung," "Google," and "Other." But multiple class values are most easily accommodated by fitting separate classification models for each possible class outcome. Then, the process would be to fit *four* classification models, with 0–1 variables for each of "is_iPhone," "is_Samsung," "is_Google," and "is_Other." Each model would be fitted to a set of historical data (ideally, the same set used for all the classification models). Again, each fitted (trained) model would have a threshold and would predict a score. If a particular model's predicted score were above the threshold, that class is predicted. In this setting, it is possible that the combined set of classifiers will indicate more than one possible class for this response.

This structuring of multi-class classification into a set of two-class classifiers means that we can focus this chapter on the latter. In the remainder of this chapter, we assume that the classification problem is to model the response as a function of a set of predictor variable values, where the response will be "no" or "yes," or perhaps 0 or 1.

Procedurally, in R, predictor variables must be numeric. So, qualitative predictor variables must be coded using dummy variables, as was done in multiple linear regression. For example, coding "student" as 1 if the loan candidate is a student and 0 if not.

What does one want from a classifier? Good performance means correct classification. Correct classifications mean correctly predicting a case of type 1 and correctly predicting a case of type 0.

Often "1" cases do not occur with the same frequency as "0" cases. Think, for example, of predicting a loan default or a cancer diagnosis. That means that errors in such predictions will occur with unequal frequencies. This complicates the characterization of performance: Do we care about the number of errors or the probability of error? These will not align if the frequencies of class occurrence are not nearly equal. Further, misclassifying a "1" case as a "0" case may have different costs than misclassifying a "0" case as a "1" case. In the loan default example, offering a loan to someone who will default (misclassifying a "1" case as a "0" case) will be much more costly than losing the business of one client (misclassifying a "0" case as a "1" case). This differential cost of misclassifying further complicates performance assessment.

Performance can be checked against two data sets, analogous to regression analysis prediction error (residuals):

- classification errors over the full data set based on a classification model fit to the full data set, or
- classification errors assessed on left-out samples via cross-validation.

For the *data-adaptive research* paradigm that is typical for classification, the latter is more appropriate but is often not the way that performance is assessed in practice. In the numerical examples in Section 6.4, we characterize prediction error both ways for comparison and see that the first approach provides optimistic error characterizations.

6.1.1 Data mining vs. predictive analytics and classification

Classification methods are often set in a *data mining* context. This topic is outside the scope of this text. In contrast with predictive analytics, data mining focuses on learning the relationship between features of an observation and the corresponding response or outcome. Careful characterization of the relationship is the emphasis in data mining, as for the data mining techniques of descriptive statistics and scatter plots.

While the subject of prediction is part of data mining, the emphasis is not on characterizing prediction uncertainty and error. Again, in analogy with scatter plots, in data mining, one fits a line, whereas in predictive analytics, one uses the *traditional research* paradigm or the *data-adaptive research* paradigm to construct prediction uncertainty intervals around a fitted line. Characterizing prediction uncertainty (classification errors) is the focus of this chapter. Because of this overlap, many classification methods are not covered in this chapter. These include support vector machines, genetic algorithms, random forests, and classification trees. These topics appear in many machine learning texts. For a brief overview, see Soofi & Awan (2017).

6.1.2 Classification errors

Since for any specific vector x of predictor variable values, a classification model prediction must be compared with a true value of either 0 or 1, measures such as $RMSE$ and R^2 will not be useful, nor will prediction intervals. Instead, we tally correct and incorrect predictions, either over a training set or over a test set, and use these values to construct a *confusion matrix*, called a *classification matrix* by Evans (2019) and others. This is a tally of correct and incorrect decisions by the classifier.

Figure 6.1 shows a schematic representation for the confusion matrix. The total number of observations is the number of positives (P) plus the number of negatives (N) in the data set that is being classified (either the training set or a test set). The model-predicted

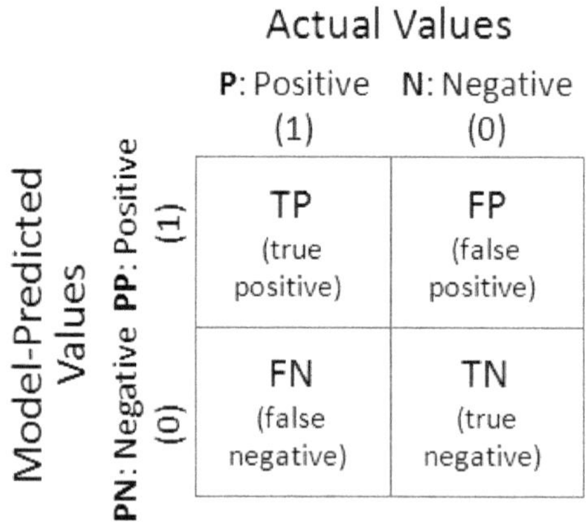

Figure 6.1. The confusion matrix representation.

positives and model-predicted negatives, PP = TP + FP and PN = TN + FN, also sum to the total number of observations in the data set being classified.

For classification error, FP or "false positives" represents the count of observations that were class "0" but were predicted to be "1" by the classification model. Similarly, FN or "false negatives" represents the count of observations that were class "1" but were predicted to be class "0" by the classification model. Correct classification counts are given by "true positive" (TP), and "true negative" (TN) give counts of correct "1" and correct "0" classifications, respectively. While the confusion matrix usually reports counts, there is also a percentage form of the matrix, with each cell holding counts divided by the total number of observations. The percentage form of the confusion matrix is typically provided for classification methods that are fitted via the caret `train()` function.

6.1.3 Classification performance

There are many measures of classifier performance that are based on the confusion matrix. Five common measures of performance are as follows:

- **Accuracy**: (TP + TN)/(P + N) is the overall fraction of correct classifications for the test or train set.
- **Sensitivity**: TP/P is the probability of detection, or, in statistical terms, $1 - \beta$. A high sensitivity means low failure to detect. *sensitivity* is sometimes called *recall.*
- **Specificity**: TN/N is the probability of negative classification of a truly negative class item (1 − false positive or $1 - \alpha$). A high specificity means a low false-alarm rate.
- **Balanced Accuracy**: ((TP/P) + (TN/N))/2 is a better measure than *accuracy*, it averages *sensitivity* and *specificity*, i.e., the detection probabilities for both positive and negative classes.
- **Informedness**: (TP/P) + (TN/N) − 1 gives zero if the sum of sensitivity and specificity is 0.5, and 1 if the classifier is perfect (sensitivity and specificity both 1). It can be computed as (2 × *balanced accuracy*) − 1.

Informedness is an important measure if your data is *imbalanced.* Data imbalance in classification means that the counts for each class are very different. How to measure data imbalance? *Prevalence* = P/(N + P) measures what fraction of the data are in class 1 (are "positive"). Ideally, this would be near 0.5, but in many circumstances it is far below 0.5. For the loan default data for example, the prevalence for default will be low.

There are other measures in addition to these six, but they will not be our focus. *Precision* measures the fraction of positives identified by the classifier that were correctly classified, TP/PP. *Cohen's kappa* (κ) presents an alternate measure of performance in the presence of data imbalance, but it has problems, including the complexity of the formula,

$$\kappa = \frac{2 \times (\mathrm{TP} \times \mathrm{TN} - \mathrm{FN} \times \mathrm{FP})}{(\mathrm{TP} + \mathrm{FP}) \times (\mathrm{FP} + \mathrm{TN}) + (\mathrm{TP} + \mathrm{FN}) \times (\mathrm{FN} + \mathrm{TN})},$$

and the difficulty in explaining what it measures to management. We discuss methods for constructing classifiers in the presence of data imbalance in Section 6.5.

Classification error has an unfortunate name since there are MANY ways to measure classification error, as seen above. This measure gives the percent of incorrect classifications over the test or train set. It is (FP + FN)/(P + N) = 1 − Accuracy. It can also be considered *MSE* for $\{0, 1\}$ classes since the sum of errors (FP + FN, each zero or one) is the same as the sum of squared errors, and the denominator in *MSE* is simply the sample size, P + N.

As discussed above, many classifiers construct a score and then base the classification on whether the score exceeds a specified threshold, usually 0.5. The performance of the classifier depends then on both the fitted classifier model and the chosen threshold.

Confidence intervals for classification performance measures

The three most common performance measures, accuracy, specificity and selectivity, are often expressed as percentages. A single out-of-sample test results in n_0 independent samples. Because across-fold samples are not independent, a conservative confidence interval can be based on the normal approximation to a binomial distribution with $n = n_0$ (sample size of $n_0 = N/10$ for 10-fold cv) and $P =$ the estimated performance measure. That is,

$$\text{Prob}\left(\hat{P} - 1.96\sqrt{\frac{\hat{P}(1-\hat{P})}{n_0}} < P \leq \hat{P} + 1.96\sqrt{\frac{\hat{P}(1-\hat{P})}{n_0}}\right) \sim 0.95, \tag{6.1}$$

where 1.96 is the 0.975-quantile for the standard normal distribution.

For example, suppose the accuracy was estimated as $\hat{A} = 0.72$ and that the 10-fold CV test set sample sizes were $2000/10 = 200$. Then, an approximate 95% confidence interval for A would be

$$\text{Prob}\left(0.72 - 1.96\sqrt{\frac{0.72(0.28)}{200}} < A \leq 0.72 + 1.96\sqrt{\frac{0.72(0.28)}{200}}\right) \sim 0.95, \tag{6.2}$$

which gives the 95% confidence interval for accuracy as $[0.66, 0.78]$.

Most texts suggest that the normal approximation to the binomial is valid if $n_0P > 5$ and $n_0(1-P) > 5$, but some suggest the number should be larger than 20. For our example, $n_0P = 200(0.72) = 144 > 5$ and $n_0(1-P) = 200(0.28) = 56 > 5$.

This interval will be conservative (wider than necessary) since the variance of the accuracy estimate is based on a single fold. It is risky, however, to use a larger value for n_0 because, in addition to variance, cross-validation estimates have bias. This bias tends top underestimate performance (actual accuracy higher) but not always. See Kohavi (1995) to learn more.

6.1.4 The *ROC* curve

There is one additional measure that *will* be of interest to us: the *ROC curve*. It is not a performance measure for a specific classifier but for a family of classifiers parameterized by the threshold value p. This curve got its name, "receiver operating characteristic," from a radar application, where the objective was to detect airplanes with high sensitivity, without a lot of false images (false alarms). In an *ROC* curve, sensitivity (TP/P) is plotted on the y-axis and the false alarm rate (FP/F), i.e., 1 − specificity, on the x-axis, as a function of the threshold value p. It characterizes the model for every possible threshold choice.

This curve would ideally lie above a diagonal line from $(0, 0)$ to $(1, 1)$. Why? Imagine a naive classifier that declares "class 1" randomly with probability p. Then, sensitivity will be p since for any class 1 case, the classifier will declare it class 1 with probability p. However, it will declare any class 0 case to be class 1 with probability p as well — a false alarm rate of p. Thus, the points in the plot are just (p, p), as shown in Figure 6.2. Purely random class guessing is the worst case one might expect for a classifier. One expects ROC curves for useful classifiers to lie well above the diagonal line.

At the other extreme is the perfect classifier, shown in Figure 6.3. Now, the classifier has 100% sensitivity with virtually zero false alarms. In realistic settings, classifier performance in somewhere in between. Figure 6.4 shows a typical pattern, along with perfect and random classifier ROC curves.

How do we associate a numerical measure with the ROC curve? The usual measure is the area under the curve, or *AUC*. As for the ROC, this number does not characterize any specific classifier, only the fitted model. To get the behavior of a specific classifier, one needs to choose a threshold. A given threshold will produce a TP and FP value, and a corresponding TP/P, FP/F point on the ROC curve. Figure 6.5 shows the AUC for the typical ROC in Figure 6.4. One can compare classification methods (not classifiers) by comparing their AUC values. A classification method whose ROC lies entirely above

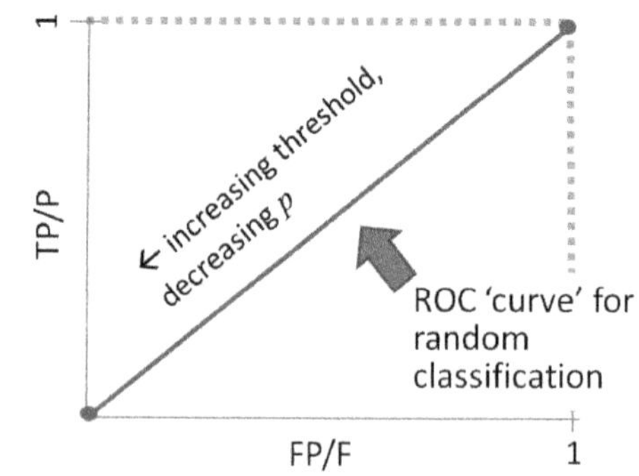

Figure 6.2. The ROC curve for a random classifier.

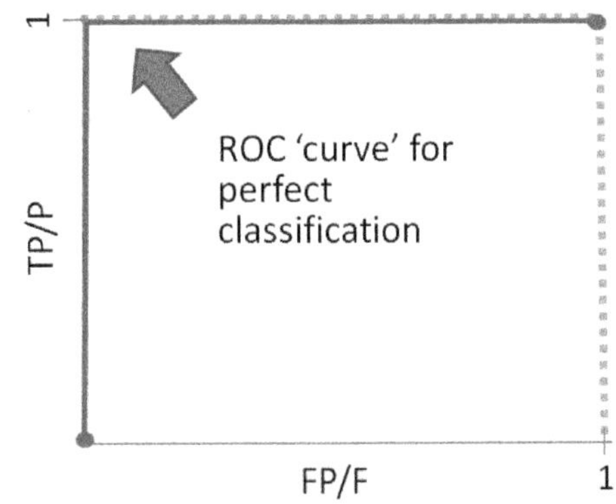

Figure 6.3. The ROC curve for a perfect classifier.

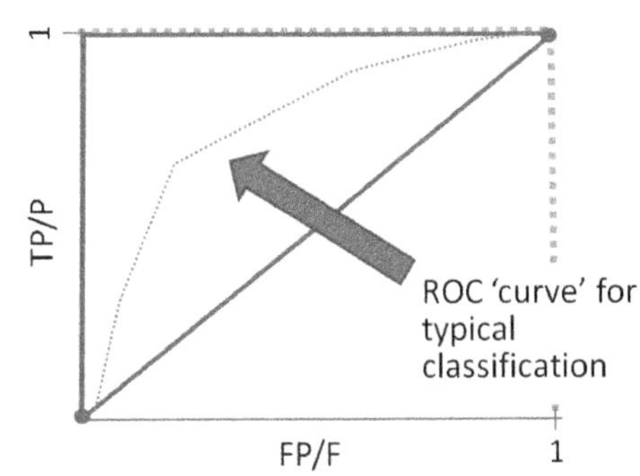

Figure 6.4. ROC curves for random, typical, and perfect classifiers.

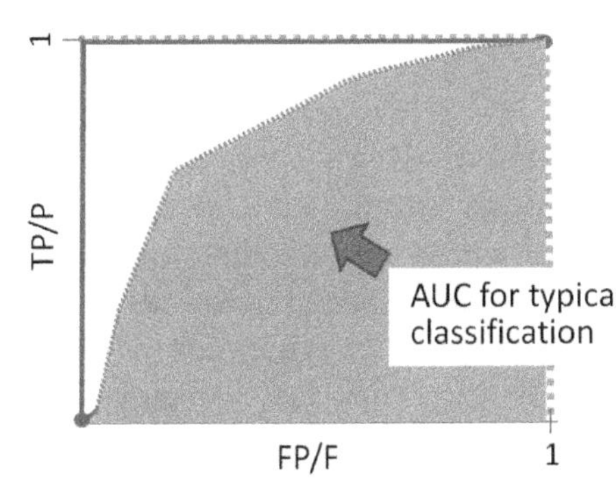

Figure 6.5. AUC (area under curve) for a typical classifier.

a competing method should be preferred. Its AUC will certainly be larger. When two competing methods have ROC curves that cross each other, the decision is not so clear. It depends on where on the curve one wishes to fix their classifier, that is, what threshold they will choose for classifier operation.

6.2 Simple Classification Methods

In this section, the focus is on the two simplest methods for classification: linear discriminant analysis and k-nearest neighbors (k-NN). Linear discriminant analysis is similar to multiple linear regression. The k-NN rule assigns a predicted class based on the class of observations with predictor variable vectors "near" the vector of values of the candidate's predictor variables.

6.2.1 Linear discriminant analysis

A natural strategy that you might think of would be to fit a multiple linear regression model using the 0–1 classification variable as the response variable y. Of course, the normal distribution assumptions would be severely violated since the random Y is either 0 or 1, certainly not normally distributed. In fact, for this setting, it is often the x values rather than the y values that are considered random! Linear discriminant analysis (LDA) looks much like ordinary regression and is erroneously presented that way in some texts (Evans, 2019). How does it work, and what are the similarities to a regression model approach?

For two classes, LDA finds a direction in predictor variable (x) space that simultaneously minimizes the within-class x variability when x points are projected on the line. At the same time, when the vectors of mean predictor variable values within each class are projected on the line, they are as far apart as possible. Remember, x is a vector containing the numerical values for all of the predictor variables.

There is an interpretation for LDA under the *traditional research* paradigm, but the normal distribution assumption applies to the x variables rather than to Y. That interpretation is typically unrealistic: the distribution of the x values are multivariate normal for

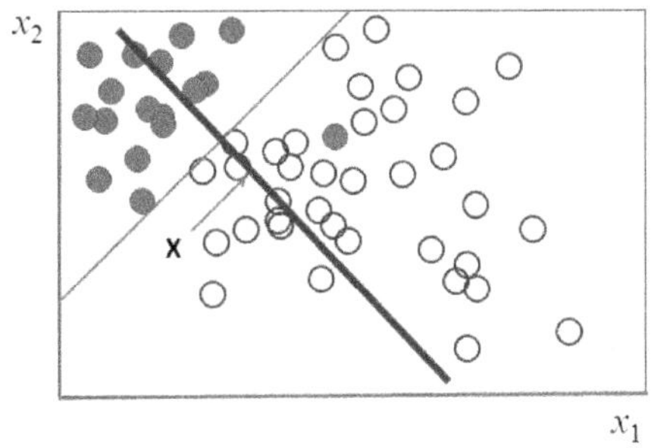

Figure 6.6. Schematic representation for an LDA classifier.

individuals in class 0 and multivariate normal (with a different mean) for individuals in class 1. So, we treat this method like the others: under the *data-adaptive research* paradigm. For good performance, it is necessary to *scale all predictors to the same range*, say ± 1.

Figure 6.6 illustrates this method when there are only two predictor variables, say x_1 and x_2. Filled circles correspond to class 1 and open circles to class 0. The bold line is the direction that gives maximum separation between the distribution means of class 1 and class 0 points in x space and minimizes the variance of each class of points when projected onto the line. To classify a new observation, say at the point "X," the point is projected perpendicularly onto the bold line. Its location on the bold line is its score.

The thin line perpendicular to the bold line crosses the bold line at a value corresponding to the *threshold.* The threshold score is often at or near zero. Points with scores above the threshold are predicted to be in class 1, while points below the threshold are in class 0. If the threshold line were moved up or down along the bold line, the performance of the classifier would change. In its current location, only one point is misclassified: a 1 is classified as a 0.

The position of the point "X" on the line is defined by a linear relationship, and that position is denoted z. The formula looks much like linear regression:

$$z = c_1 x_1 + c_2 x_2 + \cdots + c_p x_p, \tag{6.3}$$

but there is no intercept, and the predicted value (dependent variable) is not the 0–1 class indicator variable y. It is the location on the projection line described above and called z. Suppose the threshold (the point on the bold line where the thin threshold line crosses) is $p = z_0$. Then, after fitting the LDA model, z can be computed for any set of predictor variable values. If $z > z_0$, then the point is predicted to be in class 1, otherwise in class 0. For our example, z would be less than z_0, and so the individual with predictor variable values corresponding to "X" would be predicted to be in class 0.

Note that for LDA classification, the score is not considered a probability. The values are positive and negative and may have magnitude greater than 1.

The incorrect multiple linear regression approach (remember, Y is 0–1, so certainly not normally distributed) and the correct LDA modeling approach produce related coefficients. James *et al.* (2021) show the relationship as

$$c_j = b_j \frac{\mathrm{P} + \mathrm{N}}{\mathrm{PN}}. \tag{6.4}$$

The LDA coefficients are a rescaling of the multiple linear regression coefficients, which means that by adjusting the threshold, the multiple linear regression classifier can produce identical results to the LDA classifier. So, the wrong logic can produce the right classification!

One weakness of the LDA method is that it is *linear*. This means that the classifier must separate the points into two classes using a line, as in Figure 6.6, or a plane in higher-dimension x space. Sometimes, the boundary between classes is curved. Then, *LDA is not effective if the boundary between classes in x space is nonlinear.*

6.2.2 k-nearest neighbors

How does the k-NN method work? Suppose that we want to predict the class for a new observation (or an existing one) with three predictor variables whose values are represented by the vector $x_0 = (x_{01}, x_{02}, x_{03})$. In the training set, find the k observations (indexed by i) with x values closest to x_0. Distance is usually measured using the Euclidean distance formula:

$$\mathrm{dist}(x_0, x_i) = \sqrt{(x_{01} - x_{i1})^2 + (x_{02} - x_{i2})^2 + (x_{03} - x_{i3})^2}.$$

For this to perform well, it is necessary to *scale all predictors to the same range*, say ± 1. Once we have the k observations nearest to x_0. we take a majority vote on the class. If the majority of neighbors have

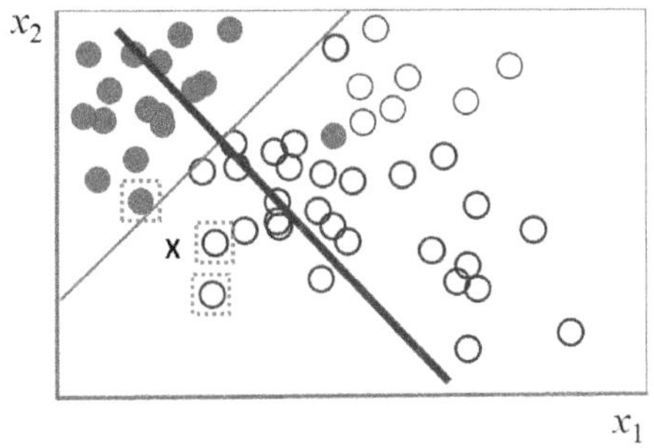

Figure 6.7. Schematic representation for a k-NN classifier.

class 0, then we predict class 0 ($y = 0$), otherwise we predict class 1 ($y = 1$). Also, sometimes the vote is represented as a percentage of total votes; then, a majority vote means a score greater than or equal to 0.5. The majority vote method means that k should be odd to avoid ties.

We revisit the data in Figure 6.6 to illustrate the k-NN method with $k = 3$. The k-NN classification is shown in Figure 6.7. For the candidate point "X", the three nearest neighbors are in dashed boxes. Two are class 0, and one is class 1, so the k-NN prediction is class 0 ($y = 0$). For this point, we get the same classification prediction for LDA and k-NN with $k = 3$.

How should one choose k? There are fancy methods, but one popular choice is to use $k = \sqrt{\mathrm{P} + \mathrm{N}}$; that is, choose k as the square root of the sample size (unless this is an even number, in which case reduce k by 1). The square root rule applied to the roughly 50 observations in Figure 6.7 would result in $k = 7$ rather than $k = 3$.

A strength of the k-NN model is that it can capture class associations that are not separable by a linear function. Also, the classification method is easy to understand and explain. But the k-NN method has a significant disadvantage over other classification methods. For future predictions, the LDA method (and neural network and logistic regression methods discussed later) only need to save the threshold z_0 and a small number of model coefficients, even if 100,000 observations were in the training set. But the k-NN model is burdened by both data and computation. It must retain the *entire* training data set. So, if there were 100,000 observations in the training set, the k-NN model must retain 100,000 sets of x and y data.

Also, for each new prediction, it must find the k nearest neighbors. If there are 100,000 potential neighbors, this is a daunting task. The conclusion is that *k-NN does not work well for very large data sets.*

6.3 Complex Classification Methods

In this section, we briefly review two more complex classification methods: neural networks and logistic regression. In this era of machine learning, neural networks are extremely popular and effective tools. Logistic regression has a long and respected history for conducting classification, and so it is included here as well. But its models often do not exhibit superior performance to LDA models and are often inferior to neural network classifiers.

6.3.1 Neural network classifiers

Neural network models were discussed extensively in Section 5.3. For classification, the y variable is a qualitative factor, typically with values 0 or 1. For classification, the output node typically employs the activation function to guarantee values between 0 and 1. Neural network classifiers have the advantage of very good performance (accuracy, sensitivity, specificity, and informedness). As for k-NN classification, the neural network classifiers can handle nonlinear boundaries between classes in predictor variable space. But the high flexibility of neural networks leads to high variability in network structure and cross-validation performance. A repeated CV approach is recommended. And while neural network fitting for classification has fewer convergence problems than for regression, *computer execution times for neural network classification mode fitting are very long compared with other methods.*

6.3.2 Logistic regression classifiers

Logistic regression (LR) models for classification are also called *logit regression* or *logit* models. The method was developed by David R. Cox (1958). The idea is to convert the dependent variable to a kind of probability of class 1. But a transformation is more amenable to regression, so instead of setting $y = p$, the logarithm of the "odds ratio" is used as y. We have all heard the "odds" concept to describe the probability of an event, such as "what are the odds" or "ten to one odds." The relationship to the probability value p is shown in Equation (6.5):

$$\text{odds} = \frac{p}{1-p}. \tag{6.5}$$

In betting, you add the two odds numbers to get the total outcome count. A ten-to-one odds actually describes the reciprocal of the odds ratio. It would be $p = 1/11$, or odds $= (1/11) \div (10/11) = 0.1$.

LR fits a linear regression model using the logarithm of the odds as the dependent variable. The regression form for classification is shown in Equation (6.6):

$$\log(\text{odds}) = y = \beta_0 + \sum_{j=1}^{d} \beta_j g_j(x) + \varepsilon. \tag{6.6}$$

Note that we are not assuming a normal distribution for ε.

Given a fitted LR model and a set of predictor variable values, prediction works as follows. The predictor variable values are used as the x values in Equation (6.6) to produce a predicted log odds ratio. Then, the equation can be used to recover p, which can be compared with the threshold:

$$p = \frac{e^{\log(\text{odds})}}{1 + e^{\log(\text{odds})}}. \tag{6.7}$$

But this comparison is unnecessary. Suppose the threshold p_0 is 0.5. Then, the odds ratio would be $0.5/0.5 = 1$, and the log of 1 is 0. So, if the predicted log(odds) is greater than zero, then classify the case as 1, otherwise classify it as 0. No need to find p; simply find the threshold for odds using Equation (6.5).

Cox developed a theoretical justification for LR so that it might be used under the *traditional research* paradigm. Since p can be derived from y using Equation (6.7) and p represents the probability of falling in class 1, the actual classifications will either fall in class 1 (with probability p) or in class 0 (with probability $1 - p$). Then, for a fixed set of predictor variable values, in a sample of n individuals with those specific predictor variable values, the count of class 1 cases will follow a binomial distribution with parameters n and p, where the probability of success p is the nonlinear function of the predictor variables given by Equation (6.6). That is why when we fit a LR in R using `glm`, we specify `family = "binomial"`.

This is a special kind of regression model: a kind of *generalized linear model* (GLIM), which includes multiple linear regression as a special case but allows more general forms. For a GLIM, replace Y in the multiple linear regression equation with a link function $g(\mu_Y))$. For LR, the link function is the logit function: $g(\mu_Y) = \log(\mu_Y/(1-\mu_Y))$. The residuals do not have to have a normal (Gaussian) distribution. For LR, they have a scaled binomial distribution.

LR is ONE KIND of GLIM, and these models have theoretical justification under the *traditional research* paradigm. However, as for LDA, these assumptions often do not hold, and so we use LR models only in the *data-adaptive research* paradigm and characterize the model predictive error empirically via cross-validation. We ignore performance measures based on *deviance* since these measures are associated with the theoretical model. Instead, we characterize LR based on the confusion matrix and related performance measures.

The advantage of LR models is similar to that of LDA models: there is a regression-like model with coefficients attached to each predictor variable. Similarly to LDA, the computations are relatively efficient and predictions depend only on the typically small set of fitted coefficients. Further, LR can outperform LDA if the predictor variables are significantly skewed or if many of the predictor variables are qualitative (0, 1).

However, there are disadvantages. The model may not perform well if the sample size is small. The *Rule of 10* suggests that the number of observations in each class must be greater that 10 times the number of predictor variables (only 3–5 needed for LDA). The *decision boundary remains linear*: a line or a plane will separate points in predictor space. Also, a log odds regression is harder to explain to management, and the intuition provided by the coefficients is less. Further, we will see in the following that *logistic regression models often have little advantage over LDA models while being more difficult to explain to management.*

6.4 Example Classification Using R and caret

This section illustrates the use of the caret `train()` function for cross-validation fitting and prediction error characterization.

Further, at the end of the section, we will see that the confusion matrices constructed in this way give a fairer assessment of model prediction error, compared with those computed with the same set of observations used to fit the model. An LDA classifier is fitted using the `lda` option, a k-NN model using `knn`, a neural network classifier using `nnet`, and a logistic regression classifier using `glm`. All four models are fit to airline passenger satisfaction data.

6.4.1 Airline satisfaction data

The data set used for analysis in this section is a subset of a survey of over 100,000 airline passengers This data set is available on Kaggle at https://www.kaggle.com/datasets/teejmahal20/airline-passenger-satisfaction.

The data set used here has a 2,000 record subset with a reduced set of predictor variables. The "test" and "train" sets were combined before subsetting to permit cross-validation fit and assessment. The reduced set of variables are:

- *Satisfied*: Airline satisfaction level (yes = satisfaction, no = neutral or dissatisfaction); this is the class variable.
- *Gender*: Gender of the passengers (Female, Male).
- *Age*: The actual age of the passengers.
- *Distance*: The flight distance of this journey.
- *FoodDrink*: Satisfaction level of food and drink.
- *SeatComfort*: Satisfaction level of seat comfort.
- *InflightEnt*: Satisfaction level of in-flight entertainment.
- *Checkin*: Satisfaction level of check-in service.
- *InflightServ*: Satisfaction level of in-flight service.
- *Clean*: Satisfaction level of cabin cleanliness.
- *DepartDelay*: Minutes delayed when departure.
- *ArriveDelay*: Minutes delayed in arriving.

It is read into R using the `read.csv` command. The structure of the data is explored in the following session:

```
> str(Air)
'data.frame':   2000 obs. of  12 variables:
$ Satisfied     : chr  "yes" "no" "no" "yes" ...
$ Gender        : chr  "Female" "Male" "Male" "Female" ...
$ Age           : int  52 13 25 36 20 26 25 44 49 61 ...
```

```
$ Distance    : int  160 460 235 2863 192 1142 562
                     3377 1182 214 ...
$ FoodDrink   : int  3 5 1 5 2 5 2 3 4 4 ...
$ SeatComfort : int  3 5 1 5 2 5 2 4 2 5 ...
$ InflightEnt : int  5 5 1 4 2 5 2 1 2 3 ...
$ Checkin     : int  2 4 1 3 2 4 1 3 4 3 ...
$ InflightServ: int  5 5 4 4 2 4 4 1 2 3 ...
$ Clean       : int  5 5 1 5 2 5 2 4 4 3 ...
$ DepartDelay : int  50 25 1 0 0 0 11 0 0 0 ...
$ ArriveDelay : int  44 18 6 0 0 0 9 6 20 0 ...
>
```

We begin with summary statistics and summary graphics, a necessary step before selecting a classification method.

```
> summary(Air)
Satisfied            Gender                  Age            Distance
Length:2000        Length:2000        Min.   : 7.00  Min.   :  67.0
Class :character   Class :character   1st Qu.:27.00  1st Qu.: 406.0
Mode  :character   Mode  :character   Median :41.00  Median : 860.5
                                      Mean   :39.63  Mean   :1212.7
                                      3rd Qu.:51.00  3rd Qu.:1780.0
                                      Max.   :80.00  Max.   :4817.0
  FoodDrink       SeatComfort      InflightEnt        Checkin
Min.   :0.000   Min.   :1.000   Min.   :0.000   Min.   :1.000
1st Qu.:2.000   1st Qu.:2.000   1st Qu.:2.000   1st Qu.:3.000
Median :3.000   Median :4.000   Median :4.000   Median :3.000
Mean   :3.224   Mean   :3.444   Mean   :3.381   Mean   :3.324
3rd Qu.:4.000   3rd Qu.:5.000   3rd Qu.:4.000   3rd Qu.:4.000
Max.   :5.000   Max.   :5.000   Max.   :5.000   Max.   :5.000
  InflightServ       Clean         DepartDelay       ArriveDelay
Min.   :0.000   Min.   :1.000   Min.   :  0.00   Min.   :  0.00
1st Qu.:3.000   1st Qu.:2.000   1st Qu.:  0.00   1st Qu.:  0.00
Median :4.000   Median :3.000   Median :  0.00   Median :  0.00
Mean   :3.666   Mean   :3.293   Mean   : 15.09   Mean   : 15.45
3rd Qu.:5.000   3rd Qu.:4.000   3rd Qu.: 13.00   3rd Qu.: 14.00
Max.   :5.000   Max.   :5.000   Max.   :493.00   Max.   :485.00
```

The summary statistics show 2,000 observations, with Satisfied and Gender as character variables. Passenger age ranges between 7 and 80, distance flown ranges from 67 miles to nearly 5,000, with rating variables ranging from 0 to 5.

6.4.2 Graphical summaries

Graphical summaries provide some idea of whether a classification model will likely be successful. One expects to see predictor variable differences between the two classes. Further, there may be differences over the values of the qualitative predictor variable Gender. It is possible to generate boxplots of quantitative predictor variables vs. Satisfaction by Gender. The following session commands generate four such plots.

```
> # do two boxplots to see joint effect
> with(Air,boxplot(Clean~interaction(Satisfied,Gender),
+                  xlab = "Satisfied, Gender"))
> with(Air,boxplot(SeatComfort~interaction(Satisfied,Gender),
+                  xlab = "Satisfied, Gender"))
> with(Air,boxplot(DepartDelay~interaction(Satisfied,Gender),
+                  xlab = "Satisfied, Gender"))
> with(Air,boxplot(ArriveDelay~interaction(Satisfied,Gender),
+                  xlab = "Satisfied, Gender"))
>
```

The results are shown in Figures 6.8 and 6.9. Figure 6.8 explores the impact of seat comfort and cabin cleanliness on satisfaction separately by passenger gender. It is clear that seat comfort and cleanliness matter because when the passenger is satisfied the scores are higher. There does not appear to be any difference between female and male passengers; however, the pairs of boxplots look similar for both genders. Figure 6.9 explores the effect of delays on passenger satisfaction. Strangely, passengers rated their experience as satisfactory even when there were significant delays! There is an impact

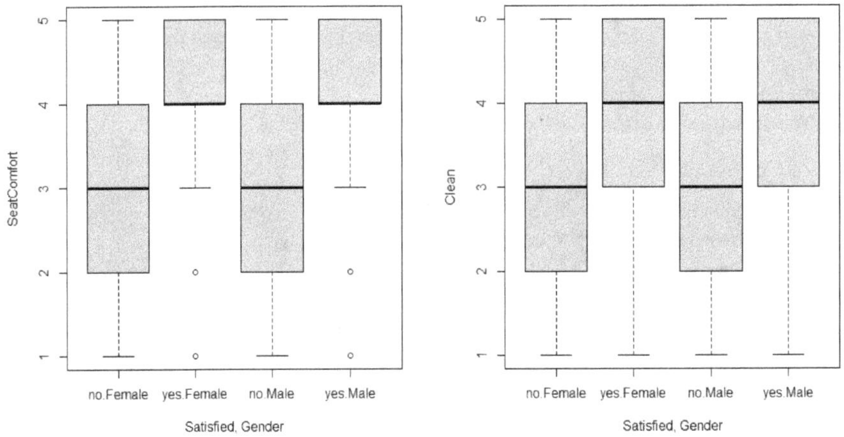

Figure 6.8. Relationship of seat comfort and cabin cleanliness to satisfaction.

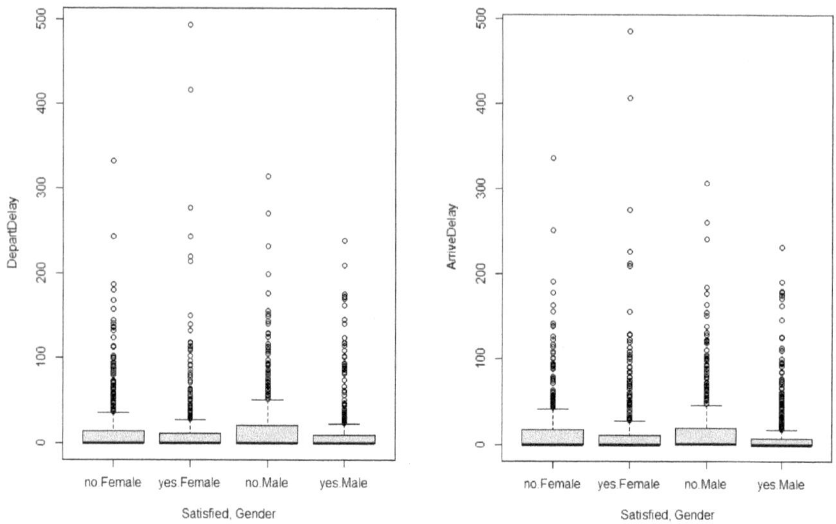

Figure 6.9. Relationship of departure and arrival delay to satisfaction.

of delay, however: a closer look shows that the "Satisfied" boxplots have a lower value for the third quartile of delay (the upper bar in the boxplot). Again, this is consistent across gender.

It is possible to explore boxplots in a broader context by gender and by satisfaction. For these plots, and for the model fitting and testing in the following section, all numeric variables are scaled to ± 1. The session commands for scaling for this example are as follows:

```
> # for remaining scatter and boxplots , rescale all
> #   numeric predictor variables to +/- 1
> # this data frame isnamed sAir
> scalpm1 = function(x){(x-(min(x)+max(x))/2)/
                        (.5*(max(x)-min(x)))}
> sAir = NULL
> sAir$Satisfied = Air$Satisfied # do not rescale
> sAir$Gender = Air$Gender       # do not rescale
> sAir$Age = scalpm1(Air$Age)
> sAir$Distance = scalpm1(Air$Distance)
> sAir$FoodDrink = scalpm1(Air$FoodDrink)
> sAir$SeatComfort = scalpm1(Air$SeatComfort)
> sAir$InflightEnt = scalpm1(Air$InflightEnt)
> sAir$Checkin = scalpm1(Air$Checkin)
> sAir$InflightServ = scalpm1(Air$InflightServ)
> sAir$Clean = scalpm1(Air$Clean)
```

```
> sAir$DepartDelay = scalpm1(Air$DepartDelay)
> sAir$ArriveDelay = scalpm1(Air$ArriveDelay)
> # convert sAir from list to data frame for plots and
> #   classification methods
> sAir = as.data.frame(sAir)
>
```

Creating a full set of boxplots for all quantitative predictor variables by satisfaction or by gender requires two additional R packages: **reshape2** and **ggplot2**. The **reshape2** package has flexible ways to reorganize data frames. To create boxplots, we need to convert the 10 columns of quantitative predictors (Age, Distance, FoodDrink, etc.) into two columns of a new data frame. One column has the measurement name (e.g., Age) and the second column has the value (e.g., 52). The qualitative variables Gender and Satisfied will remain as columns in the new data frame. Here are the session commands to create the new data frame and the first few lines of it:

```
> library(reshape2)
Loading required package: reshape2
> # melting by "Label". 'melt is from the reshape2 package.
> # do ?melt to see what other things it can do
  (you will surely need it)
> # only works for quantitative variables, need to 'id'
   qualitative ones
> sAir.melt <- melt(sAir, id = c("Gender","Satisfied"))
> head(sAir.melt)
  Gender Satisfied variable      value
1 Female       yes      Age  0.2328767
2   Male        no      Age -0.8356164
3   Male        no      Age -0.5068493
4 Female       yes      Age -0.2054795
5   Male        no      Age -0.6438356
6 Female       yes      Age -0.4794521
>
```

Remember, Age was scaled to ± 1 in `sAir`! There will be 20,000 rows in `sAir.melt` because 10 rows are needed to describe a single observation in the old `sAir` data frame: one row for each quantitative variable. Now, with this structure, we can use `ggplot` to create boxplots "by" either of the qualitative variables by using the `fill=` option in the aesthetic (`aes`) specification. The session commands to generate a boxplot of all quantitative predictor variables by Satisfied and a plot by Gender is shown as follows.

```
> library(ggplot2)

> ggplot(data = sAir.melt, aes(x=variable, y=value)) +
+               geom_boxplot(aes(fill=Satisfied))
> ggplot(data = sAir.melt, aes(x=variable, y=value)) +
+               geom_boxplot(aes(fill=Gender))
>
```

The plots are shown in Figures 6.10 and 6.11. In the first plot, it is clear that all predictor variables have higher boxplots for the satisfied passengers. The weakest relationship appears for the Age variable. The second plot shows that these effects differ little by gender, except perhaps for in-flight entertainment. These relationships suggest that good classification should be possible with the simple k-NN and LDA models.

6.4.3 Implementing knn, lda, nnet, and glm via caret

Some additional actions are needed before fitting our classification models. The code is shown as follows.

Since all predictor variables must be numeric for our methods, we code Gender as 0–1. Also, the classification methods expect the dependent variable to be recognized as a *categorical* variable with multiple observations for each level of that qualitative variable. In R, that means the object type should be *factor* rather than *variable.*

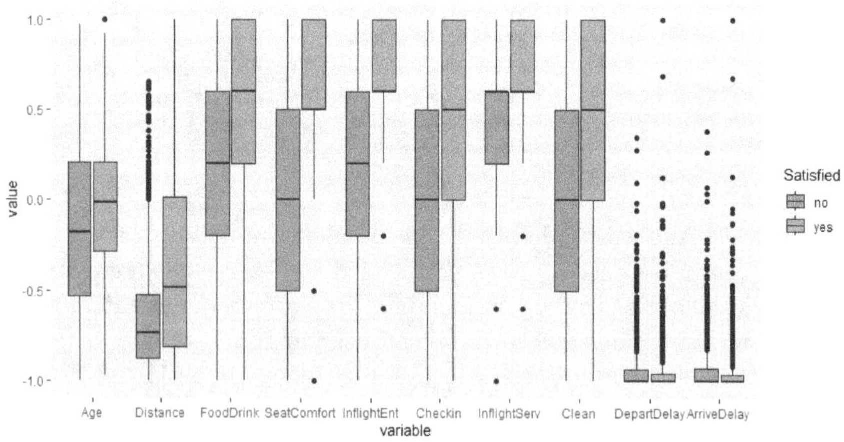

Figure 6.10. Relationship of quantitative predictor variables to satisfaction.

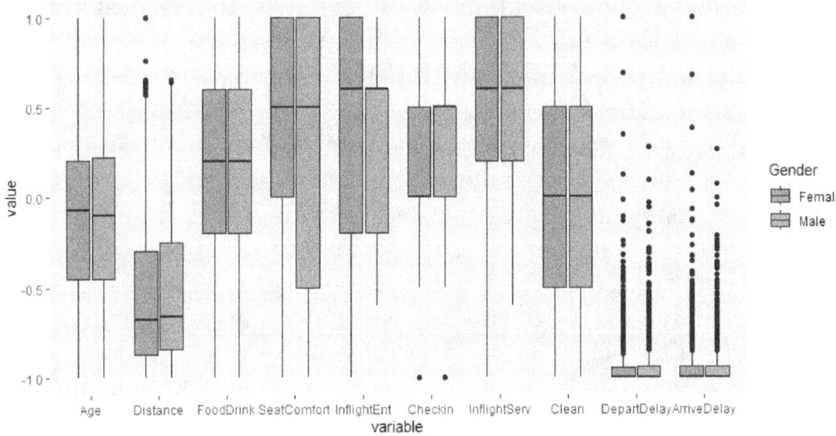

Figure 6.11. Relationship of quantitative predictor variables to gender.

One needs to make this *factor* characteristic of Satisfied explicit with the `as.factor` function in R. Finally, the classification methods take the first observed value of the classification factor in the data frame to be the class 1 value. Depending on the order of observations in the data frame, the first entry could be either "yes" or "no." The last part of this session uses `relevel` to make "yes" the class 1 value explicitly.

```
> # begin classification methods ==========================
> # convert Gender to 0-1 for model fitting
> sAir$Gender<-ifelse(Air$Gender=="Female",1,0)
> # set Satisfied to a factor -
> #     the dependent variable must be a 'factor'
> sAir$Satisfied = as.factor(sAir$Satisfied)
> # set Satisfied reference level (class 1) to "yes"
> sAir$Satisfied = relevel(sAir$Satisfied, ref = "yes")
>
```

LDA using R

We use the caret `train()` function for fitting and assessing classification models, as was done for cross-validation for regression models in Chapter 5. The model call changes only slightly to `model = "lda"`. Before showing the code, here are important aspects that are included:

- In addition to the `caret` library, you will need the MLeval library to construct the ROC curve and compute the AUC.
- In addition to the `caret` and MLeval libraries, the `lda` method requires the MASS library.
- To explore how the computational effort to fit each model type varies, we add the `tictoc` library and `tic()` and `toc()` commands to report computing time spent on the fitting (training) step.
- For any use of the `caret` `trainControl()` function with cross-validation (`method = "cv"` or `method = "repeatedcv"`), the split into test and train segments is done randomly. To get the same random splits each time you run the code, set the random number seed immediately before the caret commands. If you run the `train()` command a second time without resetting the seed, you will get a different 10-fold split and different performance (different entries in the confusion matrix) and, in some cases, (`lda`; `knn` with `caret`-selected k; and `nnet`) a different fitted model.
- To get a better fit and better assessment of prediction error, repeat the random cross validation 10-split and evaluations more than once. Here, 10-fold cross-validation is repeated five times. That requires specifying the method in `trainControl` as `"repeatedcv"` and adding`, repeats = 5`.
- To construct the ROC curve and compute AUC, class probabilities and predictions must be saved. "`, classProbs = T, savePredictions = T`" must be added to the `trainControl` options.

The full session commands for fitting the LDA model is shown next. Note that the elapsed time for the computation is reported as 0.85 seconds.

```
> # Cross-validation (10-fold) code
> #    needs train function from caret library
> library(caret)
> library(MLeval) # for ROC curves
> set.seed(80111973) # same seed for each method
> # begin LDA classification ==============================
> # set the CV method to lda
> # lda requires MASS package
> library(MASS)
> trainMeth = trainControl(method = "repeatedcv", number = 10,
+                          repeats = 5, classProbs = T,
+                          savePredictions = T)
> # monitor time to do the fitting with tic(0) toc(0)
```

```
> library(tictoc)
> tic()
> ldaModel <- train(Satisfied ~ ., data = sAir,
+                   method = "lda",
+                   trControl = trainMeth)
> # end time monitoring
> toc()
0.85 sec elapsed
```

The resulting fitted model is part of the object `ldaModel$final`. The session command to print the model structure and the results are shown as follows.

```
> print(ldaModel$finalModel)

Call:
lda(x, grouping = y)

Prior probabilities of groups:
   yes     no
0.4475 0.5525

Group means:
       Gender         Age   Distance FoodDrink SeatComfort
yes 0.4916201 -0.03638172 -0.3721061 0.4230168  0.46759777
no  0.5158371 -0.16226368 -0.6354622 0.1819005  0.02307692
    InflightEnt    Checkin InflightServ       Clean DepartDelay
yes   0.5910615 0.31396648    0.5950838  0.37765363  -0.9433227
no    0.1590950 0.03846154    0.3621719 -0.04027149  -0.9350913
    ArriveDelay
yes  -0.9433692
no   -0.9305500

Coefficients of linear discriminants:
LD1
Gender         0.07330867
Age           -0.44240309
Distance      -1.16955729
FoodDrink      0.20233326
SeatComfort   -0.26718201
InflightEnt   -1.08718949
Checkin       -0.47072435
InflightServ  -0.40211110
Clean         -0.18659065
DepartDelay   -2.46712932
ArriveDelay    2.77675497
>
```

The first element gives the Prevalence value, which in this case is 0.4475 — quite high for typical classification problems. The group means might be seen as the means for each boxplot in Figure 6.10, with the addition of the 0–1 coded Gender variable. Last are the linear discriminant analysis coefficients shown in the model in Equation (6.3): the c_j values.

k-NN using R

There are a few additional changes needed for the k-NN model fitting in the following code:

- The method is specified as `"knn"`.
- The `knn` method requires the class library.
- In this version, k (called `k2000`) is specified as the integer part (`trunc`) of the square root of the sample size. To keep things flexible, rather than simply mentioning 2,000, the sample size is given as the length of the class variable `sAir$Satisfied`. That way, if you later decide to add or subtract cases, this will still work.
- Remove the `tuneGrid = data.frame(k=k2000),` option from the `train` command to let `train()` choose the value for k that gives the highest accuracy value.

The session commands for fitting the k-NN model is shown as follows. The elapsed time is longer, at 1.84 seconds.

```
> library(class)

> # to run with fixed k, say sqrt (2000) take integer part,
> #   if it is even, subtract 1
> #   then use tuneGrid option in train
> k2000 = trunc(sqrt(length(sAir$Satisfied)))
> set.seed(80111973) # same seed for each method
> trainMeth = trainControl(method = "repeatedcv", number = 10,
+                                    repeats = 5, classProbs = T,
+                                    savePredictions = T)
> # monitor time to do the fitting with tic(0) toc(0)
> library(tictoc)
> tic()
> # note: if you choose k, use tuneGrid option, else delete
> knnModel <- train(Satisfied ~ ., data = sAir,
+                   method = "knn",
+                   tuneGrid = data.frame(k=k2000),
+                   trControl = trainMeth)
> # end time monitoring
> toc()
1.84 sec elapsed
>
```

Like multiple linear regression, the 10-fold cross-validation training does not affect the k-NN model if you specify k. If k is specified, the model is fixed. If one deletes the `tuneGrid = data.frame(k=k2000),` option from the `train` command above, then the model (choice of k) may change depending on the random fold construction. Setting the random seed before the `train()` function call ensures that each time the code is run, the choice of k will remain the same, and the resulting confusion matrix values remain the same as well.

For k-NN, the `train` exercise characterizes prediction error rather than fitting a model AND characterizing prediction error, unless you let `train()` choose the best k. There is no model to describe: only the value k. So, the model summary is brief, giving only the value of k and the number of positive and negative (or class 1 and class 0) cases in the data set.

```
> # summary of KNN results
> print(knnModel$finalModel)
44-nearest neighbor model
Training set outcome distribution:

yes   no
895 1105

>
```

NN discriminant analysis using R

There are a few specific elements needed for the NN model fitting via the `caret train()` function:

- The `trainControl` command remains the same.
- The `train` command changes to `method = "nnet"`.
- Similarly to `lda`, in addition to the caret and MLeval libraries, the `nnet` method requires the MASS library.
- Since we are doing classification rather than regression, a 0–1 output is desired, so set `linout = F` rather than `linout = T`.

The session commands for fitting the neural network model are shown as follows.

```
> # nnet requires MASS package
> library(MASS)> set.seed(80111973) # same seed for each method

> trainMeth = trainControl(method = "repeatedcv", number = 10,
+                           repeats = 5, classProbs = T,
+                           savePredictions = T)
> # monitor time to do the fitting with tic(0) toc(0)
> library(tictoc)
> tic()
> nnetModel <- train(Satisfied ~ ., data = sAir,
+                    method = "nnet",
+                    trace = F,
+                    linout = FALSE,
+                    trControl = trainMeth)
> # end time monitoring
> toc()

80.09 sec elapsed
>
```

Note that the execution time to fit the neural network was much longer than to fit and characterize the LDA or k-NN models.

The results of the neural network fitting provide detailed information on the neural network — almost too much! Here, we show how to recover the final fitted model network structure and weights.

```
> # summary of nnet results
> print(nnetModel$finalModel$n)
[1] 11  5  1
> print(nnetModel$finalModel$wts)
[1]   -1.88538295  0.38321025  0.91822387 -2.48772581 -0.61485351
[6]   -1.85968407  0.47290904  0.37849448  1.59385380  0.22090299
[11]   1.78660942  1.86673960 -0.87724430  0.48937177  2.38384674
[16]  -0.54288920 -0.65662738  4.20448145  0.60073615  2.19926916
[21]  -0.59874041  1.26617636  1.50848206  0.38425775  1.65574652
[26]  -0.28015943  0.79842596  0.73694355 -2.04326528 -0.06015405
[31]  -1.59796021 -0.47435504 -1.66364279 -1.50878599 -0.28910115
[36]   2.27837649  0.68625566  0.11462651  0.06754335 -1.87415400
[41]   0.43135049  0.33088898 -0.25350405  0.39880191  0.16648076
[46]   1.24467156 -0.39175178  2.82762088 -0.32255848 -1.26777342
[51]  -1.12288123 -1.23789281  1.01839980  1.46507073  2.80211869
[56]   1.14024424 -0.65717815  3.92775359  1.22814469  0.91305622
[61]  -0.64769297 -4.75252422 -2.73030618  3.29075194  6.92219589
[66]  -2.72068502
>
```

The network has 11 input nodes for the 11 predictor variables, 5 hidden nodes, and 1 output node. Remember, the order of the coefficients in this list goes from top to bottom and then left to right for the network. We can show a visual representation of the network

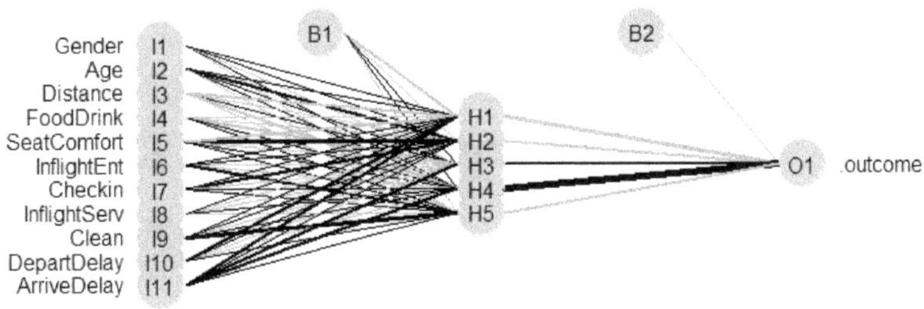

Figure 6.12. Airline satisfaction neural network and weights.

as done for neural network regression in Chapter 5. The commands are repeated in the following and the resulting network is shown in Figure 6.12. Recall that the network uses gray edges for negative weights, black edges for positive weights, and the thickness indicates the magnitude of the weight.

```
> library(devtools)
> source_url('https://gist.githubusercontent.com/fawda123/
    7471137/raw/466c1474d0a505ff044412703516c34f1a4684a5/
    nnet_plot_update.r')
> plot.nnet(nnetModel , nid=T)
>
```

Logistic regression discriminant analysis using R

There are a few comments on the specific elements needed for the logistic regression model fitting via the caret `train()` function:

- The `trainControl` command remains the same.
- No additional libraries are needed beyond the caret and MLeval libraries.
- The model specification requires two options in `train`: `method = "glm"` and `family = "binomial"`.

The full code for fitting the logistic regression model is shown as follows.

```
> # set the CV method to glm
> # no extra packages needed beyond caret and MLeval
> set.seed(80111973) # same seed for each method
> trainMeth = trainControl(method = "repeatedcv", number = 10,
+                          repeats = 5, classProbs = T,
+                          savePredictions = T)
```

```
> # monitor time to do the fitting with tic(0) toc(0)
> library(tictoc)
> tic()
> logRegModel <- train(Satisfied ~ ., data = sAir,
+                      method = "glm",
+                      family = "binomial",
+                      trControl = trainMeth)
> # end time monitoring
> toc()
1.58 sec elapsed
>
```

Note that the execution time is relatively short compared with the neural network fitting, and it is comparable to the fitting time for k-NN and LDA.

The resulting fitted model is part of the object `logRegModel$final`. The command to print the model structure and the results are shown as follows. Again, deviance values and other quantities associated with the theoretical probability model, such as degrees of freedom and AIC, are not of interest to us since we are exploring classification under the *data-adaptive research* paradigm.

```
> # summary of logReg results
> print(logRegModel\$finalModel)

Call:  NULL

Coefficients:
 (Intercept)        Gender           Age      Distance
     0.62673       0.08666      -0.52445      -1.36844
   FoodDrink   SeatComfort   InflightEnt       Checkin
     0.21168      -0.31020      -1.26558      -0.55931
InflightServ         Clean   DepartDelay   ArriveDelay
    -0.45658      -0.19820      -3.05719       3.45676

Degrees of Freedom: 1999 Total (i.e. Null);  1988 Residual
Null Deviance:      2750
Residual Deviance: 2139     AIC: 2163
>
```

The `Call: NULL` statement is not a concern: the model details from the `train()` cross-validation fitting steps are not available in the final model. These coefficient estimates are for the model in Equation (6.6). Sharing them and interpreting them for management beyond the link to this equation would be quite difficult.

6.4.4 Performance summaries in R

Some performance measures, such as accuracy, can be accessed directly from `train()` fitted models for all the kinds of classifiers that have been presented. But how items are accessed and named can be different. For consistency, all performance measures except the ROC curve and AUC are computed directly from the confusion matrix counts. These are built from the percentage version of the confusion matrix provided by `train()`. The following are the session commands for the `lda` model. The commands for the other models are similar.

```
> # build LDA CV confusion matrix in terms of percentages and counts
> ldaConfMat =
+   as.matrix(confusionMatrix(ldaModel, positive = "Yes")$table)
> print("Confusion Matrix (%)")
[1] "Confusion Matrix (%)"
> print(ldaConfMat)

            Reference
Prediction   yes    no
       yes  29.88 12.50
        no  14.87 42.75

> ldaConfMatCount = (ldaConfMat/100)*length(sAir$Satisfied)
> print("Confusion Matrix (counts) = (percent/100)x no. in train")
[1] "Confusion Matrix (counts) = (percent/100)x no. in train"
> print(ldaConfMatCount)
            Reference
Prediction   yes    no
       yes  597.6 250.0
        no  297.4 855.0
>
```

The performance measures are then computed from the count version of the confusion matrix.

```
> # derive performance measures from confusion matrix
> ldaAcc = (ldaConfMatCount[1,1] + ldaConfMatCount[2,2]/
+              sum(ldaConfMatCount))
> ldaSens = ldaConfMatCount[1,1] /
+   (ldaConfMatCount[1,1] + ldaConfMatCount[2,1])
> ldaSpec = ldaConfMatCount[2,2] /
+   (ldaConfMatCount[1,2] + ldaConfMatCount[2,2])
> ldaBalAcc = (ldaSens + ldaSpec)/2
> ldaInform = ldaSens + ldaSpec - 1
> ldaPrev = (ldaConfMatCount[1,1] + ldaConfMatCount[2,1])/
+   sum(ldaConfMatCount)
> print("Performance Measures from Confusion Matrix")
[1] "Performance Measures from Confusion Matrix"
```

```
> print(data.frame(Accuracy = ldaAcc, Sensitivity = ldaSens,
+        Specificity = ldaSpec, Balanced_Accuracy = ldaBalAcc,
+        Informedness = ldaInform, Prevalence = ldaPrev))
  Accuracy Sensitivity Specificity Balanced_Accuracy Informedness
1 598.0275   0.6677095   0.7737557         0.7207326    0.4414652
Prevalence
    0.4475
>
```

The Session commands and results below show approximate 95% confidence intervals for sensitivity and specificity based on the method described in Section 6.1.3. The calculations would be identical for any of the methods **knn**, **nnet**, or **glm**.

```
> ldaSensLo = ldaSens  - 1.96*sqrt(ldaSens*(1-ldaSens)/
+                       (ldaConfMatCount[1,1] + ldaConfMatCount[2,1]))
> ldaSensHi = ldaSens  + 1.96*sqrt(ldaSens*(1-ldaSens)/
+                       (ldaConfMatCount[1,1] + ldaConfMatCount[2,1]))
> ldaSpecLo = ldaSpec  - 1.96*sqrt(ldaSpec*(1-ldaSpec)/
+                       (ldaConfMatCount[1,2] + ldaConfMatCount[2,2]))
> ldaSpecHi = ldaSpec  + 1.96*sqrt(ldaSpec*(1-ldaSpec)/
+                       (ldaConfMatCount[1,2] + ldaConfMatCount[2,2]))
>
> print("Approximate 95% CI for Sensitivity, Specificity, lda")
[1] "Approximate 95% CI for Sensitivity, Specificity, lda"
> print(data.frame(SensitivityLo = ldaSensLo,
+                  SensitivityHI = ldaSensHi,
+                  SpecificityLo = ldaSpecLo,
+                  SpecificityHi = ldaSpecHi))
  SensitivityLo SensitivityHI SpecificityLo SpecificityHi
1     0.6368494     0.6985696     0.7490859     0.7984255
>
```

The ROC curve and associated AUC require the MLeval package. After fitting a classification model with **train()** it is easy to produce the plot and AUC value.

```
> library(MLeval) # for ROC curves
> # use MLeval package evalm routine to generate ROC plot
> ROCobj = evalm(ldaModel, title = "Plot for LDA")
***MLeval: Machine Learning Model Evaluation***
Input: caret train function object
Averaging probs.
Group 1 type: repeatedcv
Observations: 1215
Number of groups: 1
Observations per group: 1215
Positive: no
Negative: yes
Group: Group 1
```

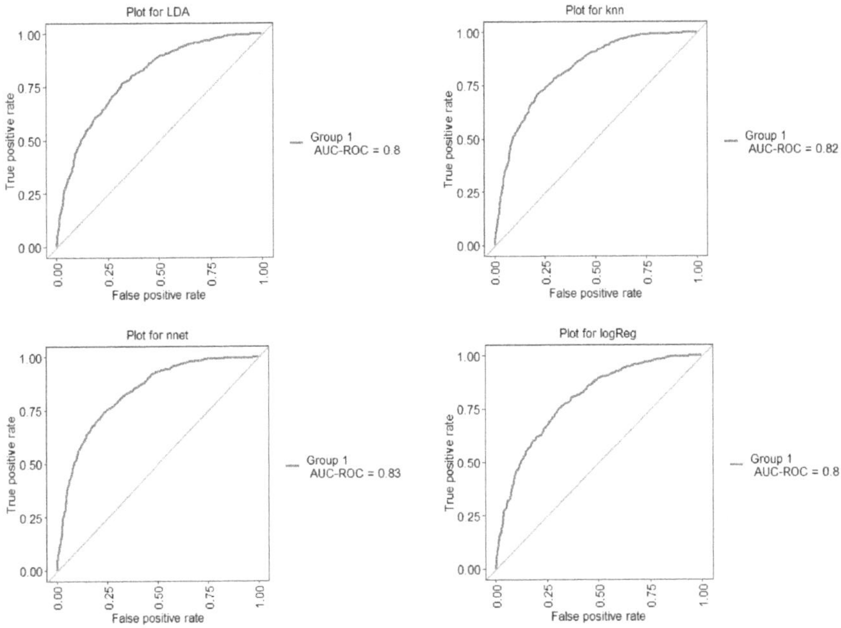

Figure 6.13. Airline satisfaction classifier ROC curves.

```
Positive: 1105
Negative: 110
***Performance Metrics***
Group 1 Optimal Informedness = 0.377169888934595
Group 1 AUC-ROC = 0.73
>
```

The information in the listing is not needed. All is contained in the plot. Figure 6.13 shows the plot for LDA along with plots for k-NN, neural network, and logistic regression classifiers. The ROC/AUC characterization of the methods are very similar: no method has a large advantage over the others for this data set.

6.4.5 Generating a prediction using a classifier

Figures 6.6 and 6.7 illustrate prediction for the LDA and k-NN classfiers. Prediction for a specified predictor variable vector is done much like it was in regression. Here, we show the predicted class for a female with "typical" scores.

```
> predvals = data.frame(Gender=1,Age=0,Distance=0,FoodDrink=0,
+                       SeatComfort=0,InflightEnt=0,Checkin=0,
+                       InflightServ=0,Clean=0,
+                       DepartDelay=0,ArriveDelay=0)
> predict(ldaModel, predvals)
[1] no
Levels: yes no
>
```

The predicted class for such a case would be "no," that is, not satisfied.

Using prediction to see the optimistic error with no cross-validation

The CV confusion matrix is based on average prediction error for cases not used for model fitting across the folds and repeats. To see that this is less optimistic than the results for the final fitted model over the full data can be computed by using the predict function. The commands and results are shown in the following for the LDA model, and the cross-validation confusion matrix follows.

```
> ldaPreds = predict(ldaModel, sAir)
> confusionMatrix(data = ldaPreds,
+                 reference = sAir$Satisfied, mode = "prec_recall")
Confusion Matrix and Statistics

          Reference
Prediction yes  no
       yes 604 242
        no 291 863
```

The option `mode = "prec_recall"` ensures that the definition of the "positive" case remains the same. Here, the prediction set is the entire sAir data. Compare this confusion matrix with that based on cross-validation folds:

```
> print(ldaConfMatCount)
          Reference
Prediction   yes    no
       yes 597.6 250.0
        no 297.4 855.0
```

The counts for the cross-validation confusion matrix are lower. Six fewer TP counts and eight fewer TF counts. We saw a similar phenomenon for regression via cross-validation. Fewer samples are used to fit the LDA model, and the test of fit is on values not included in the fitting process.

6.5 Classification with Data Imbalance

Because the caret `train()` process chooses a model based on the highest accuracy, fitted model performance may not be balanced for sensitivity and specificity when there are many more case 0 samples than case 1 samples. This imbalance is not unusual in real-world classification studies, so it is important to know how to adjust the modeling effort to get a better balance between sensitivity and specificity. There are three main approaches to adjust model fit in the presence of severe data imbalance:

- Use only a subsample of the larger class (*downsampling*).
- Increase the number of samples in the smaller class by artificially generating new ones (*upsampling*).
- Weight the classification error more heavily for cases in the smaller class (*class weighting*).

Here, we show two approaches: a combination of upsampling and downsampling employed with the `sampling = "smote"` option in `trainControl`; and class weighting using the `weights = class_weights` option in `train`. There is evidence that the class weighting approach is superior (Soleymani, 2022), but SMOTE is very popular (Chawla *et al.*, 2002).

We begin by modifying the airline preference data set, removing 90% of the satisfied cases. The following session commands make that change.

```
> # select all "no" rows for sAir_no, "yes" rows
    for sAir_yes
> sAir_no = sAir[sAir$Satisfied == "no",]
> sAir_yes = sAir[sAir$Satisfied == "yes",]
> # sample 10% of sAir_yes
> # sampling from data frame needs corpora library
> library(corpora)
> sAir_yes_part = sample.df(sAir_yes,size=trunc
                          (.1*nrow(sAir_no)))
> sAirImbal = rbind(sAir_yes_part, sAir_no)
>
```

The commands create two data frames that are subsets of the original: all the "no" entries are in **sAir_no**, while all the "yes" entries in **sAir_yes**. Then, the corpora library **sample.df** function randomly selects a subset of the "yes" data frame, with size corresponding to 10% of the total number of rows in the "no" data frame. These are then combined with the full set of "no" cases. So, the number of "yes" cases is now 10% of the number of "no" cases. The data frame **sAirUnbal** has substantial imbalance.

The following is the usual LDA model and the resulting performance summary.

```
> # begin usual LDA classification ========================
>
> set.seed(80111973) # same seed for each method
>
> trainMeth = trainControl(method = "repeatedcv", number = 10,
+                          repeats = 5, classProbs = T,
+                          savePredictions = T)
> # monitor time to do the fitting with tic(0) toc(0)
> library(tictoc)
> tic()
> ldaModel <- train(Satisfied ~ ., data = sAirImbal,
+                   method = "lda",
+                   trControl = trainMeth)
> # end time monitoring
> toc()
0.82 sec elapsed

[1] "Performance Measures from Confusion Matrix"
> print(data.frame(Accuracy = ldaAcc, Sensitivity = ldaSens,
+       Specificity = ldaSpec, Balanced_Accuracy = ldaBalAcc,
+       Informedness = ldaInform, Prevalence = ldaPrev))
   Accuracy Sensitivity Specificity Balanced_Accuracy Informedness
1 0.9155556        0.18   0.9887783         0.5843891    0.1687783
Prevalence
0.09053498
>
```

Note that while accuracy remains good at 0.92 and specificity at 0.99, sensitivity has suffered greatly. The balanced accuracy, which averages sensitivity and specificity, is only 0.58. The fitting algorithm maximizes accuracy, which is the number of correct classification decisions. However, if one cares about understanding what builds satisfaction, this is not a good predictor: only 18% of satisfied airline customers were so identified. Making the classifier more effective in identifying satisfied airline customers will require trade-offs: moving to a different point on the ROC curve. To save space, the ROC curves will not be shown for these imbalance fittings, but with the reduced data they are poorer, with AUC now about 0.77.

Next is the R session implementing the SMOTE method, which downsamples the "no" cases and generates artificial "yes" cases to create balance.

```
> # begin SMOTE LDA classification ========================
>
> set.seed(80111973) # same seed for each method
>
> library(themis) # needed for SMOTE
>
> trainMeth = trainControl(method = "repeatedcv", number = 10,
+                          repeats = 5, classProbs = T,
+                          sampling = "smote",
+                          savePredictions = T)
> # monitor time to do the fitting with tic(0) toc(0)
> library(tictoc)
> tic()
> ldaModel <- train(Satisfied ~ ., data = sAirImbal,
+                   method = "lda",
+                   trControl = trainMeth)
> # end time monitoring
> toc()
1.81 sec elapsed
>
> print("Performance Measures from Confusion Matrix")
[1] "Performance Measures from Confusion Matrix"
> print(data.frame(Accuracy = ldaAcc, Sensitivity = ldaSens,
+       Specificity = ldaSpec, Balanced_Accuracy = ldaBalAcc,
+       Informedness = ldaInform, Prevalence = ldaPrev))
   Accuracy Sensitivity Specificity Balanced_Accuracy Informedness
1 0.7145679   0.7072727   0.7152941         0.7112834    0.4225668
 Prevalence
 0.09053498
>
```

Using the `sampling = "smote"` option requires adding the themis library. Note that the execution time is more than double that needed for the usual LDA fitting. This will matter more when the data sets are larger.

We find much better results for sensitivity, with some sacrifice in accuracy and specificity. Now, all measure about the same at 0.71. Note also that informedness improved from 0.17 to 0.42 and balanced accuracy from 0.58 to 0.71.

This section does not include an R code for case weighting. Case weights are inversely proportional to the number of cases in their class. Case weighting is an option available only for certain classifiers and is difficult to implement with cross-validation via caret.

6.6 The Overall Process for Classification Predictive Analytics

Then, one can think of using a classifier in predictive analytics as having 10 steps, many in parallel with the steps for regression:

1. Determine the objectives of the predictive model based on managerial needs.
2. Summarize the data: make sure the training set is complete, with class values for every observation.
3. PLOT the data: use the `boxplot()` and `pairs()` commands in R.
4. Scale and code all predictor variables.
5. Choose a classification method (e.g., k-NN, LDA, or neural network).
6. Determine the degree of data imbalance. If appropriate, use class weights to compensate for imbalance.
7. Fit the chosen classifier using cross-validation with an imbalance adjustment if needed. Optionally, change the threshold value (default is typically determined to maximize accuracy).
8. Assess the classifier performance via confusion matrix entries and the ROC. If the performance is inadequate, choose a different classifier. If no classifier is adequate, conclude that classification is not practical for the managerial objectives and report this to management.
9. If the classifier performance is adequate for the objectives, use the classification model to predict the class for specific predictor variable values of interest. Include a characterization of uncertainty about the prediction. Do this in managerial terms.
10. Give useful overall managerial summary and recommendation on use of the fitted classification model.

6.7 Case Supporting Chapter 6

The multi-segment case ISLRDefaultData case supports the material in this chapter. All analyses are conducted under the *data-adaptive research* paradigm. This case extends over multiple weeks. The case description slides and data can be found online in the ISLRClassification folder of Barton (2023).

6.8 R Code Used in Chapter 6

```
# Full code for book Airline knn, lda, nnet, glm analyses
# Russell Barton
Air <- read.csv("C:/Users/T410/Desktop/BAN840/Book/R_codes_and_
                data/AirSatisfactionPartialSmall.csv")

# we will work with the "AirSatisfactionPartialSmall" data frame
# summarize the data
head(Air)  # show the first few lines
str(Air)   # see that the structure is a data frame
# get a summary of values (note outcome)
summary(Air)

# do two boxplots to see joint effect
with(Air,boxplot(Clean~interaction(Satisfied,Gender),
xlab = "Satisfied, Gender"))
with(Air,boxplot(SeatComfort~interaction(Satisfied,Gender),
xlab = "Satisfied, Gender"))
with(Air,boxplot(DepartDelay~interaction(Satisfied,Gender),
xlab = "Satisfied, Gender"))
with(Air,boxplot(ArriveDelay~interaction(Satisfied,Gender),
xlab = "Satisfied, Gender"))


# for remaining scatter and boxplots, rescale all
#   numeric predictor variables to +/- 1
# this data frame is named sAir
scalpm1 = function(x){(x-(min(x)+max(x))/2)/(.5*(max(x)-min(x)))}
sAir = NULL
sAir$Satisfied = Air$Satisfied # do not rescale
sAir$Gender = Air$Gender       # do not rescale
sAir$Age = scalpm1(Air$Age)
sAir$Distance = scalpm1(Air$Distance)
sAir$FoodDrink = scalpm1(Air$FoodDrink)
sAir$SeatComfort = scalpm1(Air$SeatComfort)
sAir$InflightEnt = scalpm1(Air$InflightEnt)
sAir$Checkin = scalpm1(Air$Checkin)
sAir$InflightServ = scalpm1(Air$InflightServ)
sAir$Clean = scalpm1(Air$Clean)
sAir$DepartDelay = scalpm1(Air$DepartDelay)
sAir$ArriveDelay = scalpm1(Air$ArriveDelay)
# convert sAir from list to data frame for plots and
#   classification methods
sAir = as.data.frame(sAir)

# boxplots by Satisfied and Gender for numeric predictor
  variables
library(reshape2)
# melting by "Label". 'melt is from the reshape2 package.
```

```
# do ?melt to see what other things it can do
# only works for quantitative variables, just 'id'
  qualitative ones
sAir.melt <- melt(sAir, id = c("Gender","Satisfied"))
head(sAir.melt)
library(ggplot2)
ggplot(data = sAir.melt, aes(x=variable, y=value)) +
geom_boxplot(aes(fill=Satisfied))
ggplot(data = sAir.melt, aes(x=variable, y=value)) +
geom_boxplot(aes(fill=Gender))
```

```
# begin classification methods ==========================
# convert Gender to 0-1 for model fitting
sAir$Gender<-ifelse(Air$Gender=="Female",1,0)
# set Satisfied to a factor -
#     the dependent variable must be a 'factor'
sAir$Satisfied = as.factor(sAir$Satisfied)
# set Satisfied reference level (class 1) to "yes"
sAir$Satisfied = relevel(sAir$Satisfied, ref = "yes")

# Cross-validation (10-fold) code
#   needs train function from caret library
library(caret)
library(MLeval) # for ROC curves
set.seed(80111973) # same seed for each method
# begin LDA classification ===============================
# set the CV method to lda
# lda needs MASS package
library(MASS)
trainMeth = trainControl(method = "repeatedcv", number = 10,
repeats = 5, classProbs = T,
savePredictions = T)
# monitor time to do the fitting with tic(0) toc(0)
library(tictoc)
tic()
ldaModel <- train(Satisfied ~ ., data = sAir,
method = "lda",
trControl = trainMeth)
# end time monitoring
toc()

# summary of LDA results
print(ldaModel$finalModel)

# build LDA CV confusion matrix in terms of percentages
  and counts
ldaConfMat =
```

```
as.matrix(confusionMatrix(ldaModel, positive = "Yes")$table)
print("Confusion Matrix (%)")
print(ldaConfMat)
ldaConfMatCount = (ldaConfMat/100)*length(sAir$Satisfied)
print("Confusion Matrix (counts) = (percent/100)x no. in train")
print(ldaConfMatCount)

# derive performance measures from confusion matrix
ldaAcc = (ldaConfMatCount[1,1] + ldaConfMatCount[2,2])/
sum(ldaConfMatCount)
ldaSens = ldaConfMatCount[1,1] /
(ldaConfMatCount[1,1] + ldaConfMatCount[2,1])
ldaSpec = ldaConfMatCount[2,2] /
(ldaConfMatCount[1,2] + ldaConfMatCount[2,2])
ldaBalAcc = (ldaSens + ldaSpec)/2
ldaInform = ldaSens + ldaSpec - 1
ldaPrev = (ldaConfMatCount[1,1] + ldaConfMatCount[2,1])/
sum(ldaConfMatCount)
print("Performance Measures from Confusion Matrix")
print(data.frame(Accuracy = ldaAcc, Sensitivity = ldaSens,
Specificity = ldaSpec, Balanced_Accuracy = ldaBalAcc,
Informedness = ldaInform, Prevalence = ldaPrev))

ldaSensLo = ldaSens - 1.96*sqrt(ldaSens*(1-ldaSens)/
(ldaConfMatCount[1,1] + ldaConfMatCount[2,1]))
ldaSensHi = ldaSens + 1.96*sqrt(ldaSens*(1-ldaSens)/
(ldaConfMatCount[1,1] + ldaConfMatCount[2,1]))
ldaSpecLo = ldaSpec - 1.96*sqrt(ldaSpec*(1-ldaSpec)/
(ldaConfMatCount[1,2] + ldaConfMatCount[2,2]))
ldaSpecHi = ldaSpec + 1.96*sqrt(ldaSpec*(1-ldaSpec)/
(ldaConfMatCount[1,2] + ldaConfMatCount[2,2]))

print("Approximate 95% CI for Sensitivity, Specificity, lda")
print(data.frame(SensitivityLo = ldaSensLo,
SensitivityHI = ldaSensHi,
SpecificityLo = ldaSpecLo,
SpecificityHi = ldaSpecHi))


# use MLeval package evalm routine to generate ROC plot
ROCobj = evalm(ldaModel, title = "Plot for LDA")

# simple prediction for female gender with midrange responses
predvals = data.frame(Gender=1,Age=0,Distance=0,FoodDrink=0,
SeatComfort=0,InflightEnt=0,Checkin=0,
InflightServ=0,Clean=0,
DepartDelay=0,ArriveDelay=0)
predict(ldaModel, predvals)
```

```
# lda 'optimistic' confusion matrix based on full data
predict(ldaModel, predvals)
ldaPreds = predict(ldaModel, sAir)
confusionMatrix(data = ldaPreds,
reference = sAir$Satisfied, mode = "prec_recall")


# begin KNN classification fixed k======================

# NOTE: knn librarys package "class"
library(class)
# to run with fixed k, say sqrt (2000) take integer part,
#   if it is even, subtract 1
#   then use tuneGrid option in train
k2000 = trunc(sqrt(length(sAir$Satisfied)))
set.seed(80111973) # same seed for each method
trainMeth = trainControl(method = "repeatedcv", number = 10,
repeats = 5, classProbs = T, savePredictions = T)
# monitor time to do the fitting with tic(0) toc(0)
library(tictoc)
tic()
# note: if you choose k, use tuneGrid option, else delete
knnModel <- train(Satisfied ~ ., data = sAir,
method = "knn",
tuneGrid = data.frame(k=k2000),
trControl = trainMeth)
# end time monitoring
toc()

# summary of KNN results
print(knnModel$finalModel)

# build knn CV confusion matrix in terms of percentages
  and counts
knnConfMat =
as.matrix(confusionMatrix(knnModel, positive = "Yes")$table)
print("Confusion Matrix (%)")
print(knnConfMat)
knnConfMatCount = (knnConfMat/100)*length(sAir$Satisfied)
print("Confusion Matrix (counts) = (percent/100)x no. in train")
print(knnConfMatCount)

# derive performance measures from confusion matrix
knnAcc = (knnConfMatCount[1,1] + knnConfMatCount[2,2])/
sum(knnConfMatCount)
knnSens = knnConfMatCount[1,1] /
(knnConfMatCount[1,1] + knnConfMatCount[2,1])
knnSpec = knnConfMatCount[2,2] /
(knnConfMatCount[1,2] + knnConfMatCount[2,2])
knnBalAcc = (knnSens + knnSpec)/2
```

```
knnInform = knnSens + knnSpec - 1
knnPrev = (knnConfMatCount[1,1] + knnConfMatCount[2,1])/
sum(knnConfMatCount)
print("Performance Measures from Confusion Matrix")
print(data.frame(Accuracy = knnAcc, Sensitivity = knnSens,
Specificity = knnSpec, Balanced_Accuracy = knnBalAcc,
Informedness = knnInform, Prevalence = knnPrev))

knnSensLo = knnSens - 1.96*sqrt(knnSens*(1-knnSens)/
(knnConfMatCount[1,1] + knnConfMatCount[2,1]))
knnSensHi = knnSens + 1.96*sqrt(knnSens*(1-knnSens)/
(knnConfMatCount[1,1] + knnConfMatCount[2,1]))
knnSpecLo = knnSpec - 1.96*sqrt(knnSpec*(1-knnSpec)/
(knnConfMatCount[1,2] + knnConfMatCount[2,2]))
knnSpecHi = knnSpec + 1.96*sqrt(knnSpec*(1-knnSpec)/
(knnConfMatCount[1,2] + knnConfMatCount[2,2]))

print("Approximate 95% CI for Sensitivity, Specificity, knn")
print(data.frame(SensitivityLo = knnSensLo,
SensitivityHI = knnSensHi,
SpecificityLo = knnSpecLo,
SpecificityHi = knnSpecHi))


# use MLeval package evalm routine to generate ROC plot
ROCobj = evalm(knnModel, title = "Plot for knn")

# simple prediction for female gender with midrange responses
predvals = data.frame(Gender=1,Age=0,Distance=0,FoodDrink=0,
SeatComfort=0,InflightEnt=0,Checkin=0,
InflightServ=0,Clean=0,
DepartDelay=0,ArriveDelay=0)
predict(knnModel, predvals)

# knn 'optimistic' confusion matrix based on full data

knnPreds = predict(knnModel, sAir)
confusionMatrix(data = knnPreds,
reference = sAir$Satisfied, mode = "prec_recall")


# begin nnet classification ============================

# set the CV method to nnet
# nnet needs MASS package
library(MASS)
set.seed(80111973) # same seed for each method
trainMeth = trainControl(method = "repeatedcv", number = 10,
repeats = 5, classProbs = T,
savePredictions = T)
```

```
# monitor time to do the fitting with tic(0) toc(0)
library(tictoc)
tic()
nnetModel <- train(Satisfied ~ ., data = sAir,
method = "nnet",
trace = F,
trControl = trainMeth)
# end time monitoring
toc()

# summary of nnet results
print(nnetModel$finalModel$n)
print(nnetModel$finalModel$wts)

# to show neural network structure for many network
#   (neuralnet has built-in plotting)
# use devtools for plot
# see https://beckmw.wordpress.com/2013/11/14/
#             visualizing-neural-networks-in-r-update/
library(devtools)
# NOTE - to run -place entire Web address below on ONE LINE
source_url('https://gist.githubusercontent.com/fawda123/7471137/
           raw/466c1474d0a505ff044412703516c34f1a4684a5/
           nnet_plot_update.r')
plot.nnet(nnetModel, nid=T)

# build nnet CV confusion matrix -- percentages and counts
nnetConfMat =
as.matrix(confusionMatrix(nnetModel, positive = "Yes")$table)
print("Confusion Matrix (%)")
print(nnetConfMat)
nnetConfMatCount = (nnetConfMat/100)*length(sAir$Satisfied)
print("Confusion Matrix (counts) = (percent/100)x no. in train")
print(nnetConfMatCount)

# derive performance measures from confusion matrix
nnetAcc = (nnetConfMatCount[1,1] + nnetConfMatCount[2,2])/
sum(nnetConfMatCount)
nnetSens = nnetConfMatCount[1,1] /
(nnetConfMatCount[1,1] + nnetConfMatCount[2,1])
nnetSpec = nnetConfMatCount[2,2] /
(nnetConfMatCount[1,2] + nnetConfMatCount[2,2])
nnetBalAcc = (nnetSens + nnetSpec)/2
nnetInform = nnetSens + nnetSpec - 1
nnetPrev = (nnetConfMatCount[1,1] + nnetConfMatCount[2,1])/
sum(nnetConfMatCount)
print("Performance Measures from Confusion Matrix")
print(data.frame(Accuracy = nnetAcc, Sensitivity = nnetSens,
Specificity = nnetSpec, Balanced_Accuracy = nnetBalAcc,
Informedness = nnetInform, Prevalence = nnetPrev))
```

```
nnetSensLo = nnetSens - 1.96*sqrt(nnetSens*(1-nnetSens)/
(nnetConfMatCount[1,1] + nnetConfMatCount[2,1]))
nnetSensHi = nnetSens + 1.96*sqrt(nnetSens*(1-nnetSens)/
(nnetConfMatCount[1,1] + nnetConfMatCount[2,1]))
nnetSpecLo = nnetSpec - 1.96*sqrt(nnetSpec*(1-nnetSpec)/
(nnetConfMatCount[1,2] + nnetConfMatCount[2,2]))
nnetSpecHi = nnetSpec + 1.96*sqrt(nnetSpec*(1-nnetSpec)/
(nnetConfMatCount[1,2] + nnetConfMatCount[2,2]))

print("Approximate 95% CI for Sensitivity, Specificity, nnet")
print(data.frame(SensitivityLo = nnetSensLo,
SensitivityHI = nnetSensHi,
SpecificityLo = nnetSpecLo,
SpecificityHi = nnetSpecHi))



# use MLeval package evalm routine to generate ROC plot
ROCobj = evalm(nnetModel, title = "Plot for nnet")

# simple prediction for female gender with midrange responses
predvals = data.frame(Gender=1,Age=0,Distance=0,FoodDrink=0,
SeatComfort=0,InflightEnt=0,Checkin=0,
InflightServ=0,Clean=0,
DepartDelay=0,ArriveDelay=0)
predict(nnetModel, predvals)

# nnet 'optimistic' confusion matrix based on full data

nnetPreds = predict(nnetModel, sAir)
confusionMatrix(data = nnetPreds,
reference = sAir$Satisfied, mode = "prec_recall")


# begin logistic regression (glm) classification ========

# set the CV method to glm
# no extra packages needed beyond caret and MLeval
set.seed(80111973) # same seed for each method
trainMeth = trainControl(method = "repeatedcv", number = 10,
repeats = 5, classProbs = T,
savePredictions = T)
# monitor time to do the fitting with tic(0) toc(0)
library(tictoc)
tic()
logRegModel <- train(Satisfied ~ ., data = sAir,
method = "glm",
family = "binomial",
trControl = trainMeth)
```

```
# end time monitoring
toc()

# summary of logReg results
print(logRegModel$finalModel)

# build logReg CV conf. matrix in terms of percentages
  and counts
logRegConfMat =
as.matrix(confusionMatrix(logRegModel, positive = "Yes")$table)
print("Confusion Matrix (%)")
print(logRegConfMat)
logRegConfMatCount = (logRegConfMat/100)*length(sAir$Satisfied)
print("Confusion Matrix (counts) = (percent/100)x no. in train")
print(logRegConfMatCount)

# derive performance measures from confusion matrix
logRegAcc = (logRegConfMatCount[1,1] + logRegConfMatCount[2,2])/
sum(logRegConfMatCount)
logRegSens = logRegConfMatCount[1,1] /
(logRegConfMatCount[1,1] + logRegConfMatCount[2,1])
logRegSpec = logRegConfMatCount[2,2] /
(logRegConfMatCount[1,2] + logRegConfMatCount[2,2])
logRegBalAcc = (logRegSens + logRegSpec)/2
logRegInform = logRegSens + logRegSpec - 1
logRegPrev = (logRegConfMatCount[1,1] + logRegConfMatCount[2,1])/
sum(logRegConfMatCount)
print("Performance Measures from Confusion Matrix")
print(data.frame(Accuracy = logRegAcc, Sensitivity = logRegSens,
Specificity = logRegSpec, Balanced_Accuracy = logRegBalAcc,
Informedness = logRegInform, Prevalence = logRegPrev))

logRegSensLo = logRegSens - 1.96*sqrt(logRegSens*(1-logRegSens)/
(logRegConfMatCount[1,1] + logRegConfMatCount[2,1]))
logRegSensHi = logRegSens + 1.96*sqrt(logRegSens*(1-logRegSens)/
(logRegConfMatCount[1,1] + logRegConfMatCount[2,1]))
logRegSpecLo = logRegSpec - 1.96*sqrt(logRegSpec*(1-logRegSpec)/
(logRegConfMatCount[1,2] + logRegConfMatCount[2,2]))
logRegSpecHi = logRegSpec + 1.96*sqrt(logRegSpec*(1-logRegSpec)/
(logRegConfMatCount[1,2] + logRegConfMatCount[2,2]))

print("Approximate 95% CI for Sensitivity, Specificity, logReg")
print(data.frame(SensitivityLo = logRegSensLo,
SensitivityHI = logRegSensHi,
SpecificityLo = logRegSpecLo,
SpecificityHi = logRegSpecHi))



# use MLeval package evalm routine to generate ROC plot
ROCobj = evalm(logRegModel, title = "Plot for logReg")
```

```
# simple prediction for female gender with midrange responses
predvals = data.frame(Gender=1,Age=0,Distance=0,FoodDrink=0,
SeatComfort=0,InflightEnt=0,Checkin=0,
InflightServ=0,Clean=0,
DepartDelay=0,ArriveDelay=0)
predict(logRegModel, predvals)

# logReg 'optimistic' confusion matrix based on full data

logRegPreds = predict(logRegModel, sAir)
confusionMatrix(data = logRegPreds,
reference = sAir$Satisfied, mode = "prec_recall")




# Imbalanced Classification ==============================
# =======================================================

# create imbalanced data

# select all "no" rows for sAir_no, "yes" rows for sAir_yes
sAir_no = sAir[sAir$Satisfied == "no",]
sAir_yes = sAir[sAir$Satisfied == "yes",]
# sample 10% of sAir_yes
# sampling from data frame needs corpora library
library(corpora)
sAir_yes_part = sample.df(sAir_yes,size=trunc(.1*nrow(sAir_no)))
sAirImbal = rbind(sAir_yes_part, sAir_no)


# begin usual LDA classification ========================

set.seed(80111973) # same seed for each method

trainMeth = trainControl(method = "repeatedcv", number = 10,
repeats = 5, classProbs = T,
savePredictions = T)
# monitor time to do the fitting with tic(0) toc(0)
library(tictoc)
tic()
ldaModel <- train(Satisfied ~ ., data = sAirImbal,
method = "lda",
trControl = trainMeth)
# end time monitoring
toc()

# summary of LDA results
print(ldaModel$finalModel)
```

```
# build LDA CV confusion matrix in terms of percentages
  and counts
ldaConfMat =
as.matrix(confusionMatrix(ldaModel, positive = "Yes")$table)
print("Confusion Matrix (%)")
print(ldaConfMat)
ldaConfMatCount = (ldaConfMat/100)*length(sAir$Satisfied)
print("Confusion Matrix (counts) = (percent/100)x no. in train")
print(ldaConfMatCount)

# derive performance measures from confusion matrix
ldaAcc = (ldaConfMatCount[1,1] + ldaConfMatCount[2,2])/
sum(ldaConfMatCount)
ldaSens = ldaConfMatCount[1,1] /
(ldaConfMatCount[1,1] + ldaConfMatCount[2,1])
ldaSpec = ldaConfMatCount[2,2] /
(ldaConfMatCount[1,2] + ldaConfMatCount[2,2])
ldaBalAcc = (ldaSens + ldaSpec)/2
ldaInform = ldaSens + ldaSpec - 1
ldaPrev = (ldaConfMatCount[1,1] + ldaConfMatCount[2,1])/
sum(ldaConfMatCount)
print("Performance Measures from Confusion Matrix")
print(data.frame(Accuracy = ldaAcc, Sensitivity = ldaSens,
Specificity = ldaSpec, Balanced_Accuracy = ldaBalAcc,
Informedness = ldaInform, Prevalence = ldaPrev))



# use MLeval package evalm routine to generate ROC plot
ROCobj = evalm(ldaModel, title = "Plot for LDA unweighted")


# begin SMOTE LDA classification =========================

set.seed(80111973) # same seed for each method

library(themis) # needed for SMOTE

trainMeth = trainControl(method = "repeatedcv", number = 10,
repeats = 5, classProbs = T,
sampling = "smote",
savePredictions = T)
# monitor time to do the fitting with tic(0) toc(0)
library(tictoc)
tic()
ldaModel <- train(Satisfied ~ ., data = sAirImbal,
method = "lda",
trControl = trainMeth)
# end time monitoring
toc()
```

```
# summary of LDA results
print(ldaModel$finalModel)

# build LDA CV confusion matrix in terms of percentages
  and counts
ldaConfMat =
as.matrix(confusionMatrix(ldaModel, positive = "Yes")$table)
print("Confusion Matrix (%)")
print(ldaConfMat)
ldaConfMatCount = (ldaConfMat/100)*length(sAir$Satisfied)
print("Confusion Matrix (counts) = (percent/100)x no. in train")
print(ldaConfMatCount)

# derive performance measures from confusion matrix
ldaAcc = (ldaConfMatCount[1,1] + ldaConfMatCount[2,2])/
sum(ldaConfMatCount)
ldaSens = ldaConfMatCount[1,1] /
(ldaConfMatCount[1,1] + ldaConfMatCount[2,1])
ldaSpec = ldaConfMatCount[2,2] /
(ldaConfMatCount[1,2] + ldaConfMatCount[2,2])
ldaBalAcc = (ldaSens + ldaSpec)/2
ldaInform = ldaSens + ldaSpec - 1
ldaPrev = (ldaConfMatCount[1,1] + ldaConfMatCount[2,1])/
sum(ldaConfMatCount)
print("Performance Measures from Confusion Matrix")
print(data.frame(Accuracy = ldaAcc, Sensitivity = ldaSens,
Specificity = ldaSpec, Balanced_Accuracy = ldaBalAcc,
Informedness = ldaInform, Prevalence = ldaPrev))

# use MLeval package evalm routine to generate ROC plot
ROCobj = evalm(ldaModel, title = "Plot for LDA")
```

Part IV

Predicting Dynamic Behavior

Overview

In this part, our focus is on predictive analytics methods for numerical outcomes that vary over time. Such predictions (along with characterization of the uncertainty in the prediction) can be based on history of similar values; these predictive analytics models are called *time series* models and fall in the *traditional research* paradigm. They are the focus of the following chapter.

Predicting dynamic behavior may be based on mechanistic models of a system. These are called *dynamic simulation* models and generate their own dynamic data for further analysis. This predictive analytics approach falls under Miller's *model-dependent research* paradigm, discussed in Chapter 1. The discussion is split into three chapters: creating artificial random quantities used in such dynamic models, designing and building the models, and analyzing their output.

Chapter 7

Trendline and Time Series Analysis for Forecasting

What is a time series? A time series is a quantitative outcome that is dynamically varying over time, say $Y(x)$, where x represents time, and when variations from one value to the next are not i.i.d. The predictive analytics task is to choose and fit models that can predict future values of the time series and characterize the uncertainty in these predictions. Time series models are fitted to a training data set that is a historical series of values spaced evenly in time. The outcome is usually indexed by t, say Y_t. Predictive analytics in this setting is typically called *forecasting*. The objective is always to predict for a future time: this is important in business settings to allow for advance planning for staffing levels, production schedules, ordering long-lead-time items, and other managerial decisions.

In real settings, while a pattern may be present, there will be random variations that prevent a perfect forecast. When the random variations from one time to the next are independent and the pattern is a simple increase or decrease over time, then trendline models can be used, where our usual regression approach with t is the independent variable.

But typically, there is some local dependence of the random perturbations that are part of the outcome: autocorrelation. Often, if the current outcome is (randomly) higher than one might expect, it is likely that neighboring times will similarly be high. This kind of dependence is called *autocorrelation* and is the setting for which

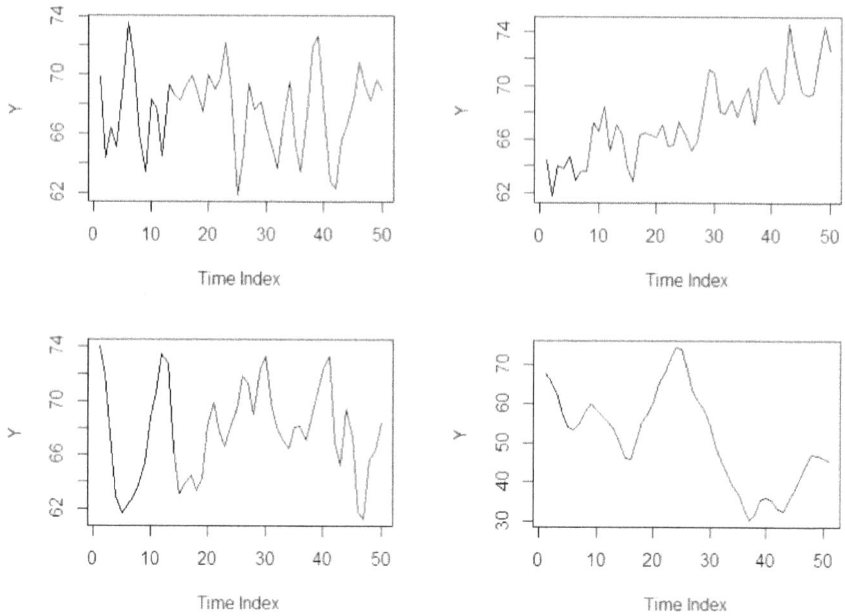

Figure 7.1. Time series examples.

time series analysis is appropriate. Figure 7.1 shows some typical time series patterns. Each was generated by a different dependence structure. These patterns are discussed in Sections 7.4 and 7.5. A time series can be modeled as a kind of *stochastic process*, and time series scatter plots are often called *run charts*.

Predicting one time step in the future is often insufficient: when setting a production or work schedule, there is a need to predict time series values well in advance, which may require predicting dynamic variations over the forecast period. Thus, we need to predict not just a single number but dynamic behavior.

In this chapter, we explore prediction using trendline models and a number of different time series models for data exhibiting autocorrelation. We will see how to fit models, characterize model uncertainty, and give predictions that take into account model uncertainty.

All of the models that we explore provide a probability model for the series, and so we return to the *traditional research* paradigm for this chapter.

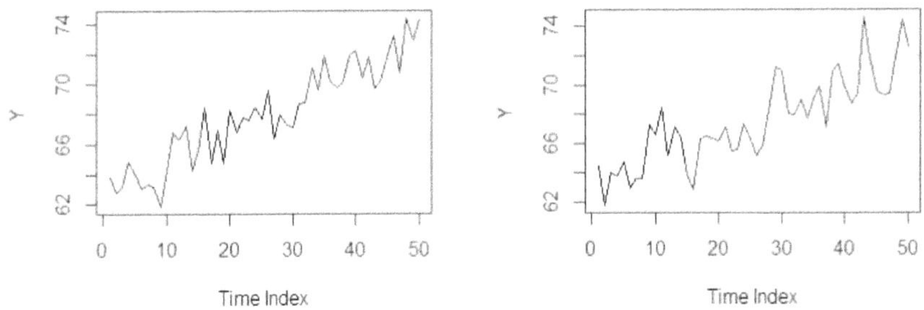

Figure 7.2. Trends with independent vs. dependent random variation.

7.1 Trendline Models

Trendline models are appropriate for time series that are experiencing a steadily increasing or decreasing trend with independent random variations. Compare the two series in Figure 7.2. One has independent random variations, while the other has autocorrelated random variations. Can you tell which is which? When the autocorrelation is positive, the data tend to wander more, rather than simply zigzagging. The series on the right (also at top right of Figure 7.1) is autocorrelated; the series on the left is not.

When you see a trend in your data without a clear wandering pattern, it is best to try a simple regression forecasting model. You do not need to be certain whether autocorrelation is present. If there is autocorrelation, it will become apparent in your regression diagnostic plots. If you fit a regression model to the data in the usual way and see problems with the autocorrelation diagnostic plot (via `acf`), then you will have to abandon the regression forecasting approach and fit a time series model from Section 7.5.

7.1.1 Linear trendline models

When there is a linear trend and the random variations are approximately independent, a regression model where Y is the time series value and x is time can give good forecast accuracy and precision. The trendline model is used under the *traditional research* paradigm. The model form is

$$Y = \beta_0 + \beta_1 x + \varepsilon, \ \varepsilon \overset{\text{iid}}{\sim} N(0, \sigma^2), \tag{7.1}$$

where β_0 is an artificial quantity corresponding to the series value at time index 0, x is the value of the time index, and β_1 is the average increase in the series from one time index to the next. There is variability in the average increase, and its standard deviation is unknown and represented by σ.

7.1.2 Nonlinear trendline models

In some situations, there may be reason to expect an exponential increase in the trend (e.g., product demand early in its life cycle) or a gradual decrease in the rate of increase (e.g., mature product demand). In these settings a transformation of x may be appropriate before fitting a trendline regression model. An exponential increase suggests regressing Y on $\beta_0 x^{\beta_1}$ or $\beta_0 e^{\beta_1 x}$ or some other power function of x. A decreasing rate of increase might be fitted with a trendline regression using $\log(x)$. Transformations to x in a regression setting are discussed in Section 3.3.2.

7.1.3 The overall process for trendline regression in the *traditional research* paradigm

How does one build and use a trendline predictive analytics model? The process is identical to that for linear regression given in Section 3.4, modified slightly for the specifics of trendline regression. The checklist for observational data in Section 3.3.6 does not apply here since a plot of the data has already indicated a trend, which is a sensible phenomenon in many business settings. There is only one predictor variable (time), so there is no *VIF* between predictor variables, and x values evenly spaced over time means there is no data imbalance:

1. The objectives of the predictive model are to predict the outcome at one or more time periods beyond the historical data: to give a forecast, along with a characterization of forecast uncertainty.
2. Summarize the data with a descriptive summary, a time sequence plot, and discussion.
3. Based on the plot and expectations (linear trend and independent random variations), propose a regression model if the expectations are met. Otherwise, consider fitting a time series model, such as an ARIMA model with or without seasonality

and/or trend. Include a mathematical presentation with βs, ε, and the i.i.d. statement.

4. Show and interpret for management the fitted regression model.
5. Discuss the practical predictive ability: fitted line plot and R^2.
6. If the fitted model has practical predictive power, perform model validity checks; plots with comments. If the autocorrelation plot shows significant correlation at lag 1 or later, it will be necessary to abandon the trendline regression model and instead fit a time series model, such as an ARIMA model with or without seasonality and/or trend.
7. If the validity checks are passed, then uncertainty characterization using the i.i.d. normal error assumption will be valid.
8. If the validity checks are passed, then continue. Show appropriate tables and discuss the sigma estimate and p-values for coefficients and the overall model.
9. Show and discuss coefficients and confidence intervals in managerial terms.
10. Show and discuss forecast prediction intervals for desired time values in the future. Remember that projections far beyond the immediate future are likely to be unreliable. Discuss the forecast in managerial terms. In the trendline setting, forecast confidence intervals are not interesting — the management cares about what will happen next, not what might happen averaged over many possible futures.
11. Give useful overall managerial summary and recommendation on use of the fitted trendline regression model.

7.2 Trendline Model in R: Weekly Product Order Volume

Consider a time series for the order quantity for a product, indexed by week. The objective is to forecast order volume one, two, three, and four weeks in advance. Accurate forecasts allow management to make staffing changes and build up inventory to meet projected demand, while at the same time avoiding overstaffing and excess inventory when they are not needed. In addition, from the predictive analytics perspective, the forecast model should provide a characterization of uncertainty in the forecast, in particular a prediction interval.

The R commands for the data acquisition summary and plot, along with summary results are shown as follows.

```
> library(readxl) # needed to read in the Excel data file
>
> # trendline regression modeling
> # read orders data weeks
> OrdersData <- read_excel("OrdersData.xlsx")  # read the Excel file
> # summarize data
> summary(OrdersData)
        Orders            Week
Min.   : 24.00   Min.   : 1.00
1st Qu.: 38.50   1st Qu.: 7.75
Median : 67.50   Median :14.50
Mean   : 65.43   Mean   :14.50
3rd Qu.: 91.75   3rd Qu.:21.25
Max.   :117.00   Max.   :28.00
>
> plot(OrdersData$Week , OrdersData$Orders,
+      xlab = "Week", ylab = "Orders", type = "l")
>
```

There are 28 weeks of historical order volume data, indexed by the variable "Week" and called "Orders" in the data frame. Order volume varies from 24 to 117 over the 28 week period. Note that unlike a typical regression model with observational data, the "x" values (Week) are evenly spaced and complete over the range $[1, 28]$.

Figure 7.3 shows the series. The pattern is consistent from week 5 onward, and the variation in the trend seems random. A regression model fitted to that period should give good prediction of the future order sizes, perhaps even several weeks in advance, meeting the objectives mentioned above.

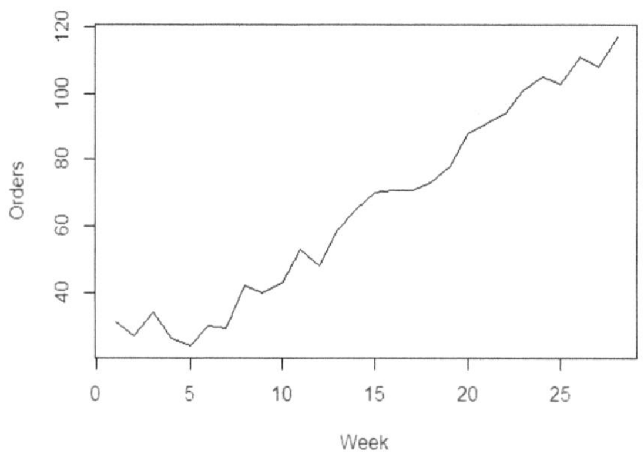

Figure 7.3. Weekly orders exhibit steady increase from week 5.

The proposed model is from Equation (7.1), where β_0 is an artificial quantity corresponding to the demand at Week 0, x is the week, and β_1 is the average weekly increase in order demand. There is variability in the average demand in any week, and its standard deviation is unknown and represented by σ.

The following code shows the R commands to fit this data starting at week 5, along with characterizations of the predictive ability: R^2 and a plot of actual vs. model-predicted values. Note: with trendline regression in R, we can treat the data as an ordinary data frame. Using R for the time series models in the following section requires converting the data into a *time series* object. That will be discussed in a separate section.

```
> # delete first four weeks from data frame before regression
> OrdersData = OrdersData[-c(1,2,3,4),]
>
> # fit the regression model
> regModel = lm(Orders ~ Week, data = OrdersData)
>
> # show fitted model
> summary(regModel)$coefficients[,1]
 (Intercept)         Week
    5.630827     3.990226
>
> # pull out the R-squared value from the summary
> summary(regModel)$r.squared
[1] 0.9815623
> # plot predicted vs actual
> plot(predict(regModel, newdata=OrdersData),OrdersData$Orders,
+       xlab = "Predicted Orders", ylab = "Actual Orders")
>
```

It is clear that the model predictive ability is high, with an R^2 of nearly 0.99. The model suggests an increase of an additional four orders per week. The plot of actual vs. predicted number of orders in Figure 7.4 confirms the high fidelity.

Because the model has high predictive power, validity checks are performed to ensure that coefficient confidence intervals and forecast prediction intervals can be based on the model in Equation (7.1). The following session creates the model validity plots described in Chapter 3.

```
> # assess model validity
> acf(regModel$residuals) # do plots to check
  model validity
```

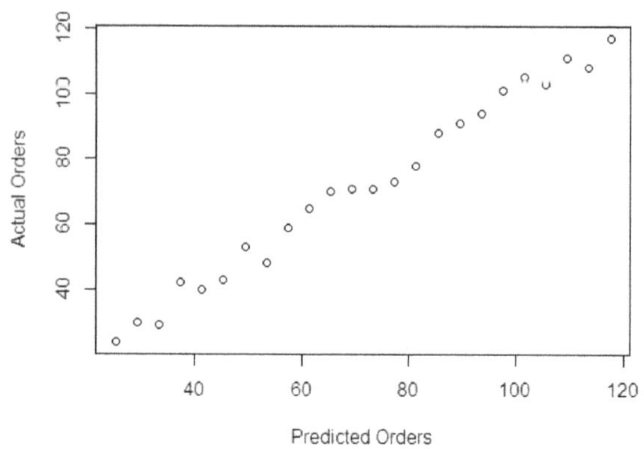

Figure 7.4. Actual vs. regression-predicted orders shows high predictive power.

```
> plot(regModel, ask=F, add.smooth=F) # more plots
> plot(OrdersData$Orders,regModel$residuals) # more plots
>
```

The plots are shown in Figure 7.5. Because the number of orders must be an integer, the normal probability plot shows some step structure, as expected. The lag 4 autocorrelation barely exceeds the $\alpha = 0.05$ threshold, but roughly one out of 20 autocorrelation coefficients might be expected to fall outside the limits with this α even when there is independence. So, this is not a concern. The other plots support the validity of the model.

With validity supported, the regression summary p-values are meaningful. The R commands for the summary as well as the 95% model coefficient confidence intervals are shown as follows, along with the results.

```
> # validity checks pass so can use p-values and construct
> #   confidence intervals for coefficients and forecast
> #   prediction intervals
> # used to show standard deviation estimates and p-values
> summary(regModel)

Call:
lm(formula = Orders ~ Week, data = OrdersData)

Residuals:
    Min      1Q  Median      3Q     Max
-5.4897 -2.4341  0.6007  2.8020  4.6425
```

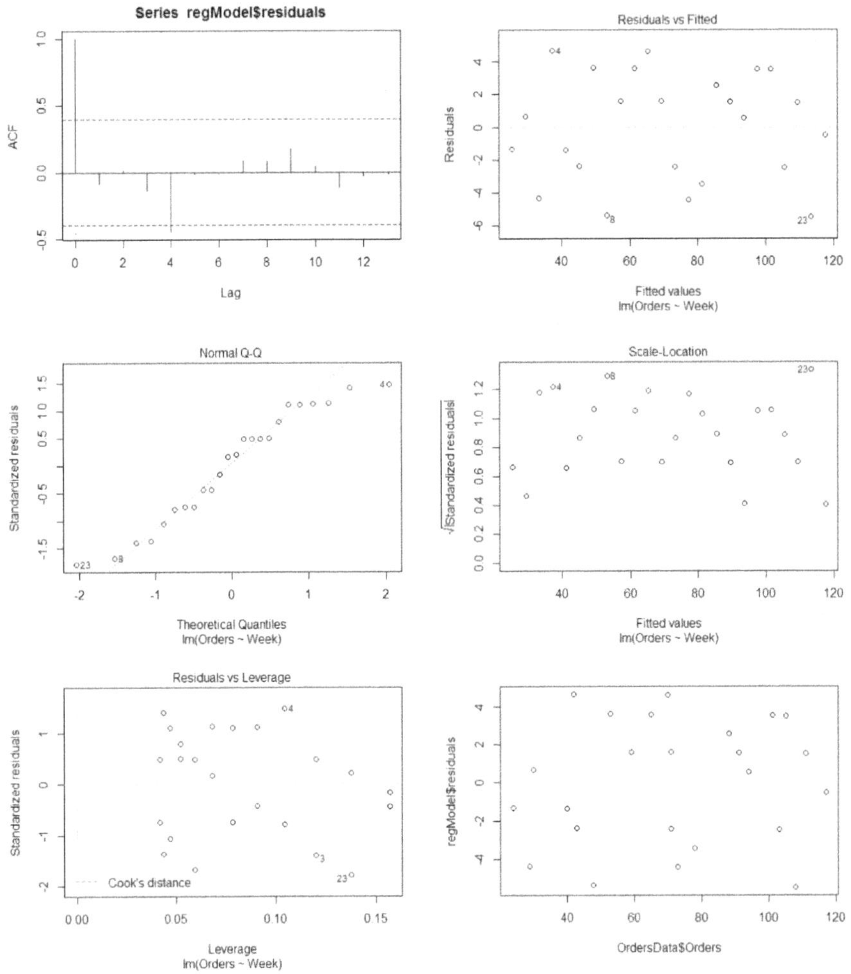

Figure 7.5. Regression residual plots support validity of the regression.

```
Coefficients:
            Estimate Std. Error t value Pr(>|t|)
(Intercept)  5.30188    1.74919   3.031  0.00614 **
Week         4.00696    0.09776  40.989  < 2e-16 ***
---
Signif. codes:  0 *** 0.001 ** 0.01 * 0.05 . 0.1   1
```

```
Residual standard error: 3.315 on 22 degrees of freedom
Multiple R-squared:  0.9871,    Adjusted R-squared: 0.9865
F-statistic:  1680 on 1 and 22 DF,  p-value: < 2.2e-16

> # compute confidence intervals for model coefficients
> confint(regModel)
               2.5 %   97.5 %
(Intercept) 1.674295 8.929473
Week        3.804221 4.209692
>
```

The output identifies the fitted model form and the data set used in the fitting. A rough characterization of the residuals distribution does not indicate any extreme outliers: model predictions differ at most by slightly over 5 orders.

Both the intercept and the trend coefficients are statistically different from zero, as expected, with p-values of 0.006 and 2e−16, or 0.0000000000000002, a very small p-value indeed! The F statistic for the overall regression model is very large, and its p-value is near zero, as expected. The estimate for σ is 3.315, which means that the standard deviation of order quantity about the model-predicted values is about 3.3.

The model coefficients and confidence intervals can be interpreted for management as follows:

- The model-predicted order volume for "Week 0" is 5.3 orders. This is a calibration constant. Model uncertainty suggests the true value would be between 1.67 and 8.92 with 95% confidence.
- Weekly order volume is increasing at about 4 additional orders each week. Model uncertainty suggests the true value is between 3.8 and 4.2 with 95% confidence.

Forecasts for trendline models are typically for a few time indexes in advance. As for ordinary regression, forecasting far outside the range of data used to fit the regression model is risky. The following code provides forecasts for order volume for weeks 29, 30, 31, and 32 and assesses the quality of the forecasts with 95% prediction intervals. Remember that in a time series setting, forecast confidence intervals are not of interest: we only want to know the uncertainty about what will actually happen in the next periods, not what might happen on average over many realizations of the next periods. No one can repeat time — there are no "do-overs"!

```
> # predict orders for next four weeks
# put desired forecast in a dataframe
> new.dat <- data.frame(Week = c(29,30,31,32))
# give forecast PI
> predict(regModel, newdata = new.dat, interval = 'prediction')
       fit      lwr      upr
1 121.5036 114.0432 128.9641
2 125.5106 117.9788 133.0423
3 129.5175 121.9098 137.1253
4 133.5245 125.8361 141.2129
>
```

The model forecasts and prediction intervals can be interpreted for management as follows:

- The model-predicted order volume for "Week 29" is 121.5 orders. Model uncertainty suggests the actual volume will be between 114 and 129 with 95% confidence.
- The model-predicted order volume for "Week 30" is 125.5 orders. Model uncertainty suggests the actual volume will be between 118 and 133 with 95% confidence.
- The model-predicted order volume for "Week 31" is 129.5 orders. Model uncertainty suggests the actual volume will be between 122 and 137 with 95% confidence.
- The model-predicted order volume for "Week 32" is 133.5 orders. Model uncertainty suggests the actual volume will be between 126 and 141 with 95% confidence.

We know that prediction intervals get wider the farther out in the future one seeks to forecast. Here, the 4-week forecast is a small fraction of the 28-week span of data, and the prediction intervals remain quite consistent. The width of the prediction interval increases from 14.92 for week 29 to 15.38 for week 32. However, for this particular data set, the consistency of the order increases gives tight prediction intervals far into the future. Figure 7.6 shows the predicted value and 95% prediction intervals out to week 50: they are increasing but still quite tight. Such tight forecasts are unusual, but they do happen in practice in certain circumstances. The code for this plot is shown as follows.

```
> # plot prediction and confidence intervals from 1 to 50
> pred_interval = predict(regModel, newdata=data.frame(Week=1:50),
+                         interval="prediction",
+                         level = 0.95)
```

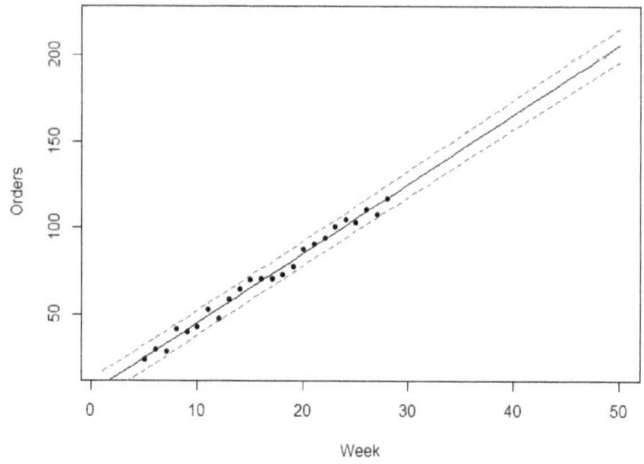

Figure 7.6. Trendline prediction intervals to week 50.

```
> plot(OrdersData$Week , OrdersData$Orders , xlim = c(1,50),
+      ylim = c(20,220), xlab = "Week", ylab = "Orders", pch=20)
> lines(1:50,pred_interval[,1],type = 'l')
> lines(1:50, pred_interval[,2], col="blue", lty=2)
> lines(1:50, pred_interval[,3], col="blue", lty=2)
>
```

7.3 Trendline Model Limitations

The trendline model discussed above had outstanding power, but that power can be fleeting. There is an unstated assumption that "the business environment changes remain consistent in the future." Remember, the predictive model is based only on past data, not on any additional predictor variables, such as market conditions, competitor actions, and price changes. The future, of course, always holds changes to the business environment that are different and likely unexpected. Such changes, when they occur, make the trendline model assumptions invalid. One does not know when disruption will happen, but it will happen. This give a reason to limit trendline model forecasts to a relatively short horizon and to be on the alert for deviations from model forecasts.

Because trendline models can often produce excellent results, management may be overly optimistic about their forecasts. It is important that you make the "business environment changes remain consistent" assumption clear so that they understand the risks that

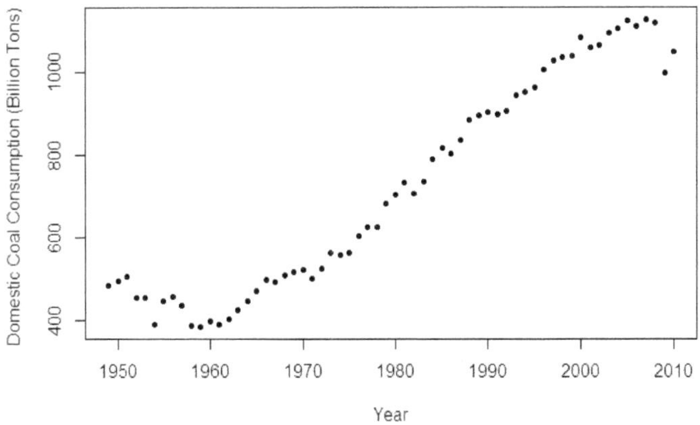

Figure 7.7. Domestic coal consumption, 1949–2011.

can invalidate model predictions. Consider the historical data set for U.S. coal consumption during 1949–2011 from the "Coal Consumption by Sector" Excel file at U.S. EIA (2023). Figure 7.7 shows consumption in billions of short tons over this period. Trendline regression would be very effective in certain periods but poor in others. Ten-year forecasts made in 1985 using 1975–1985 data would be highly accurate. But a ten-year forecast from 2001 to 2011 would give prediction intervals that would not capture the last few years of the period, when fracking led to an increased supplied of natural gas.

7.4 Time Series Data Characteristics

Time series data can take a number of forms, but all forms tend to include observed values of the series at evenly spaced points in time. We denote the random variable for the tth time series value as Y_t and the observed value for the tth index as y_t. While an observed time series data set may simply be represented by y_t, often the time series is a paired set of data: $\{y_t, d_t\}$, where d_t is the date or time of the tth value in the time series. That structure was present in the orders data in the previous section and allowed correct labeling of the week even after deleting the first four weeks before fitting the trendline model.

The visual nature of the time series plot gives hints on the likely structure and appropriate model. Figure 7.8 shows data from

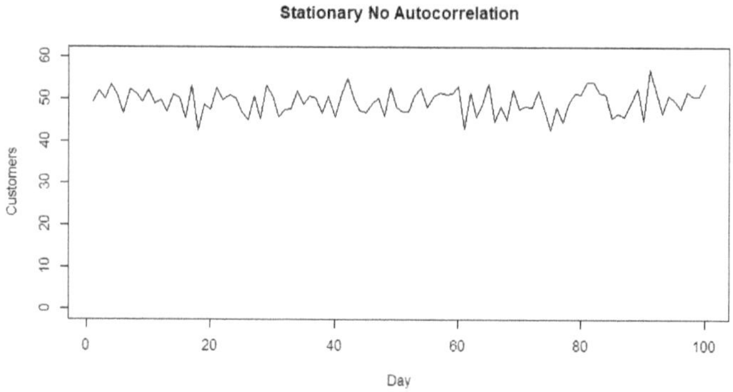

Figure 7.8. Time series with stationary i.i.d. values.

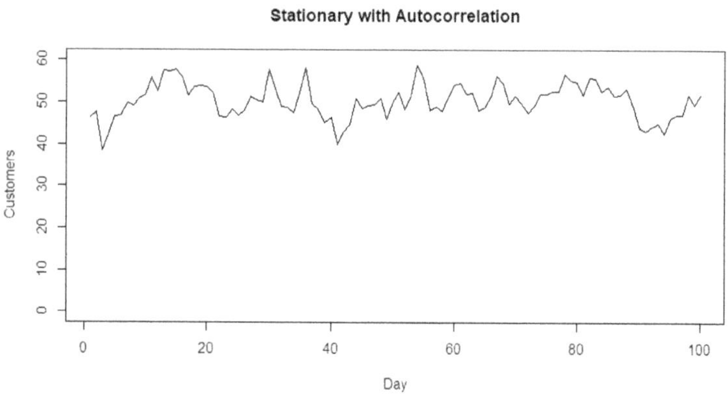

Figure 7.9. Stationary time series with autocorrelated values.

an i.i.d. process. Technically, this is not a time series. Because the values have no time dependence from either autocorrelation or changing distribution, and predictions are the same for any future period and only based on a fixed probability distribution. This is a static characterization — time plays no role.

Figure 7.9 shows no trend or cyclical structure, but the pattern wanders more than that in Figure 7.8. There random variations in this series have autocorrelation, which will require a time series model (AR, MA, or other) for good forecasts and prediction intervals.

Figure 7.10 is not stationary; the distribution's mean increases with time. But the pattern of deviations about the trend appears independent and identically distributed (i.i.d.). This kind of data

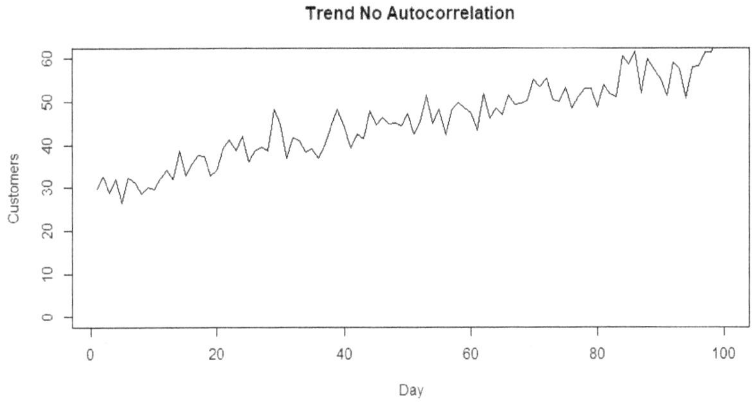

Figure 7.10. Time series with trend and i.i.d. deviations.

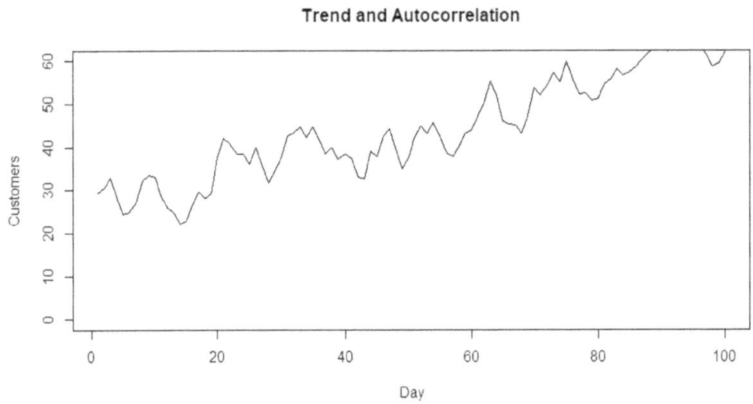

Figure 7.11. Time series with trend and autocorrelated deviations.

can be modeled by linear regression, often called a trendline regression model. When the deviations about the trend wander, as in Figure 7.11, there is indication of autocorrelation, and a time series model will be required, either incorporating a specific trend term or using a DEWMA or other ARIMA model.

In addition to trend and autocorrelation, some time series vary cyclically, from hour of day, day of week, day of month, season of year, and so forth. These cyclical variations are termed *seasonality*, although there are many cyclical patterns besides seasons of the year. Figure 7.12 shows a seasonality pattern over days of the week,

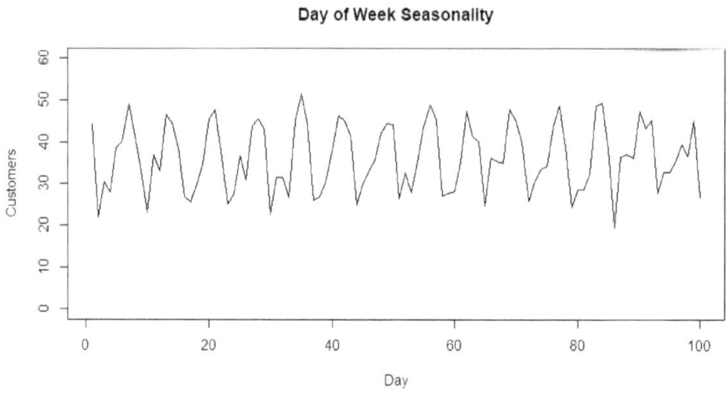

Figure 7.12. Time series with seasonality.

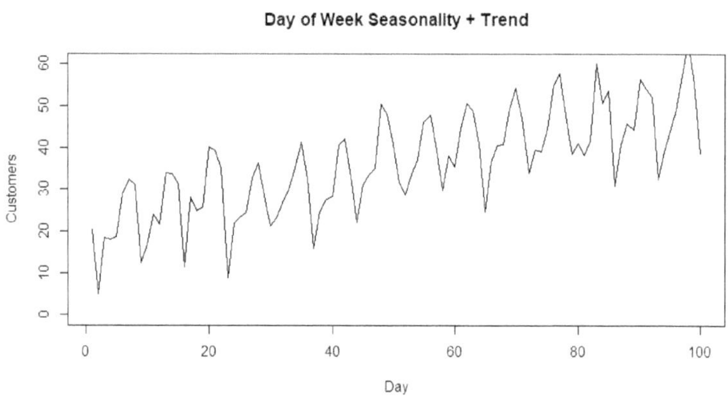

Figure 7.13. Time series with seasonality and trend.

repeating every seven days. Seasonality patterns need not be an evenly varying cyclical form. For example, U.S. online sales rise significantly during the "holiday season," say between late October and mid-December. This pattern repeats yearly but is not a sinusoidal variation. What is important is that a specific pattern of changing mean occurs repeatedly over a certain number of time periods. The length of the seasonality period (in time units) is often defined by the *frequency*: the number of time units for pattern repeats over the test data set.

Of course, combinations of these characteristics are possible, as shown in Figure 7.13. Time series models such as ARIMA and

Holt–Winters can model time series with multiple features. The next section describes a number of commonly used time series forecasting models. Models for forecasting intermittent nonzero values (e.g., intermittent demand) are beyond the scope of this text. For a review of intermittent models, see Boylan & Syntetos (2022).

7.5 Time Series Models

Many of the following models require *stationarity* of the time series stochastic process. That means that the probability model (mean and probability distribution of deviations, including autocorrelations) must not change over the duration of the time series. If the mean and/or the variance change, there are special time series modeling strategies that may be applied. This will be discussed for each of the following models.

7.5.1 Rule-of-thumb forecast methods

Although probability models can be constructed to support the rule-of-thumb forecast methods, they can stand on their own as sensible procedures.

Moving average forecasts

Forecasts using a moving average are called MA(q), where q is the number of historical time series values used to produce the forecast. The larger the q value, the smoother the forecast, but the longer it takes to respond to a change. For that reason, MA forecasts are appropriate when the time series is *stationary*; waviness comes from autocorrelation but the mean of the series and the variance of the random deviations remain constant over time. The forecast formula for a simple MA(q) is

$$\hat{y}_{t+1} = (y_t + \cdots + y_{t+1-q})/q. \tag{7.2}$$

Note that forecasts produced by MA(q) for more than one time period in advance produce the same value since to keep q constant, we need to reuse the same last q observed y values. Note that MA(q) models often use a weighted sum of the most recent q periods.

Exponentially weighted moving average (EWMA) forecasts

Rather than weight the most recent q time series values equally, one might instead base a forecast on exponentially decreasing weights for all prior time series values. This sounds complicated, but the EWMA(α) forecast formula is simple:

$$\hat{y}_{t+1} = \alpha y_t + (1 - \alpha)\hat{y}_{t-1}. \tag{7.3}$$

When this formula is expanded, each $\hat{y}_{t-i}$ is weighted by $(1 - \alpha)^i$. Note that forecasts produced by EWMA for more than one time period in advance produce the same value since all past Y_i values are used in the forecast formula.

Double exponentially weighted moving average forecasts (DEWMA)

The double exponentially weighted moving average predicts both the mean and the change in mean with exponential forecast functions. The one-period trend estimate at time t is denoted T_t. The following is the set of calculations to forecast one time unit in advance:

$$\hat{y}_{t+1} = \alpha y_t + (1 - \alpha)\hat{y}_{t-1} + T_t. \tag{7.4}$$

The trend estimate is updated with a separate exponentially weighted value β:

$$T_{t+1} = \beta(\hat{y}_{t+1} - \hat{y}_t) + (1 - \beta)T_t. \tag{7.5}$$

Since there are now two exponentially weighted updates, the method is called "Double EWMA" or just "DEWMA." The rate of decay of the exponential weights are controlled by α and β. While updates to $\hat{y}_t$ and T_t are made in t increments of one, forecasts for k time units into the future can be made by multiplying T_t by k.

Holt–Winters (EWMA) seasonal forecasts (HW)

The DEWMA predicts both the mean and the change in mean with exponential forecast functions. It was further augmented by Winters to add a seasonal adjustment term with exponentially weighted updates. Because the seasonal effect has a frequency, the update is based on the historical estimate from the prior season. Suppose the season has M periods. Then, for the matching seasonal effect at time $t+1$, we need to adjust for the seasonality estimate at $t+1-M$. If we are predicting k time units in advance, then use $t+k-M$. To predict more than one cycle of seasons in the future ($k > M$), then we subtract a multiple of M to get to our most recently estimated value:

$$\hat{y}_{t+1} = \alpha y_t + (1-\alpha)\hat{y}_{t-1} + T_t + S_{t+k-M}. \tag{7.6}$$

The trend estimate is updated as before with an exponentially weighted value, and the seasonal effect is updated with exponential weight determined by γ:

$$S_t = \gamma(y_t - \hat{y}_t) + (1-\gamma)S_{t-M}. \tag{7.7}$$

The Holt–Winters forecast model has three parameters to control the exponential decays of prior y values, prior trend values, and prior seasonal effect values. The double seasonal Holt–Winters (DSHW) model provides forecasts when there are two different seasonalities. The R `forecast` package provides `dshw`, a double seasonal Holt–Winters forecast function.

Multiplicative versions of Holt–Winters (MHW)

When applying the trend or season effect to the forecast in Equation (7.6), either or both could be applied in a multiplicative rather than an additive way. In that case, the update formulas also differ, but are not shown here. It is important to know, however, that if the magnitude of the cyclical variation increases over time with trend, then a multiplicative seasonality version should be used.

7.5.2 The MA probability model

As mentioned above, there are probability models associated with the rule-of-thumb methods. In the following, we describe one of these, the MA(q) probability model, and then consider other forecasting methods based on time series probability models.

The probability model that leads to an MA(q) forecast is

$$Y_t = \mu + \varepsilon_t + \theta_1\varepsilon_{t-1} + \cdots + \theta_q\varepsilon_{t-q},\ \varepsilon \overset{\text{iid}}{\sim} N(0,\sigma^2). \tag{7.8}$$

Forecasts from an MA(q) probability model

Since the mean of each ε_i term in Equation (7.8) is zero, a forecast for a future period is simply the estimate of $\hat{\mu}$, which will be based on the most recent observed values, as we saw in Equation (7.2).

Determining whether an MA model is appropriate

When the autocorrelation plot shows statistically significant correlations for lags up to q and small or zero correlations beyond lag q, an MA(q) model may provide an effective forecasting tool.

7.5.3 The autoregressive probability model

Autoregressive (AR) models are based on probability models. They are similar to MA models, but they describe the autocorrelation in terms of past values of y rather than past values of ε. AR forecasts lag changes in time series behavior since they rely only on averaging the past. Forecasting more than one period into the future produces different values, but forecasts far into the future approach the estimated mean. The form of an AR(p) probability model is

$$Y_t = \mu + \varepsilon_t + \phi_1 Y_{t-1} + \cdots + \phi_p Y_{t-p},\ \varepsilon \overset{\text{iid}}{\sim} N(0, \sigma^2). \tag{7.9}$$

The AR(p) model fitting process finds coefficient estimates for the $\phi_i, i = 1, \ldots, p$ through least squares matching the training set time series values, and μ is estimated as the mean of the training set time series values. The fitted coefficients are used to predict future values of the time series, but the formula usually is in terms of $y_i - \hat{\mu}$:

$$\hat{y}_{t+1} - \hat{\mu} = \phi_1(y_t - \hat{\mu}) + \cdots + \phi_p(y_{t+1-p} - \hat{\mu}). \tag{7.10}$$

Determining whether an AR model is appropriate

When the autocorrelation plot shows statistically significant correlations that gradually decrease rather than drop off suddenly (perhaps after dropping to zero then going negative), an AR(q) model may provide an effective forecasting tool.

AR or MA?

Some sources recommend choosing a time series model based on structure in the autocorrelation plot or the related partial autocorrelation plot (which removes lag-1 to lag$k$-1 correlation structure before computing a lag-k correlation). But distinguishing whether a particular AR(p) or MA(q) model (or some combination) is the best choice can be difficult to judge; therefore, both might be fitted to the time series and the performance and validity results compared. Performance and validity checks are discussed in Section 7.6. Better, the ARIMA model discussed as follows includes both AR and MA models as special cases, and the R software can automatically fit the best forecasting model using appropriate p and q for either or for a combination of both.

7.5.4 ARMA and ARIMA models

AR(p) and MA(q) models can be combined in an ARMA model. The decision on model form can be made by the fitting algorithms employed in software packages. We show how those can be used in Section 7.9.

When there is drift in the process, stationarity does not hold, and the AR and MA models are not appropriate forecast tools. The ARMA model can be modified to handle drift by differencing the time series and fitting an ARMA model to the pairwise differences. That means the left-hand side Y_t in the probability models in Equations (7.8) and (7.9) would be replaced by $Y_t - Y_{t-1}$ for first-order differences and by $(Y_t - Y_{t-1}) - (Y_{t-1} - Y_{t-2})$ for second-order differences, and so forth. Often first-order differences are sufficient to remove drift. For an ARIMA(p, d, q) model, p refers to the number of autoregressive lags in the model, q to the number of lags in the moving averages, and d to the order of differences (typically 0 or 1).

ARIMA models include AR, MA, EWMA, and DEWMA

The ARIMA class of time series models are quite flexible. In addition to moving average and/or autoregressive mechanisms, EWMA and

DEWMA models can be set in the ARIMA model framework using differencing (d):

- EWMA: fit ARIMA($p = 0, d = 1, q = 1$);
- EWMA with trend: fit ARIMA($p = 0, d = 1, q = 1$) with `include.drift=T`;
- DEWMA: fit ARIMA($p = 0, d = 2, q = 2$).

When there is trend or seasonality, their components can be combined with ARIMA models.

7.6 Time Series Model Prediction Performance and Validity Checks

As for regression, performance is based on the residuals:

$$e_i = y_i - \hat{y}_i. \tag{7.11}$$

RMSE is the square root of the average squared residual, and thus it is one measure of the predictive power of time series forecasting models:

$$RMSE = \sqrt{\frac{1}{n}\sum_{1}^{n} e_i^2} = \sqrt{\frac{1}{n}\sum_{i=1}^{n}(y_i - \hat{y}_i)^2}, \tag{7.12}$$

where the index i runs over the time indices to be forecast, either the training set or the test set.

RMSE can be interpreted as the standard deviation of prediction error. This places a heavier weight on the few large errors. Some managers prefer to use the mean of the absolute value of the errors, which places equal weights on all prediction errors in the averaging. The *MAD* (also called *MAE*) is computed as:

$$MAD = \sqrt{\frac{1}{n}\sum_{1}^{n} |e_i|} = \sqrt{\frac{1}{n}\sum_{i=1}^{n} |y_i - \hat{y}_i|}. \tag{7.13}$$

RMSE and *MAD* are measured in the scale of the data. But practical significance (vs. statistical significance) is sometimes judged based on percentage error rather than error in the original units. There is a third measure of predictive error based on the percentage error at each point: mean absolute prediction error, or *MAPE*, is calculated as

$$MAPE = \frac{1}{n}\sum_{i=1}^{n}\frac{|y_i - \hat{y}_i|}{y_i}, \tag{7.14}$$

so that the error that is averaged is percentage of the actual value. The problems with using *RMSE* based on the training set also apply to *MAPE* computed on the training set. These numbers are only indicative of one-step-ahead prediction error. *MAPE* gives a managerially interpretable characterization of the model forecast error that allows comparison of model performances over data sets with different scales. But *MAPE* should not be used to construct prediction intervals.

The computation of *RMSE*, *MAD/MAE*, and *MAPE* is done using the `accuracy` function applied to time series model objects fitted using the `forecast` package in R.

Validity and prediction intervals

Validity checks on the residuals can be used to judge whether the time series model has fully captured the dependence, trend, and seasonal structure in the data. For this, one examines the normal probability plot, the plot of residuals vs. time, and the autocorrelation plot. If these pass, it is typical to compute prediction intervals without taking into account fitting errors in the model coefficients. These approximate prediction intervals are

$$\hat{y}_i - 2RMSE \leq Y_i \leq \hat{y}_i + 2RMSE. \tag{7.15}$$

Because of the way it is computed, the *RMSE* error characterization over the training set is for single-step-ahead forecasts. For a better assessment of validity and predictive ability for more than one time period in advance, one can split the time series into a training set and a test set. The test set should be at least as long as the longest forecast needed by management. Prediction intervals based on the test *RMSE* are computed under the *data-adaptive research* paradigm, and will provide a more realistic (though still approximate) characterization of prediction uncertainty. These intervals rely less on the correctness of the time series probability model used in the forecast.

7.7 Plots and Statistical Summaries to Help in Model Selection

The R time series functions `auto.arima` and `dshw` provide great assistance in fitting time series models, characterizing performance, and providing prediction intervals. However, it is important to have a rough idea of the model or models that might be appropriate based on examination of the time series plot. Figures 7.8–7.13 are mapped into possible model choices in Figure 7.14.

These summaries show that there are many ways to find a good fit for some observed time series patterns. If there is seasonality, a Holt–Winters model can provide a good fit with or without drift. It is easier to detect drift and growth in the seasonality pattern with a plot that decomposes trend and seasonality elements. This can be done with the `decompose` function in R and is used in the following example. If there is no seasonality, the `auto.arima` function in R will fit the most appropriate of AR, MA, ARMA, EWMA, DEWMA,

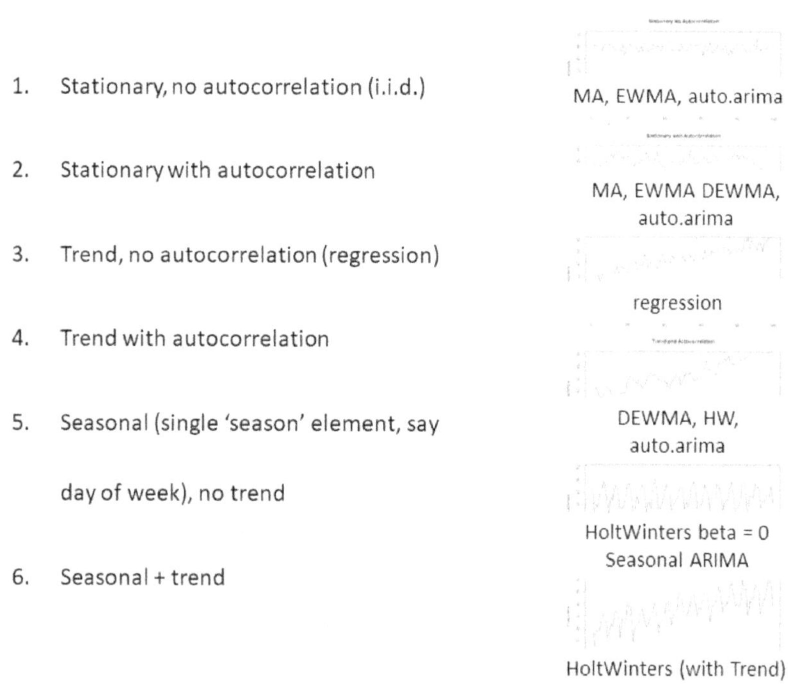

Figure 7.14. Matching time series patterns with possible time series models.

or ARIMA models. Further, by specifying a frequency with the time series data (example: `tsData <- ts(ElecLoad$SDGE, frequency = 24)`), `auto.arima` can fit a seasonal ARIMA model.

7.8 The Overall Process for Time Series Predictive Analytics

Similarly to regression, one can examine time series models in either the *traditional research* or *data-adaptive research* paradigms. The overall process is summarized as follows, including moving to a *data-adaptive* paradigm if the probability model validity checks fail:

1. Determine the objectives of the predictive model based on managerial needs.
2. Summarize the data with a descriptive summary, a time series plot, and a decomposition plot if seasonality is apparent in the time series plot, with discussion.
3. Based on the plot and expectations, propose one or more candidate time series model forms (see, e.g., Figures 7.8–7.13). This can be supplemented using `auto.arima` in R or other automated ARIMA model fitting software.
4. Show and interpret for management the fitted time series model.
5. Assess the practical predictive ability with a fitted line plot and *train* and *test* set *RMSE* values (optional: *MAD*/*MAE* and *MAPE* values), with discussion.
6. If the fitted time series model has practical predictive power, perform model validity checks: acf, residuals vs. time, and normal plot for residuals. Comment on the findings.
7. If the validity checks are passed for the training set residuals, then uncertainty characterization of one-step-ahead predictions based on the i.i.d. normal error assumption will be valid. If the validity checks are passed for the test set residuals, then uncertainty characterization of k-step-ahead predictions based on the i.i.d. normal error assumption will be valid, provided that $k \ll$ {the size of the *test* time series}. If the validity checks are not passed, move to a data-centric assessment of prediction uncertainty based solely on the test *RMSE*.
8. If the validity checks are passed, then continue. Show coefficient estimates and discuss the use for forecasts.

9. Show and discuss confidence intervals for coefficients in managerial terms.
10. Show and discuss forecast prediction intervals for desired number of steps in the future. Do this in managerial terms.
11. Give useful overall managerial summary and recommendation on use of the fitted time series model.

7.9 Time Series Models in R: Drug Sales Data

As an example, we consider data for monthly government subsidy for diabetic drugs in Australia from 1991 to 2008 (in millions of AU$). The government subsidy is proportional to sales, and so we refer to the time series as a "drug sales" series. The data set is called "a10" in the fpp package in R and can be loaded using the following R commands (they are not shown as part of an interactive session, so the > prompts are not present):

```
library(forecast)
library(fpp)
DrugSales = a10
```

Suppose that our objective is to be able to predict monthly sales two years in advance. This is important for the government to be able to determine funding needs month by month in the future. The forecast will allow the government to plan accordingly to avoid funding shortfalls or excessive borrowing to cover expenses. We check this by fitting the model to the July 1991–June 2006 data and test its predictive power on July 2006–June 2008 data.

Working with time series in R requires the `library(forecast)` statement. In addition, some data sets for testing forecasting methods are in the fpp library requiring `library(fpp)`, so those statements are at the start of the code.

A text version of the data is available at https://github.com/bozliu/Seasonal-Data-Forecasting/blob/main/drug.txt. It is instructive to begin with the text file. After reading the text file into Excel and converting the date entries from text to date format, it has the structure shown in Figure 7.15. Note that the series begins in July 1991.

The R commands used to structure the time series from the Excel file are shown as follows. The `read_xl` command assumes that the R program is in the same folder as the `DrugSales.xlsx` file and

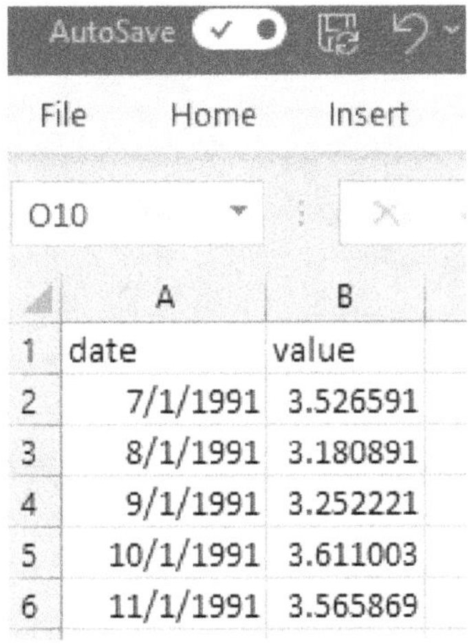

Figure 7.15. First lines of Excel file with data of diabetic treatment drug sales in Australia.

that RStudio was started by double-clicking the R program file. Otherwise, you will need to change the RStudio working directory to match the location of the file. This can be done by clicking on the `Files` tab in RStudio, browsing to the `drugSales.xlsx` folder, and then selecting `Set As Working Directory` from the `More` drop-down. The pattern we observe varies over a year, so the `ts` command sets `Frequency=12`. Because the data starts in mid-1991, set `start=1991.5` (note that fractional values for dates are understood correctly by R).

```
> library(readxl)
> library(forecast)
> DrugSales = read_excel("DrugSales.xlsx")
> DrugSales$date = as.Date(DrugSales$date)
> # annual season is 12 months for Frequency = 12
> DrugSales = ts(DrugSales$value, frequency=12, start = 1991.5)
> plot(DrugSales)
>
```

The plotted series is shown in Figure 7.16. Seasonality suggests a closer examination using the `decompose` function. That command is as follows, and the plot is shown in Figure 7.17.

```
> # notice strong monthly cycle
> #  - plot the decomposition to see other patterns
> plot(decompose(DrugSales))
>
```

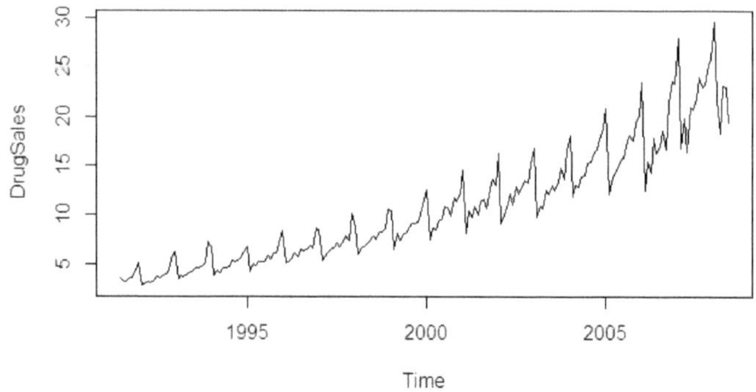

Figure 7.16. Diabetic treatment drug sales in Australia.

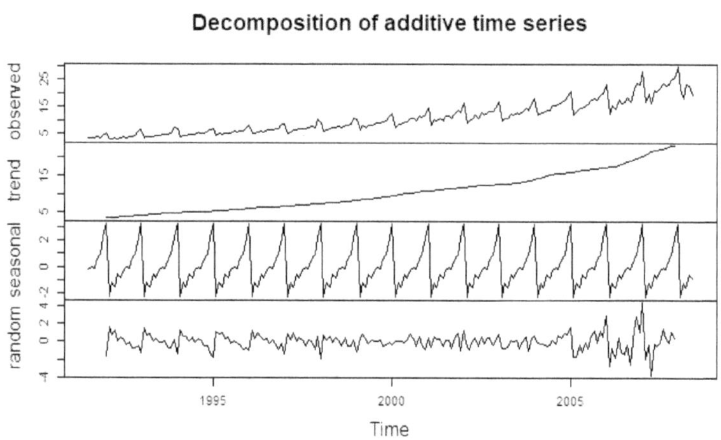

Figure 7.17. Decomposition of drug sales time series.

Figure 7.16 shows a clear increasing trend with increasing slope and also a strong seasonal pattern that increases in seasonal variation magnitude as the level of the series increases. Increasing seasonal variation spills over into the "random" panel of the decomposition plot in Figure 7.17 since the decomposition only removes a fixed magnitude of seasonality across the series. The pattern in the "random" panel is clearly not random. The "trend" panel of the decomposition plot shows a slope that increases over time. Pattern 6 in Figure 7.14 suggests a Holt–Winters model with trend. The increasing trend slope over time and increasing seasonal variation suggest the *multiplicative* version of Holt–Winters (MHW). We also compare the MHW time

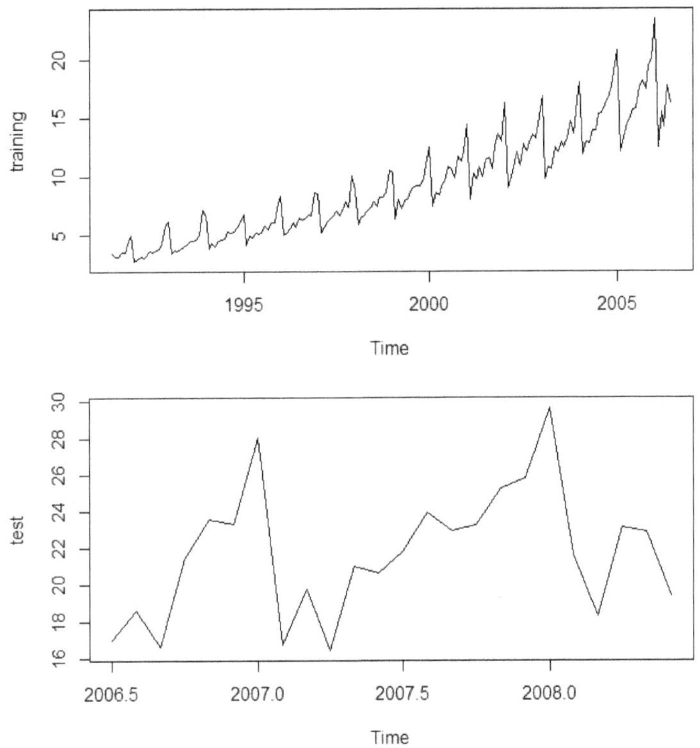

Figure 7.18. Training and test portions of drug sales time series.

series forecasting model with a seasonal-plus-trend ARIMA model and examine the difference in their ability to forecast two years in advance.

Before fitting models and testing performance, we split the time series data set into two parts: a *training* portion from July 1991–June 2006, and a *test* portion from July 2006–June 2008.

```
> #   window time limits set based on frequency,
      so c(year,month)
> training=window(DrugSales, start = c(1991,7), end = c(2006,6))
> test=window(DrugSales, start = c(2006,7), end = c(2008,6))
>
```

The training and test portions are shown in Figure 7.18. Note the scale difference for the test data plot. This scaling will make it easier to see prediction quality in plots that follow.

7.9.1 Multiplicative Holt–Winters model

We first fit a MHW model to the *training* data. The Holt–Winters model fitting command is **HoltWinters**. The multiplicative form is specified by **seasonal="multiplicative"** in the fitting command.

```
> # fit Multiplicative Holt-Winters (MHW) and show fitted model
> mhw_model = HoltWinters(training,seasonal = "multiplicative")
>
```

The estimates of α, β, γ, the level and slope used in the final seasonal cycle, and the seasonal effects estimated from the final cycle are part of the fitted model object. These commands and the resulting output are shown as follows.

```
> mhw_model$alpha; mhw_model$beta; mhw_model$gamma
    alpha
0.1538962
      beta
0.04908369
    gamma
0.4540974
> mhw_model$coefficients
          a           b          s1          s2          s3          s4
17.7599688  0.1151434  0.9957651  1.0222539  1.0417500  1.0593597
        s5          s6          s7          s8          s9         s10
1.1012265  1.1764578  1.3268486  0.7552361  0.8718484  0.8528132
       s11         s12
0.9692025  0.9318606
>
```

The values a and b are the estimated (smoothed) starting level and trend increment for the final cycle in the time series. The 12 month seasonal components (final cycle, smoothed) are shown in s1-s12.

The fitted values are used for computing accuracy measures on the training set. These are part of the fitted mhw_model object. The following commands and resulting output show the first few lines of the training fitted (prediction) values in the **mhw_model$fitted** data frame. There are column and row labels, so the fitted value (**xhat**) is the first column.

```
> # show structure of mhw_model$fitted
> head(mhw_model$fitted)
             xhat    level      trend    season
Jul 1992 3.352503 3.383485 0.06467990 0.9722573
Aug 1992 3.249847 3.509160 0.06767379 0.9085820
Sep 1992 3.514437 3.629161 0.07024218 0.9500012
```

```
Oct 1992 3.713787 3.741970 0.07233151 0.9736482
Nov 1992 4.210981 3.847605 0.07396619 1.0737995
Dec 1992 5.631531 3.946731 0.07520112 1.4002054
>
```

The performance measures returned by the `accuracy()` function include a number of measures that we will not use. For more information on these, see the `accuracy()` R documentation Web page. We specify *RMSE*, *MAD/MAE*, and *MAPE* and evaluate these first on the training data set. The commands and results are as follows. Note that there are no predictions for the first year; these are used by MHW to estimate the seasonal effects.

```
> trainAcc = as.data.frame(accuracy(mhw_model$fitted[,1],
+                                    training[-(1:12)]))
> trainAcc$RMSE
[1] 0.575485
> trainAcc$MAE
[1] 0.4370058
> trainAcc$MAPE
[1] 4.554959
>
```

Given that sales at the end of the training period have values in the range of 13–22 million AU$, the *RMSE*, *MAD/MAE*, and *MAPE* are all small, so the model predictive power is good. This is also apparent from the plot of fitted and actual data over the training set. The code is as follows, and the result shown in Figure 7.19.

```
> plot(training, col = "black", xlim = c(1991.5,2006.5),
> ylim = c(0,30), lwd=2, main = "Holt_Winters")
> lines(mhw_model$fitted[,1], col = "green", lwd=.5)
>
```

Given the good predictive power, we examine the characteristics of the residuals: an autocorrelation plot, a normal probability plot, and a plot of residuals vs. time. The code is shown as follows, and the results are in Figure 7.20.

```
> resid = mhw_model$fitted[,1] - training[-(1:12)]
> acf(resid)
> qqnorm(resid)
> plot(resid, pch=16)
>
```

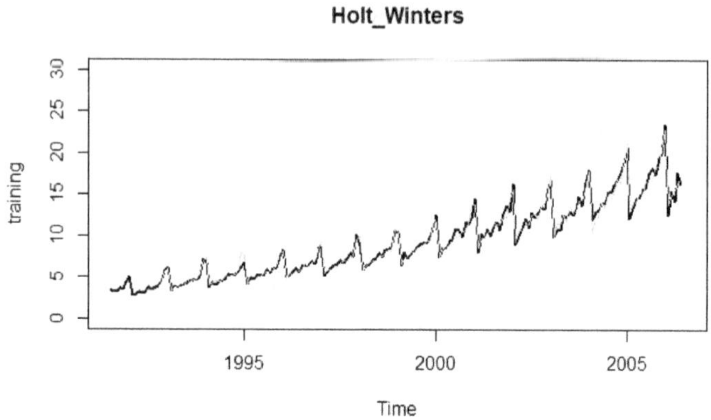

Figure 7.19. MHW fitted and actual data for training period drug sales time series.

The autocorrelation plot shows only small excursions beyond the significance limits. It is likely that there is some small portion of the autocorrelation that is not captured, but this is practically not significant. The normal probability plot looks very good. The variance of the residuals over time is not stable, however. It appears that the multiplicative model is not perfectly capturing the increasing seasonal variability, or perhaps the seasonal variability has shifted phase over time. Since the diagnostics are somewhat disqualifying, we rely on the one-fold cross-validation train vs. test results. We examine performance over the test set as a cross-validation exercise. The code and results for the test set are shown as follows. Note that prediction intervals for the test period are desired, so the `predict()` function and variable names are modified accordingly.

```
> mhw_predVals = predict(mhw_model, n.ahead = length(test),
+                         prediction.interval = TRUE)
> mhw_pred  = mhw_predVals[,1]
> mhw_predU  = mhw_predVals[,2]
> mhw_predL  = mhw_predVals[,3]
> testAcc  = as.data.frame(accuracy(mhw_pred,test))
> testAcc$RMSE
[1] 3.039528
> testAcc$MAE
[1] 2.630173
> testAcc$MAPE
[1] 11.82314
>
```

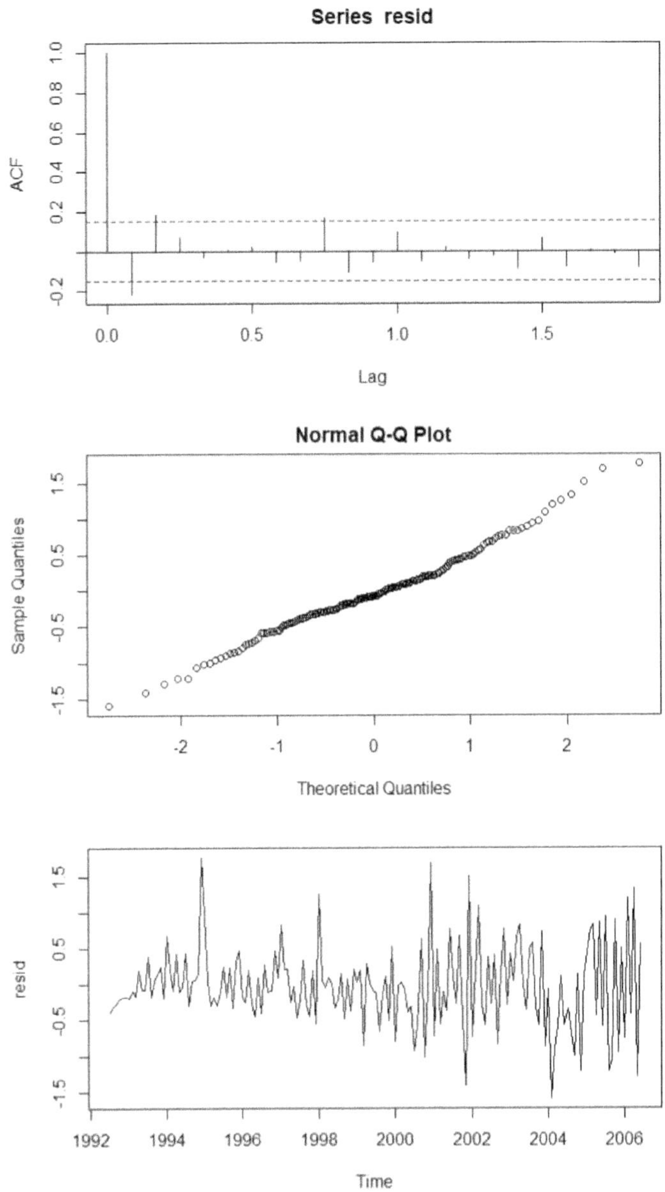

Figure 7.20. Residuals validity plots MHW for drug sales time series.

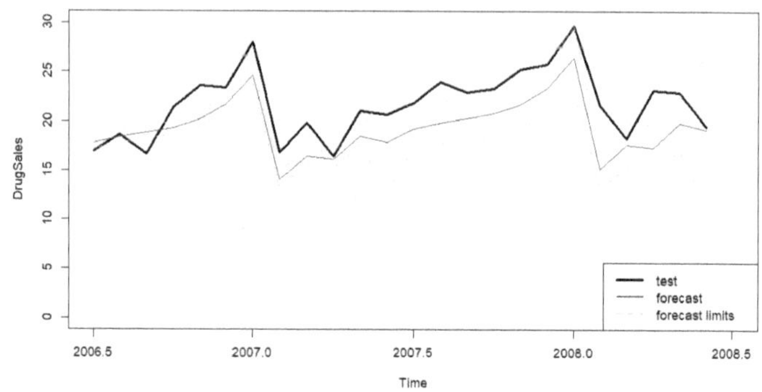

Figure 7.21. MHW prediction interval and actual data for test period drug sales time series.

While the errors are larger, a 12% average prediction error may be useful for government planning. But that is the average error. We see that the error increases over the length of the prediction period. The code for generating a plot of predictions and prediction intervals vs. actual sales over the two-year test period is shown as follows. The result appears in Figure 7.21, which shows a failure to match the increasing trend. All predictions are slightly low. This is because there has been no new data over the two-year forecast period to update the trend value. As the slope of the trend continued to increase from the last half of 2006 through the first half of 2008, the forecast used the smoothed mid-2006 value. It appears that the forecast through one year ahead, although an underestimate, is close enough to be useful to decision-makers.

7.9.2 Seasonal plus trend ARIMA model

We compare the performance of MHW with the seasonal-plus-trend ARIMA model. The reason is to test the flexibility of the `auto.arima()` function in the R `forecast` package. Because it removes the burden of model choice from the analyst, is it capable of capturing the complex pattern in the drug sales data and providing accurate forecasts two years in advance?

Much of the code structure is the same and is included in the last section of this chapter, and so some parts will not be repeated here. But there are some differences at the start.

The code for fitting the model and the fitted model coefficients are as follows.

```
> # fit season + trend ARIMA and show fitted model
> starima_model = auto.arima(training)
> starima_model
Series: training
ARIMA(2,1,1)(0,1,2)[12]

Coefficients:
         ar1     ar2      ma1     sma1     sma2
      0.0074  0.3020  -0.9112  -0.1608  -0.1716
s.e.  0.1042  0.1009   0.0599   0.0886   0.0820

sigma^2 = 0.3764:  log likelihood = -154.18
AIC=320.36   AICc=320.88   BIC=339.07
>
```

The fitted model `ARIMA(2,1,1)(0,1,2)[12]` has the following interpretation. There is a nonseasonal part that is an AR(2)MA(1) applied to first differences in the time series y_t values, the (2,1,1) part. The coefficient estimates are `ar1`, `ar2`, and `ma1`. Seasonality is a first difference (typical) and is modeled with an MA(2) model. The coefficient estimates are `sma1` and `sma2`. "[12]" indicates a seasonal periodicity of 12 was detected. The estimated σ^2 and other probability model characterizations are presented but are not our focus. We test validity by examining residuals plots if the predictive power is good.

The form of the fitted model values `starima_model$fitted` is different from the MHW `mhw_model$fitted` as seen in the following. This slightly changes the form of the commands to capture the predicted values for calculating performance, computing residuals, and generating plots.

```
> head(starima_model$fitted)
Jul      Aug      Sep      Oct      Nov      Dec
1991 3.524555 3.180248 3.251740 3.610328 3.565371 4.305276
>
> # compute MAPE, etc. for training data
> trainAcc = as.data.frame(accuracy(starima_model$fitted,
+                                   training[-(1:12)]))
> trainAcc$RMSE
[1] 1.370252
> trainAcc$MAE
[1] 1.11376
```

```
> trainAcc$MAPE
[1] 11.58426
> # plot fitted and actual over training set
> plot(training, col = "black", xlim = c(1991.5,2006.5),
+      ylim = c(0,30), lwd=2, main = "Trend + Seasonal ARIMA")
> lines(starima_model$fitted, col = "green", lwd=.5)
>
```

The training accuracy results are inferior to the MHW model. This limitation is hard to see in the predicted and actual plot shown in Figure 7.22. The extreme seasonality deviations are well captured by the MHW model, but slightly underestimated by the ARIMA model.

The results, while not as good as those of the MHW model, still have predictive power, and so the residuals model validity checks are performed. The code is shown as follows, and the results are in Figure 7.23.

The autocorrelation plot is satisfactory. The normal probability plot does not look as good as that of the MHW model residuals. The variance of the residuals over time is not stable, however. And the variance of the residuals greatly increases over time, more severely than for the MHW model residuals. Since the diagnostics are somewhat disqualifying, we rely on the 1-fold cross-validation train vs. test results.

We examine the ARIMA model performance over the test set as a cross-validation exercise. Prediction is done with `forecast()` rather than `predict()`, as shown in the code. The code and results

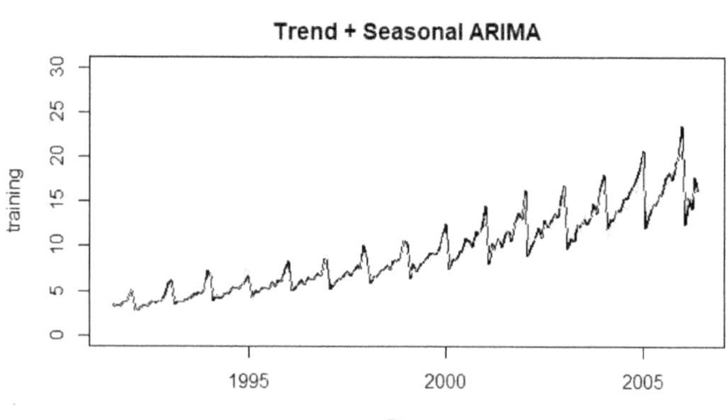

Figure 7.22. ARIMA fitted and actual data for training period drug sales time series.

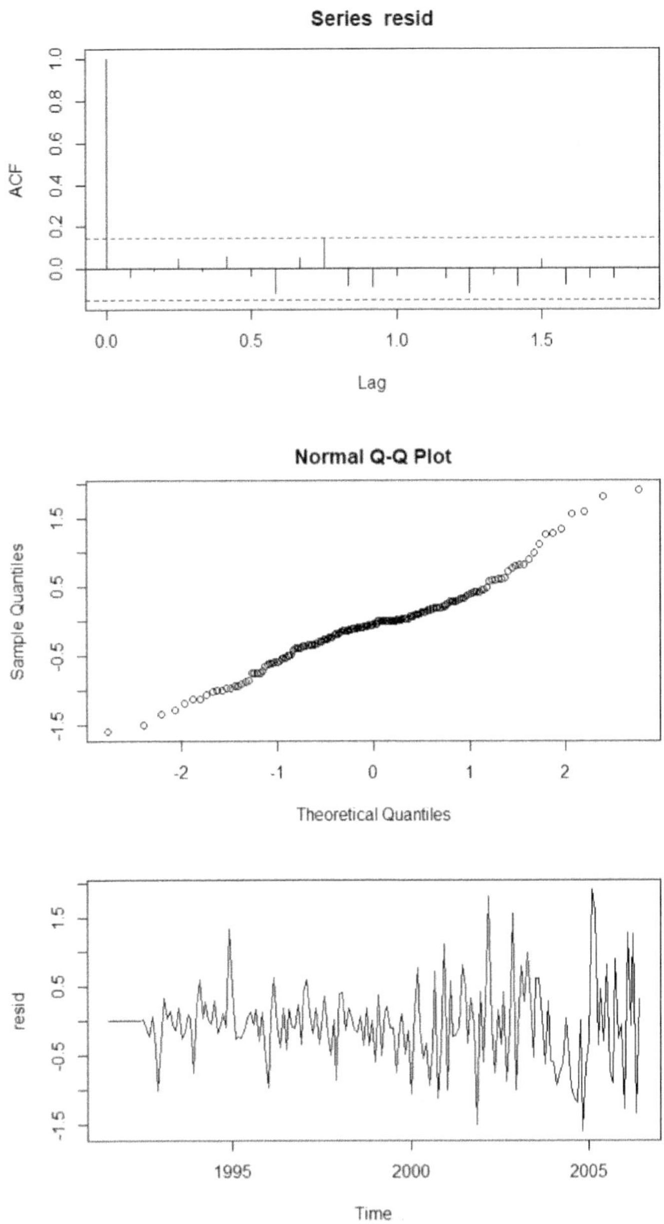

Figure 7.23. Residuals validity plots ARIMA for drug sales time series.

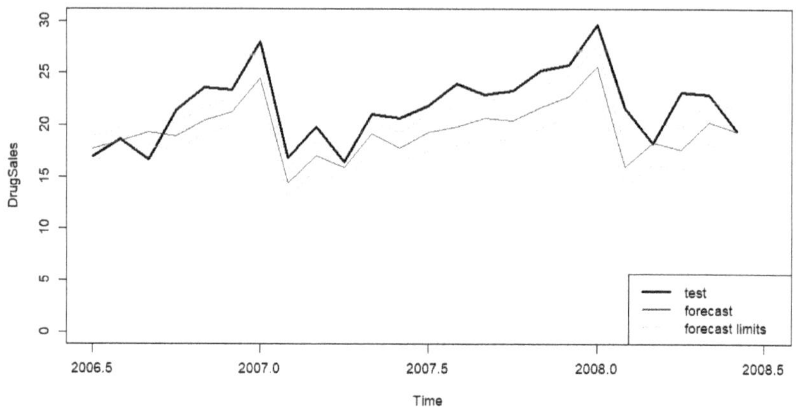

Figure 7.24. ARIMA prediction interval and actual data for test period drug sales time series.

are shown as follows. Interestingly, the errors over the test set are smaller than for MHW. The performance is clarified by looking at a plot of predicted vs. actual over the test set, as shown in Figure 7.24.

```
> starima_pred = starima_predVals$mean
> starima_predU = starima_predVals$upper[,2] # 2 gives 95%
> starima_predL = starima_predVals$lower[,2]
> testAcc = as.data.frame(accuracy(starima_pred,test))
> testAcc$RMSE
[1] 2.966683
> testAcc$MAE
[1] 2.575174
> testAcc$MAPE
[1] 11.48631
>
```

As for MHW, the result again shows a failure to match the increasing trend; later predictions are low. As for MHW, it appears that the forecast through one year ahead, although an underestimate, is close enough to be useful to decision-makers.

Overall, we can recommend to management that a one-year ahead forecast is likely to be reasonably good. It will likely underestimate sales, with the actual within perhaps 2% of the upper prediction interval.

7.10 Cases Supporting Chapter 7

The CLXLogistics case explores trendline analysis for a simple time series. It depends on Section 7.1. The case description slides and data can be found online in the CLXTrendlineRegression folder of Barton (2023).

The SDGEElecticityDemand case focuses on a double-seasonal data set: hourly electricity load for San Diego Gas and Electric. It depends on the entire chapter. The case description slides and data can be found online in the SDGETimeSeries folder of Barton (2023).

7.11 R Code Used in Chapter 7

```
# Time Series Examples ===================

# Simulate some data
p = 0; d = 0; q = 1
simData <- 67.7 + arima.sim(model = list(order = c(p, d, q),
                                          ma = .6 ),
                            sd = sqrt(5), n = 50)
plot(simData, xlab = "Time Index",ylab = "Y")

# Simulate some data
p = 1; d = 0; q = 0
simData <- 67.7 + arima.sim(model = list(order = c(p, d, q),
                                          ar = .3 ),
                             sd = sqrt(2), n = 50)

simData = simData - 5 + (1:n)*.2
plot(simData, xlab = "Time Index",ylab = "Y")

# Simulate some data
p = 0; d = 0; q = 0
simData <- 67.7 + arima.sim(model = list(order = c(p, d, q)),
                            sd = sqrt(2), n = 50)
n=50
simData = simData - 5 + (1:n)*.2
plot(simData, xlab = "Time Index",ylab = "Y")

# Simulate some data
p = 1; d = 0; q = 1
simData <- 67.7 + arima.sim(model = list(order = c(p, d, q),
ar = .5, ma = .8 ),
sd = sqrt(3), n = 50)
plot(simData, xlab = "Time Index",ylab = "Y")
```

```
# Simulate some data
p = 1; d = 1; q = 1
simData <- 67.7 + arima.sim(model = list(order = c(p, d, q),
                                          ar = .5,  ma = .8 ),
                            sd = sqrt(3), n = 50)
plot(simData, xlab = "Time Index",ylab = "Y")

# Code for Weekly Orders Time Series Models ============
# Russell Barton
library(readxl) # needed to read in the Excel data file

# trendline regression modeling
# read orders data weeks
OrdersData <- read_excel("OrdersData.xlsx")
# read the Excel file
# summarize data
summary(OrdersData)
# plot the time series
plot(OrdersData$Week, OrdersData$Orders,
xlab = "Week", ylab = "Orders", type = "l")

# delete first four weeks from data frame before regression
OrdersData = OrdersData[-c(1,2,3,4),]

# fit the regression model
regModel = lm(Orders ~ Week, data = OrdersData)

# show fitted model
summary(regModel)$coefficients[,1]

# pull out the R-squared value from the summary
summary(regModel)$r.squared
# plot predicted vs actual
plot(predict(regModel, newdata=OrdersData),OrdersData$Orders,
xlab = "Predicted Orders", ylab = "Actual Orders")

# assess model validity
acf(regModel$residuals) # do plots to check model validity
plot(regModel, ask=F, add.smooth=F) # more plots
plot(OrdersData$Orders,regModel$residuals) # more plots

# validity checks pass so can use p-values and construct
#   confidence intervals for coefficients and forecast
#   prediction intervals
# used to show standard deviation estimates and p-values
summary(regModel)
# compute confidence intervals for model coefficients
confint(regModel)
```

```
# predict orders for next four weeks
# put desired forecast in a dataframe
new.dat <- data.frame(Week = c(29,30,31,32))
# give forecast PI
predict(regModel, newdata = new.dat, interval = 'prediction')

# plot prediction and confidence intervals from 1 to 50
pred_interval = predict(regModel, newdata=data.frame(Week=1:50),
interval="prediction",
level = 0.95)
plot(OrdersData$Week, OrdersData$Orders, xlim = c(1,50),
ylim = c(20,220), xlab = "Week", ylab = "Orders", pch=20)
lines(1:50,pred_interval[,1],type = 'l')
lines(1:50, pred_interval[,2], col="blue", lty=2)
lines(1:50, pred_interval[,3], col="blue", lty=2)

# Time Series Drug Sales Examples ==================
library(readxl)
library(forecast)
DrugSales = read_excel("DrugSales.xlsx")
DrugSales$date = as.Date(DrugSales$date)
# annual season is 12 months for Frequency = 12
DrugSales = ts(DrugSales$value, frequency=12, start = 1991.5)
plot(DrugSales)

# notice strong monthly cycle
#  - plot the decomposition to see other patterns
plot(decompose(DrugSales))

# alternative way to access DrugSales: library(fpp);
  Drugsales = a10
# but this data set has 'y,m' rather than 'm/d/y' format

# set training and test portions (July 1991 - June 2006 train)
#                                (July 2006 - June 2008 test)
#   window time limits set based on frequency, so c(year,month)
training=window(DrugSales, start = c(1991,7), end = c(2006,6))
plot(training)
test=window(DrugSales, start = c(2006,7), end = c(2008,6))
plot(test)

# Multiplicative Holt-Winters================================
# fit Multiplicative Holt-Winters (MHW) and show fitted model
mhw_model = HoltWinters(training,seasonal = "multiplicative")
mhw_model$alpha; mhw_model$beta; mhw_model$gamma
mhw_model$coefficients

# show structure of mhw_model$fitted
head(mhw_model$fitted)
```

```
# compute MAPE, etc. for training data
trainAcc = as.data.frame(accuracy(mhw_model$fitted[,1],
training[-(1:12)]))
trainAcc$RMSE
trainAcc$MAE
trainAcc$MAPE

# plot fitted and actual over training set
plot(training, col = "black", xlim = c(1991.5,2006.5),
ylim = c(0,30), lwd=2, main = "Holt_Winters")
lines(mhw_model$fitted[,1], col = "green", lwd=.5)

# good results so check residuals for normal theory model
resid = mhw_model$fitted[,1] - training[-(1:12)]
acf(resid)
qqnorm(resid)
plot(resid, pch=16)

# get Holt-Winters performance for test period
mhw_predVals = predict(mhw_model, n.ahead = length(test),
prediction.interval = TRUE)
mhw_pred = mhw_predVals[,1]
mhw_predU = mhw_predVals[,2]
mhw_predL = mhw_predVals[,3]

testAcc = as.data.frame(accuracy(mhw_pred,test))
testAcc$RMSE
testAcc$MAE
testAcc$MAPE


# plot fitted, prediction intervals and actual over test set
plot(test, col = "black", xlim = c(2006.5,2008.5),
     ylim = c(0,30), ylab="DrugSales",lwd=3, main = " ")
lines(mhw_pred,col = "blue", lwd=1)
lines(mhw_predU,col = "green", lwd=1, lty=2)
lines(mhw_predL,col = "green", lwd=1, lty=2)
legend( x = "bottomright",
        legend = c("test","forecast","forecast limits"),
        lwd = c(3,2,2), col = c("black","blue","green"),
        lty = c(1,1,2))

# Season + Trend ARIMA starima================================
# fit season + trend ARIMA and show fitted model
starima_model = auto.arima(training)
starima_model

# show structure of starima_model$fitted
head(starima_model$fitted)
```

```
# compute MAPE, etc. for training data
trainAcc = as.data.frame(accuracy(starima_model$fitted ,
training[-(1:12)]))
trainAcc$RMSE
trainAcc$MAE
trainAcc$MAPE

# plot fitted and actual over training set
plot(training, col = "black", xlim = c(1991.5,2006.5),
ylim = c(0,30), lwd=2, main = "Trend + Seasonal ARIMA")
lines(starima_model$fitted , col = "green", lwd=.5)

# good results so check residuals for normal theory model
resid = starima_model$fitted - training
acf(resid)
qqnorm(resid)
plot(resid, pch=16)

# get stARIMA performance for test period
starima_predVals = forecast(starima_model , h=length(test))
head(starima_predVals)
starima_pred = starima_predVals$mean
starima_predU = starima_predVals$upper[,2] # 2 gives 95%
starima_predL = starima_predVals$lower[,2]

testAcc = as.data.frame(accuracy(starima_pred,test))
testAcc$RMSE
testAcc$MAE
testAcc$MAPE

# plot fitted, prediction intervals and actual over test set
plot(test, col = "black", xlim = c(2006.5,2008.5),
     ylim = c(0,30), ylab="DrugSales",lwd=3, main = " ")
lines(starima_pred,col = "blue", lwd=1)
lines(starima_predU,col = "green", lwd=1, lty=2)
lines(starima_predL,col = "green", lwd=1, lty=2)
legend( x = "bottomright",
        legend = c("test","forecast","forecast limits"),
        lwd = c(3,2,2), col = c("black","blue","green"),
        lty = c(1,1,2))
```

Chapter 8

Simulating Random Values

Stochastic simulation is a powerful tool for decision support. In the *model-dependent research* predictive analytics paradigm, the analyst uses a simulation model to generate artificial data based on the characteristics of actual or expected real-world data. Real-word uncertainty is captured by generating data with artificial randomness. The generated random data may be part of a spreadsheet calculation, such as number of units purchased of a particular product each month or the number of tickets sold for a particular concert. This kind of predictive analytics is called *Monte Carlo simulation.* Given historical data or estimates of uncertainty by experts, a computer program is used to generate multiple instances of the data, do business performance calculations, and produce a histogram of possible results.

Many textbooks, such as Evans (2019), describe Excel functions for generating artificial random data and using them in spreadsheet calculations to characterize possible business outcomes. Monte Carlo simulation is also common in *prescriptive analytics* studies (which are outside the scope of this text), where best decisions must be based on an uncertain future.

Artificial random values can also be used to drive the simulation of a dynamic system, such as a warehouse, a call center, or a hospital. These applications are called *discrete-event simulation* and are covered in Chapter 9.

The data generated by a computer program is *pseudo-random*: it is computed from a mathematical formula. Modern pseudo-random quantity generators produce results that cannot be distinguished from truly random quantities. Truly random quantities are typically referred to as *random variables*; artificially generated pseudo-random quantities are typically referred to as *random variates.* Both are also called *RV*s. The words *artificial* and *pseudo-* apply throughout this chapter but, for brevity, will often be omitted in what follows.

The random quantities can be used in business calculations to compute outcomes that will, as a result, also be random. Following convention, the results (or response) variables are denoted as Y. The random quantities driving calculation of an outcome Y are denoted as X.

Our focus here is determining how to generate appropriate "random" quantities for use in Monte Carlo or discrete-event simulations. This process requires several steps:

- understanding parametric probability distribution families and when they might apply,
- identifying one or more appropriate parametric probability distributions that fit a set of historical data,
- generating artificial random quantities, and
- testing the artificial random quantity generator to see that it meets expectations.

These steps are examined in this chapter.

8.1 Probability Distribution Parametric Families

Over the past 200 years, researchers have identified probability distribution families that approximate randomness in the real world. They are called parametric distribution *families* because the value or values of a set of parameters must be specified to identify a particular distribution from the family. Every parametric family has a formula (with parameters) characterizing it. If the random quantity X can take on continuous values, the distribution is continuous and is characterized by a *probability density function* (pdf) $f_X(x)$ and a *cumulative distribution function* (cdf) $F_X(x)$. If the random quantity X can only take on a discrete set of values (e.g., 0, 1, 2, 3), then the probability distribution is discrete and is characterized by a *probability mass function* (pmf) $f_X(x)$ or $P_X(x)$ and a *cumulative distribution function* (cdf) $F_X(x)$. The subscript $_X$ just indicates that the probability distribution characterizes the random quantity X. It is often omitted, writing simply $f(x)$ or $F(x)$.

8.1.1 Normal or Gaussian distribution family

The most famous example is the *normal* or *Gaussian* distribution family. If the random variable X has a normal distribution with mean μ and variance σ^2, we write $X \sim N(\mu, \sigma^2)$. This distribution family played a key role in characterizing error in Chapters 3, 6, and 7. Its justification is the *central limit theorem* (CLT). Stated informally, the CLT says that if a random variable X is a sum of other independent or somewhat independent random quantities, each with perhaps different but bounded mean and variance, then X will have a probability distribution that is approximately normal, that is, a member of the normal distribution family. The usual stated form of the CLT assumes that X is the sum of independent and identically distributed (i.i.d.) quantities, but that is not necessary for the CLT to apply.

The formula for the pdf of a random variable with a normal distribution with parameters μ and σ^2 was shown in Equation (5.1) and is repeated in the following, using X to represent the random quantity rather than Y. There is no simple formula for the cdf. It is written as in Equation (8.2):

$$f_X(x) = \frac{1}{\sigma\sqrt{2\pi}} e^{-\frac{(y-\mu)^2}{2\sigma^2}}, \tag{8.1}$$

$$F_X(x) = \int_{-\infty}^{x} f_X(u)du. \tag{8.2}$$

8.1.2 Exponential distribution family

Events occurring "completely at random" in time have times-between-events that follow a probability distribution from the *exponential* distribution family. Examples include time between calls to a call center (over a short period of time) or distance between defects in a roll of vinyl flooring. The distribution has one parameter, usually represented as an average rate of events per unit time or distance and usually with the name λ. It is written $X \sim \text{Exp}(\lambda)$. A random variable having an exponential distribution with parameter λ has a mean of $1/\lambda$ and a variance of $1/\lambda^2$. The formula for the pdf of a random variable with an exponential distribution with parameter λ is

$$f_X(x) = \lambda e^{-\lambda x}, \quad x \geq 0. \tag{8.3}$$

The random variable does not take on negative values. The cdf for a random variable with an exponential distribution with parameter λ is

$$F_X(x) = 1 - e^{-\lambda x}, \quad x \geq 0. \tag{8.4}$$

8.1.3 Uniform distribution family

Events occurring "completely at random" over a fixed interval (a, b) in time or space have locations (not the distance between them) that follow a probability distribution from the *uniform* distribution family. This family has two parameters: a lower limit, typically named a, and an upper limit, typically named b. It is written $x \sim U(a, b)$. A random variable having a uniform distribution with parameters a and b has a mean of $(a + b)/2$ and a variance of $(b - a)^2/12$. The formula for the pdf of a random variable with a uniform distribution with parameters a and b is

$$f_X(x) = 1/(b - a), \quad a \leq x \leq b. \tag{8.5}$$

The random variable only takes on values between a and b. The cdf of a random variable with a uniform distribution with parameters a and b is

$$F_X(x) = \frac{x - a}{b - a}, \quad a \leq x \leq b. \tag{8.6}$$

The cdf is zero for values of x less than a and is one for values of x greater than b.

8.1.4 Gamma distribution family

The *gamma* distribution family has a close connection with the exponential distribution family. A sum of n i.i.d. exponential random variables with rate λ has a gamma distribution with *shape* n and *rate* λ. The second parameter is sometimes replaced by its inverse, called *scale*. The mean of a gamma(n, r) random variable is n/λ, and its variance is n/λ^2. While the connection with the exponential distribution motivates the form, the gamma distribution exists for noninteger n values. To describe the pdf, we need to use the $\Gamma()$ function, a formula involving integration that is fairly complex. When n is an integer, it is just the factorial function applied to $n-1$: $\Gamma(n) = (n-1)!$. The pdf for the gamma distribution family is

$$f_X(x) = \frac{\lambda^n x^{n-1} e^{-\lambda x}}{\Gamma(n)}, \quad x \geq 0. \tag{8.7}$$

The cdf is more complex, involving the incomplete gamma function, so perhaps it is better to think of the cdf as that of the normal distribution (see Equation (8.2)). As for the exponential distribution, gamma-distributed random variables do not take on negative values.

8.1.5 Poisson distribution family

The *Poisson* distribution family is a companion to the exponential distribution family. It is the discrete distribution of the number of "completely random" events per unit length, time, or area. If the time or distance between events has an exponential probability distribution with parameter λ, then the number of values falling in unit time, distance, or area has a probability distribution from the Poisson family with parameter λ. Remember that for the exponential distribution family, λ represented an average rate, so for a random variable with a Poisson distribution with parameter λ, its mean value (the mean number of events per unit time) is λ. Interestingly, while the mean of the Poisson random variable is the inverse of the mean of the companion exponential random variable, the variance is not the corresponding inverse. The variance of a random variable with a Poisson distribution with parameter λ is λ (and NOT λ^2).

Because the Poisson family is for discrete random variables, there is no pdf. The formula for the pmf of a random variable with a Poisson distribution with parameter λ is

$$f_X(x) = \frac{\lambda^x e^{-x}}{x!}, \quad x = 0, 1, 2, \ldots. \tag{8.8}$$

Because it is a count, the random variable only takes nonnegative integer values. The cdf of a random variable with a Poisson distribution with parameter λ does not have a closed form, so it is represented as the discrete analog of Equation (8.2):

$$F_X(x) = \sum_{k=0}^{\lfloor x \rfloor} f_X(k), \quad x = 0, 1, 2, \ldots. \tag{8.9}$$

The cdf jumps at each integer value of x and stays constant for x values in between. The sum is over integer values up to but less than or equal to x, which is what $\lfloor x \rfloor$ means. So, if x were 3.7, the sum would be from $k = 0$ to $k = 3$. The cdf is zero for values of x less than 0.

8.1.6 Binomial distribution family

Another discrete probability distribution family is the *binomial* distribution family. This is a count of "successes" in n independent trials, where the probability of success on any one trial is p. The parameters of the binomial family are then n and p. A random variable having a binomial distribution with parameters n and p has a mean of np and a variance of $np(1-p)$. Because the binomial family is for discrete random variables, it has no pdf. The formula for the pmf of a random variable with a binomial distribution with parameters n and p is

$$f_X(x) = \binom{n}{x} p^x (1-p)^{n-x}, \quad x = 0, 1, 2, \ldots, n, \tag{8.10}$$

where

$$\binom{n}{x} = \frac{n!}{x!(n-x)!}, \quad x = 0, 1, 2, \ldots, n, \tag{8.11}$$

and by definition, $0! = 1$. The random variable X only takes on integer values between 0 and n. The cdf of a random variable with a binomial distribution with parameters n and p does not have closed form, so it is represented as was done for the Poisson distribution in

Equation (8.9):

$$F_X(x) = \sum_{k=0}^{\lfloor x \rfloor} f_X(k), \quad x = 0, 1, 2, \ldots, n. \tag{8.12}$$

The cdf is zero for values of x less than 0 and is one for values of x greater than or equal to n.

Figure 8.1 shows the plots of $f(x)$ and $F(x)$ for a few parametric probability distributions. Note that the Poisson distribution takes only discrete values $0, 1, 2, \ldots$ and so has a pmf, $f(x)$, rather than a pdf, and its cdf, $F(x)$, takes jumps at each integer value (no values in between are possible).

8.2 Choosing and Fitting a Distribution

In order to generate artificial random data, a probability distribution must be chosen. There are two common approaches to choosing the distribution. First, knowledge of the nature of the random variable may directly identify a parametric distribution family that is appropriate. Alternatively, historical data may be used to find a distribution family whose properties match those of the sample data. After choosing a parametric family, one estimates the specific parameter values to find the probability distribution to be used. This estimation is done using maximum likelihood, matching moments, or other methods.

There is a third way: using empirical distributions. Each of these approaches are discussed in this section.

Regardless of the method chosen, the assumption is that the sample represents independent identically distributed random values. If the sample was collected in a particular order, then two plots are required for a validity check of the sample: sample value vs. order and the acf plot for the sample.

8.2.1 Choosing the distribution family based on the nature of the random variable

The descriptions for the normal, exponential, uniform, Poisson, and binomial distribution families in Section 8.1 give guidance on when

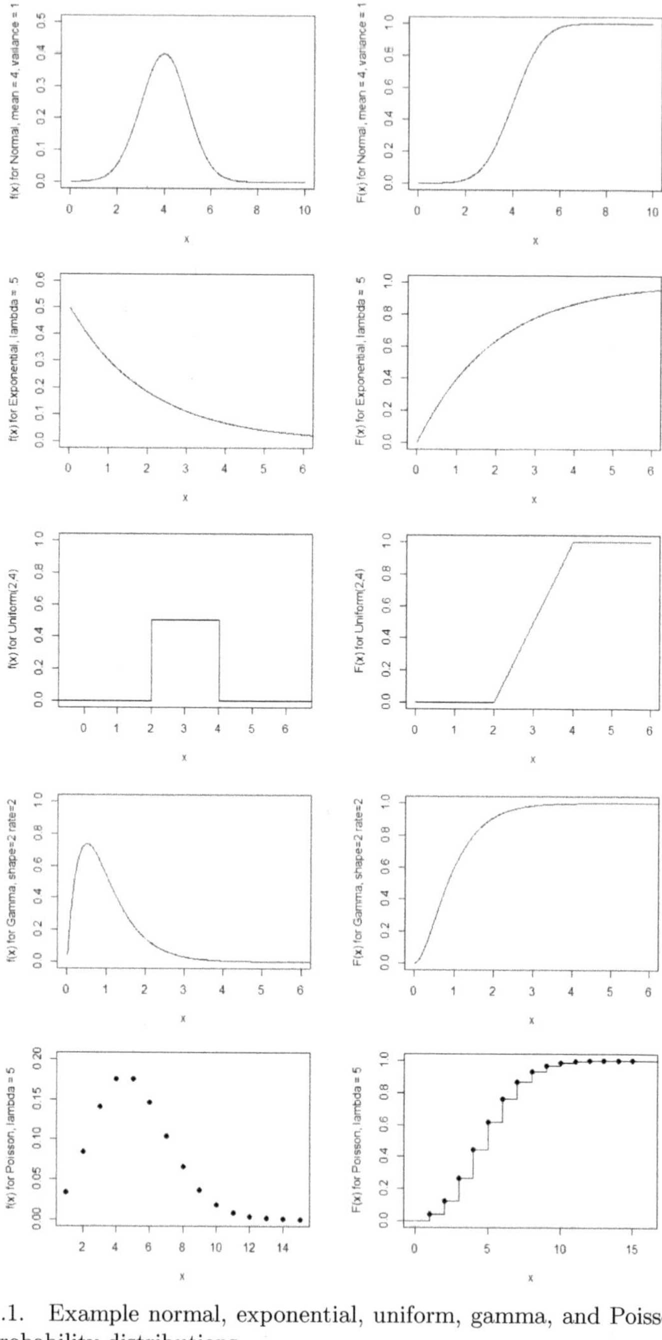

Figure 8.1. Example normal, exponential, uniform, gamma, and Poisson parametric probability distributions.

each family might be an appropriate probability distribution for a random variable X. Table 8.1 includes these five distributions and seven others, with indications of when they may be appropriate. If the nature of the data fits one of the characteristics listed in the table, that parametric distribution family is a logical choice.

8.2.2 Choosing the distribution family based on the fit to historical data

When little is known about how the random quantity is generated in the real world, it is not possible to choose a distribution family from Table 8.1. In that case, one can seek a distribution family and a specific member of that family that provides a good fit. One good way to discriminate between choices for distribution families is the Cullen and Frey graph (Cullen & Frey, 1999). This graph plots two higher moments of the data: the (squared) skewness, $\mathrm{E}(X - \mathrm{E}(X))^3$ vs. the kurtosis, $\mathrm{E}(X - \mathrm{E}(X))^4$. Different distribution families have values that appear in different subregions of the plot. One can plot a point corresponding to the squared skewness and kurtosis values computed from the sample data and see where it falls relative to various distribution families.

Figure 8.2 shows a Cullen and Frey graph for data from a gamma$(2, 2)$ distribution. The large solid circle indicates the point plotted for the sample data. It falls very close to the dashed line representing values that are possible for a gamma distribution. Thus, the recommended parametric family would be the gamma distribution family. Of course, the plotted point is based on a finite set of data in the sample. A different sample would yield a slightly different plotted point. One way to see the uncertainty in location caused by the finiteness of the sample is through a technique called *bootstrapping*, i.e., resampling randomly from the sample data and computing the skewness and kurtosis again. Repeating this 1,000 times gives 1,000 alternate values. These appear as small dots in Figure 8.3. The location of almost all of these points are near the dashed line, giving greater confidence that the appropriate distribution family is the gamma distribution family.

Table 8.1. Random variable characteristics for distribution families.

Characteristics of Random Quantity	**Possible Distribution Family**
X = *number of successes* in n samples when each trial has a common, fixed probability, p, of success (or failure)	Binomial(n, p)
X = *number of successes* in n samples when drawing from a finite population of size N with S successes in the population	Hypergeometric(N, S, n)
X = *number of samples drawn* until the first success (or failure) when each trial has a common, fixed probability, p of success (or failure)	Geometric(p)
X = *number of samples* in a fixed interval or area, when events occur completely "at random" and the average number per interval is λ	Poisson(λ)
X = *number of successes* in n samples (binomial) when n is large and p is small	Poisson(np)
X = *distance between samples* located completely "at random" along a line or in time at an average rate of λ per unit length or time	Exponential(λ)
X = *location of samples* located completely "at random" within a line segment $[a, b]$ or in a time at a rate of λ per unit length or time	Uniform(a, b)
X = *sum* of many (10+) fairly independent random quantities	Normal or Gaussian
X = *product* of many (10+) fairly independent random quantities	logNormal
X = *sum* of the squares of n independent unit normal $N(0, 1)$ random quantities	Chi-Squared(n) or $\chi^2(n)$
X = *sum* of n independent exponential(λ) random quantities	Gamma(n, λ)
X = *average of the max and min values* in a sample of independent random quantities	Logistic

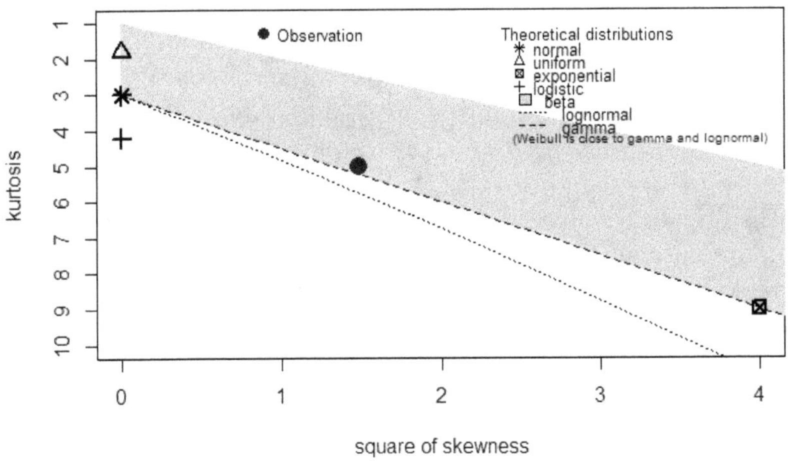

Figure 8.2. Cullen and Frey graph for a gamma(2, 2) sample.

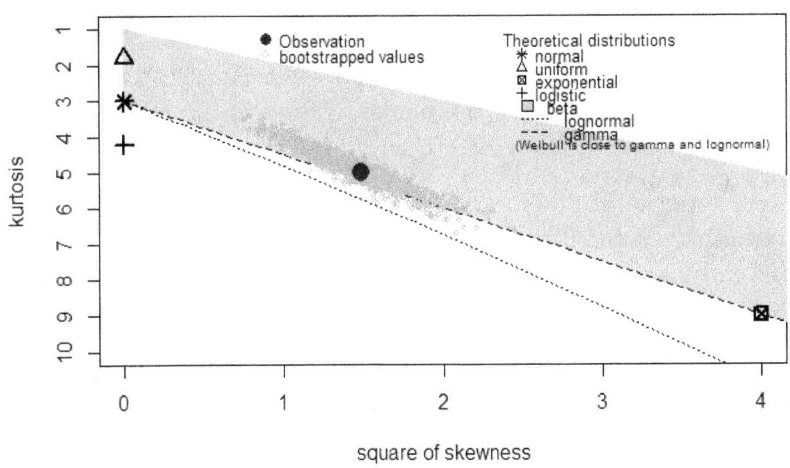

Figure 8.3. Cullen and Frey graph for a gamma(2, 2) sample with bootstrap alternatives.

8.2.3 Fitting the parametric distribution: Parameter estimation

Once a probability distribution family is selected, the particular member must be identified. That means choosing the value or values for the parameter or parameters of the distribution. Sometimes, this is straightforward. For example, for a normal distribution, set μ to the sample mean and σ^2 to the sample variance: $\mu \approx \frac{1}{n}\sum_{i=1}^{n} x_i (= \bar{x})$ and $\sigma^2 \approx \frac{1}{n-1}\sum_{i=1}^{n}(x_i - \bar{x})^2 (= s^2)$. Similarly, set the parameter λ for the exponential distribution to the inverse of the mean time or distance between sample values: $\lambda \approx 1/\bar{x}$.

Historically, analysts had to become experts in knowing how to compute parameter estimates using sample data. Now, these calculations are handled automatically by software. We use the function `fitdist()` in the package `fitdistrplus` in Section 8.7.

8.2.4 Checking the fidelity of the fitted parametric distribution

Given a fitted probability distribution model for the data, it is good to check the quality of the fit. Does the theoretical distribution match the observed distribution of the data? Three ways are particularly important:

- check for straightness of the quantile–quantile (Q–Q) plot;
- check for straightness of the percentile–percentile (P–P) plot;
- compute a goodness-of-fit statistic and check that its p-value is greater than 0.05.

The normal probability plot is a Q–Q plot for the normal distribution family. Q–Q plots plot quantiles of the fitted parametric distribution vs. the corresponding empirical quantiles in the sample data. If the probability model fits the data, these points will fall roughly on a 45 degree line. The P–P plot is similar, plotting the probability model's cdf for each sample x value vs. the empirical cdf value at that x. Again, a good fit would provide points that fall roughly on a 45 degree line. Note that the Q–Q plot is more sensitive to discrepancies in the tails of the distributions, while P–P plots are more sensitive to discrepancies at the center. We discuss how to compute a goodness-of-fit statistic in Section 8.7.

8.2.5 A third way: Use the sample empirical distribution

Sometimes, there is no parametric distribution family that provides fidelity to the distribution of the actual data. Figure 8.4 shows

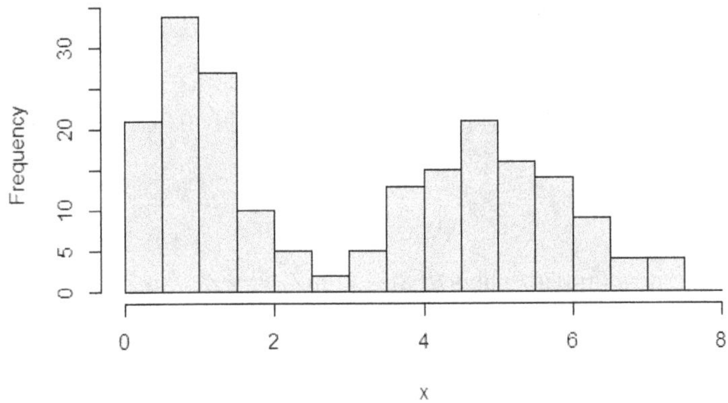

Figure 8.4. Histogram of 200 samples not fit by any parametric distribution.

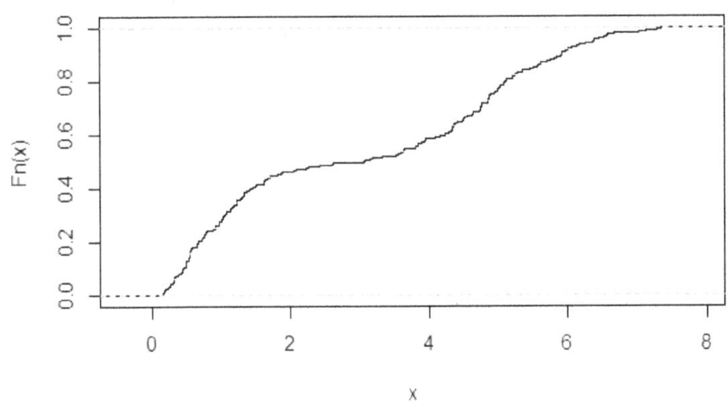

Figure 8.5. Empirical cdf for the sample data.

a histogram for a sample of 200 data values for which we want a probability model. This form is not well-fitted by any of the parametric families that we have studied. To generate random variates from a distribution that matches this form suggests using the original data to construct a cdf. This function is called the *empirical cdf* and is denoted $F_n(x)$, where n refers to the sample size and $n = 200$. $F_n(x)$ is the fraction of the total number of observations that are $\leq x$. $F_n(x)$ can be used to generate random quantities similarly to how the parametric cdf $F(x)$ can be used, as described in the following section. The empirical cdf for the data set in Figure 8.4 is shown in Figure 8.5.

8.3 Random Variate Generation

To generate artificial random quantities following a particular distribution, we use the cdf and a special property of the cdf. This property is shown in Equation (8.13):

$$F_X(X) \sim U(0,1). \tag{8.13}$$

Note that the equation says $F_X(X)$, not $F_X(x)$. So, the cdf is given a random value, x, so that the result itself is random. Why does it have a uniform$(0,1)$ distribution? Intuitively, consider the normal distribution plot in Figure 8.1. The density function on the left shows the frequency with which X values will occur: this is densest around $x = 4$. But look at where these points would fall if you traced them to the point on the cdf function. It has its steepest slope near $x = 4$ and so spreads the points out on the y axis, exactly compensating for the increased density. The result is a uniform$(0,1)$ density on the y axis. We can now state how we will generate random X values with the cdf $F_x(x)$. Since the cdf is always increasing, there is an inverse function; call it $F_X^{-1}(y)$. Now, if we replace y with a random value $U \sim U(0,1)$, we can use Equation (8.13) so that $U = F_X(X)$ and see that

$$F_x^{-1}(U) = F_X^{-1}(F_X(X)) = X. \tag{8.14}$$

To summarize, generate a uniform$(0,1)$ pseudo-random quantity, U. Then, compute $F_X^{-1}(U)$ to get a pseudo-random X.

8.3.1 Generating an exponential random variate

The inverse cdf is often difficult to compute. Fortunately, software handles this automatically for us. But to illustrate the process, we take the simple case of generating a random variate with a distribution from the exponential family. We choose $\lambda = 0.5$. The calculation is shown as follows:

$$\begin{aligned}
U = F_X(X) &= 1 - e^{\lambda X}\\
e^{-\lambda X} &= 1 - U\\
&\text{taking logs :}\\
-\lambda X &= \ln(1-U)\\
X &= -\frac{1}{\lambda}\ln(1-U) = -2\ln(1-U)
\end{aligned}$$

In summary, the process for generating a random variate having an exponential distribution with parameter $\lambda = 0.5$ is to:

1. generate a uniform$(0,1)$ random number, U;
2. compute $X = -2\ln(1-U)$.

Of course, this leaves the question of how to generate a uniform$(0,1)$ random variate, typically called a *random number*. This has been a heavily researched area for more than 50 years. For a comprehensive yet short survey, see L'Ecuyer (2017). For our purposes, the computation of random numbers U and the application of $F_X^{-1}(U)$ to generate X are handled automatically in R.

8.4 Random Variate Generation in R

Table 8.2 shows the R commands for random variables from different probability distributions. The first column gives the name and parameters of the distribution family. The second column gives the command to generate 30 random variate values. The third column shows the command to give the pmf or pdf value, $f(x)$, and the fourth column the cdf value.

Table 8.2. Parametric distribution functions in R.

Distribution Family	**Generate 30 X Values**	$f(x)$	$F(x)$
Normal mean m, std.dev. s	`rnorm(30,m,s)`	`dnorm(x,m,s)`	`pnorm(x,m,s)`
Lognormal mean of $\ln(X)$ = m, std.dev. of $\ln(X)$ = s	`rlnorm(30,m,s)`	`dlnorm(x,m,s)`	`plnorm(x,m,s)`
Exponential λ = lam	`rexp(30,lam)`	`dexp(x,lam)`	`pexp(x,lam)`
Uniform[a, b]	`runif(30,a,b)`	`dunif(x,a,b)`	`punif(x,a,b)`
Gamma(shape = n, rate = r)	`rgamma(30,n,r)`	`dgamma(x,n,r)`	`pgamma(x,n,r)`
Chi-Squared(df = k)	`rchisq(30,k)`	`dchisq(x,k)`	`pchisq(x,k)`
Poisson λ = lam	`rpois(30,lam)`	`dpois(x,lam)`	`ppois(x,lam)`
Geometric(p)	`rgeom(30,p)`	`dgeom(x,p)`	`pgeom(x,p)`
Binomial(n,p)	`rbinom(30,n,p)`	`dbinom(x,n,p)`	`pbinom(x,n.p)`
Empirical dist. for sample "xData"	`sample(30,xData, replace=TRUE)`	`NA`	`ecdf(xData)(x)`

8.5 Validating the RV Generator

Because there is always a risk of miscoding, checking the validity of generated random variates is important. There are four important checks on the validity of the generated random variates:

- the acf plot: checks for independence;
- the Q–Q plot: generalizes the normal probability plot;
- the P–P plot: plots the cdf values of the sample against the model for a series of x values; and
- random variate sample parameter estimates and confidence intervals: check that the sample parameter estimates are close to the chosen population parameters.

The Q–Q plot is sensitive to mismatch of the sample distribution from the desired distribution at the tails of the distributions. The P–P plot is sensitive to mismatch in the central parts of the distributions.

8.6 The Overall Random Variate Simulation Process

The process of identifying, building, and validating a random variate generator is as follows:

1. Summarize the sample data: make sure the data are independent and that there are no outliers or typographical errors. The acf and box plots can help.
2. Plot the data: a histogram would do, but the Cullen and Frey graph from the R package `fitdistrplus` is your most important tool.
3. Which distribution family matches the best? If none, use the empirical distribution.
4. What are the fitted parameters and approximate confidence intervals? If there is high uncertainty in the parameters, seek additional sample data before fitting a probability distribution.
5. Check the fitted distribution fidelity to the data. View the Q–Q, P–P plots of data against fitted distribution. View the data histogram against the fitted distribution. Does the distribution pass a chi-squared goodness-of-fit test for the fitted distribution?

6. If fidelity passes, use the distribution family and fitted parameters with the appropriate R variate generation code to generate random variates. Otherwise, use the empirical distribution for simulation, as shown in Table 8.2.
7. Double-check the resulting variate values for autocorrelation, Q–Q and P–P plots that are reasonably straight, and statistical measures (mean, standard deviation, skewness, and kurtosis) that are similarly valued.
8. Use the random variate generator to simulate random data.

8.7 Example RV Fitting and Generation in R

In this example, we begin with an artificial data set generated from a known distribution. This allows us to see how well our distribution fitting and RV generation process works. We create a set of (pseudo-)observations from a gamma$(2, 2)$ distribution. The R command for creating `testData` is shown as follows. Note that the gamma distribution in R is specified with *scale* and *rate* parameters:

```
> # generate sample of 200 Gamma(2,2) random variates
> sampleData = rgamma(200,2,2)
>
```

Step 1: The initial data summary commands and results are shown and in Figures 8.6 and 8.7:

```
> # data summary and box plot
> summary(sampleData)
   Min. 1st Qu.  Median    Mean 3rd Qu.    Max.
0.05179 0.51374 0.89199 1.03643 1.40087 4.26907
> acf(sampleData)
> boxplot(sampleData,xlab="Sample Data",horizontal=T)
>
```

The summary shows that all values are positive. The median is less than the mean, which suggests positive skewness. The box plot also shows that the distribution is skewed, but the outliers are not extremely far from the main part of the distribution, so data points worth investigating for typographical errors are not apparent. The autocorrelation plot in Figure 8.6 indicates that the data are consistent with the independence assumption.

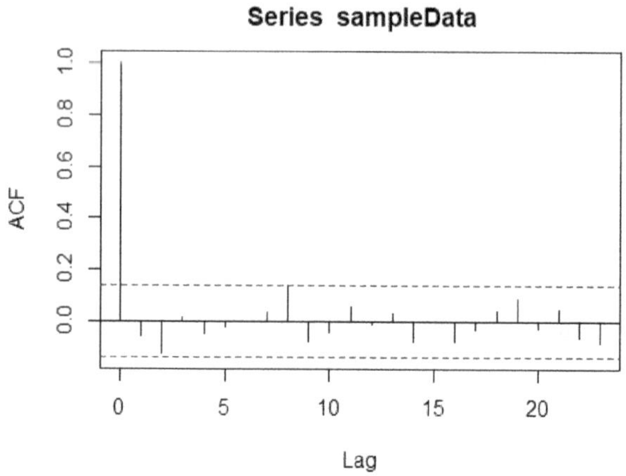

Figure 8.6. Autocorrelation plot for sample data.

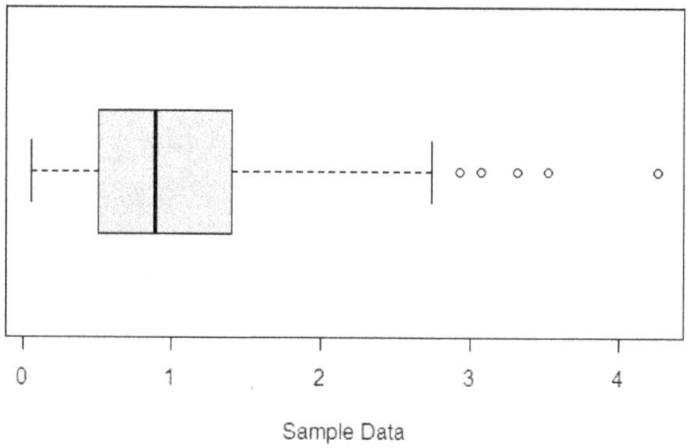

Figure 8.7. Boxplot for sample data.

Step 2: Next, we examine plots using **`fitdistrplus`** to get a better understanding of the shape and see what distribution family or families might provide a good fit. The following code shows the generation of a histogram of the data, with a smoothed density approximation superimposed, and the Cullen and Frey graph for identifying a candidate distribution family or families. The `descdist()` function also gives more details on the statistical properties of the sample, shown following the command:

```
> # use functions in fitdistrplus to choose
> #   candidate probability distribution family
> library(fitdistrplus)
```

```
> # plot histogram of data and pdfdensity approximation
> plotdist(sampleData, demp=TRUE)
> # descdist gives data summary and Cullen and Frey graph
> descdist(sampleData, boot = 1000)
summary statistics
------
min:  0.05178677   max:  4.269073
median:  0.8919876
mean:  1.036431
estimated sd:  0.7176447
estimated skewness:  1.303401
estimated kurtosis:  5.294618
>
```

The computed skewness is positive, so a normal distribution family is not appropriate. Further, the kurtosis measures the relative length of the tails of the distribution compared with the main body. Normal distribution tails give a kurtosis of 3, so a value of more than 5 suggests longer tails than that generated by a normal distribution.

The histogram in Figure 8.8 produced by `plotdist` confirms the skewness and long tail. The smoothed density estimate that is superimposed was created by using the option `demp=TRUE`. The empirical cdf is not particularly useful but is produced automatically by `plotdist`.

The large circle on the Cullen and Frey graph in Figure 8.9 shows squared skewness and kurtosis values that place the data near the dashed line for the gamma distribution family. Considering sampling error, the small dots show 1,000 bootstrapped alternative values. Again, these fall reasonably close to the dashed line, making the gamma distribution family a good choice. Falling in the gray region implies that the beta distribution family may be a good choice as well, but members of the beta distribution family are bounded above and below, like the uniform family. If there is no practical reason to expect specific upper and lower limits for the data, the beta distribution family should be avoided.

Step 3: As noted in the Cullen and Frey graph, the region for the Weibull distribution family lies between the gamma and lognormal lines. Since the sample data points and most of the bootstrapped values lie above both lines, the Weibull family is probably a poorer choice that the gamma family; nonetheless, for this example, we fit and compare both candidates.

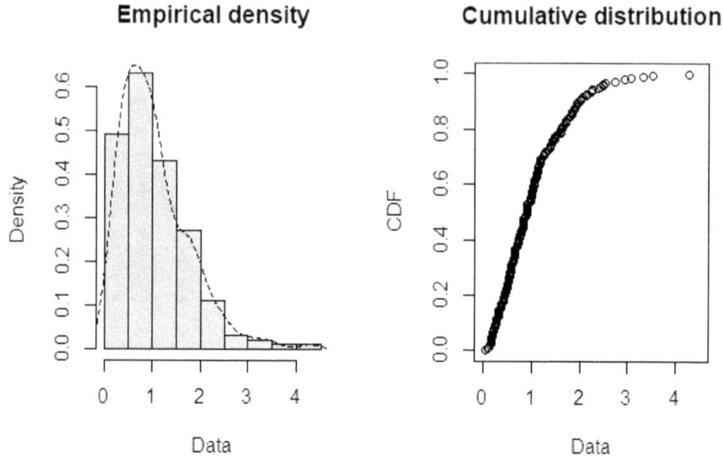

Figure 8.8. Histogram and ecdf for sample data.

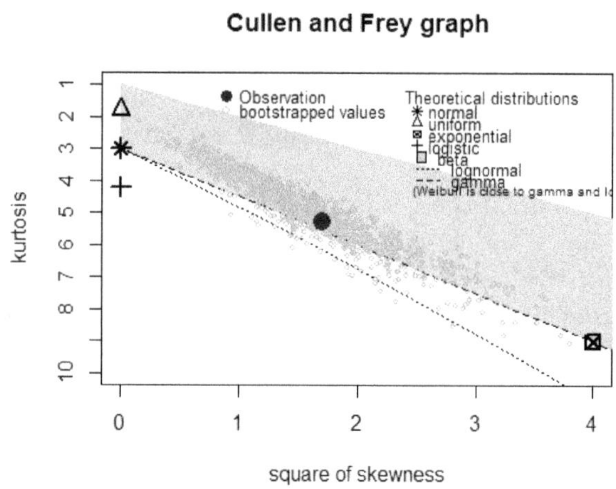

Figure 8.9. Cullen and Frey graph for sample data.

Step 4: The following code creates the fitted probability model objects `fg` for the gamma distribution and `fw` for the fitted Weibull distribution:

```
> # fit Weibull and Gamma distributions and report fits
> fg <- fitdist(sampleData, "gamma")
> fw <- fitdist(sampleData, "weibull")
```

```
> summary(fg); summary(fw)
Fitting of the distribution ' gamma ' by maximum likelihood
Parameters :
      estimate Std. Error
shape 2.090515  0.1946805
rate  2.017020  0.2121625
Loglikelihood:   -181.3652   AIC:  366.7304   BIC:  373.327
Correlation matrix:
          shape      rate
shape 1.0000000 0.8853406
rate  0.8853406 1.0000000

Fitting of the distribution ' weibull ' by maximum likelihood
Parameters :
      estimate Std. Error
shape 1.518712 0.08186046
scale 1.153810 0.05673422
Loglikelihood:   -182.927   AIC:  369.854   BIC:  376.4506
Correlation matrix:
          shape     scale
shape 1.0000000 0.3215843
scale 0.3215843 1.0000000
>
```

The `summary()` function provides four useful kinds of information:

- the parameter estimates;
- standard deviation of the parameter estimates that can be used to construct confidence intervals;
- correlation of the estimates, with a high correlation suggesting that multiple sets of parameter values will fit the data well; and
- statistical characterization of the quality of fit (Loglikelihood, AIC, and BIC), useful when comparing alternate candidate distribution families.

We see that for the gamma fit, the fitted parameters are close to the actual (2, 2) used to generate the data. Approximate 95% confidence intervals for the parameters are $2.091 \pm 2(0.195) = [1.701, 2.481]$ for shape and $2.017 \pm 2(0.212) = [1.593, 2.441]$ for rate. The intervals are relatively large because of the high correlation (0.885), suggesting that a variety of shape and rate parameters could provide a good fit to these data. For the Weibull distribution, approximate 95% confidence intervals for the shape and scale parameters are $[1.355, 1.683]$ and $[1.040, 1.267]$. The parameter estimates for the Weibull distribution exhibit low correlation, and the approximate

95% confidence intervals for the parameter values are tighter than for the gamma distribution.

Statistical characterization of fit is presented in terms of three statistics: the logarithm of the likelihood function (less negative is better), the Akaike information criterion (AIC; smaller is better), and the Bayes information criterion (BIC; smaller is better). The AIC and BIC measures will have the same ranking as the loglikelihood ranking when alternative candidate distribution families have the same number of parameters, as is the case here (both have two parameters). When the number of parameters between different candidate distributions vary, the AIC and BIC rankings give better results. The BIC measure gives greater penalty to distributions with more parameters. For our example, since the number of parameters match, all measures indicate that the gamma distribution is a better fit for the sample data.

Nonetheless, we will check fidelity for both models in Step 5.

Step 5: The following code provides the Q–Q and P–P plots for the data against the fitted distributions. These plots are shown in Figure 8.10. The histogram plot shows that both probability distributions match the histogram fairly well. But this comparison is the weakest of the three kinds of fidelity plots for discrimination between probability distributions. The Q–Q plot shows better fit for the gamma distribution at high values. The P–P plot shows slightly better fit (closer to the line) for the gamma distribution at the center of the range.

```
> # density, Q-Q and P-P plots comparing the fidelity of
> #   the fitted Gamma and Weibull distributions
> par(mfrow = c(3,1))
> plot.legend <- c("Gamma", "Weibull")
> denscomp(list(fg, fw), legendtext = plot.legend)
> qqcomp(list(fg, fw), legendtext = plot.legend)
> ppcomp(list(fg, fw), legendtext = plot.legend)
> par(mfrow = c(1,1))
>
```

Finally, we check the p-value for the chi-squared goodness-of-fit test for each fitted distribution using the `gofstat()` function in the

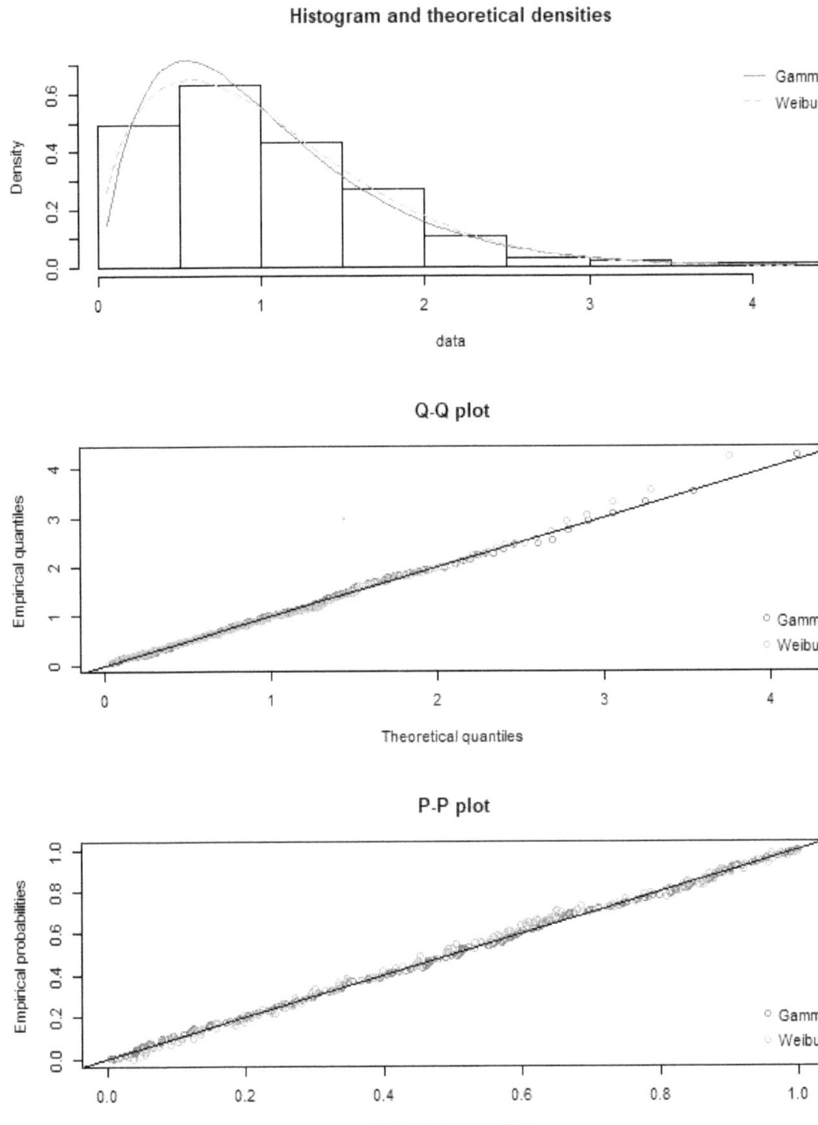

Figure 8.10. Histogram and Q–Q and P–P plots to check fitted distribution fidelity.

`fitdistrplus` library. It operates directly on the fitted distribution objects, `fg` and `fw`:

```
> # chi-squared goodness of fit test for the distributions
> gofg = gofstat(fg)
> gofg$chisqpvalue
[1] 0.7913069
> gofw = gofstat(fw)
> gofw$chisqpvalue
[1] 0.8161298
>
```

Both distributions pass the goodness-of-fit test with p-values far greater than 0.05.

Step 6: These results lead to two conclusions:

- the gamma distribution provides slightly better fit; and
- the Q–Q and P–P plots and the chi-squared goodness-of-fit p-value indicate that the fit is of very good fidelity to the sample data.

This means we can proceed to use the gamma(2.091, 2.017) distribution to generate random variates with (approximately) the same distribution as our sample data.

Step 7: We check that random variates generated from `rgamma(n, 2.091, 2.017)` behave similarly to the original data. We generate a random variate data set of the same size ($n = 200$). For samples of the same size, a Q–Q plot corresponds to sorting both data sets and plotting the paired sorted values. P–P plots show the ecdf(x) of the generated data against the ecdf(x) of the sample data for varying values of x. The data set generation and plotting code are shown as follows:

```
> # fit satisfactory, generate 200 RVs to verify
> RVdata = rgamma(200,2.091,2.017)
> # check autocorrelation
> acf(RVdata)
> # do Q-Q plot
> plot(sort(RVdata),sort(sampleData), main="Q-Q PLot",
+      xlim=c(0,5),ylim=c(0,5),xlab="RV Data",ylab="Sample Data",
+      pch=20)
> lines(c(0,5),c(0,5))
> # do a P-P plot, p varies from zero to 5 in steps of .1,
> #   i.e. (0:50)/10
```

```
> plot(ecdf(RVdata)((0:50)/10),ecdf(sampleData)((0:50)/10),
+      main="P-P Plot",xlim=c(0,1),ylim=c(0,1),
+      xlab="RV Distribution",
+      ylab="Sample Distribution", pch=20)
> lines(c(0,1),c(0,1))
> # check summary statistics
> mean(RVdata)
[1] 1.051691
> sd(RVdata)
[1] 0.7021355
> # skewness and kurtosis need library(moments)
> library(moments)
> skewness(RVdata)
[1] 1.122906
> kurtosis(RVdata)
[1] 4.432698
>
```

The autocorrelation plot is shown in Figure 8.11. It appears satisfactory. The Q–Q and P–P plots are shown in Figure 8.12. There deviations at the highest values for the Q–Q plot, but Q–Q plots often show a few discrepancies at high values, so this is not worrisome. There are only slight deviations at the center of the P–P plot, but again, they are not great enough to worry.

Finally, recall that for the actual data, the `descdist()` function gave the following result, and the RV sample values above are reasonably close.

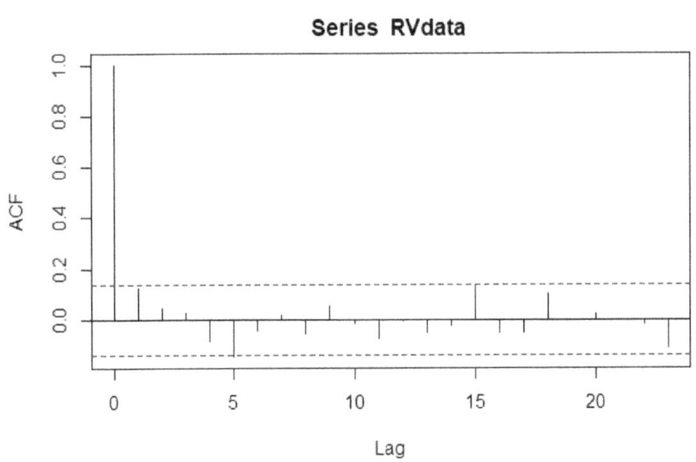

Figure 8.11. Autocorrelation plot for generated gamma random variate.

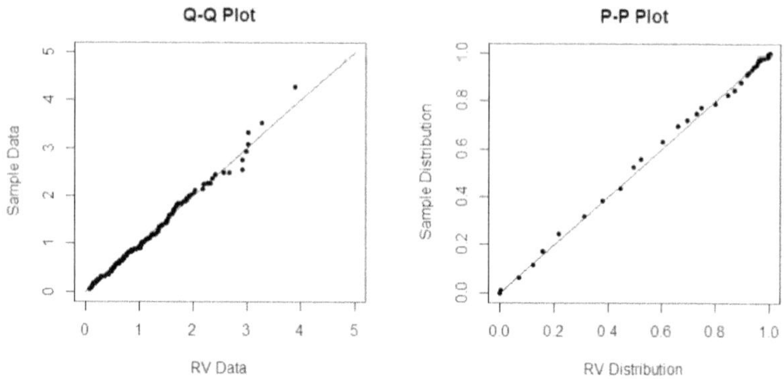

Figure 8.12. Q–Q and P–P Plots of random variates vs. sample data.

```
mean:   1.036431
estimated sd:   0.7176447
estimated skewness:   1.303401
estimated kurtosis:   5.294618
```

Step 8: The random variate generator has been validated. It is ready to use in Monte Carlo or discrete-event simulations.

8.8 Case Supporting Chapter 8

The TicketCounterRandomVariates case supports the material in this chapter. Distributions are fitted to historical data, and the artificial random variates that are generated are validated. The case description slides and data can be found online in the TicketCounterRandomVariates folder of Barton (2023).

8.9 R Code Used in Chapter 8

```
# Distribution plots for Random Variables
  Chapter=================

# Normal
x = (1:1000)/100
mu = 4
sigma = 1
fx = dnorm(x,mu,sigma)
plot(x,fx, xlab = "x", ylab = "f(x) for Normal, mean = 4,
```

```
variance = 1", type = "l",xlim=c(0,10),ylim = c(0,.5))
Fx = pnorm(x,mu,sigma)
# make a step function
plot(x, Fx,xlab="x",xlim=c(0,10),ylab="F(x) for Normal,
mean = 4, variance = 1", type="l", ylim=c(0,1))

# Exponential(.5)
x = (1:1000)/100
lambda = .5
fx = lambda*exp(-lambda*x)
plot(x,fx, xlab = "x", ylab =
"f(x) for Exponential, lambda = .5",
type = "l",xlim=c(0,6),ylim = c(0,.6))
Fx = 1 - exp(-lambda*x)
plot(x,Fx, xlab = "x",
ylab = "F(x) for Exponential, lambda = .5",
type = "l",xlim=c(0,6),ylim = c(0,1))

# Uniform (2,4)
x = (1:600)/100
fx = c(rep(0,200),rep(.5,200),rep(0,200))
fx = c(0,fx)
sfx = stepfun(x,fx)
plot(sfx,x, xlab="x", ylab = "f(x) for Uniform(2,4)",
ylim=c(0,1), main="", pch=NA) # null plot character
Fx = c(rep(0,200),(1:200)/200,rep(1,200))
plot(x,Fx, xlab="x", ylab = "F(x) for Uniform(2,4)",
ylim=c(0,1), main="", type="l")

# Gamma (scale=2,rate=2)
x = (1:1000)/100
shape = 2
lambda = 2
rate = lambda
scale = 1/lambda
fx = dgamma(x,shape,rate)
plot(x,fx, xlab = "x",
ylab = "f(x) for Gamma, shape=2 rate=2",
type = "l",xlim=c(0,6),ylim = c(0,1))
Fx = pgamma(x,shape,rate)
# make a step function
plot(x, Fx,xlab="x",xlim=c(0,6),
ylab="F(x) for Gamma, shape=2 rate=2",
type="l", ylim=c(0,1))

# Poisson (5)
x = 1:15
lambda = 5
Px = dpois(x,lambda)
plot(x,Px, xlab="x", ylab="f(x) for Poisson, lambda = 5",
```

```
pch=16, ylim=c(0, .2))
Fx = ppois(x,lambda)
# make a step function
Fx = c(0,Fx)
sFx = stepfun(x,Fx)
plot(sFx,x, xlab="x", ylab="F(x) for Poisson, lambda = 5",
main = "", pch = 16)

# create bimodal empirical data and plot
x1 = rnorm(100,5,1)
x2 = rgamma(100,2,2)
x = c(x1,x2)
hist(x, breaks=seq(0,8,.5), main="")
plot(ecdf(x), pch=NA,main="")


# code for fitting, validating,
  generating RVs===================
# code for fitting, validating, generating RVs
#   for PABR random variates chapter
# set the random number seed
set.seed(57829)
# generate sample of 200 Gamma(2,2) random variates
sampleData = rgamma(200,2,2)

# data summary, acf plot and box plot
summary(sampleData)
acf(sampleData)
boxplot(sampleData,xlab="Sample Data",horizontal=T)

# use functions in fitdistrplus to choose
#   candidate probability distribution family
library(fitdistrplus)
# plot histogram of data and pdfdensity approximation
plotdist(sampleData, demp=TRUE)
# descdist gives data summary and Cullen and Frey graph
descdist(sampleData,boot = 1000)

# fit Weibull and Gamma distributions and report fits
fg <- fitdist(sampleData, "gamma")
fw <- fitdist(sampleData, "weibull")
summary(fg); summary(fw)

# density, Q-Q and P-P plots comparing the fidelity of
#   the fitted Gamma and Weibull distributions
par(mfrow = c(3,1))
plot.legend <- c("Gamma", "Weibull")
denscomp(list(fg, fw), legendtext = plot.legend)
```

```
qqcomp(list(fg, fw), legendtext = plot.legend)
ppcomp(list(fg, fw), legendtext = plot.legend)
par(mfrow = c(1,1))

# chi-squared goodness of fit test for the distributions
gofg = gofstat(fg)
gofg$chisqpvalue
gofw = gofstat(fw)
gofw$chisqpvalue

# fit satisfactory, generate 200 RVs to verify
RVdata = rgamma(200,2.091,2.017)
# check autocorrelation
acf(RVdata)
# do Q-Q plot
plot(sort(RVdata),sort(sampleData), main="Q-Q PLot",
xlim=c(0,5),ylim=c(0,5),xlab="RV Data",
ylab="Sample Data", pch=20)
lines(c(0,5),c(0,5))
# do a P-P plot, p varies from zero to 5 in steps of .1,
#   i.e. (0:50)/10
plot(ecdf(RVdata)((0:50)/10),ecdf(sampleData)((0:50)/10),
main="P-P Plot",xlim=c(0,1),ylim=c(0,1),
xlab="RV Distribution",
ylab="Sample Distribution", pch=20)
lines(c(0,1),c(0,1))
# check summary statistics
mean(RVdata)
sd(RVdata)
# skewness and kurtosis need library(moments)
library(moments)
skewness(RVdata)
kurtosis(RVdata)
```

Chapter 9

Building Discrete-Event Simulation Models

Real systems often operate dynamically, and characterizing system performance under different management protocols can be expensive and difficult to manage. For example, in a bank operation, how much would adding one more teller reduce the waiting time and reduce the maximum and average numbers of customers in the system? Suppose an expensive software upgrade would reduce the time for a teller to complete a customer transaction by one minute on average. How much would that reduce customer waiting time with the given number of tellers?

These questions can be answered directly through operational implementation but at great cost. If an extra teller is hired but the waiting time reduction is not significant, it is bad business practice (and expensive) to then lay off the teller. The advantage of the software can be evaluated by implementing it; however, even if the software can be leased for a short term, the leasing, software transfer, and training costs would likely be substantial. Further, when designing a new bank operation not currently in existence, alternative configurations could be extremely expensive to compare through building and operating each alternative.

Instead, one can construct a computer model of the bank operation and simulate customers arriving, waiting, and being served. The simulated waiting times and numbers in the system can be collected and analyzed easily, giving a prediction of the operational characteristics of the real system. Compared with operational implementation, the cost lies in building the simulation model, which can be substantially less. In Miller's research paradigm trilogy, this is a powerful example of *model-dependent research.*

Often, such simulation models are called *digital twins*, but some use this term only when the simulation model is of an existing system (with no changes) and operates in real time in parallel with the real system, and the model and real-world systems update each other automatically. In this scenario, a digital twin can help identify if some unexpected change has happened to the real system and can be used to evaluate the impact of future management action given the current system state.

In this chapter, we explore discrete-event simulation, a computer modeling technique that is useful for many kinds of business operations: airports, construction, entertainment and sports venues, hospitals, logistics and transportation, manufacturing, retail operations, and many others. Discrete-event simulation is also used to study how communication systems and computers will perform, how diseases will spread, and how animal populations may change over time based on dynamic changes in their environment.

9.1 What Is Discrete-Event Simulation?

Discrete-event simulation (DES) is sometimes called *discrete-event dynamic simulation* (DEDS). It is a computer program that predicts the dynamic behavior of a system (think hospital emergency room, car wash, expense report workflow, etc.) over time. What does dynamic mean? It means that characteristics of the system and entities interacting with the system change over time. It is easiest to explain by example.

Consider the (slightly embellished) example given by Nelson (2013) of a video player system for presenting commercial advertisements on a network television broadcast. Because there would be serious revenue loss to the network if the commercial failed to run, a backup video player is ready to play if and when the primary player fails. The failed player enters repair by a technician, and the backup player now comes into operation and becomes the primary. Once the failed player is repaired, it is placed on standby as the backup video player.

A question of managerial interest is whether both systems can fail: the backup player in operation as the primary fails before the recently failed player has completed repair. Of course, this depends on the time until failure (TTF) of a player just put in primary mode and the time to complete repair for a player that has just failed.

When one or both of these are random, DES can be used to study the behavior and the TTF of the second unit while the first remains in repair. Nelson calls this a TTF simulation. To make it easy to follow system changes and make it possible to do the simulation "by hand," the time from start of operation in primary mode until player failure will be random, with values of 1, 2, 3, 4, 5, or 6 days equally likely. So, the TTPF can be "simulated" by rolling a die. Time to repair a failed unit is a deterministic 2.5 days. To avoid confusion, time until player failure will be called TTPF and time until system failure will be called TTSF.

You can try this simulation yourself. To record changes in the system over time, you need the structure shown in Table 9.1.

The table has a row for each *event*. An event is a change in system state, a scheduling of a new event, and/or cancellation of a pending event that occurs at an instant in time. The particular combination of these actions depends on the type of event — events have *types*. The instant in time for the event is the second column in the table. In simulation parlance, the time is usually referred to as the *clock* value. For the TTF simulation, there is only one state variable: the number of working video players. If the state drops to zero, the system fails and the simulation ends. System state is the third column in the table. The last two columns hold the next times for events of type

Table 9.1. TTSF simulation recording form.

Event #	Time (Clock)	# Operational (Sys. State)	Time Next Failure	Time Complete Repair
0	0	2	-TBD-	∞
1				
2				
3				
4				
5				
⋮	⋮	⋮	⋮	⋮

"Failure" and "Complete Repair." An event of type "Failure" triggers a state change (a decrease by 1) and schedules a new "Complete Repair" event. A "Complete Repair" event type only changes the state (an increase by 1). When an event has been processed, the simulation moves ahead to the scheduled event that occurs next.

In the TTF simulation, there are two types of events: a player failure, which reduces the state by 1 and starts the repair process, and the completion of a repair, which increases the state by 1 (and places the repaired player in backup status, but this does not add any events). In real simulation software, both types of events would be placed in a single data frame or list with two columns: time of the event, and type of the event. The data frame or list must be kept sorted by time so that the next event can be identified as the first in order. In this simple simulation, there can only be one "fail" and at most one "repair" scheduled at any time, so it is easier to keep two variables (next fail and next repair), and then the next event in time is the one with the minimum time value. These values are kept in the last two columns of the table.

The first row of the table is partially populated. At the start of the simulation, state variable values and initial events must be set. Without any events, there will be no reason to advance the time clock. For the TTF simulation, the initialization sets the clock to zero, the operational state to 2, the time to the first failure as random from $\{1, 2, 3, 4, 5, 6\}$ (written in the table as "TBD": to be determined), and since there is no repair activity at the start of the simulation, there is no upcoming event of type "Complete Repair." But we need to remove the previous clock time for "Complete Repair" or the simulation will choose that time again as the next event. When there is no scheduled event of that type, to *remove* it from the list of upcoming events, we set the time to complete the next repair to a very large number (or ∞).

Table 9.2 shows the form after processing the first event: event #1. The first roll of the die produced an initial failure time of 5 (random values from rolls of the die are underlined in bold). The next row of the form (event #1) shows a clock time of 5 (days) and a change in state from 2 players working to only 1, and it identifies the time for two new events: a roll of the die gives 3 as the operational time of the newly activated backup player (so failure time at $5 + 3 = 8$) and schedules the completion of the repair in 2.5 days (so complete repair

Table 9.2. TTF simulation form update at event #1.

Event #	Time (Clock)	# Operational (Sys. State)	Time Next Failure	Time Complete Repair
0	0	2	**5**	∞
1	5	1	5+**3**=8	5+2.5=7.5
2				
⋮	⋮	⋮	⋮	⋮

Table 9.3. A single TTSF simulation replication with TTSF = 15.

Event #	Time (Clock)	# Operational (Sys. State)	Time Next Failure	Time Complete Repair
0	0	2	**5**	∞
1	5	1	5+**3**=8	5+2.5=7.5
2	7.5	2	8	∞
3	8	1	8+**6**=14	8+2.5=10.5
4	10.5	2	14	∞
5	14	1	14+**1**=15	14+2.5=16.5
6	15	0	**STOP**	16.5

time is $5 + 2.5 = 7.5$). Looking at the last two columns with values 8 and 7.5, one can see that the next event will be the completion of repair at a clock time of 7.5 days.

A filled-in form for a completed simulation run (called a *replication*) is shown in Table 9.3. The table shows that simulated time advanced in irregular discrete steps. This is typical of DES. These time jumps are shown graphically in Figure 9.1. This is the great computational advantage of DES: time does not need to be processed in small increments to preserve time accuracy. Large time steps (when there are no intervening events of importance) speed up the computer simulation.

We can see what led to the ending of the simulation replication. In the row for event #4, one can see that the next event will be a failure at time 14. When that happens, both a failure time for the backup player is scheduled (only 1 day operation, so failure time at 15 days) and a completion of repair at day 16.5. So, the next event processed is another failure at day 15, reducing the state to zero — no operational players, a serious concern for the network. This behavior can also be represented graphically. Figure 9.2 shows

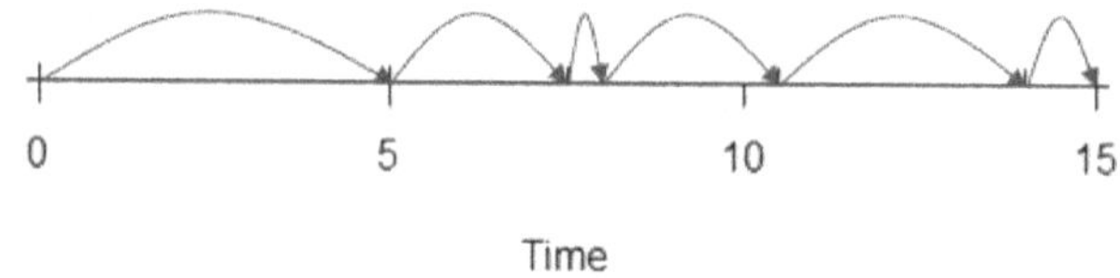

Figure 9.1. Discrete-time advance steps for the TTSF replication.

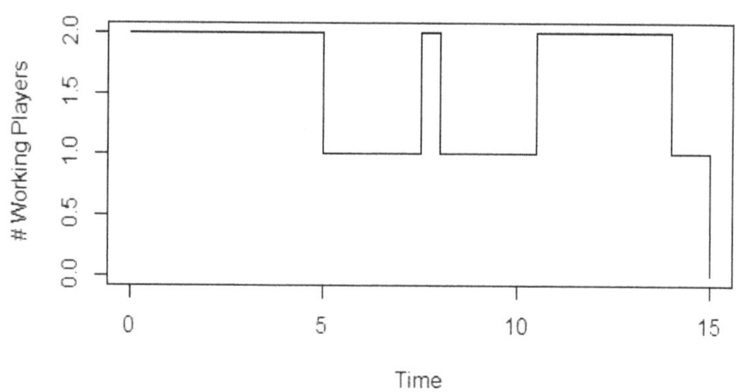

Figure 9.2. System state (# working players) for the TTSF replication.

the system state (# working players) over the simulated time. It is clear when the system fails. This figure also shows how to calculate the time-average number of working players: the area under the plot from 0 to 15 divided by 15. We will learn more about such *continuous-time statistics* in Chapter 10.

The results in Table 9.3 are one possible realization for the random events leading up to failure. To give the company insight on the likelihood of this pattern, multiple replications of this TTF simulation should be run. Then, an average TTSF, standard deviation of TTSF, and a histogram of possible TTSF values could be presented to management so that they would understand the risks.

The following code shows an R program to run the TTF simulator 100 times and produce statistical summaries and the histogram shown in Figure 9.3. The full simulation code to generate these results is included in Section 9.8; the following is the main program that calls the simulator and its output, along with the key command to generate a random integer between 1 and 6. The value of `6*runif(1)` is a single random value between 0 and 5.999999..., so the `floor()`

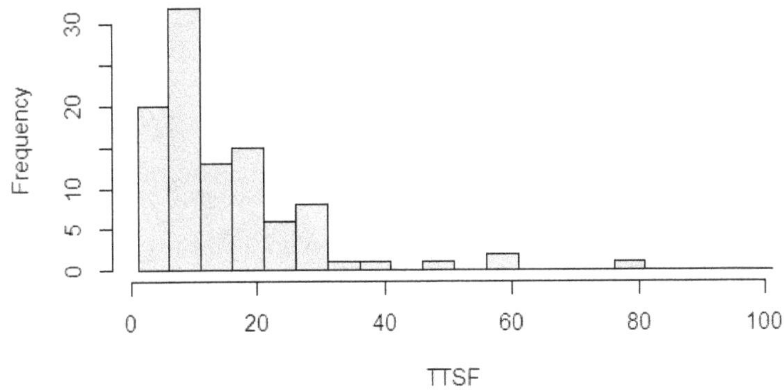

Figure 9.3. Histogram of time to system failure for 100 simulation replications.

value rounds down to between 0 and 5, and thus the need to add one.

```
> # main program completes nreps replications
> #   computes statistics and draws histogram
> # seed set for repeatable results
> set.seed(25951)
> TTSF = NULL
> nreps = 100
> for(reps in 1:nreps){
    +    simResult = TTF()
    +    TTSF = c(TTSF, simResult)
    + }
> mean(TTSF)
[1] 15.31
> sd(TTSF)
[1] 12.76493
> hist(TTSF, breaks=seq(1,105,5), main="")
>

> # R command to generate a random integer between 1 and 6
> NextFailure <<- Clock + floor(6 * runif(1)) + 1
>
```

The figure shows the skewed distribution of TTSF values over the 100 replications. Analysis of such data is taken up later: this chapter focuses on building simulation models. Chapter 10 presents the methods of predictive analytics using simulation-generated data.

There are several key characteristics of a DES model (with exemplars from the TTF simulation):

- the system has *entities* moving through *processes* (think of failed video players moving through the repair process);
- the *processes* often require accessing a limited *resource* (think of the repair technician);
- some timing aspects are random (think of the TTF of a video player);
- the system model does not model time continuously but advances time discretely to the time of the next state change (this is called *next event time advance*, or *NETA*; think advancing to time of next video player failure or to time of next repair completion, whichever occurs first).

Corresponding to these characteristics, the DES code has the following elements:

- a *system clock* that advances event by event as the simulation code executes;
- an *events list* sorted by time, from which the next event is removed using a `timing()` function;
- one *event processing function* for each event type in the simulation, often involving changing elements of the state and adding events to the events list;
- the *system state* that can be a vector of state elements, identifying the state of the system, that can be updated by event processing routines when they are activated;
- *entities* being processed by the system, typically with random interarrival times, some in process and some waiting for processing — often not separately modeled, but held (with their individual attributes) in the events list;
- *resources* used in event processing routines, typically with random processing times — usually individually modeled, with properties accessed by the event processing routines;
- various *system statistical counters* to keep track of processing times, busy/idle status of resources, number of entities in process, and so forth for use in predictive analytics (Chapter 10);
- an *initialization routine* to set the initial state vector and place initial events on the events list (perhaps including the STOP event); and
- a *stopping rule* to end the simulation based on time, state, or some other condition.

9.2 Discrete-Event Simulation Modeling Paradigms and Software

The above characteristics do not completely define how simulation models are viewed and constructed. There are three primary modeling viewpoints or paradigms for DES: event-scheduling (what we did for the TTF simulation), process-interaction, and agent-based. This section gives a brief overview of each of these.

9.2.1 Event-scheduling paradigm

In this view, the focus is on identifying the various types of events and their consequences. For the TTF example, there were two types of events: video player failure, and completion of a video player repair. Each event of each type must be processed, and the event processing may: (i) change the system state (player failure reduced # working players by 1), (ii) add events of various types to an event list (player failure added a failure event and a repair completion event), or (iii) update various statistical counters. This view of the simulation model can be represented in an *event graph.*

Figure 9.4 shows the event graph for the TTF simulation. The large circles represent three types of events: video player failure,

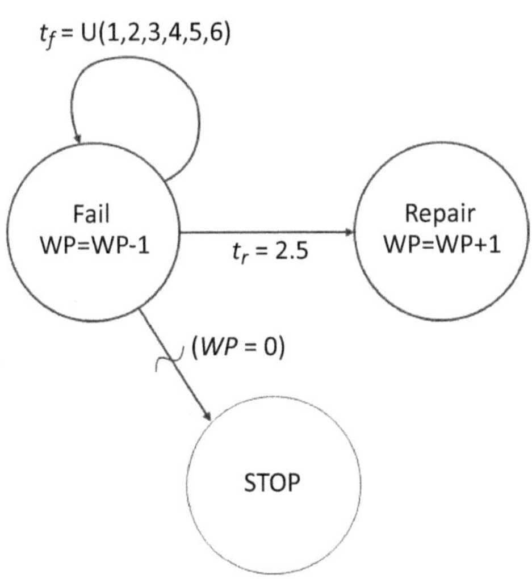

Figure 9.4. Event graph for the TTF simulation.

video player repair completion, and the end of the simulation. The lines indicate when one event triggers another. The loop on the fail event triggers another fail event, since when one player fails, the backup starts to operate, and so its failure time must be computed. The variable t_f holds the computed failure time in days, drawn randomly from $\{1, 2, 3, 4, 5, 6\}$. A fail event also triggers a repair event after $t_r = 2.5$ days. Each event also updates the system state. For the fail event, the system state (# working players or *WP*) is decreased by one. For the repair event, it is increased by one. Finally, there is a conditional trigger event from the fail node. Conditional events are indicated by a tilde across the arrow, with the condition written beside the arrow. If *WP* reaches zero, the stop event is triggered. For more about this modeling approach, see Schruben (1995) and Law (2014).

9.2.2 Process-interaction paradigm

The process-interaction paradigm views the dynamic system operation from the perspective of the entities flowing through it, being processed by system resources. For the TTF simulation, the entities are the failed video players and the operational video players. But the system behavior can be modeled simply by following a failed player. Operational players do not use resources; they simply become operating (after random time) and then (after random time) failed players. Figure 9.5 shows a process-interaction view for the TTF simulation that only follows a failed video player through the repair process. Interaction with the process resource (the technician) is made explicit. State variables are updated as the video player flows through the process. Often, it is easier to describe the operation of a process or multiple interacting processes than to think about all possible transition mechanisms for all of the state variables.

Major simulation software packages allow modeling in the process-interaction paradigm and allow visual interfaces for placement of resources and entities and routing of entities through resources. Graphical process-interaction and object-oriented programming interfaces are offered by many commercial packages, including AnyLogic, Arena, Flexsim, ProModel, and Simio. See the simulation software survey by James Swain for details (Swain, 2019a, 2019b).

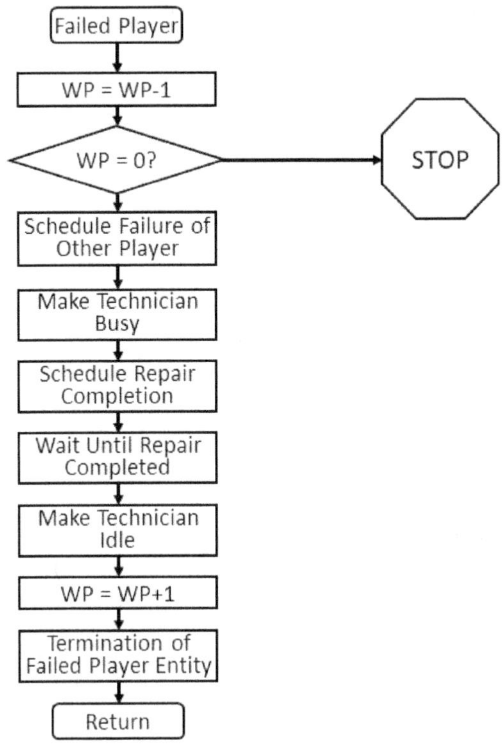

Figure 9.5. Process-interaction entity flowchart for the TTF simulation.

In the process-interaction view of Figure 9.5, one can imagine a system with more than one spare player and with more than one failed player with the system still operational. Then, the meaning of the technician being "busy" is clear: only one failed video player is repaired at a time. Other failed units must wait.

This waiting-for-resource phenomenon happens frequently in business settings, and such systems are called *queueing systems*. The waiting line is also called a queue. Entities that arrive for processing by the resource are said to "enter the queueing system" even when there is no waiting line and they are directly processed. The entities are often called "customers" and the processing resource is called the "server." There are probability models for predicting behavior for simple kinds of queues (exponential distribution for interarrival times to the queue), but many such systems are too complex to characterize with a probability model and so must be simulated to understand their expected behavior.

9.2.3 Agent-based paradigm

In the agent-based paradigm, entities are *agents* with their own operating rules. Often, the set of agents is fixed and not created and terminated as in the process-interaction paradigm. The basic characteristics of the agent-based paradigm are (Macal, 2018):

- agents, their attributes and behaviors;
- agent relationships and methods of interaction with other agents: agent connections define how and with whom agents interact; and
- agent environment: agents interact with environment elements as well as with other agents.

Each *agent* is an identifiable entity. Each agent has a set of attributes and actions (including changing the agent's own attributes) that are coded and depend on interactions with the environment and/or other agents. Agents have unique identifiers and are self-contained. In an agent-based paradigm, attributes or states can be part of an individual agent or a characteristic shared among agents of a certain type or a characteristic of the environment.

Figure 9.6 shows a graphical representation of the TTF simulation using an agent-based modeling paradigm. Agents of type

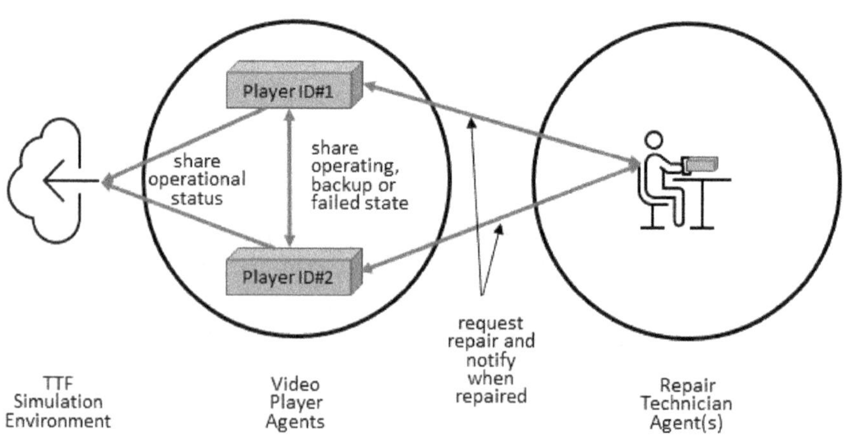

Figure 9.6. Agent-based view for the TTF simulation.

"video player" are in the circle on the left. They interact with each other sharing their state. At initialization, one video player agent is placed in the "operating" state, and it sets its failure time. When a video player agent fails, it signals the other player and also the technician to seek repair. If the other video player agent is in the "backup" state, it changes to the "operating" state and sets its failure time. If the other video player agent is in "failed" state, it makes no change. The technician agent, on receiving a signal from a failed video player, sends the player agent a time when repair will be completed, and the technician agent sets its state to "busy" until that time. The video player agents signal their status to the environment, represented by the cloud. If the environment detects that both players are in "failed" state, the simulation terminates.

Unlike the "top-down" approach used in the process-interaction paradigm, the approach for the agent-based paradigm is "bottom-up." The behavior of individual agents is modeled, and then the behavior of the overall system is discovered by running the simulation. Sometimes the system-wide behavior, called *emergent behavior*, is unexpected.

9.2.4 Modeling vs. execution paradigms

Each modeling paradigm has its advantage in thinking about the system and constructing a valid simulation model. But each of these paradigms can result in code that executes an event-scheduling method. This structure takes advantage of the next-event-time-advance (NETA) discrete-time step efficiency shown in Figure 9.1.

9.2.5 Continuous vs. discrete-event simulation

All of the modeling paradigms discussed so far have been DESs that take advantage of the *NETA* time advance efficiency. There is another class of dynamic simulation models that are used in business, engineering, and social science. These are called *continuous* or *continuous-time* simulations.

When continuous dynamic simulations ar performed on a computer, time must still be advanced in discrete steps, but the time steps are very small and they are regularly spaced. This is called *fixed-increment-time-advance* or *FITA*. At each step, formulas are used to update system state variables. The formulas may be deterministic or may include random variates. Think of modeling the level of water at a dam based on inflow rate, which itself may be a function of hour-by-hour rainfall in the dam's collection area, and outflow, which can also be controlled on an hour-by-hour basis. Such a continuous-time model would increment time evenly, hour by hour, using rainfall and outflow and delay values to update the state variable of water level behind the dam.

Often, such models are based on differential equations that describe the (continuous) change in a state variable as a function of other variables and their rate of change. In continuous simulation, the differential equations are replaced by approximate difference equations, computing the difference over small, regular time increments. *Finite-element* (may be dynamic or static) and *system dynamics* models are two such classes of continuous simulation models. But continuous simulation is outside the scope of this text.

9.3 Basic Flow of a Simulation Model

At the event-scheduling level, the structure of the computer program (often hidden from the user) has the form shown in Figure 9.7.

There is a main routine that performs initialization, setting state variables, entity and resource attributes, probability distribution

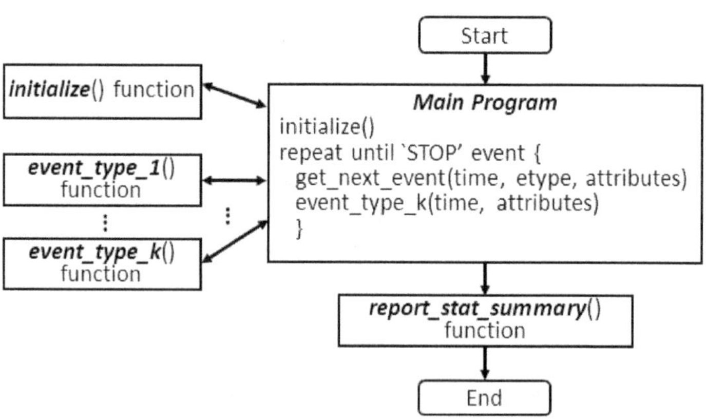

Figure 9.7. Generic event-scheduling code flowchart.

parameters, and random number seeds, and then performs a repeating loop of:

1. executing a get_next_event function to return the next clock time, next event type, and any attributes connected with that event;
2. executing an event processing function, depending on the event type and attributes returned by the timing function.

If there are no more events (i.e., the get_next_event function returns nothing) or if the event is of type "end simulation," execute a report/statistical summary function to capture the simulation results and then end the simulation program. The key functions that support the main routine are:

- the initialization function;
- the timing or get_next_event function;
- the several different event processing functions; and
- the report/statistical summary function.

This structure underlies almost every DES software package. It is included here so that you can write simple simulation code yourself, and it can be helpful in debugging simulation models written under any of the paradigms.

Next, we look at the elements of a simulation code from the process-interaction perspective. This is important for an understanding of the `simmer` package, a DES environment in R.

9.4 Components for a Process-Interaction Simulation Model

The process-interaction paradigm requires definition of three kinds of elements:

- the entities that will flow through the system, including their inter-arrival time probability distributions;
- the sequence of process activities that these entities will experience; and
- the resources needed to accomplish each process activity and resource characteristics, including how many of each resource are available and resource processing time probability distributions.

For the TTF simulation, the entities are failed players. Interarrival times of failed players to the player repair process have a discrete uniform distribution, as described in Section 9.1. The resource is the technician (only one), whose processing times are a deterministic 2.5 days. The main steps in the repair process are to seize the technician, wait for 2.5 days during the repair, and then release the technician.

9.5 Simulation in R Using `simmer`

We can implement the TTF simulation in **simmer**, a process-interaction simulation package in R. For details, see Ucar *et al.* (2019) and Ucar (2022). Coding in **simmer** requires several steps. First, the **simmer** library must be accessed, and simulation variables are set, that is, the maximum run time in days (all replications are expected to fail before this time) and the number of technicians available for repairs (here, only one). Then, the random number seed is set (to the same value as in Section 9.1). Next, the simulation object must be given a name (TTF) and initialized. The R commands for these steps are as follows:

```
> library(simmer)
> # set end time
> t_end = 500
> # set number of technicians
> n_technician = 1
> # set seed for repeatable results
> set.seed(25951)
> # initialize the TTF simulation object
> TTF = simmer()
>
```

The rest of the simulation program commands follow in a specific order:

1. a description of activities for each process, called a *trajectory* in `simmer`;
2. a model definition command that includes resources via `add_resource()` commands and entities via `add_generator()` commands; and
3. a model `run()` command that optionally specifies the run length.

The **simmer** structure takes advantage of the **tidyverse** (or **magrittr**) library's piping feature. The pipe operator, written as "% > %," takes the output of the function on the left side of the pipe and passes it as input to the function on the right of the pipe. This is a clean way to link a sequence of analysis steps. The overall code structure for the simulation is next. It is not shown as part of an interactive session, so the > prompts are not present:

```
# specify failed_player entity path via 'repair' trajectory
#   requires 'technician' resource
repair <- trajectory("failed_player") %>%
#if server already busy, stop generating arrivals, system failed
branch(
function() get_server_count(TTF,"technician")+1,
continue=c(TRUE,FALSE),
trajectory() %>%
timeout(0),
trajectory() %>%
deactivate("failed_player")) %>%
seize("technician") %>%
timeout(2.5) %>% # spend time in repair
release("technician")

# define 'TTF' simulation object entities:
#   technician and failed players, and generate player failures
TTF = simmer("TTF") %>%
add_resource("technician", n_technician) %>%
add_generator("failed_player", repair,
function() {floor(6 * runif(1)) + 1},
mon=2)
# set simulation to run for 500 time units
#   (but ends earlier if system failure)
TTF %>% run(until = t_end)
```

There is only one trajectory: `repair`. In the `add_generator()` function, entities of type `"failed_player"` are created and the command specifies that they follow the `repair` process trajectory. The interarrival time is random and specified exactly as it was in Section 9.1.

There is one technician, specified in the `add_resourcce()` command. The processing time does not appear in that statement, but rather in the trajectory description. This makes sense because the processing time might be different for different entity types (although in TTF, there is only one entity type: a failed video player).

The `repair` trajectory would be simple if we did not have to stop when the second unit failed. For the simpler case, the trajectory would look as follows:

```
repair <- trajectory("failed_player") %>%
seize("technician") %>%
timeout(2.5) %>% # spend time in repair
release("technician")
```

The following commands were added to the trajectory description to stop the simulation if a new failed player encounters a busy technician. In that case, both players would be failed and the simulation should end. To check this and act accordingly, split the trajectory into two sub-trajectories with a branch command that does the following:

- If the technician is idle (`get_server_count(TTF,"technician")` = 0), then the branch is set to 1, which has zero wait and the failed player proceeds to seize the technician.
- If the technician is busy (`get_server_count(TTF,"technician")` = 1), then the branch is set to 2, which has the action of stopping any further player failures using a `deactivate` command. The failed player does not proceed any further on the pipeline, as indicated by the FALSE for path 2 in the `continue=` parameter.

The code for the extra branches is as follows. There is no `if` statement. Instead, the computed subtrajectory number (1 or 2) is computed directly by adding 1 to `get_server_count(TTF,"technician")`:

```
#if server already busy, stop generating arrivals,
 system failed
branch(
function() get_server_count(TTF,"technician")+1,
continue=c(TRUE,FALSE),
trajectory() %>%
timeout(0),
trajectory() %>%
deactivate("failed_player")) %>%
```

There are two more code elements to explain: the 100-replication loop and the extraction of the mean, standard deviation, and histogram from the results. The code for the loop is listed as follows:

```
TTFruns <- lapply(1:nreps, function(i) {
... (code listed above through 'TTF %>% run(until = t_end)')
                })
```

The function `lapply()` is short for "list apply." This "applies" the code inside the `function(i)` definition to each of the `i = 1`, ...,`nreps` list elements. The output becomes a *list* of simulation run outputs, which can be handled by the `simmer` data recovery/summary functions.

Three data recovery functions can be used with the `TTF` or `TTFruns` objects. Their description in Ucar *et al.* (2019) are as follows:

- `get_mon_arrivals()` produces a data frame of timing information per arrival: name of the arrival, start time, end time, activity time (time not spent in resource queues)m and a flag, "finished," that indicates whether the arrival exhausted its activities (or was rejected).
- `get_mon_resources()` produces a data frame of state changes in resources: resource name, time instant of the event that triggered the state change, server count, queue count, capacity, queue size, system count (server + queue), and system limit (capacity + queue size).
- `get_mon_attributes()` produces a data frame of state changes in attributes: name of the attribute, time instant of the event that triggered the state change, and name of key that identifies the attribute and value.

To construct a vector of TTSF values for simple data analysis only requires the `get_mon_arrivals()` data recovery function. The latest (max) start time in each replication is the time when the second video player failed. The following code extracts those values into a vector `TTSF` using the R `aggregate()` function and its default output variable "`$x`." The code then computes the mean TTSF, the standard deviation, and plots the histogram. The statistics are shown. They are identical to those produced by the code in Section 9.1. The histogram is also identical to that produced by the code in Section 9.1 and shown in Figure 9.3 (note: the same random number seed and random variate generator was used by both programs).

```
> # use simmer get_mon_arrivals function to report all
    arrival and
> #   end times
> # structure of get_mon_arrivals output:
> #            name  start_time end_time activity_time finished
```

```
> #1   failed_player0          5       7.5              2.5       TRUE
> #        replication
> #                  1
> runData = TTFruns %>% get_mon_arrivals()
>
> # calculate maximum time for each replication using aggregate()
> TTSF = aggregate(runData$start_time , list(runData$replication),
     +                        FUN=max)$x
> mean(TTSF)
[1] 15.31
> sd(TTSF)
[1] 12.76493
> hist(TTSF, breaks=seq(1,105,5), main="")
>
```

9.6 The Overall Process for Simulation Model Building

As for other predictive analytics methods, the process of building DES models can be formalized, as follows:

1. Determine the purpose(s) of the simulation model. What behavior is it intended to simulate? What levels of detail and fidelity are required to be useful in managerial decision support?
2. Define a model using the event-scheduling, process-interaction, or agent-based paradigm. Construct a graphical representation of the model.
3. Verify model structure and logic with subject matter experts (SMEs).
4. Collect real system data to check model structure and fit probability distributions for interarrival times, service times, routing probabilities, and other model features.
5. Write the simulation model code. Be careful to use the same time units throughout: the simulator does not know about time, only the numbers and distributions that you supply.
6. Make debugging and validation runs of the simulation model. Validate random variate generator behavior against real system data. Choose an experiment design to vary model parameters and observe results to check expected behavior.

The result is a complete, validated simulation model. In the following chapter, we see how predictive analytics techniques from previous chapters can be applied to the design of simulation experiments and analysis of the resulting output.

9.7 Case Supporting Chapters 9 and 10

The multi-segment case BankTellerSimulation supports the material in Chapters 9 and 10. The first segment focuses on model structure and the kinds of DES model output. The second segment focuses on regression metamodeling of simulation output. This case extends over multiple weeks. The case description slides and data can be found online in the BankDiscreteEventSimulation folder of Barton (2023).

9.8 R Code Used in Chapter 9

```
# TTF example simulation ========================================
#   based on Nelson(2013) Foundations and Methods
#   of Stochastic Simulation: A First Course, Springer
#   R version by Russell Barton
#   do 100 replications, show mean sd and histogram
#


TTF = function() {
# Variables and functions
# Clock (real)  - simulation clock
# NextFailure (real) - time of next failure event
# NextRepair (real) - time of next repair event
# EventList (real) - vector of next fail and next repair times)
# S (integer) - number of operational video players
  (system state)
# NextEvent (string) - type of next event, 'Failure' or 'Repair'
#             ("End of Simulation" is not explicitly coded here)

# NOTE: since all variables are GLOBAL,
#       all assignments by <<- rather than <- or =

# initialization of clock, state, next fail, next repair
S <<- 2
Clock <<- 0
NextFailure <<- Clock + floor(6 * runif(1)) + 1
NextRepair <<- 1000000
NextEvent <<- NULL
```

```
while (S != 0){
    Timer()
    if(NextEvent == 'Failure'){
        FailureCode()
      } else if(NextEvent == 'Repair'){
        RepairCode()
      } else stop('error - invalid event type')
    }
    return(Clock)
}

Timer = function(){
# Determine the next event and advance time
if(NextFailure < NextRepair) {
    NextEvent <<- 'Failure'
    Clock <<- NextFailure
    NextFailure <<- 1000000
    } else {
    NextEvent <<- 'Repair'
    Clock <<- NextRepair
    NextRepair <<- 1000000
    }
}

FailureCode = function(){
S <<- S-1
if(S == 1) {
    NextFailure <<- Clock + floor(6 * runif(1)) + 1
    NextRepair <<- Clock + 2.5
    }
}

RepairCode = function(){
S <<- S+1
}

# main program completes nreps replications
#   computes statistics and draws histogram
# seed set for repeatable results
set.seed(25951)
TTSF = NULL
nreps = 100
for(reps in 1:nreps){
    simResult = TTF()
    TTSF = c(TTSF, simResult)
}
mean(TTSF)
sd(TTSF)
hist(TTSF, breaks=seq(1,105,5), main="")
```

```
# TTF example using simmer =====================================
#
library(simmer)

# set end time
t_end = 500
# set number of technicians
n_technician = 1
# set number of replications
nreps = 100

# replication loop: lapply does the 'simmer' simulation function
#                   nreps times (see '})' for end of lapply loop)
# "TTFruns" is the output 'object' across all replications
# set seed for repeatable results
set.seed(25951)
TTFruns <- lapply(1:nreps, function(i) {
# initialize the TTF simulation object
TTF = simmer()
# specify failed_player entity path via 'repair' trajectory
#   requires 'technician' resource
repair <- trajectory("failed_player") %>%
#if server already busy, stop generating arrivals, system failed
branch(
function() get_server_count(TTF,"technician")+1,
continue=c(TRUE,FALSE),
trajectory() %>%
timeout(0),
trajectory() %>%
deactivate("failed_player")) %>%
seize("technician") %>%
timeout(2.5) %>% # spend time in repair
release("technician")

# define 'TTF' simulation object entities:
#   technician and failed players, and generate player failures
TTF = simmer("TTF") %>%
add_resource("technician", n_technician) %>%
add_generator("failed_player", repair,
function() {floor(6 * runif(1)) + 1},
mon=2)
# set simulation to run for 500 time units
#   (but ends earlier if system failure)
TTF %>% run(until = t_end)

# end replication loop
})
```

```
# use simmer get_mon_arrivals function to report all arrival and
#   end times
# structure of get_mon_arrivals output:
#            name  start_time end_time activity_time finished
#1  failed_player0           5      7.5           2.5     TRUE
#      replication
#                1

runData = TTFruns %>% get_mon_arrivals()

# calculate maximum time for each replication using aggregate()
TTSF = aggregate(runData$start_time , list(runData$replication),
FUN=max)$x
mean(TTSF)
sd(TTSF)
hist(TTSF, breaks=seq(1,105,5), main="")
```

Chapter 10

Prediction with Discrete-Event Simulation Models

In the *model-dependent research* paradigm, a mathematical or computer simulation model generates data, often dynamic. This computer-generated data can be analyzed using descriptive analytics methods, as well as the predictive analytics methods that are the subject of this text (especially regression). But special considerations apply to both descriptive and predictive analytics for data generated by discrete-event simulation. The `simmer` bank example is used to illustrate the nature of the model-generated data and to perform predictive analytics (Garmonsway, 2022a,b).

10.1 The `simmer` Bank Simulation

A detailed example of a simulation model built in simmer is described in the tutorial Web pages (Garmonsway, 2022a, 2022b). The version used here is a simple case, with only one entity type: *customer*, and all customers have identical characteristics. There is only one trajectory for all customers, unlike a real bank, where some customers would go to the safety deposit box, some to a cubicle to apply for a loan with a loan officer, etc. Only one resource type is employed: *teller*. The number of tellers can be chosen, but all tellers are identical in their characteristics. The simulation runs for one day, with the bank doors open for 8 hours. There may be customers waiting and in service at closing time. In order to process these, no simulation end time is specified, but the generation of arrivals ends at time 480 minutes (= 8 hours). Effectively, the bank doors close, but tellers continue to service those already inside. The simulation ends when there are no events in the future events list.

We retain the interarrival time and service time characteristics used in the tutorial. The following model description shows that interarrival and service times have exponential distributions with rates of 1 and 1/4.5, respectively, suggesting that utilization will be higher than 1 unless there are five tellers or more. For example, with four tellers, the combined service rate would be 4/4.5, less than the arrival rate of 1. The code is shown as follows. It is not shown as part of an interactive session, so the > prompts are not present. Note that the entities are named "`Customer`" and server resources are named "`Teller`."

```
#
library(simmer)
# set seed for repeatable results
set.seed(80115119)
# set arrival and service rates (lambda and mu)
arate = 1
srate = 1/4.5
# set number of tellers
n_teller = 5

# define bank as simmer object
bank <- simmer("bank")
# specify entity path via 'trajectory', needs 'Teller' resource
customerPath <-
trajectory("Customer's path") %>%
set_attribute("start_time", function() {now(bank)}) %>%
seize("Teller") %>%
timeout(function() {rexp(1, srate)}) %>% # service by teller
release("Teller")

# to make simulation run, add teller resource, generate customer
#   arrivals, customers arrive over 8 hours (480 minutes)
bank %>%
add_resource("Teller", n_teller) %>%
# from_to says when to generate customers
# if arrive = TRUE (default) the first arrival will be generated
#    at start_timeand will follow dist from then on. If set to
#    FALSE, will initiate dist at start_time (so first arrival
#    will start at a time later than start_time).
add_generator("Customer", customerPath, from_to(0,480,function()
{rexp(1,arate)},arrive=FALSE)) %>%
run()
```

Simulation run control is covered in Section 10.3, but here we show the **simmer** code that allows multiple replications, that is, multiple runs of the simulation. It is not shown as part of an interactive session, so the > prompts are not present.

```
nreps = 6 # repeated runs for the same number of tellers
# replication loop: lapply says do the 'simmer' simulation function
#                   nreps times (see '})' for end of lapply loop)
# "bankRuns" is simulation output 'object' across all replications
bankRuns <- lapply(1:nreps, function(i) {
# define bank as simmer object
bank <- simmer("bank")

# simmer bank simulation code here ...
  run()
# end replication loop====================================
})  # closing for lapply
```

The `lapply()` R function takes two arguments: first, a vector or list that will have its elements fed one-at-a-time to a function; the function itself is the second argument of `lapply()`.

For the bank simulation case, the first argument is the vector of replication indices, `1, 2,..., nreps`. In the second argument, the function is named and defined within the `lapply()` argument scope. All of the simulation code is placed as part of the function definition, which is the second argument. That is why there is a closing brace for the function in the last line of the code above, followed by a right parenthesis ending the `lapply()` function. Because the random number seed is not reset inside this `lapply()` span, each of the **simmer** bank simulation replications uses different random variates and thus produces statistically independent runs. Note again that "replications" is a bit of a misnomer. If one has made two simulation runs, it is not "one run and one replication," it is "two replications."

Although the `lapply()` argument `(i)` is not actually used in the simulation run loop (it just makes sure that the loop is executed `nreps` times), the **simmer** simulation engine recognizes the `lapply()` environment and automatically adds a **replication** column to the `get_mon_` data frames. For example, see the following code showing the first lines of `get_mon_arrivals(bankRuns)`. Compared with the `get_mon_arrivals()` output shown at the end of Section 9.5, there is an additional column labeled **replication**.

```
+ # end replication loop====================================
+ })
> head(get_mon_arrivals(bankRuns))
       name start_time end_time activity_time finished replication
1 Customer0  0.1509616 1.835135      1.684174     TRUE           1
2 Customer1  0.8365957 2.943664      2.107068     TRUE           1
3 Customer2  1.3298555 3.241467      1.911612     TRUE           1
4 Customer3  3.8138326 4.383965      0.570132     TRUE           1
5 Customer4  3.8785412 5.919507      2.040966     TRUE           1
6 Customer6  6.9876002 7.008398      0.020798     TRUE           1
>
```

The order in the `get_mon_arrivals(bankRuns)` data frame is the order in which entities depart because `get_mon_arrivals()` data are recorded on departure (funny, given the name!). But that may not be the same order in which they arrived since a later customer might join the teller queue that, by chance, has customers in the line who are served quickly, and the customer who arrived a little earlier might have joined a different queue for a different teller — one with customers needing lengthy service. That is why `Customer6` appears before `Customer5` has completed. I know we have all joined a line and seen others who came after join a different line and pass us by! This is a natural feature of queues with random service times.

10.2 Kinds of Simulation Output

The data generated by a discrete-event simulation model is usually called *simulation output*, and analytics applied to such data is called *simulation output analysis*. This data characterizes the dynamic behavior of the system over time, but the analytics usually examines time averages of these data.

The dynamic data are of two distinct types:

- *discrete-time data*: numerical characterizations related to episodic events, such as the time-in-system for a departing customer at the instant (episode) of departure from the system; and
- *continuous-time data*: values that change continuously in time, such as the busy (=1) vs. idle (=0) status of a resource.

Discrete-time data is easy to average and analyze. For example, as each entity exits the simulation, one can capture its entry time to the system, its time in service at each resource, and its departure time from the system. One can compute time-in-system and waiting time

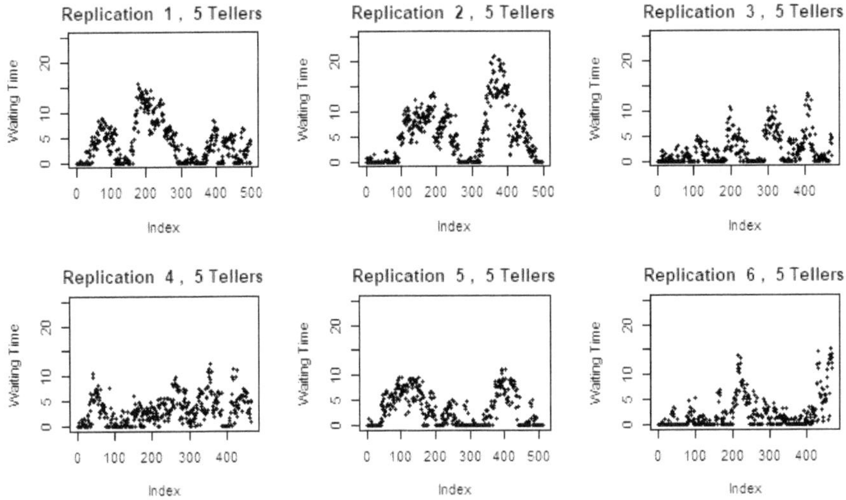

Figure 10.1. Waiting time in order of customer departure by replication.

from these statistics collected by **simmer**'s **get_mon_arrivals()**: waiting time = time in system (**end_time - start_time**) - service time (**activity_time**). These are reported for each entity that has left the system, so the plots for each entity and statistical characterizations are straightforward, as shown in Figure 10.1. Note that the plotted waiting times are ordered by customers as they depart the bank. The code is shown as follows. It is not shown as part of an interactive session, so the > prompts are not present.

```
# compute waiting time as total time minus time in service
waitData = bankRuns %>%
get_mon_arrivals() %>%
transform(waiting_time = end_time - start_time - activity_time)

# Plot waiting time of customers as the day progresses
#   for each replication
par(mfrow = c(2,3))
for(i in levels(as.factor(waitData$replication))){
    plot(waitData$waiting_time[waitData$replication == i],
    ylab = "Waiting Time",ylim=c(0,25),pch=20,
    main = paste("Replication ",i,", ", n_teller, "Tellers"))
}
```

It is important to average these measurements over all entities in a run. This is because the times are highly correlated. The following code extracts data from the first replication and creates the

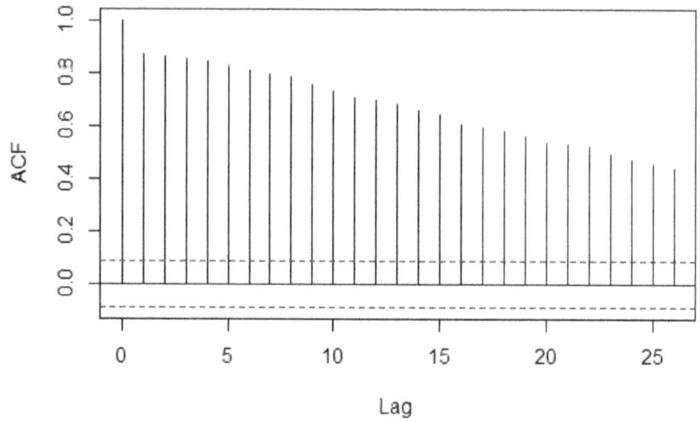

Figure 10.2. Waiting times in replication 1 have high autocorrelation.

autocorrelation plot in Figure 10.2. The high autocorrelation is also apparent in the "wandering" patterns in Figure 10.1. While results from one replication to the next are independent, *discrete-time data within a single replication are highly correlated.* Analyzing data in this form is possible but is beyond the scope of this text. Instead, our basic "observations" will be values averaged over a single simulation replication.

```
> # show serious autocorrelation problem
> acf(waitData$waiting_time[waitData$replication == 1],
      main ="")
```

Continuous-time data are associated with resources and can be computed from the `get_mon_resources()` data frame. Figure 10.3 shows the number of busy tellers as the day progresses for each of six replications. The code is shown as follows. It is not shown as part of an interactive session, so the > prompts are not present.

```
# get teller utilization information from get_mon_resources
servData = bankRuns %>%
get_mon_resources()
#
# Plot number of busy servers as the day progresses
#   for each replication
par(mfrow = c(2,3))
for(i in levels(as.factor(servData$replication))){
    stepData = stepfun(servData$time[servData$replication == i],
    c(0,servData$server[servData$replication == i]))
    plot.stepfun(stepData,servData$time[servData$replication == i],
    ylab = "No. Busy Tellers",ylim=c(0,6),pch=20,
    main = paste("Replication ",i,", ", n_teller, "Tellers"))
}
```

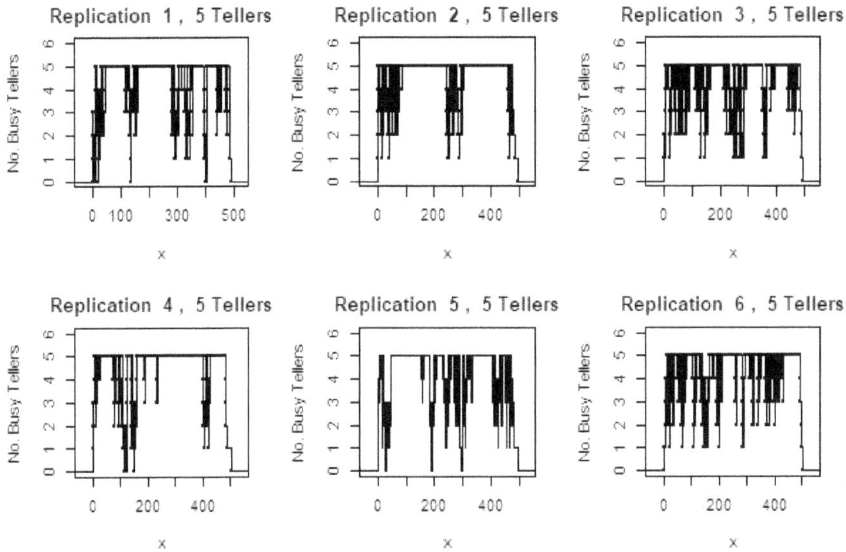

Figure 10.3. Number of busy tellers over the day by replication.

Computing the average number of busy tellers over one day is more complex than computing the average waiting time. The average number of busy tellers is a *time-average* as are all continuous-time statistics. It is the area under the plotted line divided by the duration of the plot. This calculation is done separately for each horizontal segment, then added up, and then divided by the total time duration. The time duration is computed by differencing the time values using the `diff` command in R.

R code for computing both discrete- and continuous-time statistics are illustrated in Sections 10.4–10.7.

10.3 Simulation Run Control

Before analyzing data from multiple simulation replications, it is necessary to address two issues in specifying the amount of simulation effort needed. There are two different cases, depending on whether the simulated system has a natural start and end or whether the system operates continuously. For example, the bank simulation has a natural start and end, beginning at 9:00 am and doors closing at

5:00 pm, and the last customer is served shortly after that. This kind of system is modeled with a *terminating simulation*. Run control requires determining the number of replications (runs) needed for satisfactory confidence and prediction intervals for system performance measures (e.g., mean waiting time).

On the other hand, a manufacturing plant operating three eight-hour shifts per day seven days per week never shuts down. So, there is no natural "unit" for a simulated period. This kind of system is modeled with a *steady-state simulation* and requires decisions about run length, removal of a startup period, and the number of replications required for satisfactory system performance confidence and prediction intervals.

In this section, we address the issues of removal of startup period and run length first and then the issue of determining the number of replications required, applicable to both terminating and steady-state scenarios. Determining replications is equivalent to the sample size question in statistics.

For observational studies, the sample size is often determined by the extent of existing data. Even when data collection is part of a predictive analytics study, practical or financial limitations typically constrain the sample size. But for simulation model data, the analyst is in control of the number of replications. So, the number of replications (sample size) can be chosen to be large enough to provide satisfactory predictions.

Issues in simulation run control are complex, with sophisticated theory used to suggest methodological approaches. The approach in this section is practical rather than theoretical. For a more advanced and comprehensive treatment of these issues, see Law (2014) or Nelson (2013).

10.3.1 Initialization bias for steady-state simulations

We modify the bank simulation to be a 24-hour always-open scenario. It is not realistic, but it allows us to understand the initialization bias issue without introducing a different simulation model. We use data from this artificial setting to determine an initial "warm-up" period as the bank fills. Data from this period will be deleted before the discrete- and continuous-time statistics are computed.

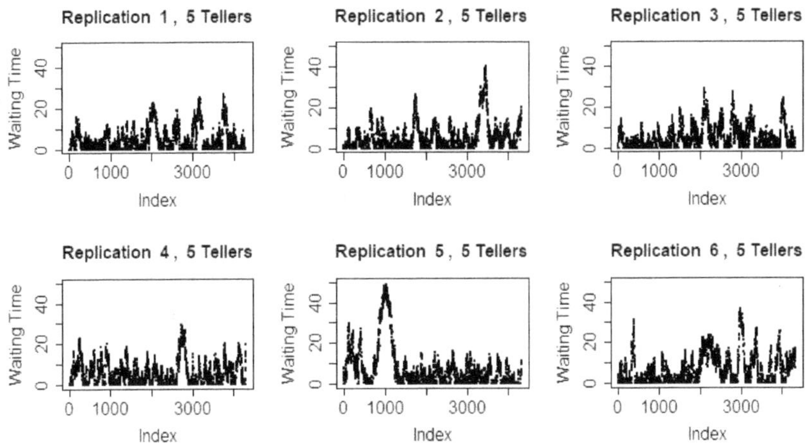

Figure 10.4. Customer waiting times over three days of continuous operation.

Figure 10.4 shows individual waiting times over three days of continuous bank operation (72 hours, approximately $72 \times 60 = 4{,}320$ customers). The issue of initialization bias is not clear in each individual run.

To see the warm-up pattern more clearly, Peter Welch suggested point-by-point averaging of the trajectories across multiple replications and then taking a moving average across time to smooth the stochastic patterns (Law, 2014). This makes it easier to see initial bias appearing across all trajectories. The following session commands show how to do a point-by-point averaging across replications and plot the result. The result is shown in Figure 10.5, and it is clear that averaging is not sufficient to visually identify the end of the warm-up transient.

```
> repMeanWait = rowMeans(cbind(waitData$waiting_time
+ [waitData$replication==1],
+ waitData$waiting_time
+ [waitData$replication==2],
+ waitData$waiting_time
+ [waitData$replication==3],
+ waitData$waiting_time
+ [waitData$replication==4],
+ waitData$waiting_time
+ [waitData$replication==5],
+ waitData$waiting_time
+ [waitData$replication==6]))
>
```

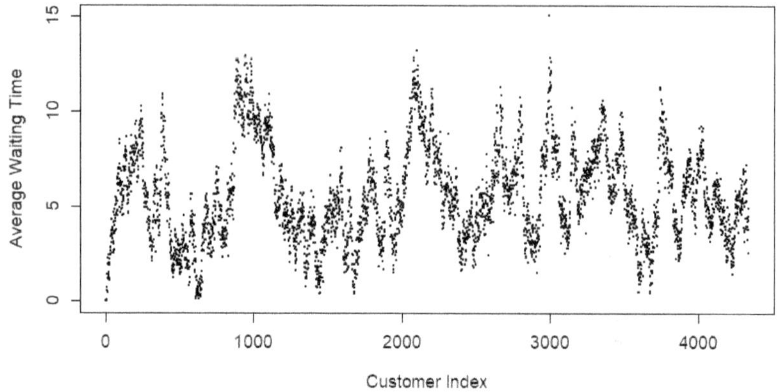

Figure 10.5. Waiting times averaged customer-by-customer over six replications.

```
> plot(repMeanWait, ylab = "Average Waiting Time",
       ylim=c(0,15),pch=20,
> xlab="Time (minutes)",cex=0.5,cex.lab=1.5,cex.axis=1.5,
+ cex.main=1.5)
>
```

Smoothing makes the pattern clearer. Rather than the moving average suggested by Welch, we use the base R smoothing spline function `smooth.spline()`. Smoothing splines are a series of linked piecewise cubic functions that approximate the response. One can let the function choose the number of pieces, called "knots," one can adjust the number of knots to get the desired visual trade-off between responsiveness and smoothness. For the data in the plot above, choosing 20 knots produced good results. The code to create the plot shown in Figure 10.6 is as follows.

```
> plot(smooth.spline(x=repMeanWait,nknots=20),
+ ylab="Smoothed Average Waiting Time",ylim=c(0,15),
  pch=20,cex=0.5,
+ xlab="Customer Index",cex.lab=1.1,cex.axis=1.1,
  cex.main=1.1)
>
```

It appears that deleting the first 200 customers puts the starting point of the remaining waiting time trajectory in the range of values seen later in the plot. The following code creates the more detailed plot in Figure 10.7. It shows the replication-averaged data for the first 400 customers with slightly less smoothing. This supports using

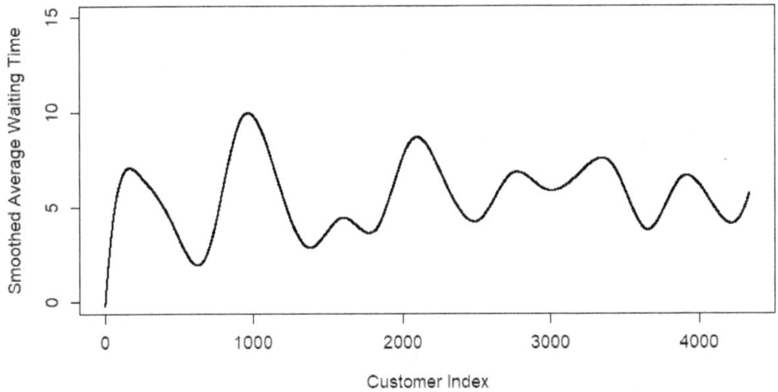

Figure 10.6. Averaged waiting times with cubic spline smooth.

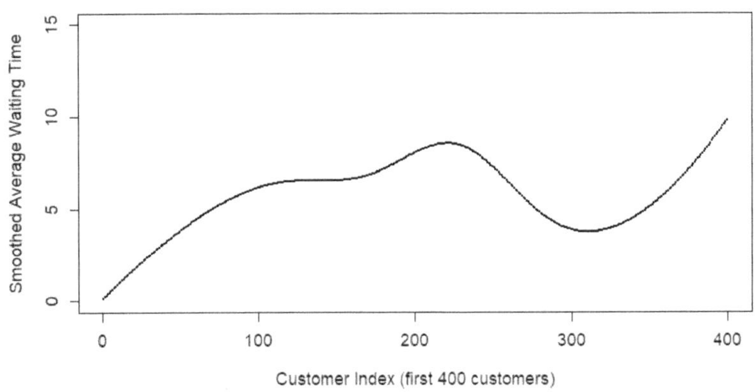

Figure 10.7. Averaged waiting times with cubic spline smooth: First 400 customers.

200 customers as the limit of the initial transient. For reasonably long simulation runs, it is not necessary to be very precise in this selection.

```
> plot(smooth.spline(x=repMeanWait[1:400],nknots=8),
+ ylab = "Smoothed Average Waiting Time",ylim=c(0,15),
  pch=20,cex=0.5,
+ xlab="Customer Index (first 400 customers)",cex.lab=1.1,
  cex.axis=1.1,
+ cex.main=1.1)
>
```

10.3.2 Run length for steady-state simulations

The deletion of a warm-up period shortens the useful portion of steady-state simulation runs. It is important to make the runs as long as possible, so that the efficiency remains high. One can define efficiency as $(r - w)/r$, where r is the length of the run (total customers or total time) and w is the length of the warm-up period. For the example above, the efficiency was (in terms of customers) $(4320 - 200)/4320 = 95.4\%$. This is a reasonably high efficiency. After the pilot study to determine the initialization deletion period, one should adjust run lengths to give efficiency of at least 90%.

One can make one single long run and break the data into contiguous subsets for analysis, gaining greater efficiency. This method is called *batch means* and is beyond the scope of this text. Because there is a risk of introducing autocorrelation in the batch "replications," expertise is required to implement this approach correctly.

10.3.3 Determining the number of simulation replications

Because the data are model-generated, the analyst has control over the sample size, here called replications. The number of simulation replications required depends on the purpose of the simulation exercise. Usually, there is some predictive analytics purpose in mind for which sample size formulas are available. These formulas require preliminary information that differs depending on the kind of analysis that will be performed. In the following, we show four common settings and the corresponding approach that gives the sample size needed. Sections 10.4–10.7 implement these methods and associated analytics for the `simmer` bank simulation.

Characterizing a single system

For a single system, predictive analytics typically entails constructing confidence and prediction intervals for some measure of system performance. Sample size determination requires some version of the following elements:

- the maximum halfwidth h of the confidence interval that you want as the size of the uncertainty about the parameter being estimated;
- the significance or *false coverage probability*: often $\alpha = 0.05$; and

- an estimate of the standard deviation of the data, typically the sample standard deviation s from some preliminary or pilot simulation runs.

In this setting, a simple estimate of sample size required for a confidence interval on the mean is based on the normal-approximation confidence interval:

$$\mathrm{CI}_{1-\alpha} = \bar{x} \pm Z_{(1-\frac{\alpha}{2})} \frac{\sigma}{\sqrt{n}}. \tag{10.1}$$

The $\pm$ quantity in Equation (10.1) is the halfwidth, h. Taking that term and specifying h allows one to solve for n:

$$n = \left(\frac{Z_{(1-\frac{\alpha}{2})} \sigma}{h} \right)^2. \tag{10.2}$$

For an approximate sample size rule for a 95% confidence interval of width $\pm h$, approximating $Z_{(1-\frac{\alpha}{2})}$ by 2 and replacing σ by the sample standard deviation s gives

$$N = \left(\frac{2s}{h} \right)^2. \tag{10.3}$$

Note the change from n (a deterministic value) to N (a random value that depends on the sample standard deviation, which is itself random). This change means that the coverage probability $1 - \alpha$ will not hold exactly, but the coverage error will decrease for smaller and smaller h values. In this and all of the following examples, the sample size estimates are approximate. They help avoid a final analysis that fails to meet statistical requirements while, at the same time, keeping the simulation computational effort as low as possible.

This sample size determination for confidence interval analysis is shown for the bank example in Section 10.4.

A similar approximate sample size formula exists for the case of estimating a proportion. Suppose that repeated simulations produce either a "success" or "failure" result. Suppose one wants to estimate the failure probability to $\pm h$ (some fractional value, as a decimal, not a percentage). Then, the analogy to Equation (10.3) is

$$N = \left(\frac{2\sqrt{p(1-p)}}{h} \right)^2, \tag{10.4}$$

where p is the observed proportion for the preliminary or pilot simulation runs.

Comparing two systems

Suppose one wanted to compare the mean waiting times for seven-teller and eight-teller systems. Is there a significant difference? One expects that there is a difference, but how many replications would be required to declare the difference as statistically significant at the $\alpha = 0.05$ level? For one- and two-sample hypothesis tests, sample size determination requires some version of the following four elements:

- the difference, d, that you wish to be able to detect;
- the significance or *false alarm probability*: often $\alpha = 0.05$;
- the power: the probability that a data set from populations with difference d will yield a rejection of the hypothesis of no difference with a p-value of $\leq \alpha$, and complementary to power is the *failure to detect probability*, β, i.e., power $= 1 - \beta$; and
- an estimate of the standard deviation of the data, typically the sample standard deviation s from some preliminary or pilot simulation runs.

For comparing two systems with equal replications, the replication-by-replication paired differences in sample means can be computed, reducing the problem to a one-sample test of the hypothesis:

$$H_0 : \mu_{\text{diff}} = 0 \text{ vs. } H_1 : \mu_{\text{diff}} \neq 0,$$

where μ_{diff} is the difference in means between mean waiting time for a seven-teller bank and mean waiting time for a eight-teller bank: $\mu_7 - \mu_8$.

Usually one- and two-sample tests are based on a *t-statistic*, and R provides a function that automatically computes sample size given the above information. When comparing two systems, the sample variances are often different, which is not accommodated by built-in sample size functions in R. However, we can determine the approximate sample size based on the characteristics of the paired differences: the standard deviation is the square root of the sum of the variances for each system. This paired test is not the same as the two-sample test: degrees of freedom are lost for the distribution of the t-statistic. But the result produces a conservative estimate (perhaps a bit larger than necessary) for the two-sample t-test.

The sample size determination and two-sample t-test calculation are shown for the bank example in Section 10.4.

Comparing more than two systems

Comparing more than two qualitatively different system simulations involves different multiple simulation models that differ by varying a system parameter (e.g., number of tellers) at multiple levels. In the latter case, regression applies. Think instead about systems with different customer priorities, different floor layouts, or different kinds of tellers. In this case, the appropriate method for statistical analysis is an *analysis of variance* (ANOVA) model, which is beyond the scope of this text. An alternative is the construction of confidence intervals for all pairwise differences. These are explored in Section 10.6.

Determining sample size in this context is beyond the scope of this text. A lower bound on the required sample size can be based on the one-sample t-test approximation for a two-sample comparison that was discussed in the previous section.

Regression across systems

Sometimes, the planned predictive model will be a regression model. How does one determine the sample size needed to find the regression coefficient(s) that are statistically significantly different from zero?

One way to estimate the sample size used by the R function `pwr.r.test` requires the following:

- an estimate of the correlation coefficient: this can be estimated as the square root of R^2 from a preliminary set of runs;
- the significance or *false alarm probability*: often, $\alpha = 0.05$;
- the power: the probability that a data set from populations with the specified correlation coefficient will yield a rejection of the hypothesis of nonzero regression coefficient with a p-value of $\leq \alpha$,

and complementary to power is the *failure to detect probability*, β, i.e., power $= 1 - \beta$.

The sample size determination and regression calculation are shown for the bank example in Section 10.7.

10.3.4 Using "common random numbers" in simulations

When comparing the behavior of different system designs, the variance of system differences can be reduced by *common random numbers*. What does that mean? If comparing average waiting time for a seven-teller bank with average waiting time for a eight-teller bank, normally the pattern of arrivals will be different for every replication of each system. So, by "good luck," the seven-teller bank might receive slightly longer times between customer arrivals over its replications than the times generated randomly for the eight-teller system. Fewer customers would result in shorter waiting times for a five-teller system "by good luck" rather than by system characteristics (we would expect waiting times to be longer for the seven-teller bank). Making the comparison fairer is the motivation behind common random numbers.

In a common random numbers scenario, the same sequence of random customer interarrival times for the first replication of the seven-teller system would be used again for the first replication of the eight-teller system. So, both systems would see the same random pattern of arrivals for the first replication. This could be repeated for each replication. Not only does the method generate a fairer comparison, but in many cases, it reduces the variance of the estimated difference in system performance, resulting in smaller confidence intervals and smaller p-values for hypothesis tests on differences.

Unfortunately, effectively using common random numbers can be complex. It requires more than just setting the single random number seed to the same value for each system before beginning that system's replications. Moreover, a poorly implemented common random numbers strategy can backfire and make things worse rather than better. Implementing a common random number strategy effectively is beyond the scope of this text. For an overview and references to strategy details, see Law (2014).

10.4 Predictive Analytics for a Single System

Predictive analytics for a single system focuses on confidence and prediction intervals for system performance measures. In this section, we focus on the case of i.i.d samples. A version of the central limit theorem suggests that run-average performance measures often vary approximately as normally distributed quantities across replications, though run lengths are not always sufficient for this approximation to be valid. Nonetheless, the overall mean of the replication means is likely to be approximately normal since the replications are independent. The process requires several steps:

1. Identify the performance measure or measures of interest.
2. Conduct a small number (5–10) of preliminary replications. These will be used to determine the warm-up period for steady-state simulations, and give a preliminary estimate for the standard deviation of the statistic for both terminating and steady-state systems.
3. Determine the confidence interval halfwidth desired at a specified significance level.
4. Use the appropriate sample size method to choose a final sample size. Make additional replications to reach the required sample size (or for greater protection, make additional replications equal to the required sample size).

To illustrate the process we use a modified version of the `simmer` bank model. In this version, an additional `for()` loop cycles through different numbers of tellers. For this and the following section, the loop includes the seven- and eight-teller cases, with a pilot run consisting of six replications each. The following code shows the parts that were added to produce the required simulation output. It is not shown as part of an interactive session, so the > prompts are not present.

```
# set placeholder for MeanWait result vector
MeanWait = NULL

for(n_teller in lotel:hitel){
    ...
    simmer bank simulation code here
    ...
    # compute mean wait for each replication
    repMeanWait = NULL
```

```
    for(i in levels(as.factor(waitData$replication))){
        repMeanWait[i] = mean(waitData$waiting_time
        [waitData$replication == i])
    }

    # assemble mean wait data for this number of tellers
    MeanWait = c(MeanWait,repMeanWait)

# end n_teller loop======================================
}
# convert to data frame
#   (create column with n_teller values for runs)
tellerNum = sort(rep(lotel:hitel,nreps))
tellerMeanWait = data.frame(tellerNum,MeanWait)
```

The resulting simulation output showing the mean wait for each number of tellers and each of the six replications is as follows.

```
> tellerMeanWait[,]
   tellerNum   MeanWait
1          7 1.47503953
2          7 0.19769941
3          7 0.24942115
4          7 0.22377235
5          7 1.06745669
6          7 0.14942073
7          8 0.05471674
8          8 0.11017305
9          8 0.10287677
10         8 0.01958222
11         8 0.07306976
12         8 0.21107580
```

The following code and output shows the calculation of the sample mean and standard deviation of average waiting time across replications for `n_teller=7` and `n_teller=8`.

```
> pilotMean = aggregate(.~tellerNum, data=tellerMeanWait, mean)
> pilotSD = aggregate(.~tellerNum, data=tellerMeanWait, sd)
> pilotMean
  tellerNum   MeanWait
1         7 0.56046831
2         8 0.09524906
> pilotSD
  tellerNum   MeanWait
1         7 0.56641921
2         8 0.06566125
>
```

For this section, we focus on the `n_teller=7` system. The objective is to construct a confidence interval for mean customer waiting time with a halfwidth of approximately $h \approx 0.1$ (.1 minutes or 6 seconds). The resulting sample mean and sample standard deviation for `n_teller=7` could be used to compute a preliminary 95% confidence interval for mean waiting time, but the R function `t.test()` operates on the original set of six replication means for `n_teller=7`. If the confidence interval meets the required halfwidth, additional simulation runs will not be required. The code and resulting output are shown as follows. Note that the default confidence level for `t.test` is 95%.

```
> # 95% confidence interval for mean wait for 7 teller system
> tel7 = tellerMeanWait$MeanWait[tellerMeanWait$tellerNum==7]
> t.test(tel7)$conf.int
[1] -0.0339522  1.1548888
>
```

Since the confidence interval halfwidth was $(1.1548888 - (-0.0339522))/2 = 0.5944205$, additional simulation runs are required to achieve a halfwidth of 0.1. The following code shows the calculations needed to compute the required sample size using Equation (10.3) and the result.

```
> h = .1 # CI halfwidth
> Z975 = 2 # actually 1.96
> s = pilotSD$MeanWait[1]
> n = (Z975*s/h)^2
> n
[1] 128.3323
```

A total of 129 replications is the estimated requirement. Combining the initial 6 replications with 123 additional replications produced the following result.

```
> t.test(tel7)$conf.int
[1] 0.3331408 0.4418950
attr(,"conf.level")
[1] 0.95
> # resulting halfwidth:
> (t.test(tel7)$conf.int[2] - t.test(tel7)$conf.int[1])*.5
[1] 0.05437711
>
```

The resulting 95% confidence interval for mean wait is [0.3331408, 0.4418950], with a halfwidth of $0.05437711 < 0.1$. In managerial terms, we can express this in seconds rather than minutes and say that "based on simulation results, with 95% confidence the mean waiting time for a seven-teller bank is between 20 seconds and 27 seconds."

10.5 Predictive Analytics for Two Systems

When comparing two systems, two predictive analytics methods are of particular interest. One might want to test the hypothesis H_0: $\mu_1 = \mu_2$ vs. H_1: $\mu_1 \neq \mu_2$, or, equivalently, H_0: $\mu_1 - \mu_2 = 0$ vs. H_1: $\mu_1 - \mu_2 \neq 0$.

The second analytics method of interest is to compute a confidence interval (typically 95%) for the difference $\mu_1 - \mu_2$. This confidence interval approach is preferred since it simultaneously accomplishes the first method: if the 95% confidence interval for the difference does not include the value zero, the hypothesis test of no difference would be rejected with an α of 5% (0.05).

The construction of the confidence interval for the difference in means is handled automatically by the R function `t.test`. The default assumes a 95% interval and that the variances are not equal. Unequal variance is often the case when comparing two different system simulation outputs. As for the single-system confidence interval, the individual replication means are provided to the `t.test()` function. The code for computing the initial confidence interval and the resulting output are shown as follows.

```
> # 95% confidence interval for difference in mean wait
> tel7 = tellerMeanWait$MeanWait[tellerMeanWait$tellerNum==7]
> tel8 = tellerMeanWait$MeanWait[tellerMeanWait$tellerNum==8]
> t.test(tel7,tel8)$conf.int
[1] -0.1285025  1.0589410
>
```

Since the confidence interval halfwidth was $(1.0589410 - (-0.1285025))/2 = 0.296860875$, additional simulation runs are required to achieve a halfwidth of 0.1.

The normal-approximation sample size calculation is simplified if we restrict the sample sizes for each group to be equal. The difference in sample means (since the simulation runs are statistically independent) has a variance that is the sum of the two squared standard errors. Taking the square root gives the appropriate standard deviation to use in confidence interval construction and sample size determination.

The following code shows the calculations needed to compute the required sample size using Equation (10.3), with $s = \sqrt{s_1^2 + s_2^2}$ and the result.

```
> # sample size needed for approximate +/- .1 95% CI
> #   for difference in mean wait
> h = .1 # CI halfwidth desired
> Z975 = 2 # actually 1.96
> s = sqrt(pilotVAR$MeanWait[1]+pilotVAR$MeanWait[2])
> n = (Z975*s/h)^2
> n
[1] 130.0569
>
```

A total of 131 replications is the estimated requirement. This is for EACH system. Combining the initial 6 replications with 125 additional replications produced the following result.

```
> # 95% confidence interval for difference in mean wait
> tel7 = tellerMeanWait$MeanWait[tellerMeanWait$tellerNum==7]
> tel8 = tellerMeanWait$MeanWait[tellerMeanWait$tellerNum==8]
> t.test(tel7,tel8)$conf.int
[1] 0.1943630 0.3081854
attr(,"conf.level")
[1] 0.95
> # resulting halfwidth:
> (t.test(tel7,tel8)$conf.int[2] - t.test(tel7,tel8)$conf.
   int[1])*.5
[1] 0.05691117
>
```

The resulting 95% confidence interval for mean wait is [0.1943630, 0.3081854], with a halfwidth of $0.05691117 < 0.1$. In managerial terms, we can express this in seconds and say that "based on simulation results, with 95% confidence the mean decrease in waiting time for an eight-teller bank vs. a seven-teller bank is statistically different from 0 and falls between 12 seconds and 18 seconds."

10.6 Predictive Analytics for Multiple Systems

We continue to pursue the confidence interval approach over the hypothesis testing approach when more than two systems are to be compared. In this case, however, there is a complication in managing

α, the overall false alarm rate. When there are five systems to compare, there are ${}_5C_2 = 10$ different pairwise comparisons among them. If there are no differences among the five means, then the chance that all five would pass a hypothesis test with $\alpha = 0.05$ would be $0.95^5 = 0.77$. That means the effective false alarm rate would be 23%, not 5%.

There are specialized statistical techniques to manage the false alarm rate for such *multiple comparisons*. Tukey's honestly significant difference (HSD) test (Tukey, 1949) is not appropriate here because it assumes equal variances for replication-to-replication output for all the different systems. We can see that the sample variance decreases as the number of tellers increase. One approach would be to use Tukey's HSD method on the log of waiting time. See Section 3.3.1, which explains the reason for this strategy.

Here, we will not apply the log transform to waiting time. Instead, we can apply Ajit Tamhane's T2′ procedure to the waiting time data directly (Tamhane, 1979). The T2′ method handles unequal variance and is available as the **tamhaneT2Test()** function in the R package `PMCMRplus` (Pohlert, 2022). The following code applies the T2′ test to 6 replications each of systems with five, six, seven, and eight tellers.

```
> fit <- aov(MeanWait ~ tellerNum , data=tellerMeanWait)
> # Tamhane T2' uses welch=FALSE tighter intervals
> #   still correct coverage with unequal variance
> library(PMCMRplus)
> waitComps <- tamhaneT2Test(fit,welch=FALSE)
> summary(waitComps)
(some comment lines omitted)
      H0     t value    Pr(>|t|)
6 - 5 == 0   -4.230 0.01041028    *
7 - 5 == 0   -4.612 0.00575875   **
8 - 5 == 0   -4.716 0.00491614   **
7 - 6 == 0   -4.501 0.00682555   **
8 - 6 == 0   -7.254 0.00016481  ***
8 - 7 == 0   -1.547 0.63075472
>
```

The Tukey and Tamhane tests in R use the output from an ANOVA model, which here is the `fit` object. ANOVA models are outside the scope of this text; see Section 3.3.5 for a brief discussion. In this case, there are six pairwise comparisons of means. Only the comparison between the seven- and eight-teller systems shows no statistically significant difference.

There is another output from the `tamhaneT2Test()` that groups statistically indistinguishable output groups. The following code shows the command and result.

```
> summaryGroup(waitComps)
(some comment lines omitted)
   mean    sd n Sig. group
5 6.246 3.166 6          a
6 0.768 0.195 6          b
7 0.275 0.185 6          c
8 0.149 0.077 6          c
>
```

It is consistent with the previous results: five- and six-teller systems have distinct mean waiting times (groups a and b), and the seven- and eight-teller systems are distinguishable from these but not distinguishable from each other (group c).

The `tamhaneT2Test()` function produces hypothesis tests but not confidence intervals, with the latter being our preference for analysis. However, in Tamhane (1979), the confidence interval formula is given. The following code implements it and produces the all-pairwise-comparison confidence intervals with overall 95% coverage.

```
> # to compute multiple confidence intervals via Tamhane(1979)
> #   for each i and j > i, CI = xbar[i]-xbar[j] +/-
> #   t(df=2n-2,alphk=1/2(.95^kC2))sqrt(s^2[i]+s^2[j])/sqrt(n)
> n_sys = 1+hitel-lotel # number of systems compared (k)
> alphk = .5*(1 - .95^(1/choose(n_sys,2)))
> t_crit = qt((1-alphk), df= ((2*nreps)-2))
> # populate upper triangular matrices with mean and s_diff
> m_diff = matrix(0,nrow=n_sys-1,ncol=n_sys)
> s_diff = matrix(0,nrow=n_sys-1,ncol=n_sys)
> low_CI = matrix(0,nrow=n_sys-1,ncol=n_sys)
> up_CI = matrix(0,nrow=n_sys-1,ncol=n_sys)
> # name the indexes as 5 through 8
> i_name = c("5 teller","6 teller","7 teller","8 teller")
> for(i in 1:(n_sys-1)){
+   for(j in (i+1):n_sys){
+   m_diff[i,j] = pilotMean$MeanWait[i]-pilotMean$MeanWait[j]
+   s_diff[i,j] = sqrt(pilotVAR$MeanWait[i]+pilotVAR$MeanWait[j])/
+     sqrt(nreps)
+   # limit number of digits to 4 decimals
+   low_CI[i,j] = round(m_diff[i,j]-t_crit*s_diff[i,j],4)
+   up_CI[i,j] = round(m_diff[i,j]+t_crit*s_diff[i,j],4)
+   print(paste("CI for",i_name[i],"-",i_name[j],
+         "is [",low_CI[i,j],",",up_CI[i,j],"]"))
+   }
+ }
```

```
[1] "CI for 5 teller - 6 teller is [ 1.251 , 9.7043 ]"
[1] "CI for 5 teller - 7 teller is [ 1.7449 , 10.1967 ]"
[1] "CI for 5 teller - 8 teller is [ 1.8771 , 10.317 ]"
[1] "CI for 6 teller - 7 teller is [ 0.1355 , 0.8507 ]"
[1] "CI for 6 teller - 8 teller is [ 0.3406 , 0.8981 ]"
[1] "CI for 7 teller - 8 teller is [ -0.1402 , 0.3928 ]"
>
```

Choosing replications for multiple comparisons

For multiple comparisons, we choose a different strategy for determining the number of replications. Suppose that we only want sufficient replications to statistically distinguish the seven-teller mean waiting time from the eight-teller mean waiting time. The mean difference is $0.275 - 0.149 = 0.126$. The current halfwidth is $(0.3928 - (-0.1402))/2 = -.2665$. This must become smaller than 0.126 to give an interval that does not include zero. Suppose we choose a target value a bit smaller, say 0.12. Since the confidence interval halfwidth goes down a bit faster than the square root of n (because the added degrees of freedom decrease the critical t value), we can compute the required sample per group as

$$n = n_0 \left(\frac{0.2665}{0.12} \right)^2 = 29.59, \tag{10.5}$$

or 30 replications per system, so 24 additional replications for each. The following results show the resulting Tamhane tests and intervals.

```
> summary(waitComps)
        H0       t value   Pr(>|t|)
6 - 5 == 0   -6.343 2.205e-07 ***
7 - 5 == 0   -7.762 9.225e-10 ***
8 - 5 == 0   -8.195 1.735e-10 ***
7 - 6 == 0   -5.373 8.597e-06 ***
8 - 6 == 0   -7.652 1.411e-09 ***
8 - 7 == 0   -3.745  0.002496  **

> summaryGroup(waitComps)
   mean    sd  n Sig. group
5 5.167 3.360 30         a
6 1.182 0.741 30         b
7 0.381 0.342 30         c
8 0.138 0.094 30         d
```

```
(confidence interval results - code omitted)
[1] "CI for 5 teller - 6 teller is [ 2.2739 , 5.6961 ]"
[1] "CI for 5 teller - 7 teller is [ 3.1065 , 6.4656 ]"
[1] "CI for 5 teller - 8 teller is [ 3.3574 , 6.7005 ]"
[1] "CI for 6 teller - 7 teller is [ 0.395 , 1.2072 ]"
[1] "CI for 6 teller - 8 teller is [ 0.6724 , 1.4156 ]"
[1] "CI for 7 teller - 8 teller is [ 0.0662 , 0.4196 ]"
>
```

The increased sample size was sufficient to declare all differences as statistically significant. Equation (10.5) is a useful strategy to find a sample size sufficient for reducing a confidence interval found in the pilot analysis to a target halfwidth.

10.7 Predictive Analytics Regression

We use the methods discussed in Chapter 3 to construct a regression model to predict the daily average waiting time for systems with five through nine tellers as well as both the grand mean (a confidence interval) and the range of daily averages that might occur (a prediction interval). Given simulation output of the same form as our previous examples, `tellerMeanWait` is appropriate for regression analysis. Again, we begin with six replications (days) per system. We follow the regression process in Section 3.4. The data summary is as follows.

```
> summary(tellerMeanWait)
tellerNum      MeanWait
Min.    :5    Min.    : 0.00042
1st Qu.:6    1st Qu.: 0.08829
Median :7    Median : 0.26653
Mean    :7    Mean    : 1.49485
3rd Qu.:8    3rd Qu.: 0.90859
Max.    :9    Max.    :10.35564
>
```

Of course, the number of tellers ranges from five to nine. Mean waiting time ranges from a low of 0.00042 minutes (less than a second) to a high of 10.36 (10 minutes, 22 seconds). The plot in Figure 10.8 shows both nonlinearity and unequal variance (heteroskedasticity) over the different systems. Section 3.3.1 would suggest a Box–Cox or

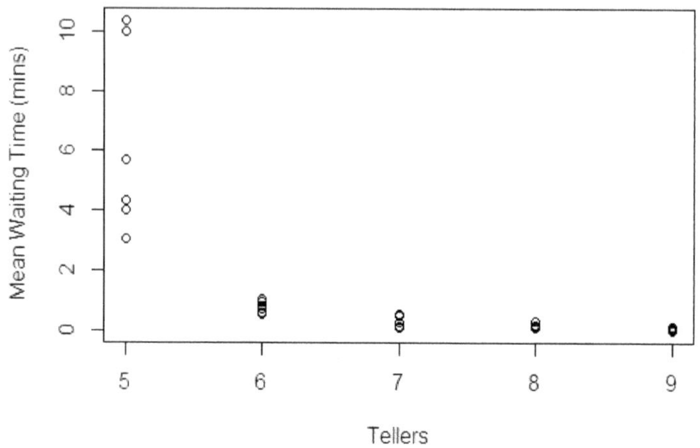

Figure 10.8. Daily average waiting times vs. number of tellers.

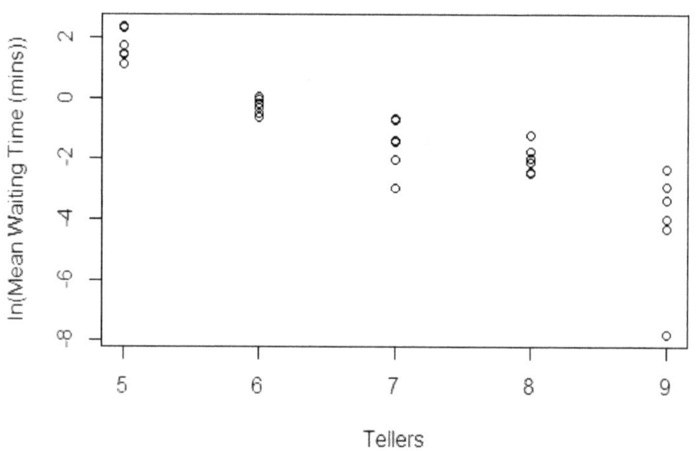

Figure 10.9. Logarithm of daily average waiting times vs. number of tellers.

log transform for this case. We try the log transform first. The resulting plot is shown in Figure 10.9 shows that the heteroskedasticity problem is gone, and the response is approximately linear, so we build the regression model using the log of daily average waiting time as the dependent variable.

The regression model fitting and summary findings are described next. The diagnostic plots are shown in Figure 10.10.

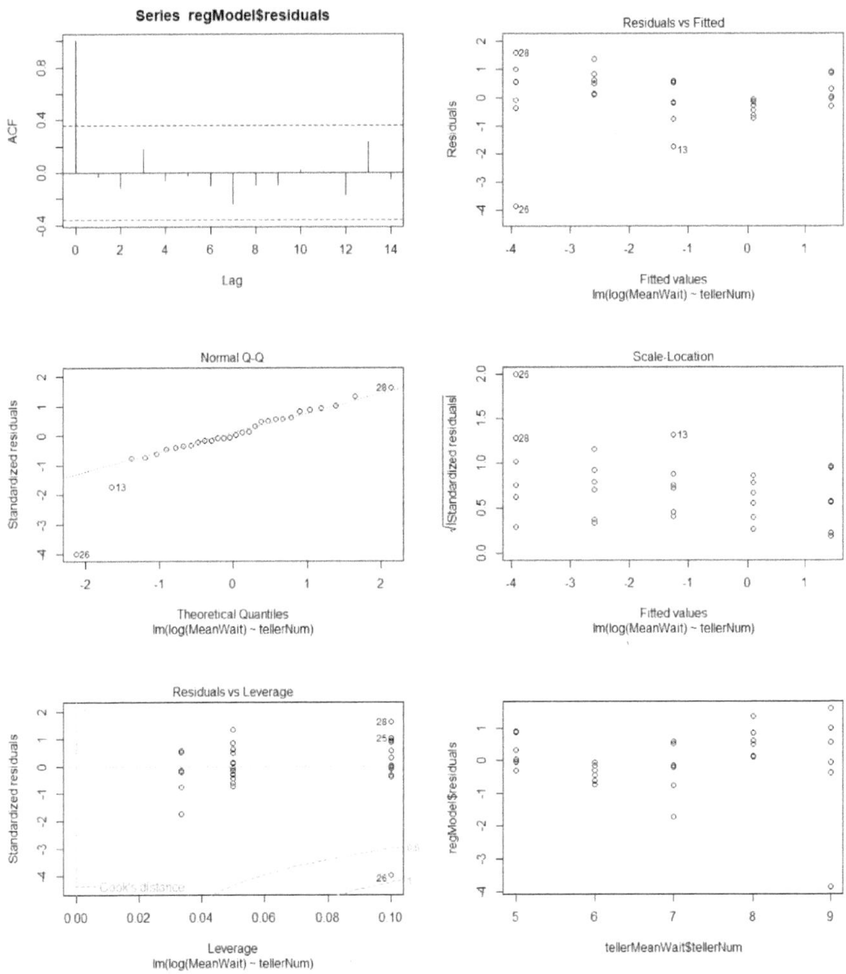

Figure 10.10. Diagnostics plots for the log waiting time regression.

```
> regModel = lm(log(MeanWait) ~ tellerNum, data=tellerMeanWait)
> summary(regModel)$coefficients[,1]

(Intercept)   tellerNum
8.13912     -1.34086
---
> # pull out the R-squared value from the summary
> summary(regModel)$r.squared
[1] 0.78692
> # do plots to check model validity
```

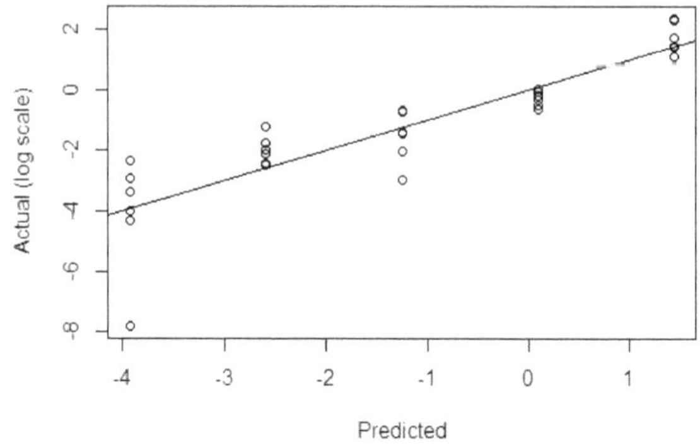

Figure 10.11. Actual vs. predicted plot for the log waiting time regression.

```
> acf(regModel$residuals)
> plot(regModel, ask=F, add.smooth=F)
> plot(tellerMeanWait$tellerNum,regModel$residuals)
```

All of the diagnostic plots appear acceptable, although some minor nonlinearity remains, as seen in the residuals vs. fitted and residuals vs. number of tellers plots. This is not a significant problem: the vertical spread of the values in the residuals vs. fitted plot all include zero. Since the R^2 is fairly high at 0.79 and the actual vs. predicted plot in Figure 10.11 shows good predictive power, we proceed with statistical characterization based on the *traditional research* paradigm.

The following code and accompanying result shows the model statistical characterization.

```
> summary(regModel)
Call:
lm(formula = log(MeanWait) ~ tellerNum, data = tellerMeanWait)

Residuals:
   Min      1Q Median     3Q    Max
-3.852 -0.312 -0.007  0.568  1.583

Coefficients:
            Estimate Std. Error t value Pr(>|t|)
(Intercept)    8.139      0.942    8.64  2.2e-09 ***
tellerNum     -1.341      0.132  -10.17  6.6e-11 ***
---

Residual standard error: 1.02 on 28 degrees of freedom
Multiple R-squared:  0.787, Adjusted R-squared:  0.779
F-statistic:  103 on 1 and 28 DF,  p-value: 6.64e-11
```

```
> confint(regModel) # compute confidence intervals for model
  coefficients
2.5 %    97.5 %
(Intercept)  6.21020 10.06803
tellerNum    -1.61096 -1.07076
>
```

A managerial interpretation can be given to these results:

- the effect of the number of tellers on the log of daily average waiting time is statistically significant, with a decrease in the natural log of daily average waiting time of about -1.34 for every increase of one teller. This is a reduction to 26% of the previous value, or a 74% reduction compared with one less teller;
- with 95% confidence, the decrease in the log of daily average waiting time for every increase of one teller is between -1.61 and -1.07;
- the estimated standard deviation of log daily average waiting time is about 1; and
- the model explains about 79% of the variation in log daily average waiting time.

Confidence and prediction intervals are computed for the logarithm of daily average waiting time but are then transformed back to original units before reporting the findings to management. The following listing performs the calculations and includes the results.

```
> # compute confidence intervals in original units
> # put desired forecast in a dataframe
> tellers.dat <- data.frame(tellerNum = 5:9)
> exp(predict(regModel, newdata = tellers.dat,
+             interval = 'confidence')) # give forecast CI
        fit        lwr        upr
1 4.1988310 2.1666774 8.1369667
2 1.0984983 0.6880555 1.7537808
3 0.2873892 0.1961453 0.4210783
4 0.0751868 0.0470940 0.1200376
5 0.0196704 0.0101503 0.0381194
>
```

These results can be interpreted in managerial terms:

- The estimated daily mean waiting time for five tellers is 4.20 minutes, but there is substantial uncertainty about this value. The true mean will lie between 2.17 and 8.13 minutes with 95% confidence.

- The estimated daily mean waiting time for six tellers is 1.10 minutes, but there is some uncertainty about this value. The true mean will lie between 0.69 minutes (21 seconds) and 1.75 minutes with 95% confidence.
- The estimated daily mean waiting time for seven tellers is 0.29 minutes (17 seconds), but there is some uncertainty about this value. The true mean will lie between 0.20 minutes (12 seconds) and 0.42 minutes (25 seconds) with 95% confidence.
- The estimated daily mean waiting time for eight tellers is 0.075 minutes (4.5 seconds), but there is some uncertainty about this value. The true mean will lie between 0.047 minutes (3 seconds) and 0.12 minutes (7 seconds) with 95% confidence.
- The estimated daily mean waiting time for nine tellers is 0.02 minutes (1.2 seconds), but there is some uncertainty about this value. The true mean will lie between 0.01 minutes (less than a second) and 0.04 minutes (2.4 seconds) with 95% confidence.

It is important to understand that these are the daily average waiting times. A more important calculation to management might be "What are the waiting times that 95% of my customers will experience?" The following is the listing showing how these times are calculated along with the results. Note that these are two-sided prediction intervals, meaning that only 2.5% of customers will wait longer than the upper prediction interval.

```
> # compute prediction intervals in original units
> exp(predict(regModel, newdata = tellers.dat,
+              interval = 'prediction')) # give forecast PI
fit         lwr         upr
1 4.1988310 0.46789546 37.679745
2 1.0984983 0.12874499  9.372780
3 0.2873892 0.03426260  2.410574
4 0.0751868 0.00881196  0.641520
5 0.0196704 0.00219196  0.176519
>
```

These results can be interpreted in managerial terms:

- The estimated daily mean waiting time for five tellers is 4.20 minutes, but there is substantial variation about this value for individual customers. The waiting time for the central 95% of customers will lie between 0.47 minutes (28 seconds) and 37.68 minutes.

- The estimated daily mean waiting time for six tellers is 1.10 minutes, but there is but there is substantial variation about this value for individual customers. The waiting time for the central 95% of customers will lie between 0.13 minutes (8 seconds) and 9.37 minutes.
- The estimated daily mean waiting time for seven tellers is 0.29 minutes (17 seconds), but there is substantial variation about this value for individual customers. The waiting time for the central 95% of customers will lie between 0.034 minutes (2 seconds) and 2.41 minutes.
- The estimated daily mean waiting time for eight tellers is 0.075 minutes (4.5 seconds), but there is substantial variation about this value for individual customers. The waiting time for the central 95% of customers will lie between 0.009 minutes (less than a second) and 0.64 minutes (38 seconds).
- The estimated daily mean waiting time for nine tellers is 0.02 minutes (1.2 seconds), but there is substantial variation about this value for individual customers. The waiting time for the central 95% of customers will lie between 0.002 minutes (less than a second) and 0.18 minutes (11 seconds).

This picture suggests that, if waiting less than 3 minutes for service is acceptable, the bank with seven tellers provides that level to more than 97.5% of customers. The recommended number of tellers will also depend on the salary, benefits, and discounted hiring and training costs for tellers. There will be a trade-off between that cost and the costs implied by excessive waiting times for some customers.

Sample size computation for regression

Given a regression fit to a preliminary or pilot experiment, it is easy to determine the sample size required to result in a satisfactory p-value for the overall model. Because we have already achieved that p-value in our pilot bank teller study, there is no need for additional replications. But we conduct the calculation to see how the process works.

For the overall regression model test, sample size determination requires some version of the following three elements:

- the number of (unknown) coefficients of predictor terms, say d, in the model;

- an estimate of R^2 for the regression model;
- the significance or *false alarm probability*: often $\alpha = 0.05$; and
- the power: the probability that a data set from population with a true regression relationship having value R^2 will yield a rejection of the hypothesis of no regression with a p-value of $\leq \alpha$, and complementary to power is the *failure to detect probability*, β, i.e., power $= 1 - \beta$.

The calculations are done using the `pwr.f2.test()` function in the R package `pwr`. An example is given by Stanley (2022). The function requires one preliminary calculation to estimate a quantity called f^2:

$$\hat{f^2} = \frac{\hat{R^2}}{1 - \hat{R^2}}. \tag{10.6}$$

The `pwr.f2.test()` function produces a degrees of freedom value v. Added to this must be the number of regression coefficients plus the intercept, so $n = v + d + 1$ (note that this uses the variable name `u` rather than d). The code and results are shown as follows. Note that $\alpha = 0.05$ was not specified. It is the default value for the `pwr.f2.test()` function.

```
> library(pwr)
> n_coef = length(regModel$coefficients)-1 # exclude the
  intercept
> R2hat = summary(regModel)$r.squared
> pwr.f2.test(u=n_coef, f2=R2hat/(1-R2hat),power=.95)

Multiple regression power calculation

u = 1
v = 4.26735
f2 = 3.693075
sig.level = 0.05
power = 0.95

> n = pwr.f2.test(u=n_coef, f2=R2hat/(1-R2hat),
      power=.95)$v + n_coef + 1
> n
[1] 6.26735
>
```

So, seven regression data pairs are required (these should be distributed over the five teller numbers). Note that n here denotes the

TOTAL number of regression samples. We already have $n = 5 \times 6 = 30$, far exceeding the required number.

10.8 Benefits of Discrete-Event Simulation

The analytic results presented in Sections 10.4–10.7 show the kinds of analyses and predictions that can be performed using simulation results. Compared with testing and predictive analytics using the real system, simulation-based analytics can be faster and less expensive. Of course, advantages must be balanced against the cost of developing and validating the simulation model.

In many circumstances, testing on the actual system is not possible, either due to the disruption and associated cost or because the system does not yet exist. Often, discrete-event simulation is used in the design phase of a production, transportation, warehousing, communication, or health service system. Paired with predictive analytics tools, discrete-event simulation is a powerful tool for use under the *model-dependent research* paradigm.

10.9 Case Supporting Chapters 9 and 10

The multi-segment case BankTellerSimulation supports the material in Chapters 9 and 10. The first segment focuses on material from the previous chapter: model structure and kinds of DES model outputs. The second segment focuses on regression metamodeling of simulation output and depends particularly on material from Section 10.7. This case extends over multiple weeks. The case description slides and data can be found online in the BankDiscreteEventSimulation folder of Barton (2023).

10.10 R Code Used in Chapter 10

Code for determining warm-up period in steady-state simulation:

```
# Simmer multiteller bank example for PABR
# Based on simmer bank example in
# https://r-simmer.org/articles/simmer-04-bank-1.html
#
# just used for warmup plot
library(simmer)
```

```
# set seed for repeatable results
set.seed(80115119)
# set arrival and service rates (lambda and mu)
arate = 1
srate = 1/4.5
# set number of tellers
n_teller = 5

nreps = 6 # repeated runs for the same number of tellers
# replication loop: lapply says do the 'simmer' simulation function
#                   nreps times (see '})' for end of lapply loop)
# "bankRuns" is simulation output 'object' across all replications
bankRuns <- lapply(1:nreps, function(i) {
# define bank as simmer object
bank <- simmer("bank")
# specify entity path via 'trajectory'- requires 'teller' resource
customerPath <-
trajectory("Customer's path") %>%
set_attribute("start_time", function() {now(bank)}) %>%
seize("Teller") %>%
timeout(function() {rexp(1, srate)}) %>% # service with the teller
release("Teller")

# to make simulation run, add teller resource, generate customer
#   arrivals, customers arrive over 8 hours (480 minutes)
bank %>%
add_resource("Teller", n_teller) %>%
# from_to says when to generate customers
# if arrive = TRUE (default) the first arrival will be generated
#    at start_timeand will follow dist from then on. If set to
#    FALSE, will initiate dist at start_time (so first arrival
#    will start at a time later than start_time).
add_generator("Customer", customerPath, from_to(0,4320,function()
{rexp(1,arate)},arrive=FALSE)) %>%
run(until=4320)
# end replication loop====================================
})

# compute waiting time as total time minus time in service
waitData = bankRuns %>%
get_mon_arrivals() %>%
transform(waiting_time = end_time - start_time - activity_time)
# Plot waiting time of customers as the day progresses
#   for each replication
par(mfrow = c(2,3))
for(i in levels(as.factor(waitData$replication))){
plot(waitData$waiting_time[waitData$replication == i],
ylab = "Waiting Time",ylim=c(0,50),pch=20,cex=0.5,
cex.lab=1.5,cex.axis=1.5,cex.main=1.5,
main = paste("Replication ",i,", ", n_teller, "Tellers"))
}

# plot average wait over first two hours
repMeanWait = rowMeans(cbind(waitData$waiting_time
[waitData$replication==1],
waitData$waiting_time
```

```
[waitData$replication==2],
waitData$waiting_time
[waitData$replication==3],
waitData$waiting_time
[waitData$replication==4],
waitData$waiting_time
[waitData$replication==5],
waitData$waiting_time
[waitData$replication==6]))

par(mfrow = c(1,1))
plot(repMeanWait,ylab="Average Waiting Time",ylim=c(0,15),pch=20,
xlab="Customer Index",cex=0.5,cex.lab=1.1,cex.axis=1.1,
cex.main=1.1)
plot(smooth.spline(x=repMeanWait,nknots=20),
ylab="Smoothed Average Waiting Time",ylim=c(0,15),pch=20,
cex=0.5,xlab="Customer Index",cex.lab=1.1,cex.axis=1.1,
cex.main=1.1)
# looks like around 200 minutes for initial rise - plot that
plot(smooth.spline(x=repMeanWait[1:400],nknots=8),
ylab = "Smoothed Average Waiting Time",ylim=c(0,15),pch=20,
cex=0.5,xlab="Customer Index (first 400 customers)",
cex.lab=1.1,cex.axis=1.1,cex.main=1.1)

# compute mean wait for each replication
repMeanWait = NULL
for(i in levels(as.factor(waitData$replication))){
repMeanWait[i] = mean(waitData$waiting_time
[waitData$replication==i])
}
# give summary statistics for waiting time
paste("Average wait for",sum(waitData$finished),"completions was",
format(mean(repMeanWait),digits=4),"minutes, for",
n_teller, "tellers.")
paste("Standard deviation of average daily wait was ",
format(sd(repMeanWait), digits=4),
"minutes, and standard error of the mean was ",
format(sd(repMeanWait)/sqrt(nreps), digits=4))
```

Code for simulation analytics:

```
# Simmer multiteller bank simulation analytics for PABR
# Based on simmer bank example in
# https://r-simmer.org/articles/simmer-04-bank-1.html
# This week the focus is on building a regression model
#   to predict average waiting time for different numbers
#   of tellers.
#install.packages("PMCMRplus")
library(simmer)

# set seed for repeatable results
set.seed(11119)

# set arrival and service rates (lambda and mu)
arate = 1
srate = 1/4.5
```

```
lotel = 7
hitel = 8

nreps = 6 # repeated runs for the same number of tellers

# set placeholder for MeanWait result vector
MeanWait = NULL

# set number of tellers
for(n_teller in lotel:hitel){

    # replication loop: lapply does the 'simmer' simulation function
    #                   nreps times (see '})' for end of lapply loop)
# "bankRuns" is the simulation output 'object'
bankRuns <- lapply(1:nreps, function(i) {
    # define bank as simmer object
    bank <- simmer("bank")

    # specify entity path via 'trajectory'- requires 'teller' resource
    customer <-
    trajectory("Customer's path") %>%
    set_attribute("start_time", function() {now(bank)}) %>%
    seize("teller") %>%
    timeout(function() {rexp(1, srate)}) %>% # spend time with teller
    release("teller")

    # add teller resource, generate customer arrivals
    # customers arrive for 8 hours (480 minutes)
    bank %>%
    add_resource("teller", n_teller) %>%
    # from_to says when to generate customers
    # if arrive = TRUE (default) the first arrival will be generated
    #   at start_time
    add_generator("Customer", customer, from_to(0,480,
    function(){rexp(1,arate)},
    arrive=FALSE)) %>%
    run()

    # end replication loop====================================
})


# compute waiting time as total time minus time in service
waitData = bankRuns %>%
get_mon_arrivals() %>%
transform(waiting_time = end_time - start_time - activity_time)

# compute mean wait for each replication
repMeanWait = NULL
for(i in levels(as.factor(waitData$replication))){
    repMeanWait[i]=mean(waitData$waiting_time[waitData$replication==i])
}

# assemble mean wait data for this number of tellers
MeanWait = c(MeanWait,repMeanWait)
```

```
# end n_teller loop====================================
}

# convert to data frame
#   (create column with n_teller values for runs)
tellerNum = sort(rep(lotel:hitel,nreps))
tellerMeanWait = data.frame(tellerNum,MeanWait)

pilotMean = aggregate(.~tellerNum, data=tellerMeanWait , mean)
pilotSD = aggregate(.~tellerNum, data=tellerMeanWait , sd)
pilotMean
pilotSD

# 95% confidence interval for mean wait for 7 teller system
tel7 = tellerMeanWait$MeanWait[tellerMeanWait$tellerNum==7]
t.test(tel7)$conf.int
# sample size needed for approximate +/- .1 95% CI
#   for 7-teller mean wait
h = .1 # CI halfwidth desired
Z975 = 2 # actually 1.96
s = pilotSD$MeanWait[1]
n = (Z975*s/h)^2
n


# result suggests 129 replications needed
# repeat analysis with nreps = 123+6 ===================
nreps = 129
set.seed(11119)
# set placeholder for MeanWait result vector
MeanWait = NULL

# set number of tellers
for(n_teller in lotel:hitel){

# replication loop: lapply does the 'simmer' simulation function
#                   nreps times (see '})' for end of lapply loop)
# "bankRuns" is the simulation output 'object'
bankRuns <- lapply(1:nreps, function(i) {
# define bank as simmer object
bank <- simmer("bank")

# specify entity path via 'trajectory'- requires 'teller' resource
customer <-
trajectory("Customer's path") %>%
set_attribute("start_time", function() {now(bank)}) %>%
seize("teller") %>%
timeout(function() {rexp(1, srate)}) %>% # spend time with teller
release("teller")

# add teller resource, generate customer arrivals
# customers arrive for 8 hours (480 minutes)
bank %>%
add_resource("teller", n_teller) %>%
# from_to says when to generate customers
# if arrive = TRUE (default) the first arrival will be generated
```

```
#   at start_time
add_generator("Customer", customer, from_to(0,480,
function(){rexp(1,arate)},
arrive=FALSE)) %>%
run()

# end replication loop====================================
})


# compute waiting time as total time minus time in service
waitData = bankRuns %>%
get_mon_arrivals() %>%
transform(waiting_time = end_time - start_time - activity_time)

# compute mean wait for each replication
repMeanWait = NULL
for(i in levels(as.factor(waitData$replication))){
repMeanWait[i]=mean(waitData$waiting_time[waitData$replication==i])
}

# assemble mean wait data
MeanWait = c(MeanWait,repMeanWait)

# end n_teller loop====================================
}

# convert to data frame for regression
#   (create column with n_teller values for runs)
tellerNum = sort(rep(lotel:hitel,nreps))
tellerMeanWait = data.frame(tellerNum,MeanWait)

tel7 = tellerMeanWait$MeanWait[tellerMeanWait$tellerNum==7]
t.test(tel7)$conf.int
# resulting halfwidth:
(t.test(tel7)$conf.int[2] - t.test(tel7)$conf.int[1])*.5

# two-sample confidence interval and sample size============
#=========================================================
# want conf int for diff in mean waits  halfwidth .1
nreps = 6
set.seed(11119)
# set placeholder for MeanWait result vector
MeanWait = NULL

# set number of tellers
for(n_teller in lotel:hitel){

# replication loop: lapply does the 'simmer' simulation function
#                   nreps times (see '})' for end of lapply loop)
# "bankRuns" is the simulation output 'object'
bankRuns <- lapply(1:nreps, function(i) {
# define bank as simmer object
bank <- simmer("bank")
```

```
# specify entity path via 'trajectory'- requires 'teller' resource
customer <-
trajectory("Customer's path") %>%
set_attribute("start_time", function() {now(bank)}) %>%
seize("teller") %>%
timeout(function() {rexp(1, srate)}) %>% # spend time with teller
release("teller")

# add teller resource, generate customer arrivals
# customers arrive for 8 hours (480 minutes)
bank %>%
add_resource("teller", n_teller) %>%
# from_to says when to generate customers
# if arrive = TRUE (default) the first arrival will be generated
#   at start_time
add_generator("Customer", customer, from_to(0,480,
function(){rexp(1,arate)},
arrive=FALSE)) %>%
run()

# end replication loop====================================
})


# compute waiting time as total time minus time in service
waitData = bankRuns %>%
get_mon_arrivals() %>%
transform(waiting_time = end_time - start_time - activity_time)

# compute mean wait for each replication
repMeanWait = NULL
for(i in levels(as.factor(waitData$replication))){
repMeanWait[i]=mean(waitData$waiting_time[waitData$replication==i])
}

# assemble mean wait data for this number of tellers
MeanWait = c(MeanWait,repMeanWait)

# end n_teller loop=======================================
}

# convert to data frame
#   (create column with n_teller values for runs)
tellerNum = sort(rep(lotel:hitel,nreps))
tellerMeanWait = data.frame(tellerNum,MeanWait)

pilotMean = aggregate(.~tellerNum, data=tellerMeanWait , mean)
pilotSD = aggregate(.~tellerNum, data=tellerMeanWait , sd)
pilotVAR = aggregate(.~tellerNum, data=tellerMeanWait , var)
pilotMean
pilotSD
pilotVAR

# 95% confidence interval for difference in mean wait
tel7 = tellerMeanWait$MeanWait[tellerMeanWait$tellerNum==7]
tel8 = tellerMeanWait$MeanWait[tellerMeanWait$tellerNum==8]
```

```
t.test(tel7,tel8)$conf.int
# sample size needed for approximate +/- .1 95% CI
#   for difference in mean wait
h = .1 # CI halfwidth desired
Z975 = 2 # actually 1.96
s = sqrt(pilotVAR$MeanWait[1]+pilotVAR$MeanWait[2])
n = (Z975*s/h)^2
n

# result suggests 131 replications needed
# repeat analysis with nreps = 125+6 ===================
nreps = 131
set.seed(11119)
# set placeholder for MeanWait result vector
MeanWait = NULL

# set number of tellers
for(n_teller in lotel:hitel){

# replication loop: lapply does the 'simmer' simulation function
#                   nreps times (see '})' for end of lapply loop)
# "bankRuns" is the simulation output 'object'
bankRuns <- lapply(1:nreps, function(i) {
# define bank as simmer object
bank <- simmer("bank")

# specify entity path via 'trajectory'- requires 'teller' resource
customer <-
trajectory("Customer's path") %>%
set_attribute("start_time", function() {now(bank)}) %>%
seize("teller") %>%
timeout(function() {rexp(1, srate)}) %>% # spend time with teller
release("teller")

# add teller resource, generate customer arrivals
# customers arrive for 8 hours (480 minutes)
bank %>%
add_resource("teller", n_teller) %>%
# from_to says when to generate customers
# if arrive = TRUE (default) the first arrival will be generated
#   at start_time
add_generator("Customer", customer, from_to(0,480,
function(){rexp(1,arate)},
arrive=FALSE)) %>%
run()

# end replication loop===================================
})


# compute waiting time as total time minus time in service
waitData = bankRuns %>%
get_mon_arrivals() %>%
transform(waiting_time = end_time - start_time - activity_time)
```

```
# compute mean wait for each replication
repMeanWait = NULL
for(i in levels(as.factor(waitData$replication))){
repMeanWait[i]=mean(waitData$waiting_time[waitData$replication==i])
}

# assemble mean wait data for this number of tellers
MeanWait = c(MeanWait,repMeanWait)

# end n_teller loop=====================================
}

# convert to data frame
#   (create column with n_teller values for runs)
tellerNum = sort(rep(lotel:hitel,nreps))
tellerMeanWait = data.frame(tellerNum,MeanWait)

pilotMean = aggregate(.~tellerNum, data=tellerMeanWait , mean)
pilotSD = aggregate(.~tellerNum, data=tellerMeanWait , sd)
pilotVAR = aggregate(.~tellerNum, data=tellerMeanWait , var)
pilotMean
pilotSD
pilotVAR

# 95% confidence interval for difference in mean wait
tel7 = tellerMeanWait$MeanWait[tellerMeanWait$tellerNum==7]
tel8 = tellerMeanWait$MeanWait[tellerMeanWait$tellerNum==8]
t.test(tel7,tel8)$conf.int
# resulting halfwidth:
(t.test(tel7,tel8)$conf.int[2] - t.test(tel7,tel8)$conf.int[1])*.5

# multiple comparisons, 5 - 8 tellers====================
#======================================================
lotel = 5
hitel = 8

# apply Tamhane multiple comparisons test - needs ANOVA output
nreps = 6
set.seed(11119)
# set placeholder for MeanWait result vector
MeanWait = NULL

# set number of tellers
for(n_teller in lotel:hitel){

# replication loop: lapply does the 'simmer' simulation function
#                   nreps times (see '})' for end of lapply loop)
# "bankRuns" is the simulation output 'object'
bankRuns <- lapply(1:nreps, function(i) {
# define bank as simmer object
bank <- simmer("bank")

# specify entity path via 'trajectory'- requires 'teller' resource
customer <-
trajectory("Customer's path") %>%
set_attribute("start_time", function() {now(bank)}) %>%
```

```
seize("teller") %>%
timeout(function() {rexp(1, srate)}) %>% # spend time with teller
release("teller")

# add teller resource, generate customer arrivals
# customers arrive for 8 hours (480 minutes)
bank %>%
add_resource("teller", n_teller) %>%
# from_to says when to generate customers
# if arrive = TRUE (default) the first arrival will be generated
#   at start_time
add_generator("Customer", customer, from_to(0,480,
function(){rexp(1,arate)},
arrive=FALSE)) %>%
run()

# end replication loop====================================
})


# compute waiting time as total time minus time in service
waitData = bankRuns %>%
get_mon_arrivals() %>%
transform(waiting_time = end_time - start_time - activity_time)

# compute mean wait for each replication
repMeanWait = NULL
for(i in levels(as.factor(waitData$replication))){
repMeanWait[i]=mean(waitData$waiting_time[waitData$replication==i])
}

# assemble mean wait data for this number of tellers
MeanWait = c(MeanWait,repMeanWait)

# end n_teller loop====================================
}

# convert to data frame
#   (create column with n_teller values for runs)
tellerNum = sort(rep(lotel:hitel,nreps))
tellerMeanWait = data.frame(tellerNum,MeanWait)

pilotMean = aggregate(.~tellerNum, data=tellerMeanWait , mean)
pilotSD = aggregate(.~tellerNum, data=tellerMeanWait , sd)
pilotVAR = aggregate(.~tellerNum, data=tellerMeanWait , var)


fit <- aov(MeanWait ~ tellerNum, data=tellerMeanWait)
# Tamhane T2' uses welch=FALSE tighter intervals
#   still correct coverage with unequal variance
library(PMCMRplus)
waitComps <- tamhaneT2Test(fit,welch=FALSE)
summary(waitComps)
summaryGroup(waitComps)
```

```
# to compute multiple confidence intervals via Tamhane(1979)
#   for each i and j > i, CI = xbar[i]-xbar[j] +/-
#   t(df=2n-2,alphk=1/2(.95^kC2))sqrt(s^2[i]+s^2[j])/sqrt(n)
n_sys = 1+hitel-lotel # number of systems compared (k)
alphk = .5*(1 - .95^(1/choose(n_sys,2)))
t_crit = qt((1-alphk), df= ((2*nreps)-2))
# populate upper triangular matrices with mean and s_diff
m_diff = matrix(0,nrow=n_sys-1,ncol=n_sys)
s_diff = matrix(0,nrow=n_sys-1,ncol=n_sys)
low_CI = matrix(0,nrow=n_sys-1,ncol=n_sys)
up_CI = matrix(0,nrow=n_sys-1,ncol=n_sys)
# name the indexes as 5 through 8
i_name = c("5 teller","6 teller","7 teller","8 teller")
for(i in 1:(n_sys-1)){
for(j in (i+1):n_sys){
m_diff[i,j] = pilotMean$MeanWait[i]-pilotMean$MeanWait[j]
s_diff[i,j] = sqrt(pilotVAR$MeanWait[i]+pilotVAR$MeanWait[j])/
sqrt(nreps)
# limit number of digits to 4 decimals
low_CI[i,j] = round(m_diff[i,j]-t_crit*s_diff[i,j],4)
up_CI[i,j] = round(m_diff[i,j]+t_crit*s_diff[i,j],4)
print(paste("CI for",i_name[i],"-",i_name[j],
"is [",low_CI[i,j],",",up_CI[i,j],"]"))
}
}

# number of replications estimate:
#  compute largest halfwidth of interval overlapping zero
#   (here only one)
hw_0 = (up_CI[3,4]-low_CI[3,4])/2
hw_1 = abs(round(m_diff[3,4],3)) - .006 # use abs if diff negative
n = nreps*(hw_0/hw_1)^2
n

#=========================================================
# multiple comparisons, 5 - 8 tellers with 30 reps========
#=========================================================
lotel = 5
hitel = 8

# apply Tamhane multiple comparisons test - needs ANOVA output
nreps = 30
set.seed(11119)
# set placeholder for MeanWait result vector
MeanWait = NULL

# set number of tellers
for(n_teller in lotel:hitel){

# replication loop: lapply does the 'simmer' simulation function
#                   nreps times (see '})' for end of lapply loop)
# "bankRuns" is the simulation output 'object'
bankRuns <- lapply(1:nreps, function(i) {
# define bank as simmer object
bank <- simmer("bank")
```

```
# specify entity path via 'trajectory'- requires 'teller' resource
customer <-
trajectory("Customer's path") %>%
set_attribute("start_time", function() {now(bank)}) %>%
seize("teller") %>%
timeout(function() {rexp(1, srate)}) %>% # spend time with teller
release("teller")

# add teller resource, generate customer arrivals
# customers arrive for 8 hours (480 minutes)
bank %>%
add_resource("teller", n_teller) %>%
# from_to says when to generate customers
# if arrive = TRUE (default) the first arrival will be generated
#   at start_time
add_generator("Customer", customer, from_to(0,480,
function(){rexp(1,arate)},
arrive=FALSE)) %>%
run()

# end replication loop====================================
})


# compute waiting time as total time minus time in service
waitData = bankRuns %>%
get_mon_arrivals() %>%
transform(waiting_time = end_time - start_time - activity_time)

# compute mean wait for each replication
repMeanWait = NULL
for(i in levels(as.factor(waitData$replication))){
repMeanWait[i]=mean(waitData$waiting_time[waitData$replication==i])
}

# assemble mean wait data for this number of tellers
MeanWait = c(MeanWait,repMeanWait)

# end n_teller loop====================================
}

# convert to data frame
#   (create column with n_teller values for runs)
tellerNum = sort(rep(lotel:hitel,nreps))
tellerMeanWait = data.frame(tellerNum,MeanWait)

pilotMean = aggregate(.~tellerNum, data=tellerMeanWait , mean)
pilotSD = aggregate(.~tellerNum, data=tellerMeanWait , sd)
pilotVAR = aggregate(.~tellerNum, data=tellerMeanWait , var)


fit <- aov(MeanWait ~ tellerNum, data=tellerMeanWait)
# Tamhane T2' uses welch=FALSE tighter intervals
#   still correct coverage with unequal variance
library(PMCMRplus)
waitComps <- tamhaneT2Test(fit,welch=FALSE)
```

```
summary(waitComps)
summaryGroup(waitComps)

# to compute multiple confidence intervals via Tamhane(1979)
#   for each i and j > i, CI = xbar[i]-xbar[j] +/-
#   t(df=2n-2,alphk=1/2(.95^kC2))sqrt(s^2[i]+s^2[j])/sqrt(n)
n_sys = 1+hitel-lotel # number of systems compared (k)
alphk = .5*(1 - .95^(1/choose(n_sys,2)))
t_crit = qt((1-alphk), df= ((2*nreps)-2))
# populate upper triangular matrices with mean and s_diff
m_diff = matrix(0,nrow=n_sys-1,ncol=n_sys)
s_diff = matrix(0,nrow=n_sys-1,ncol=n_sys)
low_CI = matrix(0,nrow=n_sys-1,ncol=n_sys)
up_CI = matrix(0,nrow=n_sys-1,ncol=n_sys)
# name the indexes as 5 through 8
i_name = c("5 teller","6 teller","7 teller","8 teller")
for(i in 1:(n_sys-1)){
for(j in (i+1):n_sys){
m_diff[i,j] = pilotMean$MeanWait[i]-pilotMean$MeanWait[j]
s_diff[i,j] = sqrt(pilotVAR$MeanWait[i]+pilotVAR$MeanWait[j])/
sqrt(nreps)
# limit number of digits to 4 decimals
low_CI[i,j] = round(m_diff[i,j]-t_crit*s_diff[i,j],4)
up_CI[i,j] = round(m_diff[i,j]+t_crit*s_diff[i,j],4)
print(paste("CI for",i_name[i],"-",i_name[j],
"is [",low_CI[i,j],",",up_CI[i,j],"]"))
}
}

# regression analytics for bank example
#==========================================================
lotel = 5
hitel = 9

# apply Tamhane multiple comparisons test - needs ANOVA output
nreps = 6
set.seed(11119)
# set placeholder for MeanWait result vector
MeanWait = NULL

# set number of tellers
for(n_teller in lotel:hitel){

# replication loop: lapply does the 'simmer' simulation function
#                   nreps times (see '})' for end of lapply loop)
# "bankRuns" is the simulation output 'object'
bankRuns <- lapply(1:nreps, function(i) {
# define bank as simmer object
bank <- simmer("bank")

# specify entity path via 'trajectory'- requires 'teller' resource
customer <-
trajectory("Customer's path") %>%
set_attribute("start_time", function() {now(bank)}) %>%
seize("teller") %>%
```

```
timeout(function() {rexp(1, srate)}) %>% # spend time with teller
release("teller")

# add teller resource, generate customer arrivals
# customers arrive for 8 hours (480 minutes)
bank %>%
add_resource("teller", n_teller) %>%
# from_to says when to generate customers
# if arrive = TRUE (default) the first arrival will be generated
#   at start_time
add_generator("Customer", customer, from_to(0,480,
function(){rexp(1,arate)},
arrive=FALSE)) %>%
run()

# end replication loop====================================
})


# compute waiting time as total time minus time in service
waitData = bankRuns %>%
get_mon_arrivals() %>%
transform(waiting_time = end_time - start_time - activity_time)

# compute mean wait for each replication
repMeanWait = NULL
for(i in levels(as.factor(waitData$replication))){
repMeanWait[i]=mean(waitData$waiting_time[waitData$replication==i])
}

# assemble mean wait data for this number of tellers
MeanWait = c(MeanWait,repMeanWait)

# end n_teller loop====================================
}

# convert to data frame
#   (create column with n_teller values for runs)
tellerNum = sort(rep(lotel:hitel,nreps))
tellerMeanWait = data.frame(tellerNum,MeanWait)
summary(tellerMeanWait)
# plot the data
plot(tellerMeanWait$tellerNum,tellerMeanWait$MeanWait,
xlab="Tellers",ylab="Mean Waiting Time (mins)")
plot(tellerMeanWait$tellerNum,log(tellerMeanWait$MeanWait),
xlab="Tellers",ylab="ln(Mean Waiting Time (mins))")
regModel = lm(log(MeanWait) ~ tellerNum, data=tellerMeanWait)
# display regression coefficient estimates
summary(regModel)$coefficients[,1]
# pull out the R-squared value from the summary
summary(regModel)$r.squared
# plot actual vs. predicted to check fit
plot(predict(regModel, newdata = tellerMeanWait),
log(tellerMeanWait$MeanWait), xlab="Predicted",
ylab="Actual (log scale)")
abline(0,1)
```

```
# do plots to check model validity
acf(regModel$residuals)
plot(regModel, ask=F, add.smooth=F)
plot(tellerMeanWait$tellerNum,regModel$residuals)

# Validity checks pass, produce coefficient conf. int
#   p-values and waiting time confidence and prediction intervals
summary(regModel) # used to show s.d. of estimates and p-values
confint(regModel) # compute CIs for model coefficients

# compute avg wiatprediction and CIs in original units
# put desired forecast in a dataframe
tellers.dat <- data.frame(tellerNum = 5:9)
exp(predict(regModel, newdata = tellers.dat,
  interval = 'confidence')) # give forecast CI
exp(predict(regModel, newdata = tellers.dat,
  interval = 'prediction')) # give forecast PI

# estimated sample size 95% detection R2=0.7869201
#   using the pwr library
library(pwr)
n_coef = length(regModel$coefficients)-1 # exclude the intercept
R2hat = summary(regModel)$r.squared
pwr.f2.test(u=n_coef, f2=R2hat/(1-R2hat),power=.95)
n = pwr.f2.test(u=n_coef, f2=R2hat/(1-R2hat),power=.95)$v+n_coef+1
n
```

Appendix A

INFORMS CAP Job Task Analysis

The list can be requested at: https://info.informs.org/jta.

Domain I Business Problem (Question) Framing
(The ability to understand a business problem and determine whether the problem is amenable to an analytics solution.)

T-1 Obtain or receive problem statement and usability requirements.
T-2 Identify stakeholders.
T-3 Determine whether the problem is amenable to an analytics solution.
T-4 Refine the problem statement and delineate constraints.
T-5 Define an initial set of business benefits.
T-6 Obtain stakeholder agreement on the problem statement.

Domain II Analytics Problem Framing
(The ability to reformulate a business problem into an analytics problem with a potential analytics solution.)

T-1 Reformulate problem statement as an analytics problem.
T-2 Develop a proposed set of drivers and relationships to outputs.
T-3 State the set of assumptions related to the problem.
T-4 Define key metrics of success.
T-5 Obtain stakeholder agreement.

Domain III Data
(The ability to work effectively with data to help identify potential relationships that will lead to refinement of the business and analytics problem.)

T-1 Identify and prioritize data needs and sources.
T-2 Acquire data.
T-3 Harmonize, rescale, clean, and share data.
T-4 Identify relationships in the data.
T-5 Document and report findings (e.g., insights, results, business performance).
T-6 Refine the business and analytics problem statements.

Domain IV Methodology (Approach) Selection
(The ability to identify and select potential approaches for solving the business problem.)

T-1 Identify available problem solving approaches (methods).
T-2 Select software tools.
T-3 Test approaches (methods).[1]
T-4 Select approaches (methods).[1]

Domain V Model Building
(The ability to identify and build effective model structures to help solve the business problem.)

T-1 Identify model structures.[1]
T-2 Run and evaluate the models.
T-3 Calibrate models and data.[1]
T-4 Integrate the models.[1]
T-5 Document and communicate findings (including assumptions, limitations, and constraints).

Domain VI Deployment
(The ability to deploy the selected model to help solve the business problem.)

T-1 Perform business validation of the model.
T-2 Deliver report with findings.

[1]These tasks are part of an analytics project, but are beyond the scope of the CAP®certification exam and are not tested.

T-3 Create model, usability, and system requirements for production.
T-4 Deliver production model/system.[1]
T-5 Support deployment.

Domain VII Model Life Cycle Management
(The ability to manage the model life cycle to evaluate business business benefit of the model over time.)

T-1 Document initial structure.
T-2 Track model quality.
T-3 Recalibrate and maintain the model.[1]
T-4 Support training activities.
T-5 Evaluate the business benefit of the model over time.

References

Ankenman, B., Nelson, B. L., & Staum, J. (2010). Stochastic kriging for simulation metamodeling. *Operations Research*, *58*(2), 371–382.

Barton, R. R. (1999). *Graphical Methods for the Design of Experiments*. New York: Springer.

Barton, R. R. (2023). PABRcases. https://drive.google.com/drive/folders/17dqhqUo-tkAXlSrLgkhXbqC_ErLJy0S2?usp=sharing.

Bates, S., Hastie, T., & Tibshirani, R. (2023). Cross-validation: What does it estimate and how well does it do it? *Journal of the American Statistical Association*, 1–12. (In press).

Baumgartner, H., & Steenkamp, J.-B. E. (2001). Response styles in marketing research: A cross-national investigation. *Journal of Marketing Research*, *38*(2), 143–156.

Becker, R. (1988). *The New S Language*. New York: Chapman and Hall/CRC.

Belsley, D. A., Kuh, E., & Welsch, R. E. (2013). *Regression Diagnostics: Identifying Influential Data and Sources of Collinearity*, 2nd edn. Hoboken: Wiley-Interscience.

Box, G. E. P., & Cox, D. R. (1964). An analysis of transformations. *Journal of the Royal Statistical Society. Series B (Methodological)*, *26*(2), 211–252.

Boylan, J. E., & Syntetos, A. A. (2022). *Intermittent Demand Forecasting: Context, Methods and Applications*. Hoboken: John Wiley & Sons.

Chawla, N. V., Bowyer, K. W., Hall, L. O., & Kegelmeyer, W. P. (2002). SMOTE: Synthetic minority over-sampling technique. *Journal of Artificial Intelligence Research*, *16*, 321–357.

Cochran, J. J. (2019). *INFORMS Analytics Body of Knowledge*. Hoboken: John Wiley & Sons.

Cox, D. R. (1958). The regression analysis of binary sequences. *Journal of the Royal Statistical Society: Series B (Methodological)*, *20*(2), 215–232.

CRAN (2022). Download R for Windows. https://cran.r-project.org/bin/windows/base/.

Cullen, A. C., & Frey, H. C. (1999). *Probabilistic Techniques in Exposure Assessment: A Handbook for Dealing with Variability and Uncertainty in Models and Inputs*. New York: Springer.

Erickson, C. B., Ankenman, B. E., & Sanchez, S. M. (2018). Comparison of Gaussian process modeling software. *European Journal of Operational Research*, *266*(1), 179–192.

Evans, J. (2019). *Business Analytics*, 3rd edn. Boston: Pearson.

Galton, F. (1885). Presidential address, Section H, Anthropology. *Report of the British Association for the Advancement of Science*, *55*, 1206–1214.

Garmonsway, D. (2022a). The Bank Tutorial: Part I. https://r-simmer.org/articles/simmer-04-bank-1.html.

Garmonsway, D. (2022b). The Bank Tutorial: Part II. https://r-simmer.org/articles/simmer-04-bank-2.html.

Hocking, R. R., & Leslie, R. N. (1967). Selection of the best subset in regression analysis. *Technometrics*, *9*(4), 531–540.

Hoerl, A. E., & Kennard, R. W. (2000). Ridge regression: Biased estimation for nonorthogonal problems. *Technometrics*, *42*(1), 80–86.

Hornik, K., Stinchcombe, M., & White, H. (1989). Multilayer feedforward networks are universal approximators. *Neural Networks*, *2*(5), 359–366.

INFORMS (2021). *Certified Analytics Professional Candidate Handbook*. INFORMS. https://www.certifiedanalytics.org/cap.

INFORMS (2022a). Best definition of analytics. https://www.informs.org/Explore/Operations-Research-Analytics.

INFORMS (2022b). CAP Web homepage. https://www.certifiedanalytics.org/.

James, G., Witten, D., Hastie, T., & Tibshirani, R. (2021). *An Introduction to Statistical Learning: With Applications in R*. New York: Springer US.

Kock, F., Berbekova, A., & Assaf, A. G. (2021). Understanding and managing the threat of common method bias: Detection, prevention and control. *Tourism Management*, *86*, 104330.

Kohavi, R. (1995). A study of cross-validation and bootstrap for accuracy estimation and model selection. In *Proceedings of the 14th International Joint Conference on Artificial Intelligence — Volume 2*, IJCAI'95, pp. 1137–1143. San Francisco: Morgan Kaufmann Publishers Inc.

Krige, D. G. (1951). A statistical approach to some basic mine valuation problems on the Witwatersrand. *Journal of the Chemical, Metallurgical and Mining Society of South Africa*, *52*(6), 119–139.

Kuhn, M. (2019). 7 train models by Tag. topepo.github.io/caret/train-models-by-tag.html.

Law, A. M. (2014). *Simulation Modeling and Analysis*. New York: McGraw Hill Higher Education.

L'Ecuyer, P. (2017). History of uniform random number generation. In *Proceedings of the 2017 Winter Simulation Conference*, WSC'17, pp. 202–230. Piscataway: IEEE Press.

Macal, C. M. (2018). Tutorial on agent-based modeling and simulation: ABM design for the zombie apocalypse. In *Proceedings of the 2018 Winter Simulation Conference*, WSC'18, pp. 207–221. Piscataway: IEEE Press.

Mahdi, S., Verma, A., Dutang, C., Kiener, P., & Nash, J. C. (2022). A 2019-2020 review of R neural network packages with NNbenchmark. Technical Report, Zenodo. https://zenodo.org/record/7415417.

Martin, J., & Hall, D. B. (2016). R^2 measures for zero-inflated regression models for count data with excess zeros. *Journal of Statistical Computation and Simulation*, *86*(18), 3777–3790.

Matheron, G. (1960). Krigeage d'un panneau rectangulaire par sa périphérie. *Note Géostatistique*, *28*, 1–11.

Merriam-Webster (2022). Analytics definition and meaning. https://www.merriam-webster.com/dictionary/analytics.

Miller, T. (2014). *Modeling Techniques in Predictive Analytics with Python and R: A Guide to Data Science*. Indianapolis: Pearson FT Press.

Nelson, B. (2013). *Foundations and Methods of Stochastic Simulation: A First Course*. Switzerland: Springer Publishing Company, Incorporated.

Pearson, K. (1903). The law of ancestral heredity. *Biometrika*, *2*(2), 211–236.

Pohlert, T. (2022). R: Tamhane's T2 test. https://search.r-project.org/CRAN/refmans/PMCMRplus/html/tamhaneT2Test.html.

Posit (2022). Posit RStudio web site. https://www.posit.co.

Ramasamy, M., Hannan, M. A., Ahmed, Y. A., & Dev, A. K. (2021). ANN-based decision making in station keeping for geotechnical drilling vessel. *Journal of Marine Science and Engineering*, *9*(6), 596.

Reichenheim, M. E., & Coutinho, E. S. (2010). Measures and models for causal inference in cross-sectional studies: Arguments for the appropriateness of the prevalence odds ratio and related logistic regression. *BMC Medical Research Methodology*, *10*(1), 66.

Rencher, A. C., & Pun, F. C. (1980). Inflation of R^2 in best subset regression. *Technometrics*, *22*(1), 49–53.

Rose, R. (2016). Defining analytics: A conceptual framework. *OR/MS Today*, *43*(3), 34–38.

Saaty, T. L. (1980). *The Analytic Hierarchy Process: Planning, Priority Setting, Resource Allocation*. New York: McGraw-Hill.

Sacks, J., Welch, W. J., Mitchell, T. J., & Wynn, H. P. (1989). Design and analysis of computer experiments. *Statistical Science*, *4*(4), 409–423.

Schruben, L. W. (1995). *Graphical Simulation Modeling and Analysis: Using Sigma for Windows*. Danvers: Boyd & Fraser Pub Co.

Semadeni, M., Withers, M. C., & Trevis Certo, S. (2014). The perils of endogeneity and instrumental variables in strategy research: Understanding through simulations. *Strategic Management Journal*, *35*(7), 1070–1079.

Shumake, J. D. (2023). r2d: R-squared as deviance explained. https://rdrr.io/github/jashu/beset/man/r2d.html.

Soleymani, A. (2022). Stop using SMOTE to treat class imbalance. Take this intuitive approach instead. https://towardsdatascience.com/stop-using-smote-to-treat-class-imbalance-take-this-intuitive-approach-inst ead-9cb822b8dc45.

Soofi, A., & Awan, A. (2017). Classification techniques in machine learning: Applications and issues. *Journal of Basic & Applied Sciences*, *13*, 459–465.

Stanley, D. J. (2022). Chapter 16 sample size for multiple regression | welcome! In *Course Notes for PSYC 4780 Advanced Research Methods & Statistics Using R*. github. https://dstanley4.github.io/psyc4780book down/sample-size-for-multiple-regression.html.

Swain, J. (2019a). 2019 simulation software survey. *ORMS Today*, *46*(5).

Swain, J. (2019b). Simulation software survey results. https://pubsonline.informs.org/magazine/orms-today/2019-simulation-software-survey.

Tamhane, A. C. (1979). A comparison of procedures for multiple comparisons of means with unequal variances. *Journal of the American Statistical Association*, *74*(366a), 471–480.

Thorpe, K. E. (2017). How to construct regression models for observational studies (and how NOT to do it!). *Canadian Journal of Anaesthesia = Journal Canadien D'anesthesie*, *64*(5), 461–470.

Tibshirani, R. (1996). Regression shrinkage and selection via the Lasso. *Journal of the Royal Statistical Society. Series B (Methodological)*, *58*(1), 267–288.

Tukey, J. W. (1949). Comparing individual means in the analysis of variance. *Biometrics*, *5*, 99–114.

Ucar, I. (2022). simmer: Discrete-event simulation for R. https://CRAN.R-project.org/package=simmer.

Ucar, I., Smeets, B., & Azcorra, A. (2019). Simmer: Discrete-event simulation for R. *Journal of Statistical Software*, *90*(2), 1–30.

U.S. EIA (2023). Total Energy Annual Data - U.S. Energy Information Administration (EIA). https://www.eia.gov/totalenergy/data/annual/index.php.

Wu, C. F. J., & Hamada, M. S. (2009). *Experiments: Planning, Analysis, and Optimization*, 2nd edn. Hoboken: Wiley.

Index

D

E

F

G

H

I

www.ingramcontent.com/pod-product-compliance
Lightning Source LLC
LaVergne TN
LVHW011658200926
848484LV00004B/981